# War Zones

*Also by Jon Lee Anderson and Scott Anderson*

*Inside The League*

# War Zones

Jon Lee Anderson and Scott Anderson

Dodd, Mead & Company
New York

No part of this book may be reproduced in any form
without permission in writing from the publisher.
Published by Dodd, Mead & Company, Inc.
71 Fifth Avenue, New York, N.Y. 10003
Manufactured in the United States of America

First Edition

1    2    3    4    5    6    7    8    9    10

Library of Congress Cataloging-in-Publication Data

War zones / [compiled by] Jon Lee Anderson and Scott Anderson.
p.    cm.
Includes index.
1. World politics—1985–1995.   2. Military history—20th century.
3. Social history—1970–    4. Interviews.    I. Anderson, Jon Lee.
II. Anderson, Scott.
D849.W35   1988
355'.02—dc19                                              87-36768
ISBN 0-396-08915-1                                        CIP

TO OUR MOTHER, BARBARA JOY ANDERSON

who made us love words

*In Memory of*
*Charles Bonnay  1930–1986*
*Allen Klots  1921–1987*

# Contents

# Authors' Note

There is always war. It is not a strange thing; in much of the world, war is commonplace and people learn to live with it.

Both of us have lived and worked in war zones. While one lived in El Salvador, the other spent time in Beirut. Our experiences gave us a desire to show how people cope when living in the midst of conflict, and we felt that the best way to do this was to let people tell their own stories in the form of an oral history. That is the idea behind *War Zones*.

Since we wanted to get an international view of war, to show the differences and similarities of war's effect on people, we chose countries in five regions of the world. The five wars included in this book span four continents and have as their causes a mixture of ideology, religion, economics and tribalism.

*War Zones* is the result of a year-long journey. It is not an academic survey. Our modus operandi was more instinctual and journalistic than anything else. Like any partnership, this book came about through quite a bit of mutual compromise; as brothers and writers, we each had different interests, experiences, and ideas.

We knew that we wanted to visit at least one war in Africa, Latin America, Europe, Asia, and the Middle East; deciding *which* wars was the hard part. In choosing from those available in Africa, for example, we had to look at over ten, ranging from the Eritrean secessionist struggle in Ethiopia to the perpetual anarchy of Uganda. It was the same daunting prospect in most of the other regions as well.

One guideline we insisted upon to ensure a balanced view was to interview people on both sides in a conflict. This criteria ultimately eliminated a number of countries from our range of choices.

Once our one-year deadline had begun ticking away, we left our respective homes in Spain and El Salvador to meet in Washington, D.C. in the summer of 1986. Then began an interesting, if bewildering, series of strategy sessions between us, meetings with various foreign embassies, guerrilla groups, well-connected friends, and colleagues.

For Latin America, our workload was already lightened. El Salvador was a logical choice, as both a compelling war and a familiar one to us both. We had already gone ahead with many interviews there, leaving us free to decide which other four conflicts to cover. We decided to try for access wherever we could to give ourselves more options.

In dealing with foreign governments, the results were often frustrating. Our American nationality didn't help in some cases. One problem was in convincing suspicious foreign diplomats that ours was a positive project, not one that would give them negative publicity—obviously, this required quite a sales pitch. Mostly, our requests languished to that greatest of stumbling blocks: bureaucratic red tape. Our request to visit Soviet-occupied Afghanistan, for instance, was filed with its U.N. ambassador, but had to be delivered to Kabul, where, presumably, final approval depended on the Soviets. Not a very rosy outlook, but we tried anyway.

More promising were the meetings we had with the representatives of guerrilla organizations. Envoys of the Afghan "Jamiat" mujahedeen group offered us a journey into Afghanistan with their forces. The Tigrean People's Liberation Front made arrangements to take us into Ethiopia upon our arrival in Khartoum, the contact point. Other rebel groups showed equal enthusiasm for our project.

For Europe, we decided on "The Troubles" in Northern Ireland. We felt that the only Anglo-Saxon conflict taking place in the world had to be included. Our rendezvous with an Irish Republican Army contact was made in the basement room of an Irish-Catholic bookstore in lower Manhattan. We were given names and phone numbers of Republican leaders to meet with in Northern Ireland.

In August 1986, we flew to London and took a ferry across the Irish Sea. In Belfast, we installed ourselves in what we hoped was a suitably "neutral" part of a divided city, a bed-and-breakfast inn run by an eccentric German immigrant. We were immediate recipients of the legendary Irish hospitality. By the second day, we were making the rounds with a well-connected Protestant reporter and, on the other side, with a Catholic IRA enforcer. With the help of our two new friends, we were quickly introduced to the darker side of life in Ulster, making contact with everyone from Loyalist paramilitary leaders to Republican gunmen. Interestingly, in a land supposedly ripped apart by sectarian strife, we were never once asked our own religious affiliations.

It wasn't all hard work. Irish-style socializing was part of the package, and a number of our interviews were conducted in pubs. Belfast was not a sipping kind of town; in a heavily-fortified Republican bar on the Falls Road, our hosts were not content until our pint drinking had reached double digits. If memory serves, this was also the night we won a bottle of vodka in a lottery to raise funds, allegedly for Ethiopian famine victims.

Our next stop was the Sudan. Although we had been assured in London just days before that our journey into Tigray had been arranged, the word in Khartoum was a little more guarded.

"The rains have temporarily washed out the road," a Tigrean guerrilla leader told us, "but if you can just wait for about six weeks . . ."

We approached the Eritrean guerrillas, but what they offered us was a guided tour of the territory under their control, far back from the battle lines. We declined. (These conflicts were actually our second choices after Uganda, but we had hoped to visit at least one of them.) For the next few days, we waited for a plane to Nairobi, whiling away the time by watching Chuck Norris "kick 'em dead" movies on the roof of the Acropole Hotel at night and swimming in the American Club pool to escape the 115 degree heat of day. In a country ruled by strict Islamic law, the closest thing to entertainment we could find was watching whirling dervishes dance in the Omdurman cemetery at the desert's edge on Friday afternoons.

The coolness of Nairobi was a welcome change from the heat blast of Khartoum. After a few days of recuperation on a wildlife safari, we made plans for the journey to Uganda. For one of us, it was a return journey; Jon had gone elephant hunting there with a gun-toting gospel minister a week after Idi Amin had seized power in early 1971.

We set off on the overnight bus to Kampala. In the middle of the night, we were attacked by bandits. At least, that's what the driver said; no one else saw them, but we did conduct evasive maneuvers—zigzagging back and forth across the road with the headlights off—until everyone on board was suitably frightened. The idea, the driver explained, was to shake off any bandits who might be clinging to the outside.

The next morning in Jinja, the first Ugandan city we came to, the headline of the government-run newspaper, *New Vision*, announced a recent spate of "witchcraft murders"; it seemed that a growing number of people were having their breasts and penises stolen in a gruesome fashion by unknown men roaming the capital at night. It set the ghoulish tone that marked our entire stay in Uganda.

We quickly found that the hotel space in Kampala not already commandeered by National Resistance Army soldiers, was too highly priced. We ended up in a kind of charity hostel for unwed teenage mothers on the grounds of Rubaga Cathedral. After a few days, we moved to the home of an expatriate Irish couple. There, our hostess took it upon herself to fatten us up; the enormous meals, complete with apple pie, were occasionally punctuated by the sound of gunfire from the surrounding hills. A frequent evening diversion was watching Musa, the aged houseboy, stomp on cockroaches in the kitchen with his bare feet and then, with a cackle, kick them under the refrigerator.

When we weren't stalking the open burial grounds of the Luwero Triangle or trying to buttonhole hostile government officials, we found relief in the combined British and American embassies' twice-weekly "pub nights." One of the friends we made there was a former mercenery who had fought in Rhodesia. Now he was running the Uganda operations of a Christian evangelical relief organization. Over Tusker beer, he swore us to secrecy.

An omnipresent specter was the soldiers. Ten months after their arrival from the bush, they still looked and acted very much like guerrillas, wearing British army surplus greatcoats, rubber boots, and sporting ragtag uniforms and weapons. They manned barricades everywhere, it seemed.

Twice in one night, while returning from the bloodied eastern province of Soroti, the trigger-happy young soldiers came close to abruptly ending our book project. Jimmy, our irrepressibly fast jeep driver, didn't see the roadblocks until too late—an easy thing to do when going seventy miles an hour at night. The worst time was when the soldiers were huddled in the middle of the road and Jimmy, heading straight for them, went into one of his inimitable, rubber-burning, headlong skids. The soldiers scrambled for their lives and simultaneously drew beads on our heads with their AK-47s.

After our Ugandan leg, we split up for a couple of weeks, Jon going to Mombasa on the Kenyan coast, Scott flying on to India. Both of these choices were probably mistakes. Jon was robbed in Mombasa, while Scott spent three hellish days on the Rajasthan desert with a crazed camel driver who had an endless supply of "desert whiskey" and opium balls.

Joining up again in New Delhi, we spent several weeks catching up on our transcribing and editing before going to Sri Lanka, which we had both settled on for our Asian chapter. In Colombo, we ensconced ourselves in the Galle Face, a beautiful, if slightly dilapidated, old colonial hotel facing the Indian Ocean. From there, we launched a persistent campaign to gain government approval to travel into the contested northern and eastern parts of the country. While we waited, we traveled around the "permissible" parts of the island, the hill country around Kandy, the ancient Buddhist city of Anuradhapura, both to conduct interviews and to see some of the sights of the culturally-rich country.

Finally, we were given permission to go to the front-line eastern city of Batticaloa. In that embattled town, Jon celebrated his thirtieth birthday. Scott, racing against curfew, scurried through the town looking for a celebratory bottle of champagne but could only come up with a bar of stale chocolate.

The next day, we made arrangements to meet up with the Tamil Tigers. Following their instructions, we began walking down a dirt road when two motorcyclists pulled up and motioned us on board. With the Tiger couriers, we sped out of town, taking detours to avoid military patrols, until we reached a lagoon. Crossing in canoes, we were met on the other side by a larger contingent of guerrillas, bundled aboard a jeep and taken to meet Kumarappa, the local Tiger leader.

The meeting was an unsettling one, both because of the youthfulness of the guerrillas, and because of the presence of Athuma, a Tamil woman the Tigers were about to execute for spying. Eleven days after our visit, government forces launched a dawn raid and the Tiger camp was wiped out.

The last country we visited for *War Zones* was Israel. We had sadly eliminated Afghanistan after realizing that we would not be able to visit *both* sides of that conflict.

In Israel, we were immediately impressed by the intense sense of history—of being right and having been wronged—held by both the Arab and Jewish communities. Equipped with our tape recorders and a rental car (along with that all-important unlimited-mileage clause) we crisscrossed the country, conducting interviews everywhere from the Palestinian slums of Gaza to the Jewish settlements of the West Bank. We were guests of honor in Palestinian homes, danced at a Purim celebration on an Israeli kibbutz, and feted at a Druze wake in the Golan Heights.

As in all war zones, there was the touch of the bizarre in Israel. This was strongest felt in the little town of Metulla, sitting astride the frontier with Lebanon. The Alpine-style hotel was presided over by a dynamic, middle-aged woman who said she was Israeli, but seemed to be Lebanese, as evidenced by the photographs of top Lebanese Christian leaders adorning the walls. Sallying past her appraising glance was a steady stream of Israeli military officers, leaders of the Phalangist South Lebanon Army, and a sizable contingent of born-again Christians from Orlando, Florida. In the dining room, while the men of war huddled to discuss tactics in that violent corner of the world, the Floridians sang religious hymns.

After we had finished writing the Israel chapter in Spain, we split up, Jon going on to Central America to work on a new investigative project, Scott staying in Spain to write a novel.

All told, we traveled some fifty thousand miles in twelve months to write *War Zones*. We conducted well over two hundred and fifty interviews and transcribed more than a hundred and fifty hours of tape recordings. In closing, there are several points about our methods that should be noted:

Almost all interviews were recorded with the knowledge and approval of those being interviewed. On those rare occasions when someone declined to be taped, we took shorthand notes.

A few of those interviewed asked for anonymity or never revealed their true identity. In other cases, we changed their names for their own protection. We have noted these instances in their individual introductions by the use of quotation marks around their pseudonyms.

We have done extensive editing of the original interviews; for the most part, those sections excised dealt with detailed political themes or local specifics that we felt hindered the basic thrust of the stories. Except for this editing, we have tried to stay out of *War Zones* ourselves as much as possible, leaving the reader to draw his or her own conclusions.

There are peculiarities of language in some of the countries, which may be a little confusing. In Uganda, for example, it is apparently considered bad luck to count one's children; when people state they have "about six children" their phrasing should be ascribed to this belief rather than to any lack of accounting skills. In El Salvador, where psychological warfare is being used by both sides, one finds even illiterate peasants using highly-politicized language. We have left these idioms in place, as we feel they lend something of the flavor of the place.

Finally, facts, figures, and "history" given in an interview are those of the speaker alone and not of the authors. The reader will occasionally note vastly different renditions of the same event. We have included these contradictions, not only because "facts" are often impossible to authenticate, but because we feel the discrepancies give an insight into the varying perceptions of the people with whom we spoke.

# Acknowledgments

We owe thanks to so many, most especially to those who agreed to share their stories with us in the lands we visited. As with our earlier book, we must thank Juana and Barrie for their patience.

Very special thanks are due to Catherine Matheson and Duncan Green for their help in El Salvador. Much of our access in Northern Ireland we owe to Margarette Driscoll. Without Chaim Shur our chapter on Israel would have taken months longer.

In addition, we wish to express our heartfelt thanks to: Jim McDowell of the Ulster Press Agency, "Francie" of Belfast and Jack Holland and all his family (Northern Ireland); Steve of Kampala (Uganda); Bhagwan Singh, the Madras AP photographer, John Retty of the BBC and Mr. "Joseph" (Sri Lanka); Hillel Schenker and Na'ama Sharir (Israel).

For their unflinching hospitality, we want to thank our friends Rex Henderson and Bobby Block in London, Ashis Gupta and his son, Arjun, in New Delhi, Angus and Keiko McSwan in San Salvador, and Laurence Birns in Washington, D.C.

And though the book is already dedicated to her, our mother Joy Anderson, whose hearth in Spain was where we found the sanctuary and comfort to work on three of our five chapters.

Finally, our editor Allen Klots, for his perpetual support and enthusiasm.

# Introduction

In the modern world, war has returned to its primitive roots. In ancient times, invaders annihilated entire populations, soldiers and civilians alike. Then, war became "civilized," a ritualized slaughter limited to opposing armies on empty ground. Today, civilians are once again war's primary victims, but their killers are rarely invaders; usually, they are the soldiers of their own governments, or the guerrillas of their local "national liberation movement."

In World War I, civilians were five percent of the casualties. In World War II, they were forty percent. Since 1945, about thirty million people have died in wars, over ninety percent of them civilians.

Our book focuses on the civilians in today's conflicts—how they live, how they are corrupted and manipulated, and how they die. Through their opinions, private thoughts, and stories, we have tried to present a portrait of their lives in five of the world's killing grounds: Northern Ireland, El Salvador, Uganda, Sri Lanka, and Israel.

These disparate places are joined by their conflicts. In each, the soldiers of either side are fighting their wars amid their unarmed countrymen. In each, war has brought an end to the common people's immunity and, with it, their innocence. Walking an unmarked and ever-shifting line between safety and danger, they must find ways to survive when the gunmen arrive. Some gather up their children and belongings and flee. Others stay and are drawn in, collaborating with food and information. Most simply wait and pray they will be spared. None are allowed to remain neutral; with their allegiance the ultimate prize, they have become war's passive weapons. These are their stories.

# War Zones

# Northern Ireland:
# A Practiced Hatred

The Catholic neighborhood of Falls Road in West Belfast is a grimy, crumbling place, its cracked walls emblazoned with revolutionary murals. Just up the hill, the Protestant district of Shankill Road looks much the same. In the Falls, women sweep the steps of their tiny, narrow row houses, as do their counterparts on the Shankill. Along the Shankill teenagers gather, idle and sullen, on streetcorners; the prevalence of alcoholism and glue-sniffing among the young here is as bad as it is in the Falls. On both streets, most of the men are unemployed, and they spend their evenings in gloomy drinking clubs complaining about British injustice and neglect.

Yet the miseries of the Falls and the Shankill are not shared ones. The two communities are divided by religion, politics, three hundred years of hatred, and high walls topped with concertina wire—"peace lines," as they're called.

Since 1969, they have been at war; Catholics from the Falls have stormed up the hill to burn out and shoot their Shankill neighbors; Protestants from the Shankill have cruised by, kidnapping and murdering whomever they happen to find in the Falls. In the war of Northern Ireland, these two neighborhoods are the fulcrum.

It is here that the paramilitary "armies"—the Catholic's Irish Republican Army (IRA) and the Protestant's Ulster Defence Association (UDA) and Ulster Volunteer Force (UVF)—have their greatest strength. Here, the worst atrocities have occurred and it is where families have been decimated by murder, prison, and emigration. The Protestants, despite their litany of complaints against Britain—for its colonialist patronage, bad housing, and lack of jobs—are willing to kill and die to remain a part of Britain. The Catholics, despite their anger at the Republic of Ireland—for its social conservatism, and for its resistance to their cause—are ready to go to prison and starve themselves to death in order to become part of that Republic.

It is here, in the place that has had the least, has always had the least, that people are fighting and murdering in the name of tradition and a borrowed national identity. Here, in the rain-swept streets, in the damp little row houses, the seeds of a practiced hatred are passed on through generations to perpetuate a conflict that gives both places, the Falls and the Shankill, a collective identity.

The two ghettos of West Belfast are only the most stark examples of how a warm and friendly people in a beautiful land have constructed little else but ugliness in which to dwell; they are, actually, only the worst abscesses of an ill and homely city.

Sprawled over a gentle valley, Belfast is hemmed in by the frigid Irish Sea and the ridges of low mountain, giving it the air of an outpost. It is an impression fortified by the low, swooping clouds, the decaying, obsolete factories, the Empire-era government buildings in the city center, and the row houses marching in lines across the landscape like thin columns of directionless soldiers wandering out from a bivouac. It is an outpost in a frontier no one cares about anymore.

Beyond Belfast, the six counties of Northern Ireland known as Ulster show a different kind of neglect. Small towns huddle in valleys. They do not share the landscape, but are braced against it and look inward. The windows are small, meant for peering, not gazing. They peer out onto rocky, windswept land, shorn of trees, penned by walls of rock; barriers of rock to defend rock.

It is for these plots of land and these cracking tenements that almost three thousand people have died since 1969. It is a war alternately described as political, territorial, and religious; history would indicate that there is some truth in all three descriptions. It is political in that the Catholic minority wants political equality in a system that they have been historically shut out of by the Protestant majority. It is territorial in that the Catholic Republicans want nothing less than the merger of Ulster with the Irish Republic, while the Protestant Loyalists want to maintain their links to Great Britain. And it is religious in that virtually all Catholics are Republicans and virtually all Protestants are Loyalists.

But perhaps, most of all, it is tribal, and the bloodletting a ritual of rehearsed animosity. The British soldiers who stalk the streets here have little maps on the stocks of their automatic weapons. They are called "tribal maps," and are divided in two colors, red for the Protestants and green for the Catholics. In this way the foreign soldiers can tell which street belongs to which tribe, and thus gauge their own level of safety.

In the 1600s, Protestant Scots began emigrating to Catholic Ireland with the blessing of the British Crown, which had recently conquered the island. Concentrating in the northeastern reaches, the province of Ulster, the Protestants quickly took total control. Catholic farmers were pushed off their land to make way for Protestant plantations, government became the domain of the Protestants, and the native Irish language of Gaelic was banned.

In 1919, the rebel Irish Republican Army (IRA) was formed to force the British out of Ireland. In 1922, the Republic of Ireland was formed, but not before the British had created an arrangement that still haunts them today.

Responding to Protestant fears of Catholic domination, Britain retained control of the six Ulster counties that had a majority Protestant population and named them Northern Ireland.

Catholic agitation for civil rights in Ulster led to street demonstrations in the 1960s, which were brutally quelled by the Protestant-controlled government and the so-called "B-Specials" security forces. As the violence spiraled and evolved into sectarian rioting between Catholics and Protestants, British military forces were introduced to "keep the peace," in 1972. The IRA, revived in the onset of "The Troubles" as a defense group for front-line Catholic districts like the Falls Road, emerged from the civil rights movement as a militant force; the issue, once again, was a united Ireland.

The continued presence of British forces, the power of both Republican and Loyalist paramilitary organizations, and the lack of movement toward a political settlement have ensured that the violence continues today. The symbols of this war are always jarring: the British soldiers patrolling, ambush-alert, across a pristine soccer pitch, the helicopters that hang high over the city, the armored convoys creeping through the streets, all seem to belong to another place, and one never quite gets used to the incongruity of it all.

It is a death-squad war waged from neighborhood to neighborhood by civilian gangs of "paramilitaries." Each paramilitary group operates like a mafia, running "social clubs" in its districts, receiving protection money from legitimate businesses, and operating its own businesses, like amusement arcades and taxi services. In return, they police the areas, beating, "kneecapping," even executing social miscreants and drug dealers. One irony is the presence of the gunmen's legal political front groups, like the IRA's Sinn Fein, which work within the British parliamentary system in order to destroy it. These "politicians," both Republican and Loyalist legitimize and incite the violence when it suits them.

But perhaps the greatest influence of the paramilitaries is upon the children. In the tough communities of West Belfast, the hard men are studied and emulated. The children are excellent pupils. Young Protestants can graphically describe the battle that won Ulster for the British Crown three hundred years ago. Catholic children can meticulously cite the centuries of oppression their people have suffered. The death of an Irish son is remembered in minute detail—his full name, the date he was killed, how many bullets entered his body. The accounts have become part of the popular folklore and, at once, further justification for the war to go on. Since the land is disputed, the surest birthright for the young is The Troubles. They already are making forays out, to shed each other's blood and their own, embracing their birthright and their identity with all the zeal of the lost generations before them.

*The name Augustus "Gusty" Spence is synonymous with The Troubles; as a top commander of the Ulster Volunteer Force (UVF), Spence was directly involved in the first outbreak of sectarian violence in Northern Ireland. After a Catholic barman, Peter Ward, was assassinated by gunmen in 1966, Spence was sentenced to life imprisonment for the killing. Spence served eighteen and a half years and became a mythic folk hero to the working-class Loyalists; imitation five-pound notes were printed up with his visage instead of the Queen's.*

*An athletic man in his mid-fifties, Spence speaks with easy assurance and puffs on a pipe, which will not stay lit, as his piercing blue eyes gaze over his stuffy Shankill Road office. His craggy handsomeness and urbane demeanor are that of a retired military officer settled to a life of research.*

*The image is jarred by the ugly blue tattoos between his fingers and on both arms. One is a faded portrait of William Prince of Orange astride a horse; the other says "Ulster Forever." Asked about them, he looks down at the marks and seems embarrassed.*

Were you ever sitting in a quiet moment and you remember something, a dark, hidden secret that you suddenly remember and you feel a cold sweat and you feel yourself squirming and you say to yourself, "You dirty bastard"? Many's the time I felt like that.

Let me put it this way. Everybody needs heroes. Each side needs heroes. And they need martyrs. People made the myth, and I stood outside the Gusty Spence people knew and the Gusty Spence that was and is. I had nothing to do with it. People attempt to mold you like putty, to make you into what they want you to be.

Take this the proper way. Despite what you think, I'm a reasonably shy person, and this always deeply embarrassed me. I couldn't believe some of the things that were written. You know, I actually squirmed. And I actually squirmed whenever I thought of some of the things that I personally had done. Become deeply embarrassed. Whenever I come out, the first thing that I had to be was the antihero. I had to trim down all the legend and myth that some people had built up for their own particular reasons. But how do you prove you're genuine in Northern Ireland?

A word of warning about Northern Ireland: you'll find it hard to find the truth. You'll find out that most people will be very frank with you, but what they see as the truth, what they actually believe is the truth, in actual fact is a lie, because both sides have been fostered on their own myths and engaged themselves in ritualistic incantations from time to time.

On the Loyalist side, I feel a certain amount of sorrow because the ordinary, run-of-the-mill Loyalist is abysmally ignorant of Irish history, simply because Irish history is not taught in schools. I vividly remember that I was completely ignorant of Irish history. Really didn't come into contact with any Catholics until I started work at fourteen years of age. It was really only after I went to prison, where I served eighteen and a half years, that I found out, number one, exactly why I was in prison and, as most things have their origin in history, I had to set out to teach myself Irish history. Which I suggest I did, very fully.

I was born and reared into a society. It was the Shankill Road, the heartland of Loyalism in Northern Ireland. And you were born and reared in a certain way. You didn't hate Catholics as such, but, on the whole, we were very, very wary of people who were Republican, because you were always cognizant that there were people that were different from yourself. And Irish Republicanism or nationalism had always manifested itself through force of arms, approximately every ten years, or fifteen, right through history. You were always conscious of this.

You didn't really come into contact with Catholics, and there was always a borderline. While there may not have been a "peace line," there was always a recognized territorial borderline. It was Northumberland Street between the Shankill and the Falls, and it had been an area of contention through the generations. And I was born into this particular atmosphere.

There was always a stern loyalty to the Queen and things British. It's a deep historical thing. I look upon myself as being British. Now, I'm a different type of Britisher than someone who lives in London, but nevertheless I have this deep emotional tie to Britain. It goes beyond emotion, it goes right through to the philosophic. It involves everything.

My own particular family had a military tradition. My father had served in the British Army for twenty-eight years; he had been through the First of July Somme.

Don't underestimate the deep impression that the First of July 1916 has left on the [Protestant] people here. They see that as their ultimate loyalty to Britain, when the thirty-sixth Ulster Division went to France and they were slaughtered. They were volunteers. There was no draft and they went along to fight and they always made sure that England never forgot that.

So my father had this military tradition, and the sons inherited the tradition. I went into the Army. And when I come out of the Army, I joined the UVF. I joined the UVF as an extension, because I had taken an oath to defend Her Majesty— great grandiose oath—to defend Her Majesty against enemies foreign and domestic. And as the IRA were always rearing their head from time to time, my service in the UVF was a follow-on to my service in the Army, because the IRA were always the enemy.

And as a result of some action and some political machinations, I finished up in prison with a life sentence to serve no less than twenty years, eighteen and a half of which I served. I got out Christmas 1984.

I was the active service unit commander of the UVF on the Shankill Road in West Belfast and I had been responsible for the organization of the UVF in this particular district. So consequently, anything that was carried out by the UVF in West Belfast I technically was responsible for.

I myself have engaged in violence, but with the shooting of young Peter Ward— and I'm looking both of you in the eyes—I didn't kill young Ward. I didn't really condemn it as such. God forgive me, I didn't. I should've, but I didn't. The police wanted me, wanted me for all sorts of things, one of them being because I was the CO [Commanding Officer], but that was good enough to put me away.

My transformation in prison was gradual. As my knowledge was gradual, the transformation became gradual. Plus the fact that I had all the time in the world to think about it in Belfast Prison.

And it wasn't only that. It was after having been in prison for a few years, and after having read the true versions of history by comparing different authors, that I begun to see that all was not right and the Loyalists were not right all the time. There were injustices on both sides.

Some men began to come into prison in 1969—that was the first really heavy volume of prisoners—and I started taking classes with them in prison. And in '70, the beginning of '71, the first Republicans began to come into prison, and this was my first real brush, other than on the other side of a gun, with the IRA, and I found out they were just people. Just folk, you know?

But most significantly, they were all working class. There were no middle class. There were no barristers or lawyers or doctors. No. We were all from the back streets, the mean back streets that led off the Falls Road or the Shankill Road.

And with me, I found I got on very well with the IRA. We could never meet ideologically; on some matters of culture we had a common identity.

You see, this is an old-fashioned war and, I don't want to sound jingoistic but, this was my country, you know?

Call it patriotism if you want—it's a much-bandied word and, fair enough, it may be the last refuge of a scoundrel—but in my case it wasn't. In many men's cases in Northern Ireland, it wasn't. Most men don't go on the street with a gun. There's a certain honesty to people who stand in a street with a gun in their hand, because they're some of the few people in Northern Ireland who are willing to sacrifice something; they're willing to sacrifice their life. That be a Republican or a Loyalist. I believe they're wholly misguided; I believe they don't have to sacrifice their lives or principles or anything, because I believe we can sort our problems out through dialogue.

That's what I would like to think the role I played whilst in prison, because even whilst I was in prison, the war went on. I like to think, and I know, that I had an influence for lesser violence, because I think it was through some documents that we sent out of prison in the beginning of '74 that led to the UVF truce in November 1974.

It was a good truce. Unfortunately, the hawks in the meantime had gotten control of the UVF, and they didn't want any truces, for whatever reason—adventurist, psychopathic or whatever—and that truce was blown up in the air, too. After that, I no longer had any enthusiasm for paramilitarism. I still remained

Commanding Officer of the prison population, because I knew also that if I had packed it in, it would have created a firestorm within the prison.

In 1977, not only did I resign the CO-ship of the prisoners, I also resigned from the UVF. That was my prerogative as a senior officer. [Now] I wouldn't want to be a part of the UVF or any other paramilitary groups, because I believe paramilitarism is a block to any progress we make here in Northern Ireland.

There was two things I always feared. I always had a very inherent fear of fascism and gangsterism. I feared that the UVF could go either way. I feared fascism more than I feared gangsterism, because gangsterism with a good police force could be cleared up.

I remember once saying to an official IRA man, "Where do you get the good office from? Where do you get the dough from?" And he says, "We rob banks, Gusty." Hell, I robbed more banks than Jesse James. In those days, you had to get funds from somewheres.

All the paramilitaries—and I'm one of the very few people can say this in Northern Ireland—all of them involve themselves in some form of gangsterism. That would be in the shape of donations or extortion or blackmail, everything. Short of prostitution and drugs. They shoot drug pushers here; it's a great, high moral crusade.

It's a dirty little poxy war, like so many little poxy wars that have been fought in the past. Poxy means VD. Poxy means it's a dirty little vicious war. A war of ideologies. A war of flags. It's not a war of religion. There may have been a religious content, but in my opinion it's infinitesimal.

SA: How long do you think it will last?

Spence: Excuse this expression, it's not often I say it: fuck knows. I'm not a saint, you know, but sometimes I'm given to use a little bit of Anglo-Saxon. I don't know. It will go on until people are prepared to take that extra step, to come out of the trench and take that extra step and say, "Well, fuck it if I do get killed; I'll know exactly what I'm getting killed for. I'll be getting killed in the interests of peace or at least trying to achieve it."

But people around these townships, they're with the herd. It's the white buffalo syndrome. They don't want to be the white buffalo. They don't want people to say, "You know, he's a different color."

I myself have come under criticism from time to time, but I couldn't care less. Some people have to stand out and say it's wrong, and I'm prepared to say it's wrong.

JLA: Even if they kill you?

Spence: Yeah. Probably happen, too. It could from anywhere.

*Anne Marie Quinn, 27, is an Irish Republican activist who left prison in May 1985. She had been there since she was seventeen years old for, she says, "possession of explosives." Short and brown-haired, Anne is feisty, tough, and hard. Her eyes are old.*

The state inside the prison was more or less all the screws were mostly Protestant bigots who were out to pick on Republicans. It was a breakdown of outside life, where the British Army is in the streets—you know, any reason to get a boot in at Republicanism—and inside prison it was exactly the same. Any change whatsoever they're totally against.

It didn't do anything to take away from Republicanism or your views. It only strengthened them, on an even closer level. I became politically more aware and more determined as a Republican.

You're gonna change from seventeen-year-old to twenty-six-year-old when you're released. I mean, there's going to be changes. Maybe your strengths as a Republican would have increased over the years anyway, but the changes are definitely that you're strengthened, you are hardened. You've been dealt too many punishments, you've got that many kicks from being in prison. You are definitely hardened from a sort of experience you could do without.

JLA: Embittered?

Anne: No. There's thousands in Northern Ireland who are the same as I. Some prisoners have done fourteen years now in the cages of Long Kesh [The Maze prison], and there's those who'll never be released. When you're in for your beliefs, you come out of prison believing in the same way. There's no way you could be bitter.

JLA: So it was nine years well spent?

Anne: Yeah, well spent. In a state such as Northern Ireland, there is only one possible way forward, and that's through the armed struggle.

*A Catholic mother of two children, 32-year-old "Doreen" is a secretary in a Belfast hospital. She lives in the hard-core Republican neighborhood of Andersonstown.*

When I was about eight months pregnant with my first child, I was walking up Finaghy Road North and a car had opened up on the Army and the Army had followed and they had chased him down Finaghy Road North where I was walking up. And the car ran off the road, smashed into a pram holding kids, and killed three of this woman's kids. And I remember standing terrified, eight months pregnant, in the road. It caused me to think, because I don't think any cause is worth taking anybody's life for.

The Troubles affects your state of mind. It affects everything, because you can't do the sort of things you want to do. You can't walk where you want to go to. You have to stay out of certain areas. The first time . . . I didn't realize how much The

Troubles had affected me and how I was really scared, afraid of what was going to happen, until I went to London. The first time I went it was November fifth, Guy Fawkes Day, and outside the flat in the street I could hear these crackers going off. Fireworks were banned here, and I just panicked. I forgot where I was, thought "My God, it's shooting." And the second time I went to London, this car drove up—I was walking along the street with my friend—and I just freaked completely out, because it was at a time that [in Belfast] they were shooting out of cars and dragging people into them. But I hadn't been aware of what I was going through here until I actually got out of it.

When The Troubles started in 1969, it was total chaos here. I was working with the Red Cross, and I went to help out. And it was a time when people were getting burned out of their homes and people were just having to get up and flee. So they were being brought to centers to be looked after, to have a place to sleep in. And I saw these women come in a total state of shock, just didn't know where they were. Older women thought they were going through the Blitz.

It was really crazy. And we had vigilantes on the road. The roads would have been empty, from one opening to the next opening, and then you would see crowds of men standing there, 'cause everybody thought, "This is it; this is when the confrontation is going to really come and the revolution is here." But at that stage people's lives were like that.

At those stages, you walked around Andersonstown in the snow, and you could see gunmen standing at your streetcorner. There were gun battles that went on practically every night. You could hear them. I lived on the other side of Andersonstown, and you could hear the machine-gun battles going on in Lenadoon. That was before there was any sort of Army presence. These were "no-go areas" at that stage, and things got so bad more troops were brought in. And everything just escalated after that.

I think it would be better to have a civil war than to live like this here. At least you could see who your enemy is, you know? But to drag on like this here for much longer, it's just . . . it just couldn't work any longer.

You have to fit into a category, whether you don't think so yourself. It's black and white; you're one or the other. You can't have a view or a different opinion. You're categorized whether you want to or not.

At this stage, it means very little to me now. I feel very sad and I feel that it would be a great loss if nothing came of it, if there was no solution or a united Ireland at the end of the day, because so many people have suffered because of it. It would be terrible sad if this dragged on and all this suffering went on without something happening at the end of the day, something of benefit. But apart from that there, I don't really care. All I'm worried about now is my children and that they don't get involved, and that's it.

I'm a great believer in putting things straight in your own house; if everybody put things straight in their own house, we would have no difficulties here at all. I don't want to have any influence on my children. I don't even want to discuss religion or Troubles, anything with them. I tell them to be careful crossing the road. That's as far as it goes. I don't tell them who they are or what they are or why people are doing this for, just that's it's not right to fight and it's not right to take lives. That's as far the conversations about The Troubles here go. But hopefully, I've been hoping this for sixteen years—is it sixteen years? I can't even remember—that something will happen so before they come of age they possibly won't get involved. Maybe I'll not be here. Maybe we'll be somewhere else.

*"John Kirk," a burly, baby-faced Protestant in his mid-thirties, is the garrulous administrator of a job-training center for youths in West Belfast. The project, funded by the British government, is designed to bring the youths from both Protestant and Catholic communities into contact with one another in a work environment. The workshops are housed in one wing of a cavernous, old linen mill, one of many in Belfast that closed down long ago.*

I'm supposed to be responsible here for job interviews, and I have to laugh at that. How can I turn around and interview a young person sixteen years of age for to have a job in here, when this here is the bottom of the barrel for them? How can I turn around and justify "You can stay and you have to go"?

I have an awful lot of referrals from Rathcoole [juvenile detention center]. At some stage, possibly every week, I have workers going to court. For instance, the Shankill riots; that's seven of my lads charged, put on remand, put in jail, at seventeen years of age. First time ever arrested, and they're kept on remand, on suspicion.

We have kids in here with problems, lots of problems. There's not one this year that hasn't been born into The Troubles. You have to consider that. This is the second generation now of adolescents which have been born into The Troubles and know nothing else but Trouble. I mean, just take the drinking situation in Belfast. The majority of young people either drink or take solvents [glue sniffing]. We've had our problems in here in the past with solvents.

For a long time there, we had about four different young people who regularly went down to prison to visit their fathers. You have to feel for young people like that there. They're missing their fathers out of the house.

So, when a supervisor comes in to me complaining about that particular lad or something, if I turn and say, "Right, you're suspended," "You're sacked," that puts that lad back years, not weeks or days. It is very, very difficult. I will do everything in my power before I lay somebody off in here. I've had to pay people off in here, hard fellows, hard men, and they was actually crying. That's hard to believe, but it's true.

Nothing could get any worse, because there's no prospects for them anyway. It makes no difference if it does get worse.

*Neil, 17, and David, 18, are trainees in "John Kirk's" work program. Both are Protestant and both have grown up in the Shankill, the most hard-line Loyalist community in Belfast. David is currently out on bail for having taken part in an antipolice riot.*

SA: What's it like growing up in the Shankill?

Neil: Conflict between the two religions.

SA: How has it affected you?

Neil: Well, you'll never forget it, like. It's an experience you'll never forget. It's made me bitter. Against Catholics.

SA: Could there ever be cooperation between the two religions?

David: No.

Neil: No way.

David: There's obviously some people cooperating. But others won't; just stand back.

SA: What about you? Do you think you could cooperate with Catholics?

David: No.

Neil: In the Workshop, you have to work with them. If you don't, you get the sack. But it's a different matter outside.

SA: How do you get along with your Catholic coworkers?

Neil: Like, you don't get too friendly with them. If people start to see you getting too friendly with them, you'll become an enemy of the other Protestant trainees.

David: Be rejected.

SA: Have either of you had any Catholic friends?

David, Neil: No.

SA: No Catholics in your schools?

David, Neil: No.

SA: Is working here the first you ever came into close contact with Catholics?

David, Neil: Yes.

SA: First time you'd ever spoken to one?

Neil: When you go places you don't ask people their religion. But in here's it's maybe the first. You know you've spoken to one.

SA: What do you think of at the word *Catholic*?

Neil: Just the Church of Rome. Right away. They have a totally different religion. They worship the Virgin Mary. Well, that's like a sin in the Bible. You don't worship a statue or any other god; they pray to Her.

SA: What about a Catholic person?

Neil: Republican. Hates British. That's it.

David: You're brought up to hear that Catholics, they're all dirt birds. (laughs) If you see two eyes close together, you know it's a Taig [epithet for Catholic].

SA: Are their eyes really closer together?

Neil: A majority of them.

SA: Do you find it strange living in a city where there's areas you can't go into?

David: We grew up in it. Just used to it. Haven't had any different for sixteen, seventeen years. That's as old as we are. Maybe older people experience it more.

SA: What about your personal experiences growing up in the Shankill?

Neil: Where I grew in the Cumberland Street, that was just off Percy Street, which was a flash-point area. And I was a little bit young to remember, but there are still points in your head that you do remember. We were at the peace line on Percy Street, where the army barracks was, and they [Catholics] come out of Ardmore Avenue and threw petrol bombs, and the police told us it was going to blow up. And that's something that always stuck in my head. That scared me.

SA: How old were you?

Neil: About four, I'd say. I can just still remember it very faintly. There's all these things that stick in your head.

SA: What about you, David?

David: When it's your whole life, you forget a few, you remember a few. I remember being lifted up and thrown away, you know, a bomb blowing up, falling on the ground with old people. There's another one once when I was up in the park and there was thirteen bombs at one time. I remember the time. Some other people killed. You remember all different things.

Neil: There's one thing that sticks in my head the most. About three weeks ago, we were standing at Leopold Street, and the Provos [slang for Provisional IRA] opened up on the peelers [police]. And that really scared me the most out of all The Troubles. 'Cause it's like everybody just started screaming and we hid behind the big concrete slabs at Leopold Street there. And they opened up twice on 'em. That's really the first time I've ever been scared. Because you don't know if you're gonna get hit or what.

SA: But you wouldn't leave Northern Ireland?

Neil: No. I was born here, and I'm not gonna leave it for anybody else.

David: I'd only leave to better myself. I wouldn't leave if I was put out of it.

Neil: Well, in that case I would, but wouldn't go for any other reason.

SA: Not if there was all-out civil war?

Neil: No. Stand. Stand and fight for your country. It's yours just as much as it is theirs.

SA: But they're not going to leave either. What could make the two communities come closer together?

Neil: Mixed trips maybe. Or else integrated schools. I think if you were to bring people up like that, when they're young, and maybe they'd learn to live with each other.

SA: So you think an integrated school would be a good start?

Neil: Aye. Teach both religions.

SA: Would you go to an integrated school?

Neil: No.

SA: Why don't you want a united Ireland?

David: Far as I can see, the Republic of Ireland is run by the Catholic Church. It's bankrupt, far as I can see at the minute.

Neil: It's run by the Church of Rome.


*Karen, 16, is a thin, dark-haired girl with a ready smile. Another trainee in Kirk's center, she was interviewed separately.*


JLA: You're from a Catholic family?

Karen: Aye.

SA: Have you made Protestant friends?

Karen: To go out at nights with? No.

SA: But you chum around with 'em at work.

Karen: No. Catholics, just.

JLA: Why is that?

Karen: Dunno, it's just the way I was brought up. (laughs)

SA: How were you brought up to think of Protestants?

Karen: I didn't know any Protestants, like, till I was about five. I thought there was somethin' different about them. And my granny's Protestant. And I met my grandmother. She had a big Union Jack sittin' in her main bedroom, and then I says to my granny, "You're Protestant," and she says, "Aye." And it's how I knew what Protestants looked like.

JLA: How is the Workshop different from the outside?

Karen: On the outside we don't mix, and here we just mix. It's like, outside you never see a Protestant unless you're riotin'. I get to talk to more Protestants, and it's good, y'know. Some's real dead on. Just like Catholics. Really dead on.

JLA: What do you think all the trouble's about?

Karen: What's it all about? In my opinion? God! (laughs) Um, I believe the cops, the B-Specials turned against the Catholics and they mostly started the trouble. And the only thing the Catholics had was the IRA men. To stick by them. And . . . we're just tryin' to get Ireland free, just to be peace. No cops. That's all that I can think.

SA: What do you think of the IRA?

Karen: I support them, is that what you mean? Aye. Probably they are murderers like, but . . . however much trouble we get into wi' the cops, we'd know they'd stick by us. They're the only ones who can stick by us, anyway.

SA: So even though they're murderers, they're still okay?

Karen: Um, they're Catholics. And they live in the area . . . so you can't just go against your own, because they're fightin' for something they believe in.

Um, when I talk to Protestants, they say they hate the cops, too. And I think, if we both get together, Protestants and Catholics, and try to get the cops and the British Army out, there'd be peace. And, um, the IRA is shootin' the cops off one by one, so they'll end up, they'll have to go out.

SA: So if the IRA has to shoot people to get the Brits out of Northern Ireland, that's okay, it's for a good cause?

Karen: The way I see it, I see that they're just fightin' for their country and they want them out. They've been doing it for long.

SA: Have you ever personally had problems from the Protestants or police?

Karen: Aye, police mostly. Used to come to our doors to lift our Dee and Jerry for fuck all—Oh, sorry!

JLA: That's okay. Dee and Jerry, they're your brothers?

Karen: Yeah.

JLA: Are they outside now, or are they in the nick?

Karen: No, my cousin's in the nick. He's doin' life.

JLA: What for?

Karen: For murder. Cops.

JLA: For IRA?

Karen: For Ireland, aye.

*Since The Troubles began in earnest in 1969, over two hundred and thirty policemen of the Royal Ulster Constabulary (RUC) have been killed and nearly six thousand have been injured. Overwhelmingly Protestant, RUC police, both on- and off-duty, are considered legitimate "targets of war" by the Provisional IRA and the Irish National Liberation Army (INLA). Since the 1985 signing of the Anglo-Irish Agreement, the Constabulary has also come under attack from angered Loyalist militants who have burned out the homes of scores of RUC officers.*

*For these reasons, policemen are not allowed to be photographed, and any interviews are conducted anonymously. The following interview is with a senior police official who works at the fortresslike RUC headquarters in East Belfast. At the time of the interview, the Provisional IRA had just extended its "target list" for assassination to include anyone entering or leaving an RUC installation.*

Recently a group of Republicans went to a guy's house and asked for a lad by name. They were armed with staves and hurley sticks. Fortunately for him, he wasn't there, because the IRA are judge, jury, and executioner. He had been remanded to us for some petty crime. Their objective in being there was to break that fellow's bones; the second thing they'd do is to blow your kneecaps. Third place is you don't get any warning and you're taken in a car to an isolated area and shot in the head.

It's not a religious war at all. It's a situation created by the paramilitaries trying to take power and bring communities into conflict with each other, create economic instability and mayhem and to bring down law and order. And it's a helluva long way off, the day before the paramilitaries are extinct.

As a policeman, you just have to be careful where you travel and when you travel. You don't just jump out of your Land Rover and try to catch some young guy throwing stones. You have always the possibility that there could be a sniper attack, because they have employed children in the past to be at the forefront, while behind there's a sniper.

Also, they'll find a sweet jar and fill it with petrol and they'll drop it out of a window when they see a Land Rover. Your engine stalls, and inside it's an oven. If you bail out, you're almost bound to be dead; there's almost always a sniper there. You don't get out.

The threats have been there for quite a number of years. Many policemen have been killed. What happens is that a lot of these police are also farmers . . . so, on their way home, they are killed, attacked from a ditch, or whatever. We've had them where a farmer is walking into a field and they'll have a booby-trapped mine. It is a very nasty situation, because when a policeman is on duty, he knows he's safe enough, but naturally the situation at his home is on his mind—his wife has to go shop, the kids have to go to school, and often, his family is ostracized in the community.

But if one were to give up hope, it's a lost cause. We will continue to be a police force and carry out law and order. Everyone is entitled to the benefit of the law, but it needs the assistance of the community and political entities. There is a vacuum at the moment, but we must carry on.

The RUC is standing right in the middle between both communities and holding this country together to enable the politicians to get together to solve the problems of the society. Whenever both sides are getting at you, like now, it's an indication that you're doing something right.

*Emma Groves sits in the austere living room of her middle-class home on Andersonstown Road, her golden retriever sprawled at her feet. Dressed in a black skirt and a frilly, high-necked white blouse, the 65-year-old woman speaks in a soft Irish brogue, occasionally overpowered by the sounds of commotion in other rooms of the house where grandchildren play. Her eyes are hidden behind oversized dark glasses.*

My children were very angry and very bitter when I was shot. But I talked to them and told them not to try to do anything, because . . . I mean, it wouldn't help me. It wouldn't help anybody if one of my children had gone out to shoot a British soldier.

I've lived a long time, and I was born in Northern Ireland. There has always been a struggle, all my life. I mean, the struggle has never stopped. It has just come to a head since 1969, but all durin' my lifetime, we had troubles, in the thirties when I was a teenager, and we had troubles in the forties. And then, of course, in the fifties . . . Do you know what I mean?

It developed into a bigger struggle. How would you describe it, the struggle at the minute? It has involved more people, but it has always been there. You know, people have never stopped fightin' for their freedom. Every generation, men have died on hunger strike. Men have spent long terms of imprisonment because they felt an injustice was being done on their country and an injustice is still bein' done. So, the fact that I was shot is all part of the struggle.

They were always raiding yer house, especially if you was a mother of boys. But on that particular morning, the British Army had just left my home when someone mentioned that a young man two doors from me had been arrested. And I ran down to see what help I could do, because his wee wife was in a very bad state and the children were all cryin'. So I tried to comfort her and made her some tea and helped her to dress the children and, just then, someone shouted, "Here are the paratroopers in."

So I went to the door, and they definitely were in, with a lot of aggression, because they had guns drawn. So they told everybody to get into their own homes, which I had to do; I had to leave the wee woman and her children and go back into my own home. And we were all put under house arrest, which meant there was a soldier put in every doorway to make sure no one got in or out.

Now, we were all lookin' out of our windows, which was all we could do, and the British Army, the paratroopers, were in the street. And they were arrestin' young boys and men, and it was—some were in their bare feet and some had just pulled on their shirts and trousers—and it was very, very frustratin' to watch, and you felt so helpless just lookin' out the window and there wasn't anything you could do. You didn't know whether to scream or cry or what to do. It was a terrible situation. So I said to one of my teenage daughters, "Would you please put on a record and boost up our morale," because, as I say, it was very frustratin' to have to watch what was happenin' in the streets.

The last thing I ever saw was one young man havin' his head beat up [on the side of] a Saracen [armored personnel carrier]. The record was only playin' minutes when a paratrooper stepped right in front of my window and fired directly into my face.

Now, all my children were present when that happened. So you can imagine what a horrible experience it was for my husband and my children to see me, because my face was a mass of blood. And I was taken to the hospital and was told a week later by Mother Teresa of Calcutta, who was in the north of Ireland at that particular time tryin' to help the situation—and none of my family were brave enough to tell me or had the courage to tell me that I would never see again—so Mother Teresa come to my bedside and told me that I would never see again.

And I just wanted to die. 'Cause when you've been the mother of eleven children and a very active woman . . . you know, even thinkin' about it now, like . . . 'twas a terrible shock to be told that you would never ever see again. So when I was taken out of hospital I just wanted to die . . . just . . . I nearly did die . . . just took to me own room and I had to take one o' me teenaged daughters out o' work and look after the house and look after the children. I just couldn't cope with the whole thing. As I say, I just wanted to die. But as time went on and the children were depressed, my husband was depressed and . . . no family life and—it was so sad, because, previously to me being shot, we had been a very, very happy family and there was always plenty o' laughter and all in the house—so I just, one morning, decided that I would just have to come to terms with what happened, for the sake o' me children. Which I did do. I taught meself to do me own washin', taught meself to do me own ironing, and taught meself to clean me own house, and then, eventually, took over the runnin' of the house.

Lookin' back on it, it was a terrible, terrible time of my life. And the one thing that still makes me very angry—because I've learned to live with the fact that I'll never see again; my children are all married and doin' well—is the injustice, 'cause the mornin' that that soldier fired that bullet into my living room, his commandin' officer knew who he was, his comrades knew who he was, because he was the only soldier who fired a shot that morning. And still I couldn't get him into the courts. I tried very, very hard to have that soldier brought to justice but I never succeeded. See, there isn't any justice here.

I have not bitterness against the soldier that shot me; I have a bitterness against the state who put him there, the system who allowed him to get away with it.

*The blinding of Emma Groves played a prominent role in the campaign to end the use of rubber bullets by the security forces. The rubber bullet had first been introduced for use in riot situations in the belief that it would provide a nonlethal method for crowd control, but before it was withdrawn in 1975, it had caused three deaths. Its replacement, the plastic bullet, was hailed as a safer and more accurate alternative but, since its introduction, it has caused at least sixteen deaths. Emma Groves is now active in the campaign to ban the plastic bullet.*

*The Sinn Fein headquarters on Falls Road has no sign. The dingy, decaying building, with its enclosing wire mesh, closed-circuit surveillance cameras, and enormous boulders on the sidewalk to prevent car-bombings, has a grim, cave-*

*like appearance. Inside is a labyrinth of small, drafty rooms, some used as offices,*
*others empty and dank. On one wall is a peeling mural in orange, black, and*
*green, a silhouette of the Maze prison marked with the words:*

> *I think how they suffer in prison alone,*
> *Their friends unavenged, and their country unfreed;*
> *Oh, bitter is the patriot's mead.*

*In a cold room upstairs, the walls covered with revolutionary posters, Danny*
*Morrison, a Sinn Fein assemblyman and reputedly a top official of the Provisional*
*IRA, organizes publicity for the Republican cause. There is a steady flow of*
*comrades into the office, and the telephone rings constantly, attended by a chain-*
*smoking aide. During the interview, one of the calls is a bomb threat, airily*
*dismissed by Morrison as a "fake." Two days earlier, a real bomb placed on the*
*street below had been defused by the British Army.*

I remember taking part in a demonstration to Belfast City Hall in which we were
demanding that old-age pensioners be allowed to travel free on the buses.

And we were gathered outside City Hall and the RUC baton-charged us. I
remember an RUC man running after and calling me a long-haired, Fenian
bastard. And I had to stop and think what a Fenian was, because he obviously
related a sectarian, political attitude to anybody coming out of the ghettos asking
for anything. He related it to a threat to the state, because Fenians are Republicans
who were involved in trying to throw Britain out of Ireland. I mean, it was totally
amazing that there we were just arguing over bus fares for old-age pensioners and
we were being baton-charged because we came out of the ghettos!

I've lived on the Falls Road most of my life, saw firsthand the pogroms of 1969,
saw people getting burnt out of their homes. We initially and naively welcomed in
the reintroduction of British troops, because we believed they were there to protect
us.

Within three weeks of the soldiers' arriving in the district I lived in at Broadway,
Loyalists gathered at the bottom of the street and threatened to march in. We come
out to the street, just to defend our houses. The British soldiers put their bayonets
and turned them on us.

Within six to seven weeks, another twenty Catholics were burned out of their
homes in the lower Falls, and we were prevented from going in to help or rescue
those people.

And then, within six months of being here, the Brits were firing CS gas into our
areas. And within ten months of being here, despite the fact that no guns in the
Nationalist community had been turned on them, and that the IRA was purely a
defensive organization, the British Army started to raid our areas for guns, which

were badly needed for defense. But it was really Internment [British security law] in 1971 and, again, after Bloody Sunday, in January 1972, when fourteen civil rights demonstrators were shot dead by British paratroopers in Derry, that had an immediate effect on members of the IRA.

The whole situation was up in the air. There was a feeling of war, community solidarity. There was gun battles every night, bomb attacks during the day, a lot of people getting killed. Many of our friends or relatives were getting killed. On my street there was forty-eight houses, and I think eight to ten families had people in jail or people killed. I mean, everybody knew somebody who was in jail or on the run, and the community was supporting the armed struggle. And it was against that whole background that I was interned in 1972. It was a short one; I was only in for fourteen months.

It's very important that people understand that the IRA didn't start the shooting. Many, many civilians were killed by the British troops before the IRA actually went on an offensive and actually killed the first British soldier.

The IRA isn't killing people because of their religion; it's killing people because they're in uniforms, because they support an unjust system.

Now, you talk about car bombs. Certainly, there have been people killed in IRA car bombs. There have been people shot dead accidentally, but I would argue that the ratio of mistakes on the IRA's part is certainly much lower and much more efficient than the ratio of some conventional armies.

The point I am making is that you have to examine it within the context of war. Within the context of war, the IRA has done its utmost, has actually canceled operations very often, to avoid civilian casualties. With Sinn Fein working away openly, agitating openly, saying fairly militant things, and with the IRA beginning to refine its operation, there have been very, very few car bombs inside city centers. There's been very few bombs planted in shops.

I can't go on television and say the IRA is right. But we will always cover ourselves by saying we believe that any oppressed people anywhere in the world have the right to resist foreign occupation.

*Desertmartin is a tiny village in the rolling farmlands of County Londonderry. "Its population," says Ruby Speer with a chuckle, "is two hundred and forty—the same as it was two hundred years ago."*

*Ruby Speer, 48, is a large, plump woman; her house is warm and inviting. She sits in an easy chair in front of a snapping fire, smoking numerous Benson and Hedges Special Filter cigarettes. In another room, a typewriter clatters—Ruby's genealogist daughter, getting an ancestral brief prepared for a foreign client.*

*On the lane opposite Ruby's two-story home sits the Orange and Protestant Hall, built in 1888. Next to the Orange Hall is a cinderblock beauty shop that used to be her husband's garage.*

It was the ninth of November. It'll be ten years this November. He had a garage—repairs and sales—opposite the house. He was getting ready to finish up that night, shortly after six, because we were goin' out. It was me daughter's birthday, comin' up in a couple of days, and we were getting ready to go out. And . . . we heard a bang, but we thought it was just a car backfiring outside the house, and his secretary ran over and she said, "Jimmy's been shot." So we ran out and he was just . . . he was dyin' on the floor. He'd been shot I think it was fourteen times.

Someone had come and said they wanted him to have a look at the car, and he turned and said, "Right, I'll be with you in a minute," and then . . . shot him on the side of the head, and then another one came in and shot him again.

JLA: The IRA claimed the killing?

Ruby: Yes, that time.

JLA: Was your husband an active Loyalist?

Ruby: Well, he was, yes. A member of the UDR [Ulster Defence Regiment, a predominantly-Protestant security force]. Part-time UDR.

SA: Did your husband's murder make you more militant against the Republicans?

Ruby: It's simply . . . at some form in your life, you have to have some form of retaliation. You just can't take murder after murder and do nothin' about it. I know after my husband was killed one of the papers rang up, and they were very nice and came on and they said, "Now, you don't have to worry about answerin' and just answer what we ask you," and then he started to ask questions, and I would just say yes or no. And then he said, "And do you plead for no retaliation?" And I said, "No, I don't!" There's no point in tellin' lies about it; I would like to see the person who killed Jimmy dead!

JLA: Do you feel more bitterness towards Catholics in general?

Ruby: I think I do. I think that's a mistake, but I think it's a thing that you can't help doin'. Because you still have that doubt, you know, even from somebody that seems perfectly sincere and everything else. You think to yourself, "If the time came, would they support the IRA, too?" You're never too sure. There is a great feelin' of distrust, on them all. And I know in me own mind that's not right, but it's very hard not to have it.

Also, the attitude of a whole lot of them, after my husband was killed, particularly people that you wouldn't have expected it from, made an awful difference. For instance, when the children went back to school the next week after their father was killed, there was quite a bit of talkin' and jibin'—you know, "We got one up there last week and we'll get another next week."

SA: To your children?

Ruby: Yes. Plus, phone calls that lasted for about three, four months. It went on night after night, "Get out, or we'll burn you out"—this type of thing. Now, interestingly enough, I had a phone call two days ago for the first time in years. Just on Tuesday.

JLA: What did it say?

Ruby: Just that, "We're going to get you!"; you know, something like that. "We're definitely going to get you," I think that was the phrase—with expressions and a few curses thrown in along with it.

SA: And do you think your children have become more active or militant because their father was murdered?

Ruby: Sometimes I wonder how, you know . . . what change would have been if he'd been still alive. Two daughters were in the security forces, part-time. The one that's got married has left now, but me oldest daughter's still in it. My son, I wonder about him, because he was in court last year for stonin' the police at the Loyalist band parade and, you know, I can't see that would've happened a few years back.

People seem to make this out a religious war, and it's not a religious war. It's truly territorial. It's not religious. There's too much hatred over the years. It's like . . . say Texas went to become part of Mexico; I mean, presumably they wouldn't want it, and they'd put up a very stiff fight not to. It's the same thing here. We've totally different cultures. Totally different. It is just separate people. It's a very hard thing to explain. It's nothing you can really put your hand on.

I mean, personally, I don't care if my next-door neighbor is Catholic, Protestant, or Hindu; it wouldn't make any difference to me—maybe that's because I'm not an avid churchgoer myself. But at the moment, when you look at Catholics, you immediately think, "Republicans, IRA," and so on. I know it's not that way, but you can't pick out who is and who isn't.

*Sean Gallogly, 40, is cautious. An elementary-school teacher, he is also a councilman in the city of Newry for the Social Democratic and Labour Party (SDLP). The moderate SDLP supports a united Ireland but opposes the use of violence to achieve it, and consistently wins a majority of the Catholic vote in Ulster's local elections. Gallogly's party office overlooks the main shopping street of Newry, where nervous British soldiers, their weapons at the ready, patrol.*

We've had twenty years of violence, and it hasn't gotten us anywhere. The IRA would claim to be going for the full measure, the whole lot, and thereby justify their armed struggle. But my simple answer to that is, in the armed struggle, people get killed. If you condone that, fine, then, okay, human life is expendable. I don't happen to believe that and, (laughs) from my point of view, when people get killed, I might be the next one, and that's where I depart from that kind of philosophy, to be quite honest.

JLA: Has the violence touched you?

Gallogly: Not directly, no. I mean, except with explosions and that kind of thing, we do tend to occasionally . . . I live quite near to the big custom station on the Dublin Road that has been bombed frequently, and I've had occasionally windows broken and structural damage to the house, but nothing other than a minor nature. Therefore, it hasn't touched me directly.

But some of my friends have been killed in bombs, and as many acquaintances have been killed. I didn't know they were involved until they got killed in their own bombs or fleeing from the authorities, or the force of (laughs) law and order, if you like. They were shot.

But nothing more personal than that, really.

*A blond, fair-skinned 20-year-old, Steve Bowler looks young for his age. Born in Woodvale, a working-class Protestant neighborhood off the Shankill Road, Bowler is currently employed for a year at Farset City Farm. "Afterwards," he says, "I'll be unemployed again. That's just the way things is."*

*The Farm, a few green acres of pasture with birdhouses, rabbit hutches, a small pony corral, and pig sty, is a government-sponsored project giving temporary employment to unemployed young people from both Catholic and Protestant communities.*

*Farset is a pastoral oasis bisected by one of Belfast's "peace lines," the ubiquitous walls erected by the security forces to separate warring neighborhoods and dividing the city into miniature Berlins. The Farset "peace line" is a giant, wire-mesh screen that separates the Protestant housing estate of Springmartin from the Catholic one of Ballymurphy.*

*Only Protestants are presently at the Farm, after some Catholic employees were beaten up by local Loyalist toughs. Two days earlier, the Farm received a telephone bomb threat, reputedly from the Provisional IRA in response to the beatings.*

I was seventeen, so I was. Down there on the road there was a soldier by the barrier. And I was comin' for my girl and we was sittin' in this house, havin' a cup a tea, just beside the barriers. And just heard a big bang. For a wee while we was scared like, y'know? And I went down and seen . . . what was left of the soldier. It was right bad, it was. Seen him lyin' there on the road, the legs, guts, and everything everywhere. It was just . . . blew apart, so he was. It was terrible. We were standin' in this garden. There was bits all in the garden. And we was just seein' the soldier down there and, later on, just seein' them people going up poppin' those bits in bags and so . . . It's just . . . it's the sorta thing that's been going on for years, y'know?

I was thinkin of goin' over to England, so I was. Weldin'. For a couple a years. There's nothin' pickin' up over here. It's just as bad over there . . . but see, over in England you seem to have a bit more freedom. You can go about anywhere you want. That's it. When I go over there, it's just—it's a good feelin' goin' anywhere you want. You're not stuck at the end o' the yard or anything. You're not scared to go this place or that place. It's a different feelin' like, an' . . . you feel better.

But then you're talkin', and you're Irish with English people, and they look at you and you sorta say, "They prob'ly think I am a Catholic or a Provvie." And I'm not, y'know? English people take all Irish people to be Provvies, so they do. It's hard to tell the difference. Well, you can't tell the difference between a Provvie and a Protestant, y'know?

*Alan Wright, 32, is, at first glance, an unimpressive man. Plump, with the unhealthy pallor of an overworked accountant and unkempt dark brown hair, he is nondescript. It is his voice that is unique. As he speaks, Wright's voice fills the room with the resonance of a natural orator. Evocative images and catchy phrases are delivered in the warm, rolling timbre of a fundamentalist preacher.*

*Wright sprawls carelessly in an armchair in his untidy living room, ceaselessly toying with a Rubik's Cube. His drab, government-owned "council house" is situated in a Loyalist estate; in the small park nearby, a Union Jack hangs from a flagpole. On his own second-story window, Wright has draped a red and white Ulster flag.*

*An electrician by trade, he is now "on the dole" and does odd jobs to supplement his welfare check. Until the Anglo-Irish Agreement, which gave Dublin a consultative role in Ulster, was signed in the fall of 1985, Wright probably would have remained obscure in his County Armagh town of Portadown, but he changed all that when he formed the Ulster Clubs. Through his power base in the Clubs, a secretive Loyalist amalgamation of survivalist vigilante groups, Wright advocates an independent Ulster republic; presumably, the paramilitary Clubs would move to seize power when Britain pulls out.*

We have a guerrilla war here in Northern Ireland. You cannot fight a guerrilla war under the auspices of civilian law. Yet that's what our police force has had to do for eighteen years, and that has proved expensive, in terms of two and a half thousand lives, twenty-seven thousand injuries, forty billion pounds lost.

Give them the proper kind of law. Then they could do something about it. They could seal that border up. Now, I'm talking about sealing the border. I'm talking about a wall from Londonderry to Newry with four crossings. I'm talking about ultimately have an interior security outfit, sole responsibility for the security of Northern Ireland, leaving the RUC free to be a police force. You may never wipe out entirely the Provisional IRA, but you take away their freedom, you take their support, and you kill them off. There may be two bombings a year, there may be six shootings a year; there's not six a week, two bombings a week.

I want a situation where we can go to bed at night without a weapon lying by the ear, where a man can come out in the morning and get into his car and go, without having to get on all fours to check around the wheels, check his engine. Where a policeman's wife can go across for a fish supper.

The government is saying that it's impossible to defeat terrorism in Northern Ireland. That's a load of crap. It's possible, but you're gonna have to be extreme. But London don't want to be extreme, because it suits their aim to get rid of us.

Now, I know to deal with them would probably be ugly. To either lift them and intern them, to either take them on and shoot the lot of them, I don't know. But I do know that I have no future, the Roman Catholics to a great degree have no future here in Northern Ireland, and I do know that politics will never, ever have any degree of any future, while Sinn Fein and their gunmen roam the streets.

I personally have been affected obviously by the loss of my father, who, in 1979, switched on his engine and was taken from the scene of the time in a horrible fashion. I talk to senior policemen all the time, and they tell me they know who they [the IRA] are, they know where they are, they know the safehouses they've got. They can't go and touch 'em. I could take you to a man whose probably down drinking this afternoon having a pint of Guinness, and from his house, under his instruction, two young fellas left to blow my father up. Now, the police know he's guilty, I know he's guilty, but they can't touch him, because the law is wrong.

Yet we have tolerated it. For this very reason: we have been brought up the British way of life, to respect the establishment. I was brought up by my father; when I asked him time and time again when he came home from duty, crying because one of his colleagues had been shot dead in front of him, "Why don't we get up and get at them?" I was brought up to respect the establishment, to believe that one day God will waken them up to do something and to protect the basic right to life itself. I sat here for seventeen years. I sat by my fire and I waited and I waited and I waited until such an occasion arose that I could not sit contented anymore.

I got my reward just last year when they pushed through the Agreement. My respect for the British establishment in Northern Ireland died at half past two on the fifteenth of November last year. I hate the establishment which governs my life, because it's a joint Irish and British coalition government, and it ain't have my interests at heart. So I'm obligated to destroy that by whatever means possible. I've gone through the political channels; that has failed. We now must enter into a campaign of civil disobedience, of passive resistance, of completely disrupting and destroying the government way of life. You cannot govern without the consent of the majority. We aim to prove that once and for all.

However, if the British government remains just as stubborn, they might well try to force us into accepting an Irish dimension. We can't ever do that. So that will mean we will have to be prepared, at the end of the day—like any patriots of old— we must be prepared to defend our country and create a peaceful and just society.

I see it basically as a struggle between Roman Catholicism and Protestantism. People say that's sixteenth-century talking. I don't believe it is. I believe in my heart of hearts that the Church of Rome is seeking to gain control of Ireland as a whole and then to move on to control Great Britain itself. And it will be a lot easier to regain control of England if they can tackle it with the full force of the island of Ireland behind them. They are a very, very shrewd establishment.

People might argue that Gerry Adams and his gunmen are socialists and are seeking a socialist republic at the end of the day. I believe they are being allowed to pursue their murderous campaign by the Church of Rome because it suits their end of the annexing of Northern Ireland. I believe the Church of Rome has the power, within its superstitious religion, to control the militant Republicans. Unfortunately, the Church of Rome wants Protestantism wiped out from the island of Ireland.

I'm aware that I've set myself up to be a legitimate target. I've been threatened and received the usual quota of hate mail. And I've been followed on one or two occasions. I check my car every morning; I've been advised to. I got a tip-off lately that I'm not exactly held in high esteem with some people, so I'm watching it at the minute. But it don't worry me, because somebody somewhere had to do something to bring some sanity to our struggle.

*Damien Gibney and Padraig O Maolcraoibhe (or "Pat Rice" in English) are Sinn Fein Councillors for the city of Lisburn, south of Belfast. Damien is a red-haired, husky man in his late twenties; Padraig is an owlish, plump man with thick spectacles, a Gaelic linguist and schoolteacher in Belfast, aside from his political duties. Padraig has dropped by Damien's home to discuss local political issues; Damien's wife repeatedly comes into the living room to check on her six-month-old daughter, crying in a playpen, and a neighbor's infant gurgling in a crib.*

*The discussion is serious, for the Councillors' constituents in Lisburn are the victims of a wave of Loyalist paramilitary attacks. In the preceding weeks, numerous Catholic families have been burnt out of their homes. The events in Lisburn remind the two men of their own experiences.*

Damien: Irishness is instilled in you. It's handed down from generation to generation. I mean, my grandmother used to tell us stories about old members of the IRA. I remember being four sitting on my granny's knee, me granny telling me about the Tans coming into the house, about how her husband, my grandfather, moved weapons for the IRA. My granny always sort of embedded in my head, when I was a kid, that this was a mysterious . . . I mean, the IRA of old were dashing warriors wearing trenchcoats—romanticized, right? All out for Ireland. Very cleverly done, probably not done consciously, but that's how I seen her instill it in me. She instilled it through romanticizing the war, which probably at that time it was a romantic thing, right?

I remember there was B-Specials living in the Short Strand, where I lived when I was a kid, and my granny always used to say, "There's the bad man." And he looked bad. He looked evil. He wore black and he carried—I always remember— a Sten. And this guy was walking up and down your street past your house, and he was saying like, "Listen, I'm always here to put the boot in." That's the impression that I got as a kid, that, "Look, this is the enemy here and we'll always be here and we'll always be kicking your doors in."

Padraig: You grew up in a small Belfast ghetto, I grew up in a predominantly Nationalist rural area, and we arrive at the same point.

In South Armagh I grew up in an area that had been Irish-speaking within the last one hundred years, and you grew up with the kinds of songs and the kind of oral tradition of the struggle for Irish independence. That was an important part of your out-of-school formation.

I've always felt in rural areas that there's a strong folk memory of dispossession, that these lands were ours, that we were banished to the mountains and the hills, but that they never quite got rid of us.

One of the places where I felt this most strongly was at the funeral of Kevin Lynch [INLA hunger striker]. Kevin Lynch's funeral was in a rural area, and a lot of the houses there would be Protestant Loyalist farms and, of course, a lot of the poorer farms also would be Catholic. And this feeling, almost like a revelation, that for these people, almost unconsciously, the struggle three hundred years later was still about who owned the land. This almost unconscious feeling that they've been dispossessed, that memory, I feel, has always remained.

Damien: You see, taking it from the Belfast context, I always felt oppressed. There was a RUC barracks that was probably the size of this street; you always had the to and fro of RUC and B-Specials. And there was always this feeling of any time there could be a Loyalist attack. And the RUC weren't going to defend you. Nor would the B-Specials going to defend you, because they would probably be leading it!

I was burnt out of two houses by Loyalists and put out of a job by Loyalists, so I can understand the fear and the apprehension that the people in this borough go through at the present time. I know what it's like. I've lived under siege.

I used to go to school in Rathcoole. Rathcoole was predominantly Protestant; it was a massive housing estate in Northern Ireland. So I'd leave the house, say half-seven in the morning, you probably got a kicking before you got to school. You then left school, went for your lunch, you probably got a kicking at lunchtime. Coming home from school you got a kicking, right? It ended up as you were frightened to fight back, because when you fought back you just got a bigger kicking. I was eleven, and I couldn't understand the Loyalist mentality.

What I'm trying to get to you is that it has always been that Catholics were intimidated. Protestants have this really in-built hatred of Catholics. And it's not just because there's a war on now; I think the Loyalists have an identity crisis and have always had an identity crisis in Ireland because they were planted here. They've lived here for three hundred and fifty years and they don't call themselves Irish. The Loyalists are afraid of the shadow that they have created themselves.

Padraig: It's always been so. I've heard it said, and I think it's true, that you always hate those you injure, more than those who injure you. And I think the Protestants were always very aware that they had come in here and taken what wasn't theirs and that they could only hope to hold on to it by keeping down those that they had pilloried, those that they had robbed.

*Slumped over the enormous conference table in the anteroom of Belfast City Hall, George Seawright, 35, splays his fingers out before him and makes tight little circles on the polished wood. Rarely looking up, he mumbles in a thick Glasgow accent, the Scottish city of his birth. He wears a suit, but it is largely concealed beneath a dark down jacket, and long, greasy hair hangs down over his glasses. While some call him a dangerous lunatic, Seawright has built up a loyal following in the Shankill, which has elected him as its Belfast City Councillor.*

SA: In both Catholic and Protestant communities, your name comes up a lot.

Seawright: No doubt they told you how nice a person I was. (laughs)

SA: Well, not all of them. Some referred to the remarks you made about incinerating Papists. Any regrets for saying that?

Seawright: No. On the contrary. I mean, it made me. Nobody knew who George Seawright was. Till that point I was maybe known in certain circles, but it made me a household name throughout Northern Ireland, if not all of Ireland.

SA: What exactly did you say?

Seawright: Oh, it was pretty insignificant; I've said worse and more controversial things. I was speaking about Fenians and maybe the Education Library Board should build a big incinerator and burn them all. But it all became contentious when people thought I should retract and apologize over it. They must realize now that they were crazy people even thinking I would apologize.

SA: What do you feel the major problem is here?

Seawright: You have two irreconcilable political forces. Irreconcilable means they can't be reconciled. So you're only wasting your time.

SA: So what's the solution?

Seawright: You see, you're assuming there is some sort of solution when there's no solution as such, other than one side being defeated.

SA: In an armed struggle.

Seawright: An armed struggle. There's no political solution. The only solution is the winner takes all.

SA: What sort of body count are you talking about?

Seawright: Impossible to say.

SA: Thousands?

Seawright: Most definitely.

SA: Tens of thousands?

Seawright: Aye. Probably.

SA: And refugees, Protestants fleeing to Scotland, Catholics fleeing to the Republic. Hundreds of thousands?

Seawright: Aye. Probably about that.

SA: And you're prepared for that.

Seawright: Aye.

SA: And that is what you—you personally—are advocating.

Seawright: It's not so much a question of advocating; it's a question of facing up to the facts. And I think an awful lot of people feel this way.

SA: What do you feel about Catholics in general?

Seawright: It's difficult to honestly explain that. I know a lot of Catholics, and I wouldn't bother too much about them. I was talking to one before I met you. It depends what they're doing. If they're involved in the armed struggle against my people, I'm quite prepared to kill them personally. Because it would be dishonest for me to ever support people doing things I wasn't prepared to do myself. My constant position has been that the Republican war machine has been involved in a policy of genocide against the Protestant people, so therefore I see them all as legitimate targets.

SA: All Catholics?

Seawright: The entire Republican movement.

SA: But not all Catholics?

Seawright: Certainly not. In fact, I think there's a danger of wasting ammunition and wasting time killing Catholics who obviously, or apparently, have no connection with the Republican movement.

SA: What about Republican sympathizers?

Seawright: Well, I think you have to be sensible in this thing. And be strategic. If you're trying to hurt a war machine, you're not going to do much damage just shooting everybody who votes for Sinn Fein. That will get you nowhere.

SA: But when you're talking about an all-out armed struggle, that's what you're talking about.

Seawright: Well, I think eventually, unless there is some sort of compromise, it must inevitably come to that. I, for me, don't see any compromise.

SA: So you're at the point, personally, where you feel, "Let's just get it over with"?

Seawright: Oh, I don't see any point in politics any longer.

SA: So you feel the Loyalist paramilitaries are necessary?

Seawright: Obviously they're necessary. Most people would like to see them do a lot more. I would. I think most people would appreciate them more as a military force and nothing else. If you speak to them, it probably comes over that they see themselves as a lot more than that, probably see themselves as politicians and community groups and a lot of rubbish that we don't have the slightest interest in. The only purpose that people see paramilitary groups for is to kill their enemies.

SA: If there hadn't been the war, would you be a much different man?

Seawright: I'd be the kind of guy the next-door neighbor wouldn't even know exists. When I stood for the election in '81, my next-door neighbors didn't know who I was. Ten years ago, it would have been inconceivable what George Seawright would have become or what he'd be doing!

But you know, it's just come home to me now, that I'm a man unemployable. There's nowhere I can go. If people stop looking at me as their representative, then I've worked all this time for nothing. But the point is I can't go back, even if I wanted to.

SA: So do you regret your outspokenness?

Seawright: Regret is not the right word. I would long, logically long, for the time when I could maybe walk around and nobody would know who I was. For someone who deep down is a quiet person—which most people don't believe—I obviously would long for that.

SA: What about raising your children in a place like this?

Seawright: It definitely affects them. Kids now grow up to be extremists without anybody trying to make them ones. I don't have to teach my kids what a Fenian is; I mean, they'll tell me after a while.

SA: Some people say they would like their children to grow up without prejudice or bigotry.

Seawright: Aye. I wouldn't like my kids to be brought to be what I am. I'd be totally against that. I'd like them to have brains and to think for themselves and formulate their own objective opinions and things. The area where I live, that's pretty difficult, but I think it could possibly happen.

SA: What if one of your children married a Catholic?

Seawright: Probably wouldn't like it and, to be frank, there's very few people in this community on either side would. They'd be telling you lies if they told you they wouldn't mind. But if somebody did . . . well, I'd like to think I was big enough to understand that it is one of those things that could happen.

You see, most extremists sometimes get disillusioned if they have adopted extremism 'round about them. That may sound like an outrageous contradiction, but that's the way I feel it. It would be nice to see my kids going off with something different or growing up with a totally different viewpoint. Even if they were liberals, that would be something I would probably take pride in. Maybe it's an alleviation of conscience.

*Three weeks after the interview, and following the Provisional IRA murder of a prominent Loyalist paramilitary lieutenant, Seawright publicly called for Protestant retaliation. Within hours, two Catholics were shot to death by Loyalist gunmen.*

*In late November 1987, Seawright was ambushed and shot in the head by Republican gunmen. He died of his injuries in December.*


*Charles, 17, lives on predominantly-Catholic Manor Street in North Belfast. He is an apprentice metalworker, and hopes to start his "own wee business" eventually. He is shy and doesn't like eye contact.*

JLA: What do you think of Protestants?

Charles: There's some dead-on, but there are some that can be better.

SA: Do you think there's any way that Catholics and Protestants can live in peace with each other?

Charles: No. You can't go anywhere, really, 'cause if you go to somewheres they might be there with a couple of mates. And then what you do? So you hang about in a crowd; that's the only thing you can do.

SA: Would you ever go out with a Protestant girl?

Charles: I'd go out with them, but I wouldn't marry. I wouldn't get married with one. 'Cause of the threat from the UDA; you end up getting yourself done.


*Seventeen-year-old John is a Protestant from the Shankill Road. His hair is in a fashionable blond "brush-cut," a gold hoop hangs from his right ear, and gaudy tattoos snake up his slender arms.*

JLA: What do you think of Catholics?

John: Some . . . well, the ones we know are okay. It's the other ones.

SA: Do you mix with them at all?

John: No. 'Specially now, you can't. 'Cause the UFF give a warning that any Protestants mixin' with Catholics is shot. It's just as simple as that now. (laughs) You don't risk it.

SA: What do you feel about the paramilitaries? Does it ever bother you that these groups are telling you what you can and can't do?

John: You get used to it. People think that the police run things . . . it's the paramilitaries run this country more than anything.

JLA: How do you know that?

John: Start toutin', get shot. Do to 'em things, you get shot. You can't do nothing or you get shot for it. It's just one o' them things.

JLA: Would you ever marry a Catholic?

John: Maybe . . . if she changed. If she changed religion I maybe would. 'Cause I wouldn't change to be a Catholic.

*With his tattoos, handlebar mustache, and thin blond hair trailing to the middle of his back, Pete looks like a biker. A barrel-chested Catholic in his early thirties, he recently spent a year in the Maze Prison accused of IRA membership, and now drives a cab for the IRA's "black taxi" line. The interview is in a noisy and heavily fortified Republican drinking club on the Falls Road, where Pete consumes a remarkable number of pints of Guinness stout.*

I run a black taxi on the Falls. It's a . . . I guess you could it a mafia. We all work for the [Falls Road Taxi] Association. We run a straight route, from the city center, up Divis, down the Falls to the end of the Falls.

We're not allowed to take off more than thirty p. [pence] from anyone. Yeah, you could call it a mafia, but it's a community service, you know? Ten p. cheaper than riding the bus. We run our line; the Proddies run theirs into Shankill. Then there are the private taxis who work the whole city. But they're mostly Proddies and usually won't come into Catholic areas.

It gets boring sometimes driving the same road all day, but it's safe; no one's going to mess with you as long as you drive the Falls. If I were to go off the route, it would be trouble, serious trouble. If, say, I were to go up the Shankill, I'd be pulled right away. I'd have to explain what I was doing there. If I had a good reason, a real good reason, they'd probably say okay, but if I didn't, that would be it. You wouldn't see me or that black cab on the street again. (laughs)

*The poster on the panelled wall shows a paramilitary guerrilla with rifle at the ready: "Fight back! Join the UDA." On the wall nearby, a calendar sports a photograph of the Queen Mother. On either side of the huge desk are flags, one of Ulster, the other the Union Jack.*

*Behind the desk and its row of three telephones is Andy Tyrie, a heavyset man with brown hair, a mustache, and glasses. Tyrie is the commander-in-chief of the Ulster Defence Association (UDA), umbrella group for the Loyalist paramilitary squads, which have gained a reputation for sectarian killings.*

*The night before, a Catholic "black taxi" driver was shot dead in his living room by the Loyalist paramilitary group that calls itself the Ulster Freedom Fighters (UFF). Freshly painted on the exterior wall of Tyrie's East Belfast headquarters, a coat-of-arms mural shows the UDA and UFF together, with the Latin motto Quis Separabit—"None Shall Separate Us." Tyrie speaks with startling candor; in the interview, he admits for the first time that the UFF is "the terror arm" of his organization.*

All conflicts that exist, they depend on the public helpin' them out regardin' finances. So what we done is, like any business community, go with what raises capital the quickest. And one of the things we stumbled onto at the early part of the conflict here . . . most pubs and clubs were being bombed and people didn't go into the center of Belfast, or didn't go outside their own districts to socialize. We then, like most people in both communities at that time, organized illegal drinking clubs. So what happened was, the security forces then decided to clamp down on these clubs. And the security forces thought we were makin' a fortune out of them, which we were not! It give us awful problems.

And, what the system done was to force us to look at businesses properly, how to run them. So what we do have, we have a lot of very well run social clubs. We have other businesses, which have been hard work puttin' together. It weren't just a matter of overnight becomin' a financial success. Some of the places in this town still give us a headache because they don't earn money.

People say that's how the Mafia does it. Well, that's how the business community does it, too. You know, you must raise finances. You have to raise finances. Robbin' banks and post offices is not a very successful thing here. We have people in jail to prove it.

Now, the UFF's a different group of people. I can't speak totally for them, but as long as UFF is not involved in sectarian conflict and shootin' people just for the sake of shootin' them, but that they are engaged in fightin' known IRA people, we will support them. We look after them any way we possibly can, but we do see them as a separate part of this organization. Not totally a part of the organization, but people who we would support.

The UFF could be shootin' people every day of the week, but they don't. All right, they shot a taxi driver last night, a known IRA man, IRA supporter, supplies money for the finance for the IRA's workin's. I mean . . . wouldn't it be just as easy for the UFF to go in and just shoot anybody on the Falls Road, or shoot any person movin', and they could've said, "Sinn Fein supporter, 'cause he voted for them," and that's justified. But they didn't. They went up and they searched and they found a fellow who they knew was a member of the IRA, was involved in the Provisional movement, financed and helped them with the taxi business he was operatin', paid into them, helps them any way he possibly can. It [killing] appears to be a sensible one; that's the difference.

But the point we make, and the reason why we have survived and not become totally proscribed is because of the size of the organization and our connections within society here. We don't simply promote violence for the sake of it, and we don't say that violence is the answer. We know that violence is not the answer to the problem here. We feel that there should be a system of government that influences and gives everybody a fair deal.

The problem is the people here see that our political leaders on both sides don't really want the settlement. If they get together, it defuses the whole situation. There's no need for UDA and there's no need for the IRA. Us? Me and Gerry Adams, if we were to shake hands with each other tomorrow and decide to form a government, it would be totally rejected by the people. They don't want to be ruled here by people who are military or paramilitary or terrorist-type organizations. They don't want to be ruled by people like us. I don't. If the UDA and the IRA ever got together to rule our society, no way would I ever support that.

*Jim McAllister, 42, has a quick laugh and an ironic twinkle in his eye as he tells the tales of South Armagh. On a two-hour tour by car around the embattled border village of Crossmaglen, McAllister points out scenes of recent mortar attacks and car bombings with all the pride of a chamber of commerce guide, eager to show off the local sights to an uninitiated newcomer.*

*As Sinn Fein Councillor for Crossmaglen, McAllister administers a dingy little office on the corner of the desolate town square. The town is best described as bizarre: looming behind the old row houses fronting the square is a giant British Army fortress, its bullet and shrapnel holes testament to its unwelcome presence in the heartland of Irish nationalism. Closed-circuit surveillance cameras atop towering steel stanchions soar above the fort and look down at every angle into Crossmaglen, its all-seeing eyes.*

*In the center of the square is perched a defiant bronze statue erected in honor of the IRA's "martyrs," while the scything rotor blades of military helicopters constantly moving in and out of the fort fills the heavy silence with a gnashing roar. Here road convoys and foot patrols by soldiers and police are in constant danger of ambush from IRA gunmen; McAllister claims that over a hundred British soldiers have died in the vicinity.*

Now, this is where the bombin' went the other day. See that tractor lyin' in the field? That outpost there, that's brand-new; that was demolished completely by those bombs. The takin' away of these hedges now are an attempt to stop the IRA gettin' in again at them. And also, some of the bunkers which are covered over there—with the tarpaulins, you know? There are underground bunkers there. They were wiped out in those mortar attacks, too.

JLA: And the mortar attacks, they were remote-controlled?

McAllister: They were remote control, yeah.

JLA: Very sophisticated.

McAllister: (laughs) It is very sophisticated. All homemade.

JLA: Were there casualties?

McAllister: They admitted to one slight injury, but the fact is the post tower was wiped out and at least one of their underground bunkers was; there was a direct hit on it. Given the fact that they allowed nobody into the area for about four days afterwards, it's a fair assumption that they lost a man or two.

And just here, see this tree? A month ago, two of them, two British soldiers, were killed there. 'Twas a car bomb.

JLA: That car below?

McAllister: That's right, yeah. The bomb was in the car. Actually, it was parked. There was a British outpost just there. The IRA parked the vehicle beside them, walked away, and left it. They came out to look at it and it blew up.

Then they [IRA] come back last week and fired fourteen mortars at them and wiped out that whole setup. They've [British Army] rebuilt it; they've extended the areas they've taken over. Their only way to hit back is build more posts, and the more posts they build the more the IRA will be able to hit them. Since they began buildin' this series of outposts around Crossmaglen, they have lost a commanding officer, they have lost two policemen, they have lost two British soldiers killed and several injured at these outposts. They've become targets and they're out in the open and, from the IRA's point of view, they're probably easier to deal with than a base in a village or town.

SA: How do you feel about all these British soldiers around you getting killed? Most of them are working-class; do you feel any sympathy for them?

McAllister: Apart from their officers, they are all certainly working-class, but, at the same time, I feel little sympathy for them, because they have minds. I understand that they don't understand what's going on here, 'cause they're—to be blunt about it—they're brainwashed by their Army officers and by the Army itself. They're fed all the propaganda about Ireland.

But nevertheless, they are here as British soldiers. They're trained by Britain, they're carryin' British weapons, and they're intent on doin' Britain's will in Ireland. So they must, unfortunately, suffer the consequences.

SA: But you're not hoping to win a military victory here.

McAllister: No. An outright military victory, no. A strategy of sapping the will of Britain and, maybe even more important, the will of those who back Britain in Ireland. The IRA's latest strategy—of hitting the British bases, hitting them hard, by mortar or whatever way necessary, by demolishing them or damaging them severely, then refusing to allow civilians to rebuild them—is hitting them very, very hard.

SA: You're opposed to people in the community working as laborers to help rebuild [the British Army posts], but where do you draw the line? What about the woman who sells sandwiches to British soldiers?

McAllister: Oh yes, she shouldn't do it. Anybody who gives direct or even indirect aid, service or whatever, to British forces should consider themselves targets of the IRA.

SA: And to your thinking she's a legitimate target?

McAllister: I think so. Definitely yes. If she knows her customers are members of the British forces and by serving them whatever it is or aidin' them, she's giving them succor and comfort and she's prolongin' the tragedy of Ireland! In South Armagh, for instance, the people have never served or worked with the British forces in any shape or form. Never! The British soldier or an RUC man could walk around Crossmaglen with a million dollars in his pocket and he couldn't buy a packet of cigarettes. They don't even bother entering a shop. Occasionally, when a new regiment comes in, you get one or two silly enough to walk in, but he's soon told just where to go.

See, the IRA couldn't exist if there wasn't a large ground swell of support for them. No, this would be impossible. You look at those outposts, the one I showed you where the mortar attack was launched last Thursday. Those mortars—the material's got to be got, it's got to be assembled, there's welding to be done, metal cuttin', vehicles have got to be got to mount the machinery on, machinery's got to be transported to the base, and a very, very large number of people have to be involved in an operation like that. That could not happen unless a large number of people in the general area were willing to let it happen.

If they were even bein' logical—aside from withdrawin' from Ireland—it would be logical they would pull back from places like South Armagh, because nobody can come in here and find an excuse for them being here. You couldn't even talk about sectarianism, since you have 99.99 percent Republican people; it's not as if the population was half and half and was at each other's throats. There's no reason for them to be here, except to be here, to prove they're here. Fulfill no role whatsoever—only as an outpost of Empire, keep the flag flyin' kind of thing. And they offer great targets for the IRA.

*"David O'Connor" is a rock musician in Belfast. He was born a Catholic.*

I'm twenty-four. My name's David O'Connor. I was born in the Dockland of Belfast. Lived there till I was nine. Moved to a place called the New Lodge Road. Lived there three years. My father died when I was twelve, so my mother moved up to Twinbrook, and I've lived there for twelve years.

I had a good childhood, you know. I'm one of the lucky ones, 'cause I stayed clear of it. But the situation here, what I found is a lot of kids they're just born and they grow up and they don't see anything other than Trouble. But I've been lucky. Playing in the band, I met a lot of people, went to London, made a lot of English friends. I've been okay.

Regards the political aspect of it, I'm not a Republican by any means. I'm not a Loyalist by any means. I'm sort of in the middle. But I'm an Irishman. I was born on this soil, and I'm Irish. And that's about the end of it.

You got young blokes coming over, joined the British Army because they can't get a job. And what do they do? They get blown away. Same situation as Argentina. Argentina is Argentina, right? And like Ireland is Ireland. And I stress the point, I'm not political-minded, but I still think that Ireland's Ireland. But I don't agree with murder, with wiping people off.

It's easier for a politician. Like I could be a politician and I could sit and say to yous two, "Well, the situation here, and such and such." But there's guys going out risking their fucking lives for that, working-class people. If I had my way, I'd get a fucking big bucket. I'd put them all in it and burn it, you know. Or float them off to sea.

I'm totally fucked off it. I'm thinking about getting out altogether. I'm just fucking fed up with it. You go out and you see Brits all over the street, and the Brits shouldn't be here.

Tell you a wee story. I was coming down from my girlfriend's house one night about three years ago. It was about three in the morning, pissing rain, and there was a foot patrol coming up the street and it was inevitable that they were gonna stop me and ask me my name. So they did stop me and I told him my name. And the wee Brit, he was just crouching there with his rifle, and I just turned around to him and says, "What the fuck are you doing here?" And he turned around and said, "I don't fucking know." And it was coming towards Christmas, and I said, "Would you not want to be with your family?" and he says, "Yeah." I said, "Do you know what's going on here?" "No." And he was eighteen. Fucking eighteen years of age, and he's fucking handed a gun, go out and walk the streets! It's fucking crazy.

From a nonpolitical point of view, it's common sense that it's Irish soil and it's an Irish country. But why the fuck fight for a lump of soil? I mean, why the fuck fight for a lump of dirt? A lump of fucking soil that you can hold in your hand, that you can fucking squeeze it and throw it in the bin again. I think it's a heap of shit, people going out and getting themselves killed over it. I wouldn't do it. I'm too interested in having a good time.

I've not harmed anybody in my life, although when I was a kid I threw bricks at the soldiers, 'cause that's all I knew. But, thank God, at the end of the day I stayed clear of it. I said to meself, "There's something fucking funny here. There's something going wrong. Steer clear of it. You have to better yourself in life." The night before my father died, he said to us three boys, "Stay out of it." And the next day he died, so we were stuck with that policy.

Oh, sure, as a kid, I thought to myself I have to do something and before you know it, somebody says to you, "Why don't you do this? Why don't you join up?" So, automatically, the person who asks you is connected. It's very easy to join . . . well, I wouldn't say that; like, I know nothing about it. But, thank God, I stayed well clear of it. . . .

 Okay, I'll tell you the real story. I had every opportunity to get involved in the

IRA. When I was a kid, I was involved to a certain extent. I didn't take an oath or anything. Like this is when I was twelve, thirteen . . . used to go out and took collections and stuff. For the IRA, right? Then it was called the Fianna Eireann; basically it was the junior wing of the IRA. I wasn't active, right? It was just going out and doing collections and stuff like that. I only did a few. Going around house to house, saying I was collecting for Fianna Eireann. Everybody knew who we were talking about, and everybody gave. It was like running around selling the newspaper . . . like, I've never told anybody this before, not even my girlfriend.

So that lasted for about a year, and then I started to wise up, started saying no. But then it was fun. Then you thought you were somebody. You wore your little green beret and socks and everything else. But now it's all diminished. There's no Fianna; it's just the IRA, active service.

I used to think there was a cause. I used to be a Republican. Yeah, I did. Hated fucking Protestants. Hated the fucking Brits. At twelve years of age, just wanted a united Ireland. Okay, I was fucked up, right? 'Cause I lived in a fucking ghetto. And only from my father dying, I'd probably be there now. Probably doing fucking life or something.

So that was my childhood.

*The Catholic Finnegan family lives in the Lenadoon housing estate of West Belfast. Seamus is 29, Martin is 27, and Kathleen, their mother, is 62.*

*In an earlier meeting, Martin seemed hard-bitten, his blue eyes calm and knowing; now, in the presence of Seamus, he is the deferential younger brother, fixing everyone cheese sandwiches and endless cups of tea. Throughout the interview, he watches Seamus intently.*

*Kathleen, a thin, white-haired woman, sits on the carpet near the fireplace, and, at times during the five-hour interview, cries quietly as she listens to Seamus.*

*Seamus, muscular and bespectacled, sits in an overstuffed armchair and speaks in a soft, flat voice with little emotion as he tells his family for the first time some of the details of his years in The Maze. In an incredulous tone, as if disbelieving his own ordeal, he describes his experience as a prisoner on the IRA's "blanket," a four-year protest for improved prison conditions and recognition of IRA inmates as political prisoners. "The Blanket Men" refused to wash, leave their cells, use toilet facilities, or wear the prison uniform, and wore only blankets instead. Seamus also speaks of two friends arrested with him who died on the IRA hunger strike of 1981; one of them was Bobby Sands, the first of the ten men who starved themselves to death and now a Republican martyr.*

Seamus: There was six of us altogether; that's who was finally charged. Um, I was arrested with a pistol in the car, four of us. The other two were caught up the street, in possession of nothin', but yet they were charged with "unknown weapons." They were found in the vicinity, but not in our possession, and we all refused to recognize the court and we all got fourteen years for possession with intent. But . . . as the papers have said, it was a bombing mission. It was a big commercial sort of target for the IRA, and when we were apprehended the RUC and their special patrol group and the military police just opened fire indiscriminately and it was very, very lucky that there wasn't other people killed or shot.

SA: You were just driving down the road and they opened fire?

Seamus: No, we were . . . I was in the street where the bombs were, and I was drivin' out when the MPs stopped us.

SA: You were in prison during the hunger strikes. Did you consider going on hunger strike?

Seamus: Yes, very much so.

SA: And decided not to?

Seamus: No, well, I did. And, I was selected to go on hunger strike, but just at the last moments I decided to withdraw. Because it had been a long, drawn-out period, and I think that the deaths themselves had taken so much out of me that I didn't know whether or not I would be able to go through with it. And that indecision on my behalf could have resulted in the deaths of other people by being weak and . . . also, because of a brother of mine on the run from the British Army and the British government. He's an escapee from the H-Blocks. Dermott. I've a brother dead, who was killed in a car crash just after bein' released from prison, which was John. . . .

And that there, and everything else, I think it woulda killed me mother at the end of the day. You know, the effects of all that there, you know? I mean, I just couldn't. You know what I mean? It may've been okay for me to give my life, but knowin' that it might kill her—that there, and also the indecision, swayed me to withdraw at the end of the day. And it broke my heart, because so many of my comrades and friends had died on it.

It's a very frightenin' experience, like. You sittin' down tryin' to condition yourself into believin' that you're gonna die. . . . I mean, you'll be forgotten about . . . especially, like, I've been in jail from I was sixteen and . . . You had no life, you know what I mean? But it wasn't a decision you came to lightly, because you're talking about givin' your life for something.

SA: (to Kathleen) Did you know that Seamus was considering going on hunger strike?

Kathleen: Yes, he was that told me.

SA: What was your reaction?

Kathleen: Well, no matter he would do, I was behind him every way. I would've stood by him. But as soon as he went, I would've tooken my own life.

SA: This was 1981. Was Dermott also in prison at that time?

Seamus: Well, Dermott was arrested in February 1981 for the killin' of an RUC man and the attempted murder of an RUC man. And he was released four months later and went back into prison on the twentieth of August after he was caught in active service after shootin' at a British soldier just on the road here. He got eighteen years for possession with intent, and he was only in for two years before he escaped.

JLA: And today, he's . . .

Seamus: He's on the run. We don't see him.

JLA: And you had another brother who was also in prison who later died.

Seamus: John. Well, John died in 1972, a fortnight after he was released. He returned to the IRA. He was in active service and he died the first night of the [IRA] cease-fire in 1972.

SA: (to Kathleen) If Seamus or one of your other children, if they were active now in the IRA and if they were called to go back on active service, what would your reaction be?

Kathleen: I'd be behind them.

SA: Even though—

Kathleen: Even though it would mean prison again.

SA: Or possibly their death.

Kathleen: Or death, yes.

JLA: Why?

Kathleen: Well, I know what has happened since 1969. Because you went to bed at night and you didn't know when your door was going to be kicked in. You didn't know when it was gonna happen. You went to bed at night and you were afraid to go asleep. I coulda put my teapot on for my house being raided every week and, when my husband was dead, they even came and they put a Union Jack on my tree out there.

JLA: (to Seamus) Was your father involved in the earlier Republican efforts?

Seamus: It's funny, because the only thing about that . . . My father would be what the Catholic Church would call a very strong, conservative, Catholic family man. And he was; and he was a good man. And I'm very thankful for all that he's ever given me, 'cause he was a good man. But he lived for his family, and maybe he was afraid to express himself at all politically for fear of it leadin' to us becoming involved. . . . I think he found it hard to understand because he loved us so much and it really. . . . I think maybe that's what killed him at the end of the day, too, that he saw the whole family bein' torn apart and people losing their lives and having to sacrifice their lives in prison or whatever.

Like, I saw my father twice in jail before he died in 1976. Once was just after I was caught and I told him that I expected twenty to twenty-five years. The last time I saw him was the week of my trial, and I told him that I was going on "the blanket" and that I wouldn't see him for a long time. And he told me he couldn't go to the trial because it . . . he had to mind the kids. And that was the last I saw of him. That was a really emotional visit for me. After I'd heard of the first heart attack, I'd planned to get him up that Christmas, but I never, ever got to see him again.

On the death of me father, the British Army came to raid the house, to arrest Dermott. The hassle was so great that night in the house, my father ended up takin' a heart attack afterwards and died. So, I mean, I blame the British Army for his death.

Kathleen: Yeah. I blame them, too.

JLA: What's it like getting out?

Seamus: Well, I've never really talked about it to my family, but . . . the first thing that I sensed was the apathy. Not towards the Republican movement, but towards life in general. I think one of the things I underestimated in jail was the effect of this last seventeen years on our people.

JLA: What about your prospects? Can you remain active on any level, legitimate or otherwise, in the Republican cause without getting burnt?

Seamus: I'm a public target now, as it is, because I've been . . . you know what I mean? When I was in jail, the last two years of my imprisonment I was classified as a top-risk security prisoner. If they believe I haven't been rehabilitated — and the fact that I've been in prison twice already, you know, I'm a red light. . . . And I believe I am under surveillance. They know who I am.

Well, I am a Republican. I mean, I haven't been broken by imprisonment. And I still believe in everything that I ever fought for. And I will become politically active again.

JLA: Even if it means going back?

Seamus: Well, anybody can go to jail here. You know, all they have to do is arrest you and get a statement out of you. The prisons in the North here are full of innocent people, too. So, if I'm gonna go away to prison again, I want it to be for something.

JLA: So you plan to stay in Northern Ireland.

Seamus: I plan to. I plan to stay in Ireland. I'm not going to leave it for them; it's our country.

SA: What about your brother [Dermott] who's on the run? What sort of future does he have?

Seamus: None. Prison. Prison or . . . the grave. There's very little options available to 'im.

JLA: Martin, what about you? Have you been arrested?

Martin: Everybody's been. Anybody you talk to on the street will tell you they've been arrested, whether it's for four hours or seven days. So, I've been arrested, like, but only by the British Army, for screenin'.

Kathleen: But they knew who you were.

Martin: Yeah, and they know I'm here. There's nothin' stoppin' them from comin' tomorrow morning and pickin' me up and takin' me away. But . . . I

haven't been affected the way the likes o' Seamus and my brother Dermott has.
. . . But it's a fact a life; for them, it's been bein' away from the house . . . for me,
it's been losing them, growin' up without 'em. . . . It's just that type a thing, the
way it's affected me, you know? Losing a family, a brother, and . . . there's no
future for you at all.

SA: Has the experience of your brothers made you apprehensive about getting
involved, or more willing to be?

Martin: Apprehensive. Maybe it's possibly a fear of bein' arrested and put into
jail and taken outta circulation or bein' put six foot under, you know?

SA: Seamus, having spent almost twelve years in prison, what would you like
to see Martin's role in the Republican cause to be?

Seamus: I would give him all the advice and help that I could, but it would be
his decision, at the end of the day, as to what role he would like to play. But no role's
too small or too great. I think he, and everyone else, has a contribution to make,
were it be passive or active.

SA: But obviously you wouldn't want to see Martin go through what you did
with twelve years in prison. Would that outweigh—say, if Martin were to want to
become active in a military sense, would you try to persuade him not to?

Seamus: No, I wouldn't prevent him, because I think Martin is at a stage in life
where he's old enough to make his own decisions. I would try and make him aware
of the dangers, the sacrifices, the hardships, and the consequences of it. About
bein' a Republican, like . . . that's not a question you can answer in a few
sentences because . . . I mean, how do you explain pain?

Being a Republican . . . I wouldn't say it's a massive burden, because it's a—
it's an honor, you know I mean? Because I do honestly believe we are fightin' for a
very noble cause. And it should be an honor for anybody to be a member of the
IRA, in my opinion. But the IRA Volunteers have great responsibilities to live up
to. And that life is not an easy life to lead.

Kathleen: Not only that. When they were on the blanket . . . it was very hard for
me as a mother to go up and see my son comin' out to me with hair way past his
shoulders and beard down to there and the eyes all glazed and a pale, pale, face and
the eyes sunk away in the back o' the face. I don't know what it was like for them,
but I know what I felt when I come home. I just couldn't think; I just couldn't do
anything.

SA: Did you ever consider asking him to come off the blanket?

Kathleen: No, I didn't. Never would. Because what he was doin' was for what
he believed in, and I was behind him all the way. But I just couldn't describe to you
what they went through. It would be very hard for me to do it, because there's
nobody knows that, only themselves. . . . And this is the first time I've ever heard
him speakin' about anything.

Seamus: As I said earlier, it's a very, very hard road to travel. But even trying to analyze your role or your struggle . . . This thing about—of taking life and the morality of war . . . you can become so deeply entrenched in it at times that if you don't control that, it can do you damage psychologically at the end of the day.

I think you always have to remind yourself that it's a war of attrition . . . and there's no time limit to it.

*"Supergrasses" are turncoat members of Ulster's paramilitary squads who inform on their comrades to the British authorities; after testifying in court, the informant is protected, relocated, and given a new identity. In recent years, there have been a number of Supergrass trials, with mixed results; some defendants have been linked to specific crimes and sentenced, but many more have been acquitted on lack of evidence. The system has been roundly criticized for the dual system of justice it represents: men and women going to prison in Northern Ireland on hearsay, "evidence" that would be thrown out of an English court.*

*Both Catholic and Protestant militants have been the targets of Supergrass trials. Evelina Sayers, 47, Ruth Hewitt, 43, and Mary McCrossan, 44, are the Protestant wives of three alleged Ulster Volunteer Force (UVF) members who were arrested in different Supergrass dragnets. Their husbands, Norman, Jackie, and Jim, respectively, were imprisoned "on remand" for periods ranging from twenty months to thirty months before they were all acquitted. Norman Sayers and Jim McCrossan had previous arrest records for paramilitary activities.*

Evelina: Know how it works? Say you two, you were setting on the bar and you two were setting and talking. And there's someone listening turned Supergrass, and he says, "I heard them two setting, plotting a murder at such and such a bar, at such and such a time," and you two would be lifted, arrested, put into prison, and held for up to two years, if not longer! On his word alone! And you couldn't do nothing until your trial comes forward, and it's up to the District Prosecution Office before they set a date. And that's just Internment, to get people out of the Road. That's all it is. Internment by remand.

JLA: All three of your husbands were held on a Supergrass. How does that make you feel about the British government?

Evelina: I feel regret, because I've always been British and intended to stay British. But then, whenever the trials came out, British justice actually came through in the end.

Mary: But it took a long time.

Ruth: You know, the hardest part is that these men have been cleared of these charges. Say we got out in the cars and we're stopped at a roadblock. We're held for a while. Because these men are "terrorists," "known terrorists." You have to set until your name's all cleared, and the passengers in the car, and all their names are taken. So even when the trials are over, it's an effect you don't forget, for it's a mark against you.

Evelina: And it's a mark against your children. I have three teenage sons. Now, my oldest boy is just going into twenty and he has applied three times for the Royal Air Force and three times he has got the runaround. One time he didn't have enough qualifications. Now, he had five O levels [high school exams]. Hadn't enough qualifications. Got more, went to college, went back again, and they said his eyesight wasn't too good and he needs a stronger pair of glasses. We went out and got that. The third excuse was that there was no vacancies. Now, it's advertised every Thursday night in the *Belfast Telegraph*: "Make your career in the Royal Air Force." And he went back the third time, and they said they had no vacancies. All they had was for cooks.

Now, the youngest boy. He's just going into sixteen. He does his O levels next year and he has his heart set on the Royal Air Force. And he hasn't a hope. They don't want to know ye. You can't get a job in the electricity service. You can't get a government job as a civil servant, no matter how many qualifications you have, because they put you down as a security risk. And that's your children, what has nothing to do with it.

SA: So what are your futures here?

Ruth: Zero.

Evelina: If I had the money, luv, I'd pack my kids off across the water to my brother. And the wee lad is only back from America. I'd pack him back again to the people that had him over there. Them people over in America wanted to keep him, and he wanted to stay. But he also wanted to come home to us. He was torn between the ones in America and torn between us.

You know who I blame for all this? Maggie Thatcher. Maggie Thatcher! If I had her now by the throat, she'd never walk away again.

JLA: What was it like visiting your husbands in prison?

Evelina: Hated it.

Mary: Heartbreaking. You get yourself dressed up and wear a smile and say everything's all right, while it's heartbreaking. My Jim was in the [Maze Prison] Blocks. They weren't allowed to wear their own clothes. They weren't allowed shoelaces on their boots.

Evelina: When mine was in Crumlin Road [prison] David wasn't even two. And then I think of the children don't get to see their daddies. Through time, children forget about their fathers if it's a long time. The children, if you don't take them oft times they forget about them.

I had that experience with my bigger ones. With my bigger ones in school, I wasn't keen on taking 'em off school. And then when they didn't come, maybe a couple of months later I said, "Norman, go see your daddy." "Oh, I don't want to go to Crumlin." You know, they had no interest. They'd lost interest in their daddy.

Mary: They don't understand prison when they're babies. But as they get older and they're at school, I think they feel it.

Evelina: There was one time my Emily—now, Emily is ten now—and the children were all playing on the street. They were playing cops and robbers. Now, it was all right when she was the police, chasing the other children, but, you see, when it came to her time to be a robber and the other ones chasing her to catch her to put her in jail, she went into nerves! Really screamed! "I don't want to go to jail! I don't want to go to jail!" She was terrified, you know, after going to that prison every week.

Ruth: And we have the job of bringing the young ones up. You're trying to teach your child one thing, and when your husband goes in on a Supergrass you're trying to explain, "Your father's not guilty." "Well, why was he put in jail?" . . . Kids just don't understand it.

Mary: They're confused. They don't know who's telling the truth and who's telling the lies. In the playgrounds . . . you know, children can be very cruel. And one week, one of my wee ones went to school and it was all over the school—"Oh, your daddy's in for murder." And that wee lad, it broke his heart and he didn't want to go back to school. And you're trying to talk your way out. Well, all on account of these Troubles it's the young ones that suffer. Suffer very badly.

JLA: What do you think would happen if it became a united Ireland?

Mary: (laughs bitterly)

Evelina: There'd be a bloodbath.

Ruth: It'll never happen.

Evelina: There'd be a civil war. Because the Loyalist people will not give up. Why should we give our country up?

Ruth: Okay, a lot of Republicans died, but there's been good Loyalists died. You don't forget all this, you know? People have fought for their country. I was brought up a hard-line Loyalist, I won't deny that. I was brought up British and I'll always be British. And that's the end. We don't need changes.

JLA: What is going to happen now?

Evelina: Well, if there's not a peace situation very soon, there'll probably be a civil war. I'd say it's coming very quickly. That's my feeling.

Mary: I think it's getting worse instead of better. We had something that we want to hold on to, to be British. And no way we intend to give that up. We're getting forced in. It's getting took off us behind our backs, and we're not going to stand for it. The Protestant people will not stand— We're getting pushed too far, and I think it's coming to that time.

We're not taking off nothing from the Roman Catholics. We only want to hold on to what belongs to us.

*The Rossville Flats are three high-rise apartment buildings that stand on the slope below the picturesque walled city of Londonderry (or Derry, as Republicans prefer). They are an ugly testament to 1960s urban planning gone bad, where the overflow of inhabitants in the cramped Catholic ghetto of the Bogside were placed.*

*Today, one of the three towers is being demolished and there are plans for eventually razing the other two. Republican militants simultaneously decry the conditions of Rossville and laud its reputation as the city's bastion of resistance against "official repression."*

*On a frigid, windy morning, Rossville residents are meeting on the concrete walkways to discuss and inspect the damage done by the security forces during a predawn raid this morning. Marty Malarkay, a Republican activist in his mid-twenties and a resident of Rossville Flats, shows neighbors the bootprint and broken hinges on his front door.*

All the other raids I think they arrested. This was the first time they didn't actually arrest anyone. Most of them are just blind, sort of indiscriminate sort of things, you know? 'Cause if they did know anything about anyone, they'd come and just knock on their door politely and handle them without wakin' the whole neighborhood up.

But the whole idea is just to teach everybody in the Flats a lesson. They see us as a hard-line Provo area, and anybody at all—I mean, even walkin' and it's a Sunday, there's people that walk through these Flats—and when they walk through here they get searched. It's just anybody. Could be a priest or anything, if you're just in the vicinity. You're not wanted; you will be taught a lesson.

They [the British Army] don't like this as a sort of terrain for them, because they can't keep a close eye on it. They've used the helicopters now for the last month at night over these Flats, with spotlights. You can't sleep with that. They shine onto the house, and the whole courtyard lights up. With the shinin' and the noise of it, there's no way you can get any sleep. But it's different to them; they just regard the Flats complex as jes' training grounds.

*Martha McLelland is an expatriate Irish-American who, over the past thirteen years, has developed the accent of her adopted homeland. She is active in the Republican movement in Derry and, on a tour of the ancient walled parapets of the city, which overlook the Rossville Flats and the Bogside, she sees the British government's "sinister designs" everywhere.*

You see that, the way the screens are set up? If they wanted to protect two communities from conflict, right, they would have the screen right there so that nobody could throw bricks over, or petrol bombs that way, right? But instead, the Loyalists can sit here and fire bricks across there, right? And nobody could really get to you; you could smash every one of the windows.

See the woman in that blue flat? She was ironing, right? She got a brick and it just missed her head. Had she been sitting at her desk instead of standing at it . . .

And see where that mark is on the door; the blue flat below there? The boy was thirteen sittin' on his bed and the window came in on him with a brick. And, for two or three Wednesday nights in a row that was happening, you know?

That was during the winter, that bit. And the Loyalists would just be up here. They had the advantage. I gave chase one night, but I can't run very fast, and they're away before you know it.

You see there, now? Now, if we threw petrol bombs from there, given that the gates are all blockaded off by Brits and soldiers—RUC, right?—anything that we throw back is stopped by those walls. But yet they're on the walls and they can attack us. They command the heights.

That there got a lotta bad publicity, you see? That's a Protestant church, right? The roof o' that there was an SAS post. Undercover soldiers were camped out there and they could fire into the Flats, right? When the Bogside people found that, they burnt out that church, right? I don't know if it was being used at the time, but it got international publicity: "Bogside Youths, Young Catholics Burn Out Protestant Church." But it wasn't that at all, you know; it was the fact that when you've got houses where undercover soldiers can hide, it's actually quite dangerous to people. They fire out on you.

You see here, the difference in the planning here? See the difference in the breadth of that street? It's deliberately a really wide avenue, really broad carpark in front, a carpark when even now, when a lotta people have cars, that's how few cars are in that carpark. Okay, now, the difference for that is that you can't really hide anymore, right? Those flats, the flat-roofed ones who were built a bit earlier? That's a better place if you want to riot, right? 'Cause it affords some cover. All that broad area there, that is deliberately . . . it's like a scorched-earth policy that separates groups of people and they [the security forces] can go in and do those flats, then they can go and do another small area, right?

The flyover; if you'll notice the flyover, right? It deliberately cuts into the Bogside like that and, again, that was deliberate. We didn't actually need a flyover in the middle of the Bogside. That was actually done deliberately to bisect the community, you know?

You'll see also in the new estates, in addition to the single entrance and exit, they have really broad green places. And it's not that they want to give people playing spaces or children playgrounds. They're just broad green spaces so that you can maneuver vehicles in them but you can't hide in them. And so they can seal off whole areas and anyone entering or leaving would be immediately caught, you know? Because it's like a scorched-earth policy. The fact that it looks nice and green is a bit superficial, you know? It just looks nicer . . .

*Jeremy Atkinson, 19, Geoffrey Burnham, 29, George Douglas, 18, and Joe Barrow, 22, are among the lucky few young people in Belfast who have full-time jobs. They are employees of a construction company that is currently rewiring a five-story building in downtown Belfast. It is their lunch hour, and they sprawl out in a dimly-lit storage room cluttered with their tools.*

*Jeremy is a tall, serious boy, his eyes thoughtful behind horn-rimmed glasses. Geoffrey, the oldest of the crew, looks tired and occasionally massages his jaw with a dusty hand. George has an open, innocent face, and the rosy-cheeked Joe wears a constant half-grin, as if awaiting the perfect moment to tell a cherished joke. All are Protestants.*

Jeremy:  You've got very little worries in this country, you know. No more than if you were a black in a white area in the States. I certainly would never worry.

Geoffrey:  Well, most people's lives have been touched by The Troubles—oh, aye—to a fairly major degree at some stage during the last fifteen years. I mean, everyone gets affected by the police checks, and you can't park your car in the security zones and all that sort of thing, but I would say just about everybody has known someone who has gotten killed by The Troubles.

I would say my life is definitely different. Sometimes I think its soul-destroying. You're working away trying to get a few pound together, trying to get on your feet, and you think to yourself, "There isn't really any point in doing all this." You could spend the next five years beating your head against the wall trying to make a few pounds, and then it turns up being a united Ireland or whatever, and your property isn't worth anything and it's all gone up in smoke. Sometimes I wonder why I stay here at all.

George:  A lot of people would feel bitter if something in their family has happened. Because I've had quite a few relatives blown up or shot or something. In fact, a couple of weeks ago, the policeman shot down in Newry, I went to school with and I was very friendly with. And he was shot.

Here, you think to yourself whenever you go out—say you're out chasing it and meet some girl—you're always very cautious. Who she is, where she comes from. If she comes from a bad place at all, you just go away.

Jeremy:  Same as any other place in the world.

George:  'Cause, for all you know, her father could be in the IRA.

Joe:  I've always to be careful. You know, who I go out with from the Falls or whatever, 'cause the place I live in, Ballyclare, it's nearly all UDA men. And if they heard you were mucking about with someone from the Falls, you would get done in.

I've no worries against ordinary Catholics. No problem. There's quite a few Catholics live in Ballyclare that I jump about with. But it's the Republicans, the Catholics from the Falls and that, who really are bitter against you.

Jeremy:  We come from a sixty percent Protestant, forty percent Catholic estate, and there wouldn't be any trouble in this estate. Although some people . . . there's rumors going around that two of them—do you remember a Catholic taxi man being killed a few years ago?—there's two boys up for it in our estate. But in the actual estate you would find no fight between the Catholics and Protestants. Although, across the way, a couple of Catholics were burned out of their houses. But not in our estate.

Geoffrey: I was brought up in a fairly middle-class sort of background, and I didn't have a clue what the difference between a Protestant and a Catholic was until The Troubles really started, when I was about ten or eleven. I knew a Catholic was a Catholic and I was a Protestant, but as far as the history of Ireland or why there was Catholics and why there was Protestants, I hadn't a notion. And, in fact, I still have very, very little knowledge in Irish history and that sort of thing.

George: I'm lucky, because my father, he used to be a lecturer in the Orange Clubs and, whenever I was being brought up, that was one of the first things he ever taught me. What to do and what not to do. And he's always on at me, whenever any time I go out, he's always on at me, "Be careful, never say anything that could get yourself done in. Just keep yourself to yourself."

Jeremy: Personally, I have nothing against Catholics. Republicans, yes. They're a totally different race of people.

George: Their eyes are narrower together. (laughter)

Joe: You're joking there now, but an awful lot of them have squinty eyes. There's some look about them.

Jeremy: We've always fought for our country. Even in the Battle of the Somme and all, the Northern Ireland people were about the first to volunteer to fight.

Joe: My dad's got this speech thing of what Winston Churchill said after the war. He says that if it hadn't been for the Ulster people, we would've lost the war, because we were able to keep the shipping lanes open whenever the Nazis were barricading everything off. And everybody over in England were all drafted in, forced to go in. Everybody in Northern Ireland wasn't; they all went in as volunteers. They volunteered for their country.

Jeremy: The Ulster people would be far more loyal to the Queen. They think more of the Queen than the majority of the English.

Joe: They would. That's right.

Jeremy: Far, far more loyalist to the Queen.


*Small and thin with intense brown eyes, Fiona was brought up in a hard-line Republican household with four brothers and three sisters. Soon she will be entering Queen's College in Belfast to study French. She is 18.*


I don't think my life has been affected by The Troubles that much. It probably affected the lives of my family more than me, because I don't bother with it that much. But they're pretty bitter. I mean, they don't go out and shoot people, but say there's something on the news about some RUC men had been shot or blown up or something. They would cheer and say, "Good on 'em." Sick.

Like my younger brothers would have absolutely nothing to do with Protestants. And they're all for the IRA, and they think, "We're right behind you." If they hear of a Protestant or somebody from the Army or somebody from the RUC getting hurt, there would be cheers. This would be great. And if there was a Catholic or an IRA man that had been killed, it would be "Let's get out and get them. They done this and let's make them pay for it." My parents would be the same.

If you said to one of my wee brothers, "Why do you not like Protestants?" they would just say, "Because they're Protestants." They wouldn't really know why they don't like them.

On the ninth of August there, we had a spot of trouble. Just outside my bedroom, it was. And it wasn't anything. It was more just young people out for kicks, like. They found tins of paint in somebody's coal shed and milk bottles, and they filled up the milk bottles and chucked the paint all around the place. It wasn't for any cause or anything; it was just, "Let's go have a fun time." But they made it out to be "We're out to get the trespassers on Irish soil." I think it's just excitement, adds a bit of excitement into their lives.

I mean, when I was a kid during the hunger strike—that was, what, about five or six years ago, so I was thirteen then—one of the hunger strikers lived on our street and so we were among the first to hear that he had died, and I was *the* first person with my bin lid out, banging my bin lid at the end of the street. And that was when I was thirteen. That was because my family did it and everybody around me did it. But then, I've developed me own views now and I wouldn't be the first one there now; in fact, I probably wouldn't even be down . . . although I might go down for the excitement. It's a good crack.

The people look to the likes of the IRA. 'Round where I live there's a problem with joyriding and stuff and there's groups of eighteen-, nineteen-year-old boys that go out just terrorizing everybody, and the people look to the IRA to protect them.

And the IRA does. You hear about kneecapping and stuff like that? That's what that is. It's in the newspapers and made out that these boys are innocent and they've just been victims of the IRA and they haven't done anything, but the people appreciate that kind of thing. I mean, even I would say.

There's times when I think I would disagree about the way the IRA goes about things. The way it seems sort of sly, some of the things they do. Like they just pounce on people and blow them up or whatever. But when we did history in school, that has always been the way the Irish have fought. I suppose if they came out into the open they would have no chance. . . . They seem to represent hope for the people, but I don't know what they're hoping for. I would probably—I might support what they're fighting for, but I wouldn't support the way they're going about it. And I'm not even sure if I would support a united Ireland, because the south of Ireland isn't exactly perfect. I'm just happy with things the way they are.

*John McMichael is a burly pub owner in Belfast. At 38, he is reputed to be the real strongman of the paramilitary Ulster Defence Association (UDA), of which he is a prominent leader. He speaks in a booming voice, but the words themselves are tentative and made of conflicting passions. There is a report circulating that he was spotted near the scene of a recent sectarian murder of a Catholic taxi driver. The murder was claimed by the Ulster Freedom Fighters (UFF), the terrorist wing of the UDA; before the interview begins, McMichael rails about the report and says it has earned him a "top priority" on the IRA's death list.*

I have been arrested many, many times and taken into custody for questioning, usually general questioning. Um . . . I've been in prison a couple of times. On remand. Always, the charges were dropped. I've had all the misfortunes that a lot of people in Northern Ireland come up against.

My life's been wasted by it, you know? My life's been wasted. Because it's all taken up with the problems in Northern Ireland. All I've been doin' is holdin' the line, eternally defendin' the frontiers . . . not allowin' things to get . . . we're holding on to Northern Ireland. We're sorta fightin' for existence. Now, that's no way to live! So it's not. In fact, you're not livin' at all; you're just existin'.

Now daily, there are people mutilated, there are people killed, and the tragedy is you can't even remember the last person that was killed! It's just that your memory's been tested, thousands and thousands to test it.

Now, at the minute, people worry when they come into me house. It shocks 'em when there are bolts on the doors, maybe six bolts on a door, and there's contraptions that you put in so that the door, no matter what happens, you can't force the door open . . . and I have to look underneath me car, and I have to keep an eye out, to watch over me shoulder. You watch out for the kids in the street . . . if anybody comes up the path, you wonder who it is, and you don't open the door, unless you know who it is. And you're probably livin' with more adrenaline floatin' about in your body at any given time and you're sort of on a high all the time. . . .

If I go away, say for a fortnight somewhere, if I take a holiday, it takes the fortnight just to try and wind down! I always look forward to comin' back, because I really love this place . . . but sometimes, I would like to stay away a bit longer, you know, just to get unwound. I find if I go to London or anywhere in England or Scotland—I went there last week—that you find it strange. It's unnatural! Everything's so peaceful!

Well, I'll tell you somethin' that crossed my mind more times than enough.

[Over there] you're not worried about cars sittin' about; you can park in places that you can't park here. You can go in a shop; you don't get searched. You're not seein' people runnin' around with guns all the time and Land Rovers full of . . .

Something crossed my mind when I was away a number of times is . . . that you look 'round, y'know, and everybody's goin' about normal . . . peaceful, right? You start to wonder, what's their drivin' force, you know? What's important to 'em? Are they actually—are they playin' any real role?

*On the evening of December 22, 1987, McMichael got into his car to drive to his favorite pub. It was ripped apart by a car bomb and McMichael was killed instantly.*

*They are anachronisms and outcasts on the tough streets of Belfast. Gary Nolan is an unemployed 25-year-old Protestant from the Springmartin estate of West Belfast. Maggie Darragh is a 19-year-old Catholic from adjoining Ballymurphy, a staunchly-Republican neighborhood. Together, they represent one-third of the Youth for Peace, the youth branch of the Peace People.*

*Founded in 1976 by two Belfast housewives, one Catholic, one Protestant, the Peace People led a series of bipartisan marches which called for peace and reconciliation in Northern Ireland. Winning the Nobel Prize for Peace in 1976, the Peace People captured the imagination of the world's media, if not that of Northern Ireland; the movement has long since been moribund, if not yet extinct. The Youth for Peace branch, which once attracted hundreds of activists, now consists of six young people, including Gary and Maggie.*

Gary: I never got any hassle or anything in school. The main problem was outside school, around the area in Highfield. I was beat up twice since I got involved in Youth for Peace, because they saw it as . . . well, I don't really know what they saw it as—sort of seemed to think it was something set up by the IRA, to dupe people into some false sense of security. But the IRA Republican newspaper, they called it "Operation Peace People." They said it was a British plot.

Maggie: I used to hear it from home a bit. "You Peace Person, you." They gave up after a while, because they knew it didn't bother me. Can you imagine living in a hard-line Republican district—just imagine it—and somebody in your family has totally different views, who doesn't believe or want to hear what Sinn Fein are putting forward, who doesn't want to hear anything about the violence, doesn't think it's great whenever some policeman has been shot dead? I remember times when somebody would come along and go, "Oh, we got three of those old peelers today." But once you sit down and think about it, those are people doing a job.

They're just doing a job, for they need money. They're ordinary people, too. I just could not accept it.

And then, when the Peace People came to the school, I thought it was really good. It was different, that was the main thing. I wanted to find out what this alternative thing was. And once you do get into it, you just can't go back to see rioting again.

I can't stand violence now at all. It's in my district all the time, and I'm not in my district. I stay out of it as much as I possibly can. I know the people in my district. I wouldn't walk past anybody without saying hello or anything like that, but their views are so totally different to mine, I feel I just can't accept it and I don't want to sit down and have an argument, because these are people I live with. I don't know if they want any part of me. I know there's a lot of people who feel the same way as myself in the district, who would like to see something different, but who aren't bothered to get off their backsides and do something about it. Which is what I want to do, and I feel this group, that's exactly what they're doing. They're bringing people together.

The first camp I went to, after the first couple of days you couldn't be bothered with religion. Religion just sort of went out the window. And what you've got to remember is that's going to stay with that kid for the rest of his life. So whenever that kid grows up, marries, has children, he's not going to pass on the same views to his children that his father passed on to him. It's maybe not this generation, maybe not the next generation, but maybe the one after.


*Frank McCoubrey, 20, is a hard youth with an air of sullen defiance. He lives in the Loyalist neighborhood of Springmartin and is a painter by trade. He slouches in a chair and clasps his hands before him, the bony knuckles adorned with tattooed blue dots.*


JLA: Has your life been affected by The Troubles?

Frank: No, not really. Just . . . not really. Just that . . . when we were young, like, my dad was put in jail. He was a Loyalist prisoner for three and a half years. We never saw 'im. 'Bout once a month we saw 'im. That was it, the only real problem we've had.

SA: Have you ever had Catholic friends?

Frank: No. I try my best to keep away from 'em, like. I know you shouldn't, but I try my best to keep away from 'em. Just can't mix wi' 'em. I can't trust 'em. Just can't do. Think they're too sneakin', so I do. Just can't trust a Taig—or a Catholic, whatever you want. And I think the Protestants are run down, so I do.

JLA: What do you think should be known about the Protestants?

Frank: We are civilized! If you look around our estates, like they're clean and tidy. You take a trip up to Ballymurphy, they're stinkin,' so they are. And they're just livin' in slums there.

SA: What do you think would happen if there was a unification of Ireland?

Frank: Obviously there'd be a civil war and there'd be a lotta people killed. It'll be a bloody war, so it will.

And I don't like the thoughts of their Tricolour. An' I don't like the thoughts of bein' run by a government like the South. I'd kill meself before, so I would.

But if the civil war came and was over tomorrow, you're still gonna have bitterness somewhere, so you are. It'll never be over. That's my point of view. It will go on for years.

SA: Would you ever think about leaving Northern Ireland?

Frank: No. There's no way. Where could ye go to? There, a Protestant is dirt, so you are, when you go to England. They class you as an IRA man once they hear your accent. Don't want anything to do wi' you. Once they hear the accent, they're lookin' their shoulders at ye, you know what I mean? You're classed as Paddies.

We were evacuated in 1973, to Liverpool, when The Troubles were bad. They treated us like dirt. I remember. I wasn't a child, so things like that stick in your mind, so they do.

JLA: So you feel you have to do something on your own?

Frank: I do. Takes people to speak out, so it does, on the Protestant side. I've lived up here all my life, and I've saw it. I've saw it all, so I have. Bullets comin' through yer window. Everything. You go down the road outside o' your house, you'll see all the holes where the bullets went in it. Know what I mean? Leaves a scar on yer head, and you always remember it, so you do.

*"Betty" is a 31-year-old Catholic divorcee and mother of two children living in a strongly Republican West Belfast district. She works sixteen hours a week for a small Falls Road business and receives twenty-two pounds ($32) a week in government financial assistance. A bright, vivacious woman, her nerves seem frayed and her fingers tremble as she chain-smokes Silk Cut cigarettes in the kitchen of her small rowhouse.*

I was out in a drinking club one night and I was sitting with my sister and her husband, who's English, and we were just sitting there having a drink and there was a band playing. And the lights went out and the group stopped playing and we were told to keep still and nobody to leave the hall. And we saw all these masked men coming inside with balaclavas. We were absolutely terrified. Everybody froze. We've got about a hundred people in the hall; it was a social night. We didn't know what was happening. Everybody I was sitting with, every fella I was sitting with, drained. Pure white! Everybody thought, "They're coming for me," you know the way people think?

My poor brother-in-law happened to be at the top of the hall to talk with someone and, him being English, these guys went straight up to where he was and he thought "My God, I'm English; they're coming for me!"

But it was the fella sitting beside Nigel.

All I seen was, "Stand up! You, stand up! Put your hands on your head!" And this guy stood up and put his hands on his head. His face was pure white! And they frog-marched him out. And I'm going, "My God, this is awful."

You know, people don't like witnessing that, no matter how bad the person is and what he's done. Because you know what's going to happen to him when they get him outside. They break his legs and arms with hurley sticks.

And we were going, "Oh God, we come out to enjoy ourselves, not to witness this. Things are bad enough. You try to escape the tensions of the house and to come out to relax, and you see this?" Which is really upsetting.

And my sister said to me, "If I hear any gunfire, I'm going home." We were so upset. And I read about it in the paper the next morning and they had broken nearly every bone in his body.

But anyway, the lights went back on, the music started again and everybody resumed drinking. Fellas were going, "God, I thought they were coming for me, because you know, they looked so menacing with those cudgels and balaclavas.

And we're still talking about it when the lights went out again and the man who was responsible for the hall said, "Ladies and gentlemen, the club has now been surrounded by the RUC, and we advise all patrons to leave now in case of a disturbance."

I thought—I mean, I am paranoid anyway at the best of times, and this country has really made me totally paranoid—"Oh, by God, the RUC is going to come in and fire rubber bullets, shoot in here." That's the way you're geared to think here. You really don't trust anybody.

It was really terrible. It was my birthday, actually. I went out to celebrate my birthday, and that's how it ended up. A totally bad night.

The Troubles have made me really paranoid. I really hate . . . the thing I really fear is sectarian murder. It really terrifies me. Just people getting murdered. Because I've known people that got murdered. Went out to drink and were found next morning, hooded, shot through the head, their hands behind their back. I mean, when sectarian murders start up it's awful, because when you're walking down the road at night in the dark, I'm really scared when cars slow down, you know, in case they're going to try to pull you in or shoot you. I've got this fear all the time. I actually left Belfast when I was eighteen because I couldn't stick it anymore. I went to live in Dublin.

This is such a backward place. I find it hard to understand. I mean, we pick up a paper and find out a Catholic has been mutilated and badly tortured just because he's a Catholic. Only certain people can do this. They must have this really intense hatred of Catholics to be able to do anything like that. I don't think the Catholic community is capable of being that vicious.

Protestant people have a deep fear of losing. They've a lot to lose—let's face it—if this did become a united Ireland. They own the best land. For hundreds and hundreds of years, all the best farming land is owned by Protestants. They've got the best jobs, so they have a helluva lot to lose. And that's why they can be vicious.

People years ago used to hide it all from their children. You weren't allowed to mention Protestants or Catholics. If someone said Protestant, you'd go, "Where did you hear that? What's a Protestant?" But now, I want my children . . . I mean, I—they can't understand, they think— My two children went with my mother last Sunday down to the big march for the ninth of August. Well, there were colorful bands and everything, and my children said to my mother, "Granny are they the Protestants?" They still don't really understand.

They have a fear of soldiers and big armored cars, because they have seen rioting on television. But they think the police are doing it to the people; they don't understand that they're fighting back, that the people are retaliating with bricks and bottles. They think it's the soldiers, and they're wary of them.

My daughter was lost one time about two years ago, and I couldn't see her and I couldn't think straight, all these masses of people in the town. I mean, you could tell on my face, I just couldn't think of where she'd gone. You know, you think someone's snatched her. . . .

This woman seen my face; I looked so really anxious. She said, "Have you lost a little girl?" and I said, "Yes." She said, "She's up there; a policeman has her." And I thought, thank God the policeman has her. And here he was carrying her and she was trying to get away from him and he said to me, "She wouldn't tell me her name." And I says to her, "My little one, why did you not tell the policeman your name?" She said, "I thought he was going to shoot me with a plastic bullet." She was only three or four. And that there brought it home to me; it's a terrible situation that we're living in here.

I just feel that I'm a puppet in between all these politicians, organizations. I am completely disillusioned with the whole thing, to be quite honest. I haven't got faith in their word. That's the way I think, and that's why I don't like living in Belfast anymore. I hate it, absolutely hate it. How can people be so stupid?

About eleven years ago, I lived in London; (laughs) this sounds like a fairy story! I was in a restaurant on Carnaby Street and an Arab came in. I didn't know he was very wealthy at the time.

And he couldn't speak good English and he asked could I order him a meal, and I ordered for him what I was eating. And he was very grateful, and he asked would I go out with him. But I was a bit wary, and I said, "No; I'm going back to Belfast shortly; there would be no point." And he asked for my address in Belfast, and I give it to him and he sent a postcard from Italy.

I was feeling a bit depressed here about the beginning of last year, and I discovered the postcard and I said, "I think I'll write this guy and see if he's still alive"—I mean, this was after eleven, twelve years.

I was sitting here one night and the phone rang and he phoned me from Saudi Arabia! I have been keeping in contact with him ever since, and he said to me on the phone last week—I wrote and I told him about Belfast, about the lack of employment and what it was like—and he phoned me back and he says, "How's Belfast? Is it cold there?", and I says, "It's absolutely freezing!"

He said to me at one stage on the phone, "Betty, (imitates his accent) is there anything you want! Is there anything you need?" And I thought, "My God, (laughs) I could use a lot of things," but I didn't say it—put him off!

But he said to me—he must be a bit stupid, you know—"You want to come to Arabia, I find you work. What would you like to work?" (laughs)

I don't know, and people keep saying to me, "God that's your meal ticket out of here!" This is the way you come to think, you know? So I think to meself, "God, I'm gonna stick with this guy. He might get me out of here."

But it really is strange, and I think, wouldn't it be wonderful and . . . Oh, I don't know . . . I'm just waiting for another letter.

I mean, am I going to die in this place?

*Of all the paramilitary groups in Northern Ireland, the Irish National Liberation Army (INLA) is perhaps the most despised by authorities. Beyond the goal of Irish unification, INLA seeks to establish a socialist revolutionary state and draws its inspiration from Marx and Lenin. The INLA was responsible for the bloodiest attack in the history of The Troubles, a pub bombing in the village of Ballykelly in which eleven British soldiers and six civilians were killed.*

*"Jerry," one of INLA's top-ranking officers, is an overweight 25-year-old man with small, close-set eyes and short sandy hair. The interview is held at a secluded table in a "safe" backstreet pub of Belfast. Jerry leans closer across the table and talks evenly and rapidly, retreating several times to the restroom to confer with his comrades, who are scattered throughout the club. He is humorless and severe.*

What you have to remember is for generations our people have been suffering at the hands of British oppression. And every generation, from when Queen Elizabeth sent the first troops to Ireland, young Irish men and Irish women of all ages have shouted our right to be free of this oppression. You know, there has to be something better for future generations. And yes, that is worth all the work, that's worth all the pain, and eventually it comes down, it's worth dying for. Because you can't allow your children . . . I'm not rearin' children to be shot dead by plastic bullets when they're four or five years old! You know? You have to look at it from that point of view. But until we get rid of Britain, British imperialism and British capitalism, things in Ireland aren't going to change!

We can't allow— Having given so much, so many people having died, we owe it to ourselves and our children to finish it now. And that makes it worth it, to think that we'll have been the last. We have to think that we'll be the last, we have to believe that we are going to win, to stop it. Because otherwise it'll go on and it'll go on, ad infinitum.

SA: Your organization makes no bones about having an assassination list, right?

Jerry: Yes, it's classed as "Those who incite Protestants to murder."

SA: Which people fall into that category?

Jerry: A number of people certainly do. Members of the security forces actively involved in the oppression of the Nationalist people, those who associate themselves with the security forces in their off-duty hours, those who serve them drink, those who would go to dance halls with them, are all classed as legitimate targets.

SA: So you're including civilians.

Jerry: Well, the most notable attack of the INLA was on the bar in Ballykelly, which received a number of warnings over a number of weeks. And every Monday night for a number of weeks the place was evacuated because of an INLA bomb scare, and still the people went to the bar and still the people served the soldiers drink. So, regrettably, the INLA was forced to detonate a bomb within the premises which resulted in seventeen deaths.

Uh . . . this is unfortunate, but it's also a fact a life. You can't allow these people to have safe havens. At the time of the Ballykelly explosion, a number of children and people in Derry had been shot and injured by plastic bullets and a number of them had been killed. For people in the area to be sittin' down and drinkin' with the people that done that was abhorrent and still is abhorrent. That has to be clearly understood.

JLA: What will happen if INLA takes over?

Jerry: The whole thing would have to be collectivized and run by the state. We are firm believers in the old adage, "From each according to his abilities and to each according to his needs." This would be the precept that would run the country, so that no one would starve and no one would be superior. But on the other hand, no one would be inferior. We'd be very wary of falling into the traps of . . . the so-called Russian elite society, and things like that there. I think the best model would be Castro's Cuba. But no Loyalists would be oppressed.

SA: So what would happen to the Loyalists?

Jerry: Loyalism is ah . . . miseducation. In the event of the INLA taking power, I would imagine that there would have to be a massive reeducation program. You'd have to draw the line, say, "All right, look, you're wearin' blinkers here. This is the way it is. We're not the enemy. Unemployment's the enemy; bad housing's the enemy. This is entirely engineered by British oppression."

JLA: On the policing of neighborhoods, how do you deal with criminals?

Jerry: What do we do? These people are involved in crimes against their own community. . . . You must be seen to act on behalf of that community when the pressure becomes too great.

Now, because there's no jails, you can't just take them away and lock them up for two years. But if you put a gun to the back of somebody's knee and take his kneecap off, it's gonna cause great physical pain for three or four days. He will walk with a bit of pain and a limp for about a month until his new plastic kneecap becomes adjusted and then he'll be as right as red. Hopefully, he will have learned his lesson.

But on occasions people don't, and then you must think of more severe terms to deal with them on. You must not allow hoodlums to dictate to the people in the area just because the security forces aren't prepared to come into an area because of the fear of ambush from the INLA or the IRA.

SA: How does the punishment for hoodlums graduate?

Jerry: At first, they're kneecapped. The next stage would be they'd be knee-capped again, only this time in both legs. In very severe cases, they'd be shot in both legs and both arms, and in the ultimate infringement, which would be after all these warnings, they'd still be committing serious crime, such as going into houses, beating on . . . It's only ever been done once by the Provos; the guy who was doing all those things was a total animal, so he was stiffed.

SA: What is your life like?

Jerry: It's, ah . . . you're continually stopped, harassed, continually arrested and taken to Castlereagh [detention center] for interrogation. Daily you run the risk of being assassinated by Loyalists; therefore, extraordinary security precautions must be taken. Every time you hear a motor bike, you're jumpin' in the doorway. . . . You know, you just do not have an opportunity for living a life. I've been at this from when I was about fourteen years old, so I couldn't draw a comparison with a normal life. It's not complete hardship, but it's one where you're continually looking over your shoulder.

JLA: Where does the INLA get its funding?

Jerry: Our funding's limited. And funds from time to time must be . . . liberated from British institutions such as post offices . . . uh, banks, savings banks. Never from areas that would cause Nationalists or ordinary Loyalist people hardship.

SA: You mentioned that you were on active service. Can you describe an INLA operation?

Jerry: Uh . . . what type of operation? A robbery, a shooting, a bombing?

JLA: A shooting.

Jerry: Well, a shootin' is . . . obviously, because of security reasons I wouldn't be so blind as to tell you anything what I been involved in meself . . . but, it's not just a case of somebody getting a gun and going out and shooting police or anything. The whole thing's totally thought out, it's totally planned. It's carried out on a military basis, which is why so few people are caught during operations. The risk to the volunteer would be minimal and the chance towards success would be high.

JLA: What about the emotional effects, if any, each time you've shed blood?

Jerry: You don't allow yourself to think. It's the first thing that you train yourself to do, is you don't think. You think merely in terms of uniforms; that's all you do. You don't think of the human being. You can't afford to let yourself think of the human being. You don't allow yourself that emotional leeway. You have to be totally sure you're politically correct before you can pull a trigger and plant a bomb. You have to be sure of your reasons, because if it was plainly an emotional thing, first slap in the head you'd got at Castlereagh, you'd be telling all. So you must be sure that you're politically correct; you must be able to justify it to yourself.

And you must think of the end and offer nothing. And you must keep your mind single because, at the end of the day, the guy you're pulling the trigger on or planting the bomb on is probably a family man like yourself, is probably a fella with children. You cannot allow yourself to be blackmailed by the tears of children.

Think of the end, not the means by which you're using to gain that end, but think of the end result. Which, at the end of the day, is not just an end to the security forces, it's a liberated Ireland, an Ireland where will be able to exist all the strands of religion that we have, a gentle place where you'd be proud to bring your children up.

# El Salvador:
# Turning the Masses

To cross the Torola River in northeastern Morazan department, one has to wade or cross the submerged stones in a four-wheel-drive Jeep. There has been no permanent bridge since it was blown up by the rebels in the early days of the war. Periodically, the army puts up temporary bridges, and the rebels blow them up.

The Torola is one of the few visible dividing lines in El Salvador's civil war. The frontlines are almost always invisible; the war swirls in eddies among the people, their towns and villages. Eight years of civil war has left little neutral ground.

South of the Torola, the government's army controls the towns and patrols the countryside, but a roadblock a mile from the river marks the outer limits of its authority. On the north side, all the way to the border with Honduras, there is no permanent government presence; at a roadblock manned by Farabundo Marti National Liberation Front (FMLN) guerrillas, travelers are cleared before venturing on into the FMLN's domain. Here, along with the roving rebel units, live as many as twelve thousand civilians. They are both pawns and victim on a battlefield that was once their home.

It is a war between two bitterly opposed ideological forces, a war to win the hearts and minds of the five million inhabitants of Central America's smallest nation. The cost on the courted constituency has been high: at least sixty thousand dead and more than half a million displaced from their homes. These have found new homes along railroad sidings, road edges, and the eroding walls of old volcanic rifts. Many have left El Salvador altogether, while thousands more are political refugees inside their own country, living in compounds nominally protected by church or state.

A blue-green file of volcanoes dominates the narrow country. These spectacular mountains form a cool, central escarpment between the cotton and sugarcane fields that abut the swampy Pacific coast, and the broken hinterlands that gradually rise to pine mountains along the Honduran border. The towns, watched over by crenellated forts and solid old churches, are surrounded by plots of cultivated land, claimed long ago from the jungle. Here, coffee and cotton; there, cattle, sugar, or corn. El Salvador's peasants, both coveted and killed by the two warring factions, till the fields and ply the pitted roads on lopsided oxen carts with ancient wooden wheels, as stray dogs trot in the carts' cool shadows. The peasants are so obviously of the past; yet, here they are, omnipresent.

The people are everywhere. They fill the overworked land and have transformed it into a verdant, unending slum. It is for the precious land itself, so little for so many, that the war is fought. But the more the struggle is prolonged, the more people lose access to it; El Salvador's cities have swelled with the war's human effluvia from the countryside. There, uprooted and unemployed, they live in shanty slums or refugee camps, awaiting the distant day when the land will be in peace.

The origin of today's civil war cannot be separated from a revolt that occurred a half-century ago. Then, as in recent years, the Central American isthmus was riven by bloody binges as nationalist and Communist rebel leaders sought to wrest political power from the region's conservative dictators. In response to a revolt in 1932, the Salvadoran military, in a savage frenzy of reprisal, slaughtered as many as thirty thousand peasants and Indians in a matter of days.

For the wealthy landowners, the so-called Fourteen Families who virtually owned El Salvador, the revolt was a dire warning; new laws were introduced to clamp down on the peasants and make their access to land less attainable than ever before. Peasants deemed vagrant were forcibly conscripted into manual labor on the oligarchs' plantations. To the military the uprising which ended in *La Matanza* ("The Slaughter") was proof that El Salvador was a target of "international communism" and they stepped up their vigilance accordingly. Afterwards, a succession of "military presidents" hand picked by the oligarchy ruled the country.

By the mid-1970s, the disenfranchised had begun to organize more openly in an attempt to pry open the locks of the closed political arena. The opposition ranged from Christian Democrats to Marxists among academics, students, clergy, peasants, and labor activists. A series of fraudulent elections, growing economic pressures, and political frustration gave a focus to the growing dissidence, which was quashed by increasingly organized and brutal repression. The torture-murders and disappearances of dissidents by the armed forces' death squads became commonplace. A rural paramilitary vigilante group called ORDEN, formed in the late 1960s to root out communism from the peasantry, played a bloody role in the campaign of terror. By 1979, El Salvador was ripe for revolution.

The triumph by the Sandinista guerrillas against the Somoza dynasty in neighboring Nicaragua that summer spurred events in El Salvador. A cabal of junior military officers overthrew the Salvadoran military president and installed a "revolutionary junta" which included leftist civilian politicians in an attempt to prevent a total sweep to victory by the militant left. A series of decrees were issued, aimed at ending the oligarchy's control of the land and the military's means of repression. But the coalition was doomed as enraged rightists in the military and ruling families launched a counterattack. It came in the form of mass murder. Death squads were unleashed with an unbridled vengeance, killing peasants, students, leftist politicians, nuns and priests; even the country's popular liberal archbishop, Oscar Arnulfo Romero, was gunned down in 1980.

As the army's killings intensified, so did the militancy of the leftist groups, now armed and openly calling for the overthrow of the hamstrung junta. The leftists in the coalition resigned, and in 1980, the left announced the merger of five guerrilla groups into a single armed force, the FMLN. They took as their namesake Farabundo Marti, one of the executed leaders of the 1932 revolt. In an ominous parody, the military gave one of their death squads the name of the dictator who had ordered La Matanza, General Maximiliano Hernandez Martinez.

Former National Guard major Roberto D'Aubuisson emerged to lead the Salvadoran right. A boyishly-handsome thug, his name had already become synonymous with the death squads, and he is widely believed to have ordered the Archbishop Romero killing. By 1981, the death-squad killings reached eight hundred a month and the FMLN, now fighting in the hills, had embarked on a national war for power against the ill-equipped and badly prepared army. A call to the "final offensive" in January 1981 failed to bring the FMLN the total victory it sought, and evidence that it was receiving arms from Cuba brought the United States into El Salvador more directly than ever before. Just before leaving office, Jimmy Carter renewed military aid to the Salvadoran regime after having suspended it due to its grotesque human rights abuses. The entrance of the Reagan administration ensured that American aid would not only continue but increase; American military instructors began training Salvadoran troops to counter the guerrillas' more effective tactics. By 1988, nearly two billion dollars in military and economic aid had been sent to El Salvador in a bid to protect what Reagan called "an area vital to our national security."

U.S.-sponsored voting resulted in the 1984 election of Christian Democrat Jose Napoleon Duarte as president. Simultaneously, the United States brought pressure on the military to dismantle its death squads. With electoral support and the firm backing of the American government and the armed forces, Duarte seemed determined to win the war, militarily if necessary. A short-lived "dialogue for peace" brought him and top rebel leaders together twice in 1984, but a political settlement, a popular notion with a majority of Salvadorans, appeared increasingly remote.

By 1986, a new pattern began to emerge. The military, emboldened by increased numbers, better weaponry, and improved tactics due to U.S. training, had turned the tide that once ran in the rebels' favor and opposed any "deal" with the FMLN. The guerrillas, still determined, announced they would embark on an indefinite war of attrition to bleed the country's resources until "the enemy" was brought to its knees.

To combat the guerrillas' political clout with the peasants, the government has turned to psychological warfare. Aware of the near-impossible task of a military victory, it hopes to weaken the FMLN by causing desertions in its rank-and-file. This strategy is partially successful; several high-level defections to the government have rocked the FMLN. The military, while still unwilling to acknowledge its control of the death squads, has largely ended their use. The ORDEN vigilantes have been mostly done away with; rural vigilantes are now called "civil defense." The government has also studiously avoided clashes with street demonstrators, in contrast to the wholesale massacres of just a few years ago, and no massacres by government troops have occurred since mid-1984.

Although the war has decreased in intensity, this is due to stalemate, not reconciliation. The guerrillas have largely achieved their primary goal of economically devastating the nation; the military has largely broken the rebels' sanctuary among the peasantry, through massacres and death-squad actions before, by forced resettlement and aerial bombing now.

But if the death toll is ebbing, the damage to Salvadoran society is not. For the people, the war continues to dominate their lives, a horrible but apathetically accepted state of affairs. Truly a civil war, virtually everyone, it seems, has a close friend or relative in the opposing armed camps. For the peasants, the backbone of the country, the war has meant an end of innocence. Manipulated by the "hearts and minds" campaigns of both sides, they are forever changed, and no "people's victory" or "U.S.-style democracy" will return to them what they have lost. In the meantime, those with the guns, fervent in their beliefs of righteousness, vainly try to deal each other mortal blows.

*Dr. Francisco Garcia Rossi, 63, is a medical doctor and president of the ultra-rightist Salvadoran Coffee Growers' Association. The Association is a last bastion of the wealthy clans (or "Fourteen Families"), who controlled El Salvador's destiny along feudalistic lines until agrarian reforms broke up their holdings in the early 1980s. Garcia Rossi is a spokesman for the landowners in their opposition to the Christian Democratic government's policies, and, especially, state control of their seized private land. Blind in one eye, he wears dark glasses and constantly eats candy from a bag he carries with him.*

In the first place, there isn't any war here. In Great Britain, there's a war. In Iran, there's a war. But I wouldn't call this a war; I'd call it a group of crazed fanatics dedicated to destroying and causing terrible damage.

What motivates this destruction? For me, who is causing this destruction is a rabid dog, a crazed fanatic.

If we classify the guerrillas under the definition of crazed fanatics, they're motivated by the same things as in Ireland, blinded by hate . . . destroying. And what are they going to achieve with that? Change the religion? Are they going to create another religion? Are they going to make a Catholic become Protestant or a

Protestant a Catholic? Is it justifiable that they are placing those bombs and assassinating innocents for religious motives?

What these people want is to become notorious by causing this destruction. But motivation they don't have. I've never thought they had any motivation, or justification, for acting the way they are acting. Violence doesn't have any justification in any part of the world.

And now the Christian Democrats come along and say that it's social injustice which has caused this. It's not that! In this country there are opportunities.

Look, my grandmother made her cents selling sweets in fairs. In the Metapan fair, in Jutiapa. We inherited this kind of commerce from the Spaniards. Everyone who produced something would have their place in the fair. My grandfather was an Italian who came here. They bought some land, and together they bought it, from their sweets and sacrifices. They made their money. That's the economic origin of my family. It was humble. Sure, I was born into another set of diapers, but the families here are like ours. They developed through generations, reach a climax and then begin their descent.

I love my country. The All-Powerful One has given me things I never thought I would have. I'm not fighting. I have lived sufficiently. To leave here, well sure, but . . . you look back, and—This is an agreeable country! It is a country with a smile! It's lies that all of those liars say about this country. . . .

Sure, we have people who are unjust. What society in the world doesn't have its difficulties? We didn't discover it! It is a country just like any other in the world, but it is exceptional in every sense. We don't have any underground wealth; the only thing we have is people, people with the capacity to work for something. It's just marvelous. . . .

If being a rightist is to ask that the State returns to within the law, if being a rightist is to ask that it complies with the constitution, then I am a rightist! I say that those who destroy the economy should have the full weight of the law fall upon them. And to those behind the subversives asking for human rights, I say, "All right, and what about the rest of the citizenry whose human rights aren't being respected?" What would happen in the United States to someone who goes and blows up a bridge, or simply a high-tension tower which they put dynamite to? What would happen in the United States? Do they treat them with their human rights and not hurt them? I seem to remember quite a few times when they have had to put in the National Guard and kill people.

I am not a member of ARENA [ultrarightist Nationalist Republican Alliance party], but in particular I have a great gratitude to [Roberto] D'Aubuisson, because at the moment that we were completely confused and frightened by the circumstances, Roberto D'Aubuisson came and began to show us the nationalism within us. It was in me. I recognize D'Aubuisson's great defects, but I also recognize my gratitude. And not only that; he's the only bastion we have to defend ourselves from this collective madness which they are trying to impose on us, this imposed, collective insanity.

I believe in free enterprise. For me, free enterprise is the only means with which to develop the economy. What would it be like in the U.S. if one fine day the state decides to put the tanks on the street, steal all the banks, and then tell their owners "You can't come in; this is confiscated"? Is that democracy? Here they'd confiscate your long fingernails from you if you had them!

*Garcia Rossi was killed in a car accident in the United States in 1987.*

*Refugio Sanchez is one of the leaders of ANIS, an indigenous rights association representing El Salvador's dwindling Indian population. While technically several other tribes still exist, it is Sanchez's Nahuatl tribe, concentrated in a few towns and villages of western El Salvador, which has most retained its cultural identity.*

*Thousands of Nahuatl were brutally massacred in 1932 by marauding government troops after participating in a short-lived Communist-led uprising against the western landowners; the Nahuatl remember the butchery simply as La Matanza ("The Slaughter"). There have been other massacres since 1932. In Sanchez's village of Santo Domingo de Guzman, troops entered and gunned down sixty-nine people in 1981. In 1983, an ANIS-run agricultural cooperative called Las Hojas was the scene of more killing. It was the last known large massacre in El Salvador's ongoing civil war.*

*Sanchez lives in a mud-walled, dirt-floored hut in Santo Domingo de Guzman; his bed is a straw mattress on a wood frame strung with twine.*

I was born on the thirtieth of March of 1938 in the hamlet of Carrizal, jurisdiction Santo Domingo de Guzman, at one in the morning.

Firstly, I am an Indian who has *lived*. Now, I am worn down and I have seen many things. In some ways, brother, those who are in the mountains [the guerrillas] are right. But it's not true that by grabbing a weapon we'll get liberty; there are alternatives to exhaust first. If the alternatives dry up and we can't do any more, then we would look for another thing to do. Really, for me, the war is . . . well, is right on the one hand. The governments who have passed were guilty, because they never, never have given us an equitable life.

I will try to make a little sketch of the situation. This property at first belonged to Mr. Candelario Castro. We entered into negotiations with him in the year 1977. A year we negotiated, because this property was totally disorganized; it was forgotten by its owner. So we bought this property on the thirtieth of October of 1978. On the west side of this property is a landowner who is named Alfonso Araujo, and on the other side lived a gentleman who was named Raul Renderos. These gentlemen, in view of the fact that Candelario Castro had forgotten about the property, let their cattle graze here. So, when we entered and our cooperative took possession here, we put up fences around it, and there was no way for the cows of Alfonso Araujo nor those of Raul Renderos to get in.

That's when the rancor began, and the cooperative was soon accused of not being a cooperative at all; they said that what was being installed was "the communism." So, in view of this, Mr. Raul Renderos, through his sharecroppers, was trying to get us to open the gates for his cattle. The patrollers [armed civil defense force] were warning us, "Anytime soon," and "These people in this cooperative aren't good people. They are guerrillas, because they have come from various places."

So this thing began with the two instigators, Mr. Alfonso Araujo and Raul Renderos. They made their plan to turn this into chaos. Then comes the twenty-second of February of 1983, when at six or so in the morning more than two hundred soldiers entered, fully equipped. They brought a list and they began taking the boys from over there, and there, and took them away. The patrollers — the civil defense, that is — the fingerers, came with the soldiers. So that was how the thing went.

A comrade who wasn't on the list came and told us at our office. As we came, the three truckloads of soldiers passed us, and we saw that they didn't have the comrades with them. So we said, "They aren't bringing the comrades; they must have let them go, they must be back in their homes." When we arrived, about one in the afternoon here in the cooperative, we found all the women whose sons had been taken. We found them very distraught, all . . . crying, and they said, "In the distance we heard gunshots." So we went on asking where the gunshots had been heard, and the people told us they had heard it come from the "little hill" about one kilometer from where we are now. So we went on, and it is true that when we got there we found the first cadaver, disconsolate, with the hands tied behind, with the head destroyed. And they had put a stake through its back, besides.

So we continued searching. We found seven cooperativist comrades completely destroyed, and the rest who were floating in the river. We counted twenty-eight like that, floating! The cartridges were there, thrown about.

About three we returned and went to find the judge so he could witness. But he didn't find twenty-eight; he found more! Later, with the Human Rights Commission and the Red Cross, the search found a total of seventy-eight dead people. And when we divulged the information, that's when the persecution of us, the indigenous leaders, began.

*Refugio Sanchez's version of the events at Las Hojas are widely accepted as factual. None of the men he named, nor any of the soldiers who carried out the murders, has been imprisoned. According to President Duarte's interpretation of the 1987 regional peace plan, those responsible fall under an amnesty provision and can never be prosecuted for their crimes.*

*Big and burly, Jorge Camacho is a veteran and controversial labor leader. With his trademark wicker cowboy hat, he is gregarious, loves salty jokes, and has a booming voice. Among the peasants and Indians with whom he has spent his life, he is a natural leader; everyone calls him simply "Camacho." He travels with a bodyguard, a young man with darting eyes who never leaves his side, for Camacho, a consummate political maneuverer, has made many enemies, on the right, on the left, and in the military. Following Duarte's election as president in 1984, Camacho was vice minister of agriculture, part of a deal whereby Duarte had obtained Camacho's union's electoral support. A truculent trio of white geese guard the doorstep of his house in a middle-class suburb of San Salvador.*

All my life I've had links with the two great tendencies in El Salvador. It's something that's just happened; I can't explain it.

My name is Jorge Alberto Luis Camacho. I have forty-nine years of age at the moment and twenty-three to twenty-six years of working with the unions in El Salvador, mostly with the peasant organizations.

My origins, I was an agricultural worker. I worked on a *finca* [farm] of the Alvarez Zaldivar family in the 1960s. There was a house for my wife and children. I was paid two hundred *colones* a month and my wife one hundred a month to run the clinic. Electricity and firewood was free. How beautiful it was! We had study sessions in the evenings to teach the workers the alphabet. We formed a cooperative. We convinced the boss to give each worker a little plot so they could grow vegetables. But then the persecution began there.

As a foreman, one would have to go around with a revolver in one hand and a machete. You had to instill respect in the people. The peasant, they used to say, didn't respect anything but the loss of his life. So, on the finca, one had to go around well-armed, well-assured. And there were even N tional Guardsmen detached to the fincas to instill respect.

So one had to learn how to shoot, to show off he was a good shot, and a good fighter with a machete. You had the *corvo* really done up in a nice sheath and you had to really know how to throw it around. You know how the peasants are always cutting into trees with their machetes? It's to show how well they can slice; a peasant never machetes a tree for nothing!

Typically, the image one had to present to the people was a good sombrero. A good *jipijapa* hat, not one of palm leaf. All the foremen had them. Also, you had to have your good revolver, preferably a .38 long, a special. If it were possible, with white stock, to give it that extra look. Even though the old guys said a white stock wasn't good—because if they wanted to shoot you it could be seen from afar, so a dark stock was better—but even so, white was preferred for the impression it made. And also a belt, completely full of bullets and, on the other side, your machete! I still have my machete in the house, really sharp and pointed!

The bosses' orders were never take out the revolver unless it was to kill. And many of the foremen on the finca have anecdotes of having killed one, two, three people. In situations like . . . a peasant was demanding more pay, or saying that the finca was stealing his money, he'd have to be killed in front of all the other workers so they wouldn't get the same idea. At the very least, they'd shoot off his ear.

If a worker went and took an orange from a tree, it was the death penalty. He had to go and ask the owner; if he took it without permission, they'd kill him.

On all the haciendas, there is a law called agrarian law. In that law, the peasant is described as a bum, a ne'er-do-well. Before, if a National Guardsmen asked, you'd have to tell them where you worked. If you didn't have work, they had the authorization to take you to a place where they needed laborers, whether you liked it or not. If you didn't work, they put you in jail. In that law, if the owner needed the assistance of the security forces, they were obliged to help, in capturing escaped workers and things. And that law still hasn't been taken off the books.

From the finca, I was recruited by the American Institute for Free Labor Development, around 1965. They had me go to a course on agrarian reform. In 1966, they invited me to the U.S. and sent me on a tour to get and know the labor groups there. This was so I could come back and put together all the loose ends of labor unions we had here. I met Cesar Chavez and drew a lot of experience from that meeting. I went walking with him in the field; I participated in some strikes with him. I learned a lot from his movement. . . .

So, with that experience, I returned to El Salvador and here tried to get going, through seminars and social projects for the peasants. I had learned about picket lines, and so here we used them on the landowners who refused to go along with the legal reforms.

So we watched the worker grow into another kind of worker, using his own experiences, you know? I had been very impressed with the visits to workers' houses by Cesar Chavez, so this was done here, too, among great numbers of people, to show that, united, the peasants could find solutions to their problems. So that's when the idea was born to found the Salvadoran Communal Union [UCS]. It was planned to give better social and economic conditions to the people, as an agrarian union which would permit a just distribution of the riches of El Salvador. Because there had been studies made here that if something wasn't done to channel the demands of the working masses for their freedom—better living conditions and land—this was going to explode. So this was a way to forestall violent revolution.

Through the UCS the first cooperative was born. But in those days, what was thought would ameliorate the situation didn't do more than alert the power groups and make them view the peasant organizations as germs of international communism and terrorism, and they were attacked. One of the first things the landlords did was to start raising the cost of renting land. In less than two years, they tripled the price to seal off access to the peasants. This naturally started the great struggle in El Salvador. The peasants sought other means of organizing themselves; they formed alliances, and then came the repression and, by 1979, all the leadership of those organizations were "beheaded."

Of all the comrades I knew who were at the heads of those organizations, almost all are dead! I've only seen two of them still alive. . . . The other ones, I don't know, because they took up weapons and right now they are in the mountains fighting. So many of our people were leaving for the mountains, because the armed struggle was already on the horizon. Open armed struggle was proposed as of June 1979, in which the armed groups could be seen in the streets. Many of our people went to sign up. They'd come back and tell us, "Yes, I went to sign up as a future combatant of the Revolution, because neither the government nor the gringos want to do anything."

I remember an anecdote in one village. The FMLN was going to be in a certain place and all the peasants who wanted to take up arms were to meet in that place and the countersign was a half-peeled orange. So all the peasants were all over there carrying oranges. We saw them and thought, "Where have all these people gotten so many oranges; why are they all sucking on oranges?" But that was the countersign, that if you had an orange, you would take up arms. So they were doing a census, the FMLN, on how many combatants it could count on. So with this census, it was going to go and negotiate for weapons abroad, to calculate how many arms it needed.

And I am witness that many, many working people were in their unions trying to negotiate for reforms but as these possibilities to negotiate with the *patrones* [landowners] closed, as all the means were closed, this radicalized them more, to the extent that by September 1979, we lost an entire cooperative! All of them left to join up! So this is how things went, to reach the historic moment of the Salvadoran war. And in this war, it is the peasants who are killed fighting; the majority of the commanders and their aides are of peasant stock. The best combatants both in the armed forces and with the guerrillas are our peasant brothers!

Naturally, we have been persecuted for our ideas; there wouldn't be three or four days to pass without an attempt on my life. I am grateful for the backing of the AFL-CIO, which gave me sufficient bodyguards, because, at the time, there was only four paths left, as we say here: leave the country, go with the right to the death squads, go with the left to the mountains, or go to shit!

So we received threats from both the totalitarians of the right and the anarchists of the left. There was a time when we didn't know what would happen to us, and in that time fistfuls of people died! Fistfuls! People who believed in some kind of political solution to the conflict through elections.

Right now, all of these military guys who are doing all the killing, I've known them all since they were kids, since they were cadets. Two times they have sent me warnings, signed by the death squad, but I knew it was the police. One said: "For being a CIA agent and an agent of the guerrillas." That was in 1981.

Another time when they located me, I was in a slum on the outskirts. They just shot from a passing car, an armored car. They were hooded and everything. Once, they came straight to the house—about twenty-five soldiers—and they had me and my whole family surrounded. So I called the AIFLD director, and he sent people and got me out of it. Then there was a while where me and D'Aubuisson were having a fight, he trying to fuck me over, me trying to fuck him. And the son of a bitch came and tried to kill my wife, tried to run her off the road. We knew it was his car. . . . The last time, well, it was machine-gunning at the house itself; it was just a volley of nine millimeter, and then they left.

Another time, they sent a guy to enter my house and assassinate me. But he fell in love with my daughter. He ended up not doing any harm. Now they have children, my grandchildren. He's in the house now. That's how it is. Now he watches out for me. He really watches out for me.

*An enigmatic civilian intelligence officer, middle-aged Dr. Lice (his real name is Llach) is a crew-cut, stocky man with pale skin. He is an unofficial but integral presence at the Arce Infantry Battalion headquarters in embattled San Miguel. Lice's origins, academic background, and exact duties are the speculation of the few who know of his existence there, but it is known that his primary task is to politically indoctrinate the U.S.-trained Arce officers.*

I am what you would call a "politologue"; I used to be a lawyer. Now what I do is consciousness-raise. As I am talking to you, this is what I am doing.

It is important that we study ideas. . . . We are still in time to continue respecting the idea of the peasantry. It's false that the war is being fought because of hunger and malnutrition. If this were the case, Mexico and India would have war every single day. The cause of this war is ideological warfare, fanned by international propaganda, with lies and falsehoods. The first lie of this campaign is that here there were the Fourteen Families who ruled everything. False! Because in the agrarian reform, they took five hundred farms from five hundred families, each with over five hundred hectares! Second, there was never any military dictatorship. Never was, never has been! There have always been civilians directing national politics.

The enemy is a paper tiger made out of propaganda. They are just becoming aware now that there is no contradiction amongst us on this side, not between the United States and D'Aubuisson or Duarte, nor between any military man here. What they don't realize is that we are all the same thing, all aboard the same ship. Here, what we need is for the peasant to go back to cultivating his land, peacefully.

*Jose Luis Grande Preza is the middle-aged leader of the National Workers and Peasants Union (UNOC), a progovernment labor federation formed in 1986. His former leftist comrades call him a traitor, but, in fact, he has long had links to the ruling Christian Democratic party. One of his arms is shorter than the other, the result of what he describes as "a rightist assault." He drives a Jeep with smoked-glass windows, with a pistol between his knees and a bodyguard because of threats from the guerrillas.*

Now there are some changes in behavior that one can feel. Last year, we had an experience which I think was unique. We had a strike in some textile factories. In these places, the company has its own security, armed men. So what happened there was, to get rid of the union, the company ordered that there be a mock firing squad of the nine union leaders. They put them against the wall and shot above their heads; one of the comrades escaped and came and told us. So we called President Duarte and told him what had just happened, and General Golcher, who is now head of the Treasury Police, was put in charge of the rescue of the comrades.

And what happened was incredible! A force which had repressed the workers for so long and now did an act of this kind? Golcher went and gave five minutes for the company to open the factory gates or the armored cars would go in to rescue the comrades. So, that's a thing that happened that demonstrates to us that sometimes, when there is someone on the top who follows an order, then there can be those at the midlevel or subalterns who can perform a good role, too.

I recount this because, for me, it was historic. I sometimes think I only believe it because I saw it myself. If I were just told about it, I wouldn't have believed it, that a security-force group would go and rescue nine labor leaders! Well, that's how it was. . . .

Afterwards, though, the repression in the factory against the comrades was so bad we had to have them abandon it. The only thing we achieved was that they were paid their indemnities.

As a union leader, one can play politics, but it's really a risky situation. It can be really dangerous, because if one isn't careful, it can lead to the disappearance of the organization.

There have been four attempts against my life. The last operation I had was to extract a bullet in my knee. They lowered my ankle because I was having trouble walking. I have torture scars from the Treasury Police. In the last attempt against me, two were arrested. It was established that they were a National Police sergeant and a National Police agent.

And in my family there have also been cases. Father Rutilio Grande was my uncle, the first Jesuit priest assassinated here in the country. Later, my mother was at the funeral of Monsignor Romero and a bomb exploded and the whole left side of her body was burned; she lost a kidney and had to be operated on. My younger brother disappeared in 1982; he was found murdered in Guazapa. He had graduated from high school two days before from the National Institute. In the Institute, there was the Revolutionary Student Movement, but I understand he didn't belong to it. But the fact that he was from the Institute and had been combative for the students' rights, well, that was still a crime. So . . . this is what we have suffered.

A cousin, a nephew . . . so, in this there is my eldest son, as well. Because my house was ransacked many times by the army until 1982, my son had a nervous breakdown and he has remained with the problem ever since. The doctors tell me that what happened was a complete breakdown of the nervous system. About four or five months back, he got better—not completely—but before, he used to awaken screaming every night that he had been placed facedown [prelude to death-squad execution] with my mother.

But that is the price one pays at times for belonging to trade-union movements. I have been in this now for twenty years. I've been the leader of many unions, and I hope to have better luck in this opportunity now.

*"El Gato" is the underworld pseudonym for a former police detective. He has agreed to meeting in a spare office in a nondescript building in the sleazy market district of San Salvador; across the street, an* aguardiente *store spews out drunken men and prostitutes at all hours. Under the newspaper on El Gato's desk, bare except for a telephone he occasionally answers, lies his revolver.*

*In his mid-forties, short and slightly heavy, El Gato has a hustler's face and way of talking. His eyes are those of a detective or a criminal, both of which he has been; he is basically a gun for hire. He spent time in El Salvador's anti-communist death squads—first the security force–operated Maximiliano Hernandez Martinez Brigade, then Roberto D'Aubuisson's Secret Anti-Communist Army (ESA)—and still maintains links with his former comrades. Although he denies having personally executed people, it is undoubtedly mere shyness on his part.*

At first, it was to eliminate subversives, you see, but eventually it got bad. Corrupted. And people sought in it ways to make money. I remember how the vehicles of the dead were shared out among the personnel. Three guys I know are still driving them today.

There was one slobberbucket from the Treasury Police. He used to grab people out of the *pensiones* [hostels] and, after robbing them, he'd kill them. He used to brag about it to me. Finally, his own companions killed him to shut him up. A lot of the comrades have been killed by their own units, some because they talk too much, others because they know too much. And over money. Me they haven't eliminated because they know I don't talk. And, anyway, there is this belief that I am a great marksman. It's not really true, but I might as well let them believe it.

Once I was in the Santa Ana police station and they had about ten dead people there and I found the guy they call "El Niño"—he's kind of a dumb guy they raised and he became one of them—fucking the body of a dead woman. I yelled at him and I said, "What are you doing?" And he just kept on fucking her but looked at me and said, "The corporal gives me permission after we go on a mission to fuck the best-looking of the women."

Later, in Santa Ana one day, El Niño, he came over to one body and tried to touch it. A girl. She screamed, because she wasn't dead, and the new people who had taken charge found out about him. So he had to be weaned off of all of that because they didn't like it.

Sure, what one would like to do on seeing that is to eliminate him, because you can see he's just a beast. But to say anything would be to reveal your feelings and you'd be eliminated immediately. This Niño, he's a little crazy, you know. He likes to go out on missions with them so he can maybe get something, like a ring from one of the bodies afterwards. They'd always take him along. He's still there today, in the Santa Ana police station.

After a while, what one grows to feel is disgust towards the whole corps, toward the chiefs who didn't care about their underlings working within the law. It was on their orders, anyway.

Once, in Santa Ana, I was in the police station, and three of the guys had a guerrilla suspect there. After interrogating him, Jesus [El Gato's friend] laid him down on the floor right there in the dormitory of the S-2 [intelligence section] of the Santa Ana police station. He had him facedown on the floor, and with a knife, he cut—deeply (shows a three inch depth with his fingers)—MHM, the initials of the Maximiliano Hernandez Martinez, into his back!

I saw it. I watched. And in the morning, the cadaver wasn't there; it was on the road outside the city with the initials and the [death sentence] piece of paper. It wasn't the knife that killed him; he was strangled.

Then there was the slaughter at the Santa Ana Fair! There was about twelve victims there. They just went in and picked up the employees after dark—there were queers and everything, those who ran the stands at the Fair. They went to take them out at night and that dawn they killed them. They said the reason was that they were connected with the left, but it was uncertain, I think.

Once the death squad had them, they were always dead. They'd say to the client [victim], "Tell the truth." And if he did, he died. If he didn't, he died as well. They tell them, "Tell the truth," and put the pistol against the head, but the client would always think they were just trying to frighten him, even though they were told, "We're going to kill you." And then if he didn't answer, the guys would just pull the trigger right then and leave them. They were dead from the minute they were grabbed.

One time they told me—I was hanging around the lobby—"We're going out to work," and one knew what that meant. If they just saw you, they'd tell you, "Come on, you're coming tonight, asshole." If you tried to make like you had something else to do, they would threaten you. So this night, they made me go and then, out in the truck, they had about ten tied up and they said, "These are already convicted." And they made me go, and when they had them out at the place we went to, they said, "It's your turn," and tried to give me the gun. I refused and they started threatening me. "Look at this guy, acting like a priest and trying to tell us what to do," and, "You'll get yours, asshole," and then they just blew them away themselves, right there.

The memories affect me because I remember each scene clearly, the faces of the victims as well as those who did it. And them . . . some of them who fell wounded and then . . . them coming near and giving them the coup de grace. It's hard, that; it is pitiable. There has been a lot of depravation. Much lack of respect towards people.

It got out of control. Each did as he wanted, but no one could try to put right these atrocities, because if you said anything they'd kill you. It was better to say nothing. It's completely painful for me; for example, the case of that man who they they cut the initials into. It was better to laugh and let it happen. One would spend entire nights thinking that at any moment your own comrades would come to kill you because you saw it. I am still afraid, because just in Santa Ana I saw them do about five things [killings], and I went with them for a while.

*The Christian Democratic mayor of San Sebastian, a small town in central San Vicente department, Manuel de Jesus Cordova is a small, tidy man in his late fifties. He speaks with the practiced circumspection of a veteran civil servant.*

*In 1982, San Vicente was the focus of an ill-fated government campaign to win back the area from the FMLN rebels. A key part of "Operation Well-being" was to form armed Civil Defence units with local civilians in order to force them to abandon neutrality in the conflict and fight the guerrillas themselves. Often, the units were commanded by regular army officers. While the U.S.-sponsored program faltered due to guerrilla attacks, several towns, including San Sebastian, still have Civil Defence units today. The interview is in Cordova's small, Spartan mayor's office facing the town's sunstruck central plaza.*

The Civil Defence is organized here. It is always ready, but not in the outlying hamlets. We don't arm them, because it would mean their destruction. That's the error we made before, to arm those hamlets; then the guerrillas came and destroyed them.

Before, the duties of the Civil Defences were to guard day and night in the trenches waiting for an attack. Not anymore; the situation is better now. Now we have the National Guard. Now they protect us. . . . They aren't like before. Then, they saw us as animals and they treated the civilians like less than human. Now they are trying to get along with us. They are fulfilling their duty.

Now there is more security. The military is doing big monthly sweeps with five battalions. Here there are about eighty [Civil Defence] reservists; if there was an emergency, they can help. But there hasn't been one since April of '84. . . .

But a real bully of a commander came here. He was very demanding. This was about six months ago. He was from the Fifth Battalion. If one of the men arrived late or drunk, it was three days in jail. He just ordered everyone around and treated the people with repugnance and bad manners. He was dangerous to have here and, finally, we were able to get rid of him. When he left, the unit was dismantled. But the boys are always ready. But not so they can be treated like pigs. The commander we have now, he behaves himself with us.

Now, to maintain the Civil Defence, everyone here who have jobs or some money have to pay a quota, ten to thirty colones a month [two to six U.S. dollars]. There are about ten in the Civil Defence now. They are supposed to get two hundred colones each a month. The quota is always expected and demanded, but not like it was before. That one [commander] who left used to come around demanding and threatening the people that if they didn't give he would drag them out at midnight and take off their heads.

Now the civic committee collects the quota, ever since that one commander who killed a lady here. He did evil things, so he was stripped of his post. The quota system isn't legal. The army could pay them a salary, but it doesn't; so it has to be done. It is necessary to do so.

*Elias Marinero Alfaro is the present commander of San Sebastian's Civil Defence unit. He is 21 years old. He is wearing a T-shirt which says "I want to live in peace" in Spanish. He explains that it was given to him by one of his "gringo" instructors. The interview takes place in the stockade directly across the plaza from Mayor Cordova's office.*

I myself was a Civil Defenceman four years ago; I am from [nearby] Santa Elena. The terrorists murdered my father, so I came here to lend my services.

The government ordered this whole town to organize the Civil Defence. The man who headed it before me was Sergeant Antonio Ordoñez Molina. Later, they cashiered him, I don't know why. I never saw him have any problems with the civilians. He handed over to me on the thirteenth of June of 1985.

I now have 160 inactive men. They tell me they won't come back without a salary, because if they die in a guerrilla attack, their families will be left destitute.

Right now I have six with me. They earn two hundred colones each a month [forty U.S. dollars]. There is a Self-Defence Committee of teachers and store owners, and they agreed that ten colones should be paid by each for the men who give service day and night.

I am just now dominating the people.

*Tall, thin, and a chain-smoker, Jon Cortina is a Jesuit priest from the Basque region of Spain who has lived in El Salvador since the 1950s. Besides his parish work in San Salvador's slums and Church-run displaced persons' camps, he teaches engineering at the Jesuit Central American University (UCA) in San Salvador.*

*Cortina's liberal Catholic order is viewed with suspicion and enmity by El Salvador's rightists, and its members were the targets of numerous death squad attacks in the late 1970s and early 1980s.*

At the beginning, there were peaceful demonstrations for labor and salary demands, simple ones. These were mostly by the peasants. The peasants were then normally machine-gunned. They were repressed with violence, and, little by little, they saw that the only possibility they had was to confront the established power in a violent way.

For the country, the war has been, and is, one of the most cruel phenomenons that can be. You have to realize that twenty-five percent of the people are either outside of the country or internally displaced. This is really a phenomenon of horror. In terms of death, the war is the greatest cause of death. The figure that is talked of is over sixty thousand. This is to say that we have lost a very important part of the country, people who could have given something. And, as always, the war is taking its worst toll amongst the poorest people, upon those people who, even before the beginning of the conflict, were suffering the consequences of the existing injustice. This toll is on both sides, the army and the insurgents. The insurgents, they are from the peasant strata, the poorest people, but it is also the peasants who are dying in the army. There is no one from well-off families, of the middle class, who are participating in the army as soldiers.

There is another aspect, that of persecution of the Church. To defend the value of life on either side is something which gives one a certain "color." To defend the cause of the poor, of the peasants, is, for many people, enough to say that one is with the extreme left. But it is not to be with the extreme left; it's simply defending something which is absolutely logical. Even, from the moral and ethical point of view, something which must be done. We have forgotten totally and absolutely of all the moral and ethical aspects of life.

The persecution of the Church in this war has taken the form of the murders of bishops, priests, catechists, lay preachers, who, for the fact of being catechists, were assassinated. In many places, to have a Bible in the house was sufficient reason to imprison people. To have a picture of Monsignor Romero [the liberal archbishop who was assassinated while giving Mass in 1980] was a crime, sufficiently serious for a person to be taken to prison. For my people, to be a Christian and to belong to the Christian communities has been a crime which has brought about their deaths. There were moments. . . . there was even a slogan: "Be patriotic—kill a priest"!

When a person wants to defend an ethical or moral position, this person is accused. He is not allowed to speak; to do so can be crime enough to be taken to prison, or to be made to "disappear." Apart from the deaths the Church has suffered, there have been house searches, bombings, machine-gunnings in different Church locales, in parishes, universities—in sum, everything which has had ecclesiastical relation with the defense of the poor.

As Jesuits, we have felt it. Our house has been machine-gunned. In our residence, they have placed bombs, many bombs. Our residence has been ransacked and we have been obliged to live outside our house for a long time. There have been death threats to many in our community.

Why this? Well, I would say that the fundamental reason is because we have tried to be faithful to a vocation. We have tried to defend something which for many people is indefensible. In this country, what one can see is that the life of the rich person is valuable, but the life of the poor isn't worth anything. So, he who would defend the life and rights of the poor is accused of being "Red" and of belonging to the FMLN, of having links with the FMLN, and that is an intolerable crime. . . .

Liberation theology is merely a way of putting into black and white the problems we are living through here. A priest has an obligation to defend his people, and he is obliged to maintain the hope of his people, and is obliged to accompany his people and make their faith grow. I do believe that in the Salvadoran church [hierarchy] there exists a lack of interest in the situation of the poor. This may have been born out of a certain comfort: the poor are bothersome, their problems are bothersome, to defend them will cause inconveniences and bother.

I began working as a priest in the poorest *barrios*, with the simplest people, and with the peasants. And on seeing their life and the way they lived their faith, I began understanding that those people lived their faith in a very deep and radical way, that they fulfilled their Christian duty in a way that was much more radical and sincere than our own!

The fear is the same for everyone. The only difference between that felt by a priest and everyone else would be that a religious person assumes death as something that will come for being faithful to his Christian past. But . . . fear will always be there, will always exist. But, even with this fear, it doesn't paralyze him and he will continue acting as he should act, even though he knows that by doing so it will lead to his death. But he believes in something more, in the Resurrection, and this gives him strength to continue his work. But the fear of death is there. It is the same for me.

The Church has a duty to decry these things, in order that God's plan might in some way be accomplished. But the person who heralds the Kingdom of God is taken away.

*Andrea, a woman in her late twenties, is one of El Salvador's estimated seven hundred thousand civilians displaced from their homes due to the war. She has been living for several years in a Catholic Church-run displaced persons camp. Like many there, Andrea is an FMLN supporter; her husband is a guerrilla fighter.*

It's been a long time that I have not communicated with my husband. In the confusion, we lost each other. I understand he has not died. It's one and a half years I don't know anything of him. . . .

Persecution made us all come here. In '80, where I came from it was a crime to listen to Monsignor Romero and to belong to the [leftwing] Christian communities. When the people wanted to live with a more humanitarian sense, others didn't want it and many had to abandon their places, because their children were killed by the security forces and they destroyed their houses.

At the beginning of '80, they killed almost all of my uncles in the place we lived. There, an ORDEN commission was formed. My husband was a catechist; the ORDEN people, when they looked at the religious work, said it was just the opposite.

Once, around five A.M., we heard shots. They were shooting at some boys of our Christian community. They killed three, so we ran with the children. When we returned, all the houses had been burned, the animals were dead, and there were ten people dead, their throats slit. One was being eaten by dogs. There was a sign saying that just how they have begun with the first ones, they were going to finish the rest. Many people didn't flee, and these were the people who saw them take some of the girls tied up, and others they took by the hair, and they raped them and killed them.

Those people hated us, because we didn't have the same idea as they had. The word of God is love, liberty, and justice, but they lived those macho and repressive ideologies. They think that God's will is to kill others and live under slavery. Although they live badly, some think that it is God's will and accept that they remain in slavery. It is pathetic to see people who, although really knocked about by life, continue believing that the army and the government is everything.

The soldiers are our enemies. The North American aid comes to convince people that we are communists and that communism is bad. Here, the one who takes charge of the war is the North American government. We know that

Salvadorans don't manufacture planes to go and bomb, nor train these new battalions.

El Salvador is sick, and it needs special medicine to cure it. The guilty ones are the oligarchs, always on top of everything; the people don't forget this. A mother is not going to forget her children. This is uncurable.

*Lieutenant Marco Palacios is an athletic 28-year-old officer in El Salvador's elite naval commandos, a U.S.-trained naval antiguerrilla force.*

When I was younger, I thought that a revolution would be correct, but later I changed my mind. I saw that the movement was influenced by Marxism-Leninism.

Our cause is . . . we believe in God, and we are anti-Communist; they don't believe in God and the personal freedoms of man.

*Maria Nieves Espinal is 76 years old. She lives in the nearly deserted town of La Villa in northern Morazan. After the fighting started, the saints in the Catholic church of La Villa, the first town to be seized by the FMLN, were evacuated to the safe south side of the nearby Torola River by the church caretaker. To see their saints, the faithful of La Villa have to make a precarious bridgeless crossing of the river, a no-man's-land, and walk several miles to the church at San Simon. On the locked-up La Villa church's walls there is rebel graffiti in red paint. One scene shows a rebel shooting at soldiers and the slogan "Our people advance; the enemy retreats."*

All my life I have been a Catholic. I cried when they took away the Virgin from the church. Now I am evangelical, because there are no more saints.

*Father Miguel Ventura, 40, is a Salvadoran priest who chose as his flock the FMLN guerrillas and their followers. Working with the enigmatic revolutionary Belgian priest, Father "Rogelio" Poncel, Ventura has accompanied the rebels for several years. He espouses "liberation theology," a Catholic splinter credo that has adopted certain Marxist tenets.*

*Ventura speaks in the sacristy of the Perquín church while the People's Revolutionary Army (ERP), a branch of the FMLN, occupies the town. Outside the nail-studded door of the office, a rebel bodyguard crouches. Inside, Ventura sits beneath a poster of assassinated Archbishop Romero. On the desk are a Bible, religious books, and candles. Against the wall leans an M-16 automatic rifle.*

Here the FMLN exercises full control, and this has had a noteworthy effect on those who dwell here. Father Poncel and I decided that these people needed to be accompanied religiously, because they are a very religious people.

Our task is to feed the hope of the people, in that the day will come when this situation will change. There will be a new day. What we do through the Mass is feed their hope. We celebrate the Word, with the catechists, using biblical texts chosen as appropriate for the situation the people are living in. This is so that they can see this is just a phase which must be gone through.

For example, to understand the war better, we chose Chapter Twenty-Four of Matthew, where he speaks of the end of the world. We did this because many of these people believe this war heralds the end of the world. "It is written," they say, but we show them that this is not a Christian vision, but one of passivity.

You see, popular religion confronts these situations without a role, without any sense of criticism, so we have to distinguish between what is faith and what is religiosity. How to interpret a bombing? A religious person might say, "It is the will of God." The person of faith, though, sees in the bombing the incarnation of sin and he sees the structures of the sin. So he sees how to confront and vanquish that sin.

If people are still living up here, it's because they have begun understanding the revolutionary process and the need for a change. Because, as the war is prolonged they are learning that running from one place to another is not a solution; what they have to understand is that everybody participates in the solution of the problem. This is why you see them living here. Even though there are bombings, they don't leave. This is helping them raise their level of consciousness.

*Adan Vigil, 50, is a peasant farmer living in northern Morazan.*

This is the fulfillment of a prophecy, the war is. So neither side can be blamed. Anyway, I don't understand the political reasons for it.

*Adrian Esquina Lisco is a tiny Nahuatl Indian and the head of ANIS, the indigenous rights group. The chief of all El Salvador's indigenous people, he is a longtime activist for Indian and peasant rights.*
*In his sixties, Lisco lives with his parents in the village of his birth—Santo Domingo de Guzman. His mother is 105; his father, several years older, still works in the fields. Lisco is seeking justice for the 1983 massacre of seventy-eight Nahuatl Indians at Las Hojas and says, "I'm going to keep talking about it until I die, and I know they're going to kill me."*

In the Matanza of '32, my *nana* [mother] and *tata* [father] escaped it, but the rest of their brothers and sisters, nephews, cousins, were killed. The Señor Victor Alfaro was a great landowner in that time. Alfaro was the owner of everything from those hills you can see there (points out window) all the way to the sea! All of this where we are—Sonsonate—was his.

So when the massacre came in 1932, my tata says, the indigenous people went to his house to defend themselves. When the troops passed, they called the people out to get into lines. The army had a book and read out the names. He who appeared in the book they made stand apart. And so, in the end, these Alfaro gentlemen turned in a lot of people. After, they took them out there, behind the fence, and the shots were heard. They killed them! And so this is what my tata told me in my childhood, and I listened. And so from there I saw that we must fight for our race.

We've always been a target, ever since the Spanish conquest! The number of our indigenous brothers they have killed here in El Salvador!

So how is it possible that when one has a conscience, I won't say things the way they are just because I'm threatened? I have to speak out. When I was young, I worked on a hacienda, for two cents a day. One day, finally, I rose up against the foreman and saw the need for Indian unity. Because what good does it do if I don't confront it, to defend my race against the injustice that is being done against them? Defenseless people! It's not possible.

I am first a Nahuatl Indian; I'm not first a Salvadoran. I am a Nahuatl Indian and, after, a Salvadoran! And this I defend however I can.

I am an Indian who owes no one. I have not robbed anyone. I can't read things so well that I can do things that the intellectuals do, so what I say is, well, *tata dios* helps me.

With Latins, I sometimes feel discriminated, when only they are the ones who speak and one himself doesn't have the opportunity. I don't feel satisfied. There are others who—especially politicians—they clap you on the back like a friend, but really there is nothing there. . . .

In my community, nobody speaks Spanish; everybody speaks Nahuatl. My nana and my tata, from the moment they rise in the morning, they speak, they communicate, spiritually through nature and, afterwards, they begin to speak. At the moment of dawn, everybody kneels as the sun rises, to illuminate the mind and think about what they have to do and, through the rays of the sun, they see what is going to happen in the day or the future. At the midnight when the years change, our parents go out and sit down and they tell us, "This year, this is going to happen." And sometimes I myself am surprised and I go to my tata with my brothers and I say, "I am going to plant a tree," and he says, "Don't plant it because the moon is not good." And he doesn't read! Not of books, not of anything, but he says, "It's not good," and so I must obey. . . .

So one sees life through nature. I believe much in the spiritual life . . . of the sun, of the Mother Earth, as we call her, the air, the fire, the trees, the little birds, the water. This is our God.

I will try to tell you what my tata tells me. He tells me, "We know what has occurred here." He talks of the Matanza of '32 and that after that, in '34, there was the cyclone here in El Salvador. The cyclone was a great water that fell, when the trees came down and the corn came down, so that the dry rivers filled up. Why did that happen? "To wash," he says, "away the many slaughters that happened. To wash away all of that that came to rest upon the Mother Earth. And so, with the power of the very Father God, he sent all of that and it was cleaned."

That was called The Cyclone. The earth began to tremble and, after that, came the locusts when the corn was sown and then those animals, the locusts, they fell upon the corn and in five minutes there was no more corn. The next year came The Hunger. And so all of this, he has told me, are things which happen because of all that has been occurring.

I know that he who has more wants more, and the gods of those who have more is money. They don't believe that nature exists. And we, we are like a weed, the wild grass. They chop us down and we always grow and grow!

We are all part of nature, but what happens is that the *ladino*, because of his studies, wants to be above all the things. They want to be more than Father Gods, you see? It is those who are taking our nature to ruin. And when they unite, when the armed forces come, they try to finish with those of us who are like weeds. It's what my tata has talked to me of, and I have been able to understand that this is right.

We are part of nature, brother, and this helps us to survive. It's like the corn; it blossoms at the time it must and it will, even though you put your hand on it. And we are like this. We must grow and nobody can stop us. And this is because we are part of nature.

You must not, like in the books of the whites — as the Indians call them — stop to believe in yourself.

*Tall, green-eyed, and supremely self-assured, Colonel Jesus Natividad Caceres is the army commander of Sonsonate department. On his office wall is a scroll of Psalm 23 and a photograph of his meeting with U.S. Vice President George Bush. A born-again Christian as well as a career officer, Caceres takes his beliefs to the war; in early 1986, he showed his faith by having the entire city of Chalatenango, his former command, painted white.*

I will begin by telling you what war means to me: in this sense here, the war is a whip with which to awaken the people. Before, there were many things we didn't know about in El Salvador; the conflict has made us wake up and know ourselves better.

There has been much talk of fifty years of military government in El Salvador as being a cause of the war. I ask if we really know what is a military government. We cannot accept that we had military governments here for fifty years if we don't know what one is. If we have had military presidents, that is a completely different thing.

But, in the long run, this image is exploited by the left and, for other reasons, by the right. Many people maintain that it was us, the armed forces, who installed the military presidents; I am completing twenty-four years of service and nobody's ever asked me who I wanted as president, except when I voted! So, we can conclude that the armed forces did not install the military presidents. What has always happened is that the rightists chose an individual in the military and, for them, that person had certain leadership qualities and it was easy to launch him on an electoral campaign and to make him president. That is the reality, but that still doesn't mean they were military governments.

We have been blamed with everything bad that has happened in El Salvador. Whatever has been good, we have never done. Good has been done by others, by congressmen, ministers, and so on.

On the other hand, the left in El Salvador continually sought, ever since way back in 1932, since the Communist Party was founded, to exploit the conflict which existed, and, at the same time, to create causes which would win them a following. They had the gift of gab to agitate the masses and raise questions among the people. They learned how to offer land. They learned how to offer equalities in an infinity of ways at the same time that they knew these things were impossible. . . . So the years passed and the class struggle was fomented in El Salvador.

That the armed forces has been partly to blame for what has happened, yes, it's true. The high command has accepted this; I personally accept that there is something in this. The subversives make it seem as though all the members of the armed forces are included in these acts. That's just not true! In every profession, even among priests, there are some who are better than others. Among human beings, in every family there are some better than others, so why should we all be the same in the armed forces? That is where the left has been adept, in exploiting these acts, and that gave them a lot of worldwide publicity, to the extent that in Europe it was said the Salvadoran armed forces grabbed live children and threw them in the air and killed them! I think it is impossible that a human being could do that. He'd have to be crazy. First he would have to kill his own children, and I think that is completely illogical!

Here is the part where the war is like a whip that awakens the people. This war has awoken us in the armed forces. All of these things I am telling you, we began to see and meditate on and we began then to find the way of rectifying our steps in the sense of what the people mean to us. We began to realize that we are the ones who live with the people, because we are throughout the country.

I think that the war has humanized us more. . . . You have to see how we visit all the schools here, talking with the people. We celebrate Mother's Day, Day of the Secretary, Day of the Telegraphist, of all of them, for the people!

We want the people to feel what we really mean for them and what we are for them. This identification with the people is achieved mutually, by the fact that we both live in a war. In 1980, an army patrol would move through a sector, and if it asked people if they had seen the subversives, nobody would have seen anything, nobody ever heard anything. In 1982, the people began to see and hear. By now, we don't have to search for subversives; the people come to us, and this is why we are winning the war and that is why action with the subversives is less now. If you ask any child in Chalatenango to say something that would hurt us, he won't, I assure you, because he knows that the colonel, the captain, the major and the soldier go to his school for a piñata for him. They take him a clown and they give him candies, a book, a pencil. So even though someone might want to teach him that we are bad, they can't convince him, because bad people don't give out candies, don't do them favors nor share things. There is the solution.

Recently, the people came here on the Day of the Soldier. A school came and brought cakes and, another, wine, and a soda pop for every soldier, and then there was thousands of children singing The Soldier's Hymn and there were 279 gifts which the people brought for the troops. Isn't this flattering? Isn't that beautiful?

What the people see is that we are concerned for them. I believe that it isn't difficult to chat for five minutes, to have a coffee with them. For this, the people have a great admiration and, for those five minutes and a cup of coffee, they'd be ready to do anything for you. So why shouldn't one do it?

I could kill all the terrorists and still I wouldn't win the war, because even if all those in the mountains died, but there was still the will for people to go and take up those guns, then it would be an endless cycle. So, with that in mind, we began to reach out to the people. We began going to neighborhoods with our musical band and talking with the people, to whom we explained our intention, and in this way, little by little, everyone began understanding.

But I still thought, "How to generate a new image for Chalatenango?" because Chalatenango signified darkness, amputees . . . and then it occurred to me that the people should express their desire for peace, at the same time as they showed their purity, their soul, and also their cleanliness. So I decided that we should paint Chalatenango white!

At the beginning, many people weren't in agreement with the color white. For this reason, we held meetings, and I tried to convince them that it wasn't an obligation, but a demonstration of unity. When brides marry in our country it is in white, and people think higher of them—the ladies understand. It signifies purity, so many things . . . and so the people began to comprehend. Those who didn't have money for paint we helped out. . . . The mayor has been at my side always, also the governor . . . here there is unity. So, for this reason, when you see the white fortress, it is of the people. And if the city is white, then the fort should be white, too.

I have my Bible here. I have my New Testament here. Without God, we can't do anything; I don't believe that even a leaf of a tree dies without the will of God. If a leaf dies with God's will, then how is it possible that the life of a man can die without it?

There is no contradiction between my faith in God and the fact that I am a soldier. You remember David and Goliath. You know that David killed Goliath in the name of the Lord. Also, we have Solomon, and all the other warriors of the Bible. If God helps them, why won't he help me? If you come at me with a weapon to kill me and I defend myself, why shouldn't God help me? A good Christian, for me, should be a good soldier, and a good soldier a good Christian; the two things go together perfectly. So I can conceive that if I am confronted by others shooting at me, I have to be convinced that I can kill them all and not feel anything in my conscience, because I have fulfilled a duty and God will not hold me responsible for that.

That is my life. It is the life of a soldier who asks for peace.

*Colonel Sigifredo Ochoa recently quit the armed forces to take up politics in Roberto D'Aubuisson's ARENA party. The interview is in an office of ARENA headquarters; Ochoa is dressed in casual civilian clothes and lays a* mariconera *(a man's purse) containing a pistol on the table next to him. He has a rigid face and remarkably cold, hazel eyes.*

What are the results of the billions of dollars in aid that has come from the United States? We don't see positive results. On the contrary, what we see is that with this amount of money the government has its hands tied by the North Americans. I think we're serving as guinea pigs, in a laboratory where we are doing the bleeding and in which, in a given moment, the very same Americans will abandon us. I believe that here in El Salvador, everybody sticks their hands in, like we were whores! Everybody has the right, for a few dollars, to fondle us. The Mexicans, the Panamanians, the gringos, everyone!

We advocate a Salvadoran solution, and I can assure you of one thing: without the weight of the North Americans, we would resolve this problem! In our own way!

A war cannot be humane! They are talking about humanizing the war; to humanize the war, it must be ended! And to end it, there are two ways: be beaten or win. There is no other way. We have to clean up the country; the country is in disorder!

I can assure you that, in the United States, if there was a problem like this they would declare it an emergency! And they'd stick in all the National Guards and they'd smash that thing and imprison the leaders and, if possible, for rebelling against the state security, they would shoot or put in the gas chamber a whole bunch of people! For what reason is it that the Americans don't let us resolve our problem?! We have to think as Salvadorans and we have to fight and die here in our country!

*Antonio Martinez Marquez, 46, lives in La Ceiba, a hamlet in the eastern department of San Miguel.*

I am a carpenter. I am the father of four children. I make benches and guitars. The army arrested me, saying everything I did was for the guerrillas, and destroyed my workshop. They took my tools and they broke twenty-five guitars I had made. Everything else, things like the chickens, they took as well, and they threatened to make me disappear if we didn't leave.

Now I can't work in my little workshop. Now I have to work in agriculture with a machete. Now, well, I am living, suffering . . . I make three colones [sixty U.S. cents] a day working, from six-thirty in the morning to two in the afternoon. I used to sell my guitars for eighty colones each. I could make twelve guitars in eight or nine days. I also made violins and furniture. To put up the workshop again it will take me three years to save the money.

Before, we lived in Carolina [larger town in San Miguel]. In those days, I used to travel all the way to Guatemala to sell my guitars. Then on the twenty-first of December, 1983, I was attacked. The soldiers came there and they violated my wife in front of the children. The pretext was that my house was on a corner, and when the guerrillas would come there they would ask for water or something. Just for this they accuse you of being a guerrilla yourself!

When afterwards I went to see Colonel Monterrosa [then area commander], he said, "These things happen in war, and this is a war," and he told me that it was my problem.


*Maria Julia Coreas, 48, is a strong woman with penetrating eyes, but with the premature agedness that poverty brings. She is the undisputed leader of her squatter's community, 21 de Junio, named for the date the camp was established. Already displaced by the war in 1983, Coreas was among the 200,000 Salvadorans who lost their homes in the devastating October 1986 earthquake.*


I have come from Mercedes Umaña. I have been four years now in San Salvador, but the reason for my coming is because I was afraid of the situation that was happening in the village. I had to come here because of the guerrillas. The *muchachos* would come in at midnight, in lines, shouting, you know, "Long live our town, because this town is ours," and so on.

Then my husband was hurt and so I alone was looking after our seven children. And I have two boys, and this was what worried me because they [the guerrillas] were stealing the boys. At that time, one was eleven and the other fourteen.

And so, when I saw that I was alone and that other people were arranging their things to leave that town, I thought, "What will I do here alone with my children, seeing how these people are coming in and that they may bother me?" when all of a sudden there was a great bombardment on the [nearby town of] Berlin. That was when they [FMLN] took Berlin, right? You could see those great balls of fire falling from helicopters and the next day we could see the great numbers of people coming from Berlin, with their children on their backs and all their things with them. The street was full of people.

I came out with coffee and bread, giving it to the people, but at the same time I was crying because I thought, "Just as these people are having to leave, we may have to as well." The park full of people, the houses were filling up with people asking for help, and the bombs falling for three days and nights. So, finally, seeing all this I felt a great anguish and I thought, "I can't let my children be like this." So I got together our little things and some bread and we came to San Salvador.

We stayed in a park. Finally, after three days, I located a relative and they found us an abandoned house on a *finca* [farm]. We were there a week, without even the bread of every day for my children. Later, a woman who worked in the market gave me money and facilities so that I could sell in the market, and in this way I began to survive with my children.

We finally ended up in a *barrio* in the Cerro San Jacinto, and we made a hut and everything was all right until the earthquake on the tenth of October. That was frightening, because all the huts fell down. We went to a piece of land, and we were over five hundred families of refugees there. Some institutions helped us with materials.

Afterwards, the owner of the land told us to leave. He said if we didn't leave he was going to unleash his "dogs" [hired gunmen] to get us out. We knew what kind of dogs they were, so we left. Some went to some field and the rest of us went back to the Cerro again, even though the institutions told us people couldn't live there anymore. But since we didn't have anywhere else to go . . . and the children . . . so we went.

Then the rains came and the earth was inundated with water and some families were buried—about three. So, upon seeing this, we felt bad and we didn't have any support, and we said, "How will we resolve this? We don't have anywhere else to go."

That was when the other communities helped us and we went out looking for a piece of green area and that was when we found this place. So that was how we came, about eight in the morning, in one single move—you know, the families cutting grass and making huts. And three days of silence passed in which no one told us anything.

After three days, the mayor's office called us to ask us how we were, and we explained that we had come because we had nowhere else to go. We found they wanted to get us out of here because this neighborhood didn't want to see this eyesore here. Since then, it has been silence.

So we are waiting. But we can't stay like this. We need water, and the children have missed school. Now what I hope is that our life changes. I ask the Lord, who is the only one who can help us, to find a solution to this problem so that we can live peacefully. Even if for our last days, you know? So we can have a different life than what we have had. That is all.

*Steve Salisbury is a 25-year-old American correspondent for the paramilitary* Soldier of Fortune *magazine. He has lived in El Salvador for five years and regularly fights with Salvadoran army troops against the FMLN guerrillas.*

To me, in a personal way, the war here has meant an opportunity to try and develop myself. I have established myself as an "action journalist" and I've written some good stories out of it and taken some good pictures.

It's been a growing experience for me, I have to say, because when I came down here, I was just like any other twenty-year-old kid. I was looking to make a name for myself, to establish myself in the career of journalism. Then I started to see what was happening here, and I've always been a conservative but, uh, I've seen that the Communists can be their most ruthless and that we have something very special in the United States with our democracy and our lifestyle and our values and they deserve to be defended.

What's most important to me is doing what's right for the United States— patriotism. I would suppose that my role, and *Soldier of Fortune*'s role overall, is the democratic answer to the Communist's call to internationalism. I see myself as a freedom fighter; I don't see myself as a mercenary. When I go out in the field and carry a weapon, that's because the Communist guerrillas have threatened to kill members of *Soldier of Fortune* magazine! So carrying a weapon is for self-defense!

I want to see what's best for the Salvadoran people, and I feel that what's best for the Salvadoran people is a democratic form of government and the opportunity to choose what religion they wish, career they wish—and also, the free enterprise system. It's just one more contribution that I'm making to my country and the effort to bring about and defend democracy in this world.

There's many things involved here. We all gotta die for something, and why not die for something noble?

To carry a gun . . . in your heart, it gives you a feeling of pride. It gives me, when I was able to defend myself . . . it removed fear from me. A weapon is there so that you can defend yourself. As long as you have a weapon, the other guy's gotta think that he can get popped, so he's gonna . . . it's a . . . it's used to go out and find the enemy and kill 'em or . . . and to defend yourself at the same time.

I tell you what really gets me and what really pulls at my heart, what, at times, comes close to bringing tears to my eyes, is, well, like I've seen a lot of bodies, you know, a lot of war casualties, a lot of wounded, a lot of dead and . . . after a while, one . . . one body, one victim of this war becomes just like another. Like, I've seen bodies hacked apart and riddled with bullets, but what really gets me is when you have the loved ones grieving over the body. That is what's the most difficult.

But when I get into a combat situation, there's an immediate rush, an immediate push of adrenaline, starts pumping—your heart starts pumping, your—expecta- tions grow, your senses become more acute, your hearing becomes more acute, to pick up the twitching of the grass. And when the bullets start to fly, it really pushes that adrenaline going! You feel exhilaration. You feel courage. You feel—It's, it's a sense of freedom, too!

On this last operation I went out on, this night operation, we got close to the guerrillas, maybe ten, twenty meters apart from them. And I was with this sergeant, just on flat, barren terrain! Scrub brush . . . and under the cover of darkness . . . and we were on the verge of losing our existence, possibly, but I felt, shoot! I felt exhilarated and . . . I felt freedom! And I felt courage! And . . . you don't have those sensations living the life in the United States!

*Father Flavian Mucci, 52, is an Italian-American Franciscan priest with a heavy Boston accent. The interview is at the open-air café he runs on the road named after him leading into the town of Sonsonate. Just beyond is his large Agape compound, with homes for unwed mothers and old people, youth workshops, and hospital. Mucci, who has lived in El Salvador for twenty years, also runs a series of SOS Children's Homes for orphans and is building homes for indigents.*

The killings about four, five years ago . . . I remember, 'cause every time I went to the capital there would be bodies all over the place on the roads. Every Monday—'cause I was building in Santa Tecla my second children's village and every Monday I went there—and there were bodies. I remember all the . . . all the bodies on the . . . on the roads. It was really scary in those days.

My Santa Tecla project is all war orphans. When we first took those kids in, I remember we were sitting at the table at supper and all of a sudden a helicopter went over and the kids ran out and they start wavin'! The [surrogate] mother called to them and says, "Get in here!" That was about three, four years ago when they were killing, so the mother got them all in the house, and they says, "No, no, you gotta wave, you gotta wave!" And she says, "Well, why do you have to wave?" They says, "We don't wave, they throw bombs!" So there they are, all these little kids (chuckles) wavin'! That's what they were accustomed to! I mean, these kids come from the inside. They seen those helicopters come round, and so they were trained by their parents to wave!

I was very, very strong . . . during the killings. . . . I am a little weak now, uh . . . insofar as, I'm scared. I'm scared. I'm scared all the time. But during the real killings, when we were in martial law—do you remember that?—I was, you know, I was—hey—jus' going around, doin' my things. They were killing priests in that epoca. But it was then they told me to be careful, and right now I'm still trying to get outta that.

One time, I had one guy come in. He comes up to me. He says, "Father, I wanna see you personally in an office or by ourselves." So . . . we're sitting down. "Look," he says, "Father, I have to tell ya something," he says, "I don't want you to go over to the port." I says, "First of all, who are you?" He says, "I'm a private detective," or secret service detective, or whatever. Whatever. So I says, "Well, why can't I go to the port?" The port's only twenty kilometers. He says, "Because I don't wanna kill you." I says, "You don't wanna kill me; what did I do?" He says, "Look, I have orders to kill you if you go that way." I says, "I didn't do anything; I'm not even political." He says, "I like the work you're doing, but we just had a meeting this afternoon and, well, I don't know if I should tell you, but every time you leave this house, I have to be behind you and I have orders the minute you start going towards the port, you're dead," he says, "so please don't let me kill you."

Apparently, some priest was going down there, and they thought it was me. But it wasn't me. I wasn't going, I wasn't, you know, teaching any . . . but he wouldn't tell me. He says, "Just don't go." I was already marked to be killed. . . .

I know I was being followed. First of all, my church was taken over four times by the guerrillas—if you want to call them guerrillas. They took over the church, and I told em, I said, "Look, I'm coming in every two hours. You touch my walls"— 'cause I'd just painted them—I says, "and you're gonna have trouble." I said, "I'll stay away. You want a telephone, there's one. You want a bathroom, use the bathroom. I don't want a dirty church." I says, "I don't wanna get in trouble with you guys, but I'm coming in every two hours." And I did go in, and I would spend hours with them talking.

I says, "Why you in this stuff?" And he says, "Give me a job." I says, "Whaddya mean, give you a job?" And he says, "Well, look, we get twenty-five colones a day to take over churches. If you give me a job—even the half—I'll take it." So I says, "Whaddya mean, you do this as a job?" He says, "Yeah; why do you think there's not that much killing in November through February?" He says, "Because we cut coffee. We drop our arms, we go and cut coffee. We cut sugarcane, then we come back to the mountains again. It's a job." That's what he told me.

There was always a girl, the leader. Always the girl; they were the tough ones. So . . . then they took me by gunpoint, twelve o' them, all the way to the port. That's when I really—You know, you go through things like that and . . . I had a van. They wanted to come out o' the church—no soldiers around, you know, nothing—so they were all down below and twelve pistols to your head. You know, I'm shivering; it's twenty kilometers! I said about forty rosaries going! I said the African church and I said everything. (laughs) I just kept on praying, like this. (shows a frightened image) They says, "Come on, Father, keep going, keep going." And I was going. Thank God, one by one, they got off. Then the last guy has to get out way in the woods. I said, "This is it; there's no way I'm gonna be saved." He leads me all the way and he says, "Okay, now you can leave." And he gave me directions to get back. My heart was—I mean, things like that . . . it breaks you little by little, all those little incidents.

*Ruben Guardado is in his late fifties, thin and silver-haired, with a gold tooth and vibrant, intelligent eyes. His fat young grandson sits on his knee. He is from Guazapa volcano, a longtime guerrilla stronghold sixteen miles from the capital of San Salvador. In 1986, the armed forces launched a mostly-successful campaign to wrest control of Guazapa from the FMLN; they called it Operation Phoenix. Guardado is now in a Catholic Church-run displaced-persons camp.*

I come from Guazapa. I had a sixteen *manzana* farm and I had three children who were studying. I lived well with my children; none of them were drunkards or gamblers or womanizers. One they killed. Also they killed a pregnant daughter.

I had thirty cows; they killed them all or they robbed them, the security forces did. They robbed me also of seven thousand colones [fourteen hundred dollars] I had saved. They killed a grandson of five years and a daughter-in-law. Once they shot me with a bullet, but not seriously. We have suffered hunger, tortures, bombings, machine-gunnings, mortarings. . . . Today you find me without a home; they burned it all. We have five and a half years of suffering in the war; every day we had to go into the bush with the woman and children with a few tortillas. Finally, I decided to leave; they gave us a place here. But we suffer from the food. They give us beans, cabbage, and tomatoes. I have lost ten pounds here.

Today I am living on charity, and that is hard. Sometimes, the children ask us for things, and the only thing I can do is to lament.

They consider us *masa* [guerrilla supporters] because sometimes we gave food to the guerrillas. For this, the armed forces persecuted one, for living in conflictive zones they saw one as a subversive.

I never thought I would end up here, to mourn and beg. I tried to return to Guazapa fifteen days ago, but we had to hide from the aviation for five hours as they bombed. I have left one son there to look after things. I stay here only so as not to leave my other children alone.

There are times I cry at seeing my own disgrace, but we all have to suffer some for the love of God.

*The minister of culture and communications, Julio Adolfo Rey Prendes, is a close aide and old friend of President Jose Napoleon Duarte. A founder of the Salvadoran Christian Democrat party, Prendes is an affable but cunning political animal; he plans on being the next president when Duarte's term expires in 1989. During the interview at his rambling home, he shows off his new laser disc player and periodically stops talking to stand in front of the speakers at crucial moments of Tchaikovsky's 1812 overture.*

*Prendes is a black sheep of El Salvador's traditional landed oligarchy, having chosen not only to go into politics but to espouse certain reforms. He is now in charge of coordinating the government's "hearts and minds" campaign to win away the peasantry from the guerrillas.*

When we joined the Revolutionary Junta in 1980, it was difficult. We were sharing power with the military, and about six hundred Christian Democrats had been killed already by the security forces and the death squads. Enemies don't become friends overnight, and the security forces were still allied with the ultra-right, which was trying to destroy the junta. But even though we knew all that, we had to make a sacrifice in order to have power and we hoped that, gradually, we could implement the needed reforms and curb the excesses.

Now, the new stage of the struggle is the battle to win the hearts and minds of the people. I call it "ideologization," the final and decisive battle to instill El Salvador with social and democratic concepts. People don't fight for what they have, but for hope and illusion. War will end when a majority of the population takes a negative view of the guerrillas. That view is growing. That's the only way to begin ending this war. The war will end when one side or another wins the hearts and minds of the population.

I asked for the president to create the post of culture and communications for me in order to penetrate the hearts and minds of the people. It is a new challenge in my life, to build the society which I aspire for, and for which I have fought for so long.

You need to "conscienticize" people from top to bottom. The Communists understand this, so why can't democracies also use their power to penetrate a culture? The biggest difficulty has been to convince the armed forces of the need for ideologization of the people. To me, this achievement is the big goal, the ideal, but it is a job that needs five or ten more years of work.

*Evelyn is a quick-eyed woman in her early thirties, bright and dogmatic in her revolutionary beliefs. She is a political officer and literacy instructor in northern Morazan for the People's Revolutionary Army (ERP), one of the FMLN's five factions.*

I used to be a social worker and I worked two years clandestinely as an ERP cell member in San Salvador. We had a house, my husband and I, and the leaders would go there for meetings. Once, Villalobos [top FMLN commander] came; I didn't know until afterwards that it was him!

At the same time, I was a student at the National University. With the Final Offensive [abortive January 1981 rebel campaign], I finally incorporated as a combatant. In the city, we appeared to be just a normal married couple; not even the neighbors knew what we really did. Meanwhile, we were a communication base for the ERP.

On the second of January [1981], it was decided to go to the theaters of war. First it was decided that only my husband would go to the front, but I said, "Why not me?" so it was discussed and it was decided that I could come, too.

We went by car. We just took bathing suits and things to make it look like we were going to the beach. We went as far as a place on the road near Santa Rosa de

Lima [in eastern El Salvador], then we went into the bush, to Morazan. After a while, we reached a safe house, where we stayed. It belonged to a peasant comrade, and we waited the night before continuing. It was all just like a movie! I remember how fat we both were; just from the city, we weren't used to walking at all!

My husband was an electrical engineer and had brought with him—this was the whole purpose of his coming—the electronic apparatus to set up the first Radio Venceremos [the FMLN's clandestine radio]. It was he who announced the initiation of the Final Offensive on the tenth of January, 1981.

My first duties were in communications; later, as a literacy instructor. I have never been in combat. I've only fired about fifteen rounds, but I *have* been on some operations. Today, I have a higher level of motivation than ever because of the constant school of war.

*From the grassy knoll beside the basketball court, there is a sweeping view of coffee plantations and grazing sheep. Aldea Infantil SOS is an orphanage run by Father Mucci on the flanks of the San Salvador volcano near the town of Santa Tecla. It is home to just over a hundred children, about half of them war orphans; two of these are Luis Lopez Rodriguez and Atílio, both 16.*

Luis: My mama, before . . . she was a butcher and she didn't have time to take care of us . . . and so in the nursery, my little brothers and sisters were looked out for during the day. So the people there knew us; when they heard of the deaths, they came and took us in.

JLA: Whose deaths?

Luis: Uh . . . my parents.

JLA: What happened?

Luis: Well, the truth is, I didn't know. I just remember that that last day I was with them, we went to go collect money that her clients owed. We returned about nine at night and we prayed the rosary before going to bed and then, about eleven, they came to take them outside. I didn't know who they were. And near there, about three hundred meters, they gave the death to both of them.

JLA: How old were you then?

Luis: I was seven.

JLA: And you did not know why they died?

Luis: I still don't know why.

JLA: But you have been told that it was because of this conflict?

Luis: Yes, I believe it's because of the conflict (voice low, fades out).

JLA: Do you know who took the lives of your parents, from which side they were?

Luis: Uh . . . if I'm not mistaken, they were from the guerrillas, because there were some . . . neighbors who I believe participated in that and they had sentenced my parents to death.

JLA: How has the loss of your parents affected you?

Luis: Before, I felt very nervous. I felt very . . . alone. I stayed for a while without friends. A long time. Afterwards, I began forgetting everything. . . .

JLA: (to Atílio) Do you want to tell me a little about yourself?

Atílio: Well . . . my mama and papa, we lived together. We lived in a little village, and my papa worked in agriculture. My mama was a domestic in the house. And they . . . killed her because . . . the soldiers killed her because . . . I mean, there, near where we lived, guerrillas would come. Of the guerrillas, there was one who knew my father. But my papa wasn't anything. This guerrilla passed over to the armed forces and after . . . he came with other soldiers and said my father was a subversive and so my father—he was working in agriculture a ways away—and my mama told them he was away working and they didn't . . . believe her. They took her and they killed her.

JLA: And were you there when that happened to your mother?

Atílio: Yes. I was in the house, but I didn't see when they killed her since they took her out. . . .

JLA: Do you feel bitter?

Atílio: It would just get worse to take a vengeance or something like that. . . .

*After earning his Ph.D. in the United States in education, Ricardo Stein returned to El Salvador in 1978 to work as a statistician, keeping count of the nation's war toll. His war documentation center, operating out of San Salvador's UCA university, disseminated information about the conflict throughout the world.*

There is one date I will never forget. It was January eighth, 1980. Salvador Samayoa, who was an officemate of mine and a person for whom I had a great deal of respect, had been acting as minister of education. Prior to the coup, we were both thinking of buying a car at the same time, and I had asked him to be my cosigner to get the car and I was the cosigner for his car. When he resigned from the junta, he had a spate of malaria and was in bed for a few days.

We met on a Sunday—January sixth—in which he said, "Look, there's going to be a press conference on January eighth. I want you to listen very carefully and not be surprised by what's going to be said. Just be aware. I probably won't see you for a long time, so good-bye, thank you for everything. . . ."

It was five o'clock in the afternoon, and I was listening to the radio broadcast transmitted from the National University and Salvador Samayoa began making a statement which ended by announcing that he was a clandestine member of the FPL, that he had decided to join and that he was now moving into clandestinity. I felt that at that point I was going to die, literally! For the next year and a half, I always kept payments on my car two months in advance (laughs) just in case anybody decided to check out who my cosigner was!

I don't think that there's anybody in this country who hasn't lost a friend. Yeah, I've lost friends. Of all political types. People who were connected to the left, people who had their houses destroyed by rightist terrorist acts and who we kept until they were able to get out of the country. People who we knew on the right and who were targeted by guerrillas. . . . If I would add up, between friends and acquaintances, I think the list could easily go over a hundred.

In retrospect, I think I escaped from that reality by immersing myself totally into what I was doing and, to a certain point, not thinking of the risks one engaged in. My wife played a very important role in bringing caution to my life. I think that if I would not have been married in those days, most probably I would've been one of the corpses found somewhere. She was always forcing me to reflect upon the risks that I was taking and upon the responsibilities I had and . . . Eventually, what becomes worth dying for? That once you're dead, you become one statistic—a statistic that I myself was picking up in my work.

A sense of survival also emerges. I wouldn't be able to explain, but I think I . . . I think that I am a survivor. I can deal with situations of intense psychological pressure, of intense fear or intense terror, intense pressure of any form, and remain whole. I probably won't and can't explain what my escape mechanisms are, but they *have* been operating.

I think the most valuable moments for me personally have been those very depressive moments in which, when you begin to question your whole world, you begin to find answers which round up your political countenance. My father used to say—very supportive and very respectful, never pressing me to abandon whatever it was that I felt correct—but he used to say, "You'll discover in time that there is almost a natural process in life in which one goes on from being an incendiary student to a professional fireman." I don't think that is quite accurate; it's just that the accumulation of experiences begin to give you a sense of political nuance. You do not think of situations in terms of blacks and whites. The blacks and whites, in fact, begin to be rejected and one develops an appreciation for the hues, the tones of gray that are interspersed. And in that process, one also begins to feel that what is important is not necessarily to explain, but to act. In that sense, I feel that I would be a totally different individual today if I had not lived these six, seven, eight, very intense years . . . very intense years! They seem to be more like twenty or thirty. . . .

I never had any personal attempts on my life. The closest I came to anything like that was on September sixth, 1983, in which the death squads began a series of terrorist attacks. It coincided with a campaign that the FMLN had launched attacking the installations of the Third Brigade in San Miguel. Several bombs exploded that night, one near the Jesuit residence, a second one in the home of the secretary of communications of the university, and I just could not get it out of my mind that if there was another target, I just couldn't think of anybody in that university that wouldn't come next but me.

We found the room that was farthest from the garage that night and put a series of mattresses against the windows and against the walls and the doors. The children were very, very upset. That was also the closest that I came to thinking, "I have to get out; this is destroying me," probably the first time that I thought seriously of just how destructive it could be in personal terms, of how my family relations had become so strained. Reflecting on what had become routine for me. Checking whether I carried home every night papers that could be incriminating. Making sure that the library at home had all—books that had certain semanticized words which are taboo in this society—the Industrial Revolution was bound to be a text that would be confiscated and get you accused of having subversive connections because of the word *revolution*. The history of socialist utopias was another one that could've been the most dangerous thing in your possession.

I remember an incident. My name appeared publicly connected with the very high-profile rebels in the early part of 1983. To have your name in that connection inevitably meant that not only did they [the security forces] have a file on you but that you probably would be subject to persecution. My sense at that moment was that I should say, "I am here and come and get me. My vulnerability is my greatest protection; I have good friends to vouch for me."

But my wife was very much . . . emotionally shattered. It was like the straw that broke the camel's back. She wanted to get out of the house, so we invited a very good friend of ours, a journalist from *The New York Times*, to spend the night over at our home and to be an eyewitness if anything was to happen. And that night, I remember being very calm and thinking, "Richard's coming to sleep over— simply to calm my wife! I mean, if they come, this is going to do absolutely nothing!"

But a routine was established as of that day by which we had an emergency network that could become operational at any moment of the day with one phone call. The network could be connected and people could do something about it.

One night, after this network had been established, around three o'clock in the morning, the doorbell rang. All the descriptions of people feeling fear are nothing compared to the feeling of fear that one has when the doorbell rings at three o'clock in the morning and there is a curfew which started at ten o'clock at night. You know the descriptions about your throat being totally dry, your tongue sticking to the ceiling of your mouth, being awakened at that moment and having to react with all your reflexes totally alive! Do the phone call and do it in such a short time that you can present yourself to the door and confront the situation without giving a trace of suspicion to the people that are knocking, except the fact that you were asleep and trying to put a night robe on. Hoping that the telephone would be picked up immediately after you had dialed, hoping that they didn't cut the lines. All these thousands of thoughts going through your mind! The whole house in absolute turmoil . . . lights going on . . . and to discover that it was this individual, some child, who was going along the houses of the block ringing bells! It's one of those experiences which . . . literally strains you, but . . .

You've asked me to approach the situation from a totally different perspective than I always approach it. I always try to keep my own personal feelings very much out of it, trying to be as cold and objective as possible, and now, just trying to give my own internal sense of feeling, I don't feel very comfortable with it. Not that I don't engage in that sort of thing, but they are soft voices, spoken to myself.

*Maria Ofelia Marroquín, 24, is a political prisoner in the women's prison of Ilopango on the outskirts of San Salvador. During the interview, her little girl, the result of her rape by her military captors, squirms in her lap. Maria is a member of the National Resistance (RN), one of the FMLN's five factions; she has a bad limp from a gunshot wound suffered in prison.*

My name is Maria Ofelia Lopez Marroquín. I came here when I was twenty-three. I just became twenty-four and so, unless something happens, I'll be here to become twenty-five.

I am from Suchitoto, Department of Cuscatlan, the zone so well known as Guazapa. There I grew up and there I began to form. At twelve years old, I began to study with the priests. I was one of the catechists and I, and my papa as well, were persecuted for this situation, because he was a catechist, and I worked together with him.

The persecution began in 1980—pardon, since May of 1979. Members of the death squads—at that time they were from ORDEN—they watched us, where we gave catechism, to the extent that at the school where I studied, they went there to get us and we went running in the midst of the shooting and hid in some hills there.

About three months later, they starting putting ambushes where I lived because their objective was to finish with my whole family. But by pure luck, my mama felt something was going to happen and she left with the littlest children. Only my eldest brother stayed and they did kill him there. They took him together with a brother of my father and they killed them together. Since then, we couldn't live a normal life. Then, a war began and then, in 1980, the first comrades began rising up. In any case, we had to defend ourselves so that the death squads wouldn't finish us.

It began with five armed men, men who carried short arms [pistols] and one or another with a mechanical rifle. Then we began to organize everything—health committees, brigadists, radio operators. There was all the infrastructure. There were those who were security, who made food, tailors . . . there was a sewing workshop and everything. So this is how we formed our structure to the extent that about fifteen truckloads of armed people of the government began arriving to take us out of where we were.

There came fifteen truckloads of the army, and we with only five weapons, nothing more. So we ran. What they did was to rob. They took the maize we had in the granaries, the animals, the cattle, the chickens, everything. When we came out, there was nothing left—no chickens, no pigs or cows, nothing. That was how the meat for food in that area ended and, with all the war there has been and the North American aid to the government, the repression has increased.

We have lived a mountain of experiences. In the beginning, we had to run for whole nights. We couldn't return, because the army was installed in our houses, eating everything. At first we went for three days, but, little by little, the time increased that we had to run and there were times when it was months. Now, there isn't even a fixed place to stay. I don't know how it would be there today, but I tell you that is where my brother and father died and the other younger brother. There are two brothers dead already. One was killed by a bomb. My father, they killed him with volleys of bullets.

What I did in that zone, I did with the end of helping the population. And the army, well, why not say it—the truth is that necessity obliges one and the brothers have to incorporate [join the FMLN] upon seeing all the things done by the army of the puppet government. They killed children. Of course, this makes one indignant to the point of having to take up an arm to defend those people.

I didn't carry an arm; I carried a first-aid kit. I carried intravenous bottles, syringes, pills, a whole kit with even a small surgery outfit. After '81, the masses began to return. Little by little, the people began coming back, so there was a mountain of people we had to attend to with our medicines. There were some really serious cases—paralysis, for example, strokes—and we had to fight the sicknesses with just natural medicine. We had a mountain of containers full of weeds—one for headache, one for stomachache, for grippe, for sore throat, toothache, and for "the itches," as we call them.

For a time I was in charge of the military hospital. I wasn't there long, though, because I became pregnant. So another took over that responsibility and I went to the hospital for the masses, which is not as heavy work.

After I had the girl I didn't work for four months. Three days after she was born I had to run from an army invasion. I couldn't stand it, but still I ran. Luckily, we didn't have to go far, and we returned all right. Later on, with more invasions by the army, aviation, and everything, the things got harder.

Right next to where we were evacuated from, there was a horrible massacre. They killed twenty-three children from eight days old to seven years old. They left their little heads on one side, their little feet on another, and the little heads cut off—well, split. The little boys, they tore off their little parts [genitals] and they left them thrown there, and later we heard them go away laughing as they were marching, and we, silent so they wouldn't find us. They were making jokes about what they had done; they enjoyed it. "Those little son of whore insects," they said. "They're in pieces there now, so now there won't be any more guerrillas." That was in September '83.

I came out in December of '84. When I was here in the city, I lived in the refuge [Church-run displaced person's camp]. When they captured me, I had gone to visit an aunt.

I was in a place where there were always a lot of people, when suddenly I saw three cars which were polarized [smoked-glass windows], and from one of them came two men dressed as civilians. Well, if they'd been armed I would have run, but, no, they were in civilian [clothes], so I was walking slowly when from behind they grabbed me by the shoulders and they put their hands over my face so I wouldn't know them. And then I didn't return home.

They took me to a lonely place, and at the moment I thought in my mind that I was in a place where they throw garbage, where there is a precipice and where below passes the dirty waters.

From the moment they captured me, and put me in a vehicle and blindfolded me, I couldn't see anything, not even the faces of the men. Then in that place, they said to me, "Where do the weapons come from?" and "Where are the comrades?" They wanted me to give up my comrades and my family . . . they asked me for everything, for safe houses, that I give them up. When they listened and I told them that I didn't know anything of safe houses, they got mad and started to hit me.

They started to say to me that I was such and such and they told me the pseudonym. "You are Caína," and I said, "No, no, my name is this," and I had my identity card with me. "No, that's not your name and that's not your photo," and they asked me, "When were you born; who is your mother?" and I told them the same, ten times, the same thing. When they didn't get anything out of me, they put on the *capucha* [quicklime-coated cloth hood] and told me that when I wanted to talk, I should move my fingers. For a fact, when I couldn't stand it any longer I moved my fingers and they took it off and began to ask me again and again, and I said, "I don't know what you're talking about," and they put it on me again and another time—three times. I moved my fingers to make them think I was going to talk, but then I didn't tell them anything. But they did let me rest, for at least one minute, but then, again they put it on.

Every time they got more indignant and they said to me, "Look, whore, you don't want to talk and we know what you're doing and how you're called, and if you don't tell, we're going to kill you and here you'll be left." With what they told me, I imagined I was next to a riverbed; it was psychological pressure. "We're going to leave you thrown here, and nobody's going to know you're here. You'll see, if you don't talk, you're going to go to a place where they will get the truth out of you and there you will be a thing to give pity, little mama." Just psychological pressure. . . .

Then I told them, "Man, but I don't know anything, so what am I going to tell you!" "You don't know anything, right?", and they hit my head, they twisted my arms. All the time, I felt that in front of the car where they had me was the other car. I heard them open the door and come to where I was. "Leave this bitch to me; she'll soon see who I am." And those who were at first with me left, and the other two stayed with me. Then, well, one began to beat me. "You're going to see, bitch; you'll talk to me!" At first he put the capucha back on me, loosened my handcuffs, and told the other, "Lift her up," because they had me thrown on the bed of the car. They lifted me up and began to undress me without taking off my blindfold. Then from all the times they had put on the capucha, I had a pain in the chest, or maybe the lungs, such that I felt when I breathed it attacked me and I hurt inside and it had bitten me all up. My face and cheeks bit.

Once I was nude, they kept asking me the same questions. I said, "I don't know, I don't know," and I almost couldn't answer them, because I felt when I breathed that I didn't have enough air. So then one said to the other, "Look, maybe we better just kill this bitch." I think they had me there about an hour and a half. Then those two violated me. Afterwards, they continued asking me, so I screamed at them, and they said to me, "Wait, bitch, this isn't all; we're going to kill you."

So then they took me down from the car, blindfolded. They took off my handcuffs and gave me my dress to put on and they said, "You're going to throw her there; throw her over there." I thought they were going to kill me right there, but maybe they had pity. So they put me down and they said to me, before taking me to the barracks, that I shouldn't say anything because I would regret it. And they asked me, "Are you going to say anything, bitch?" I didn't answer. "If you say anything you know what you'll get, right? You have to promise you're not going to say anything." After a while of their asking me, I told them "No"; because of the very fear, one has to accept everything. "Well, then, little bitch, you know that with us you're not going to play around. You haven't told us anything, and now you have to go talk there and you'll see it's not good. You already know what's the good part." And then they took me away.

They took me to the barracks of the National Police and there they had me five days, day and night, day and night, interrogating me, asking me the same, my name, birthdate, place of birth. They didn't let me see the International Red Cross during the whole time I was there. When they came, they'd keep me in a small and dark room until the Red Cross left. Then they took me back again. That's how they had me.

I felt good. I don't know . . . I was just very optimistic, and even more when I entered "The Fifth Front of the War" [rebels' name for prisons]. I felt good but, yes, the experience I had to endure was very hard.

The month after I came here, we had the threat of a search here in the [political prisoner's] Section and so we had to give an immediate response to the enemy. As a result, three of us were wounded—me the worst, unfortunately.

I had to spend three months in the hospital. For me, it was hard to live in a hospital—without medicine, everything dirty; it's terrible. Even more, because there they discovered my pregnancy.

I wasn't prepared for it. I wasn't expecting to have become pregnant. In the beginning, I reacted negatively, but, little by little . . . I don't know, I began preparing myself psychologically and I changed my mentality and, later, when my little girl was born, for good reason!

After I got out of the hospital, it was sad, because I had to drag around on crutches and with my stomach all heavy. It was hard to get around. I rested finally, when my girl was born. I still walked on one crutch, but it was easier to get around without the stomach.

I still don't know if I'll be here two years or more. I don't know. I don't know about if I get out because, in the first place, I don't have anyplace to go. I know that within a short time the refugee camps will disappear because of all the threats from the government [to close them down]. I don't know when I'll get out, nor where I'll go; I don't know. It worries me, and that's the worry of all the political prisoners here, that on getting out free, where will they go? One doesn't have a family that lives normally, because the truth is that my home is on Guazapa, if it still exists, which I doubt. Because . . . when my papa was still alive, every time the army operations ended, he always found the house burned, always, always, and he would fix it again. When they arrived again, they'd burn it again, in that style. So, since today he is dead, I suppose that the house is useless since there's no one to fix it. And, anyway, I can't go there.

But I don't know . . . they tell me I will be able to leave here so that they can do a good operation on my leg, because the truth is I can lose it if I'm not careful. I have to walk carefully so I don't fall. If I am half careless, my leg doubles on itself . . . but I don't know what possibilities there really are.

The truth is, I'm not prepared. That's a certainty. I can't run, and my desire is to go back [to Guazapa]. How wouldn't I want to go if that's my place, eh? I am delirious to get out of here! The problem is I know I'll just go out to be a victim there because I can't run. If I knew I could walk tranquilly without any problem, I would go there. That's my dream.

*Colonel Peña Arvisa is a member of the armed forces chief of staff, formerly the U.S.-funded Psychological Warfare program run out of military headquarters. Peña Arvisa looks like somebody's kindly uncle: bespectacled, aging, a kind of military "Oxford don."*

*The "psy ops" campaign got going with a vengeance in the summer of 1985 as part of a concerted effort to capitalize on the army's battlefield gains, by attempting to both demoralize and cause defections in the rebel ranks and woo away peasant supporters from the FMLN. The program includes "civic action" by soldiers in disputed villages, a military radio propaganda station, the aerial leafletting of rebel strongholds urging guerrillas to give themselves up under the government's amnesty program, and a broadcast campaign with taped messages by ranking rebel defectors.*

We try and influence the emotions and sentiments of the risen-in-arms, without coercion. We try to say nothing more than the truth. Those who do give themselves up, we give them a psychological warfare questionnaire, like the polls in the United States. We want to know why some surrender and others don't. The questionnaires go into computers, and we then analyze the information. Most of those who have surrendered complain that their commanders don't mix with the troops and that they are made to feel inferior. So we incorporate that kind of information into our campaign.

The greater number who surrender is a triumph for us; we win more with leaflets than with bullets—at least, that is my pretension. What we offer them has to be a kind of "white propaganda," like commercials in the United States. Like Seven-Up!

Now, we don't call them "terrorists" anymore. Rather, "combatant" or "comrade," although this was a hard thing to make some of our commanders understand. This has to be done like they sell Coca-Cola in the United States. We are trying to sell them a product, and the product is peace.

*Maria Concepción Sanchez Chicas, 45, lives in La Laguna, a war-ravaged community in northern Morazan.*

All of my cousins, uncles, and relatives were killed in the massacre of La Joya [by army in 1981]. Two years ago, my daughter, she was fifteen, was killed by the soldiers when she was picking beans in Canton de los Quebrachos, near Jocoayti-que. She had been looking for me. I had been running because of that massacre. Now I am poor of solemnity. I don't have anything; I live on the charity of this town.

What a bad government which kills in this way! How ungrateful! Now, I am alone.

*Napoleon Romero (alias Miguel Castellanos) is a guerrilla defector, the highest-ranking rebel officer to have betrayed his cause. He is a short, acne-scarred man, and intensely ambitious. The interview is in the suite of a govern-ment-owned hotel in San Salvador. The door to the adjoining room is ajar, where his armed security agents wait. Both the interview and the location are pre-*

*arranged through the Salvadoran government, which holds Castellanos in protective custody. Castellanos, in his late thirties, was the political-military commander of San Salvador of the Popular Liberation Forces (FPL), one of the FMLN's five branches. As a guerrilla officer, he received special instruction in Cuba and Vietnam. Now he is a star of the government's psychological warfare campaign to woo other rebels from the FMLN's ranks. He and other defectors are heading up a government-backed Institute of the National Reality, which publishes analyses of the war on the government's behalf.*

JLA: What was a typical day for you when you were with the guerrillas?

Castellanos: The activities of one within the guerrillas are programmed for the day's twenty-four hours; there's almost no time for personal life. One has a schedule mapped out. One day, meeting with, for example, the committee that deals with the masses, see? One analyzes the current situation, how the masses are confronting it, in order to give them policy directions for the next five- or six-month period. With the military part, it's the same. Looking over whether or not the plan ordered by the high command is being applied, seeing how specific operations are going. That is, whether it's, say, an execution or a sabotage—you know, seeing how it's going, what needs there are, to help them.

JLA: What about today? Are you an employee of the government?

Castellanos: No. More than anything, I collaborate in analysis, you know? Because . . . they ask me how I see the situation.

JLA: But your bodyguards are provided by the government?

Castellanos: Yes, they came with the amnesty; part of it was that they stay with me. And a safe house.

JLA: I've heard that something happened to your woman and that this had something to do with your decision to come in.

Castellanos: In the organization, one has certain relationships, right? Because one leaves everything else behind, one's life, normal ambience. Because . . . I was married when I left; now, I have returned to her . . . and I have a daughter with her. But . . . one leaves all this, because you have to submit and . . . yes, I had some companions and . . . it's natural when one is . . . And so, yeah, that companion who is referred to, yes, she was a companion with whom I was with for . . . a time. But I think that what happened to her was part of the process.

JLA: And what happened to her, exactly?

Castellanos: That is to say, she was captured, see? She was captured and . . . nothing more was heard of her. That was in '83.

JLA: And that affected you?

Castellanos: No! To me, that is, how do you say it . . . that, having lost her, it affected me because I loved her a lot, you know? I loved her and . . . later . . . But one manages to overcome these things, you know? That is, one is prepared for these eventualities, that the companion will fall, or even one himself. I mean, you're in a war and you know that from one moment to the next . . . one talks about it . . . and when you get together, that situation is anticipated, that one can fall in combat or any other situation. So I managed to . . . assimilate that fact, you know. . . .

Sure, if one is thinking about it happening, it's different, because it is very painful, to lose a companion. Even more when one esteems her and loves her, you know?

JLA: Was there one day when you finally made up your mind to come in?

Castellanos: No. That is, the decision wasn't just one moment. It was over several days that one is thinking, before taking the decision . . . because it means leaving . . . the ideological thing . . . and the friends and those who respect one . . . It isn't easy, to leave them behind. But one of necessity has to erase all that. When one reaches a threshold, like in my case, one just passes night after night thinking. Night after night. Because one has formed a whole world there, you know.

JLA: Are you a traitor?

Castellanos: That is . . . I knew, since we had already done it to other persons who had surrendered . . . so I knew they were going to call me one. But I thought later on the FMLN would see that I'm not a traitor, in the sense of turning my back on the people who need to achieve social justice. So in that sense I don't think I'm a traitor. But sure, for the FMLN, anyone who leaves its ranks and doesn't agree with it is a traitor. And if one starts to criticize, it's worse. That is sanctioned, and the maximum sentence is death. And I knew I would confront that sooner or later. But I know that it is the people who will be the judge, if one is really a traitor or not.

JLA: You were in charge of the urban arm of the FPL, and many of the actions you carried out were assassinations. What is it to execute somebody?

Castellanos: An execution has various principles. First, the political-ideological aspect. Because it's part of the armed struggle, one's enemy has to be eliminated. That's fundamental. Second, this element [person] who is going to be executed, what role does he play, concretely? Is he an element of the security forces, or a functionary? So there are grades of importance. Those who are most against the FMLN have to be executed; that's the criteria.

For example, within the military plan, there is what is called eliminating "heads," those who think. On that list, those who go are the [U.S. military] advisers for their importance. Then the pilots; they are top priority for executions. Second ladder are public functionaries: ministers, the president, vice president, chief of staff, colonels. And other state officials, the intermediate level. Afterwards, a third level are those intermediate officers of the armed forces, and also people in the government, who are identified for execution. But at this level, one tries to win them over more if there's any way to recruit them, in order that they lend a hand. And a fourth level are the "base people"—for example, the watchmen and "ears" [informers], as they are called—who are dangerous and known in a community. Also, there go labor leaders who are contrary.

So that is the political foundation; now, the execution is another thing. Where will it be done? How? The general thing is to do it with firearms, right? It's unusual to recommend carrying it out with knives, because this gives it a criminal or personal appearance. So it is not recommended to do it with knives or blunt instruments, but firearms. And usually to do it as quickly as possible and with few bullets, giving him the coup de grace. You can easily see the difference between a normal routine murder and an execution, because when it's a real execution there is the coup de grace. There may be two or three bullets in the body, but there is going to be a bullet right in the head, shot point-blank or fairly close. This is done so that the element stays [dies] and the mission is accomplished.

JLA: And you were in charge of making those kinds of decisions?

Castellanos: The problem is that, although one might have certain observations, the first thing is to fulfill the mission. This is the way of thinking. So it has to be done. Sure, there are the things of one's own, like asking for the target to be checked out completely, if it's really justified. . . . But the people below are saying, "No, let's do it, do it as quick as possible!" Because these are people who want to act, and that's their task, right?

But when one is in the leadership, you hear things about types just because of their appearance—"He's an [U.S.] adviser," for example. I'd say, "No, this isn't sufficient. This has to be verified." So they'd say, "No but to this place foreigners go!" and so on. In my case, I never approved this. No, sir. My criteria was the information had to be one hundred percent verified—or at least ninety percent—that for sure it's a person who merits being executed. Of course, that was the mission and everything, but sometimes, when I reflected, yes, I had doubts about all of that. Even more if the person hit was unarmed. That gave me doubts as to just how far that information was correct.

JLA: What did you feel the first time you took a life in this war?

Castellanos: You mean when someone is eliminated? Yes, well, (laughs) when one does that—and one isn't the one in charge, but the one executing—when one begins, it's a change.

It was hard for me. We went with some comrades that day, to do that execution, right? But it remains, a deep impression of that person who was executed. It remains really engraved, that action, and, afterwards, the idea leaves you that human life is a phenomenon which one can't affect. That is, life becomes a means toward an objective. Eliminating these people isn't something for which some God is going to punish you later; rather, it has to be seen as a measure to be taken in carrying out a political-military policy which is, supposedly, adjusted to the popular interests. That is the scheme. The first step is hard, maybe, but not later. It's not such a big thing . . . no, you accept it, as part of a job, a way of being.

But one overcomes it, you know. One overcomes it. Human life becomes this . . . one doesn't even think about it; it's a war. But now, at this point, I think one thinks about life and how to live it. Respecting life. For example, that of eliminating someone unarmed, no? There's no justification for that. Now, for me, even violence itself is rejectable, on either side. The dogmatization of violence.

*Luis, 25, is a thin, bearded former university student from San Salvador. He is now an area commander for a rebel unit belonging to the communist Armed Liberation Forces (FAL), one of the FMLN's five factions.*

*Luis's area of responsibility includes the rich, coffee-growing area of northern Usulutan department in eastern El Salvador. As part of his job, he deals with the area's landowners who, on demand, supply him and his forces with money, food, boots, or clothing. Luis also enforces an FMLN-decreed minimum wage for the peasant workers. If the landowners renege, they are forced to leave or have their crop burnt, or are abducted and held for ransom. Sometimes they are killed.*

I have been in this for eight or nine years; before, I was in the student movement.

We have grown a lot this year in this zone. Three and a half years ago, we were six; now we cover the whole area from the Pan-American [Highway] to the Littoral [coastal highway].

This area we consider a disputed zone. We don't control it, but neither does the armed forces. Before, we operated in large groups; now, we are mobile, in small units. We used to have a permanent instruction center in this area, but since the big [army] operation at the beginning of '84, we now have mobile schools. Our squads are ten-man; before, we used to go around with forty or more.

Even now, we defend controlled zones, like Jucuaran [town to the south], but not fixed positions, because they have a much greater firepower than we do. But we don't abandon areas completely, even so; we just move to one side.

With small units, the military objectives we have become much greater. The enemy has improved and has gained experience in these years of war. He has bettered his intelligence networks, and with the planes which take photos we have had to break down in size.

Before, the guerrilla columns didn't give enough time to politics and their links with the people were few because they were fighting all the time. We were beginning to have a relationship with the population like that of an army of occupation. The boys had little political involvement; they didn't fulfill their duty of organizing, agitating, and raising the consciousness of the population. So measures have now been taken so that the work isn't just going to be military, but also political. Under the new scheme, all will participate in the political work, as well.

On the urban front, it is up to the unions. They, the urban masses, are the other leg of the revolution. The first demand is always economic. When these demands aren't met, they have demonstrations, and these demonstrations convert into political demands, which is when the movement acquires its highest level. Then, actions are taken, like a general strike, and insurrections. . . .

Now, the conditions are right. They have to continue to be developed. The economic crisis is being achieved, but we have to get to the point where the movement is organized in one single army and in one single political party. . . . The high command believes that the place for strategic growth is in San Salvador, in terms of recruitment and incorporation. Here in the countryside, it is a constant trickle, but it is still not the needed quantity.

We have to use mines, massively; it is a policy of the command structure. All guerrillas have to know how to use explosives. It's an order. All of the columns have to have at least one or two "miners." At first, it was really dangerous; the comrades were afraid and many died when we first started using them. But now, the popular inventiveness is making some that are really safe and practical!

In this zone, they've not been used yet, because there are a lot of civilians. We have to educate them first; we're involved in that campaign right now. We have to get the people to lay the mines for us. What better than a peasant who can watch when an army patrol comes here? He can see what trails they use. He can plant a mine without any problem. We need to have the people involved.

There are squealers, "ears," here. Last month, we uncovered a network, and four of them we executed. But it wasn't because they were relatives of the military, as has been said; there are plenty of military relatives living here with no problem. They were executed because their duties were, one, to monitor the population and, two, to monitor the movements of our forces and to detect our encampments.

We know that there is a danger that the closer we get to the population, the danger of a North American intervention grows, which is their last card to play. But we will not restrain ourselves because of this. We have to expose ourselves in order to triumph.

The new concept is popular revolutionary warfare. Frontal attack against the enemy. All the forms of struggle have to be developed. It must be popular, in every sense of the word. It is the official line of the FMLN.

*It is midmorning in the coffee-growing town of Jucuapa in northern Usulutan. The night before, a large force of FMLN guerrillas attacked the National Guard fort here and set fire to the telephone and mayor's offices. Five guerrillas were killed; their bodies are stretched out in a line in a nearby coffee grove where jackbooted Guardsmen watch over the peasants commandeered to dig the grave pit. Las Marias, where the FAL field commander Luis (preceding interview) operates, is just down the road; without doubt, his force participated in the attack.*

*Lieutenant Sebastian Alvarado, 44, is the commander of the Jucuapa garrison. He is a burly, stern-faced man with suspicion in his eyes.*

For me, they are men just like us. The only thing is, maybe he who does wrong ends up badly, right? Maybe for this reason they suffer more casualties, you know? Because he who seeks the bad will find it.

As humans . . . they have the right to life and they have the right to be respected. Everyone has the liberty to think as he wishes and as he thinks is convenient for him. But, for example, what occurred last night, those guilty for those who died are they themselves. We were here and they came to look for us. It was a duty and a right of ours to defend ourselves, because apart from the obligation we have to defend the population . . . well, we always have, as humans, the right to defend our own lives.

*Down a small dirt road leading away from Jucuapa, a line of white chalk marks the spot where Jose Francisco Antonio Martínez, 16, was killed by a guerrilla mine blast in last night's attack. A group of small, excited boys lead the way to the dead boy's home.*

*The parents, Jose de la Cruz Martínez and Ana Francisca Corea, talk with visitors to one side of the tree-shaded adobe house. Inside, Francisco's body lies in a coffin surrounded by candles. Perhaps a result of shock, they are rather dispassionately theorizing about the exact cause of their son's death.*

Ana: Since there was a karate movie last night, you see, he and the other boys went to see it. Four of them. When they were coming back, the firing began, so I think maybe it was bullets which fell onto them! You see, he has holes like this (shows small holes with her fingers), one below his belly button.

JLA: But they say he stepped on a mine.

Ana: But that would have torn him apart. And he's all there. (She turns to a woman washing a pair of pants in a nearby bucket.)

Ana: Show him the pants.

(The woman comes forward, holds the pants out, and sticks her fingers through the several holes in them.)

Ana: See? It's from a small bullet. I say it's a bullet hole, not shrapnel.

JLA: So what do you feel now? Are you angry?

Ana: Well . . . God wanted it this way, right? That it be the will of God. Because there were four of them coming, you know, and he was ahead and it was his turn, right?

*Paolo is a Western European man in his late thirties fighting with the Revolutionary People's Army (ERP) branch of the FMLN. Tall, extremely thin, and bearded, Paolo has been with the guerrillas for several years and has political duties.*

We are not here to build schools; we are here to make a revolution. At first, the people thought, "Well, good, now that these ones are the new power here, they are going to do these things." And it took us quite a bit of political work to make them understand that, in reality, the FMLN has very little to give to them, apart from instructing and orienting them, or maybe giving them a permission to cut down a tree or something, so they can build a school.

*Fernando Ponce, 42, represents an FMLN-advised "civilian directorate" that teaches literacy to children in northern Morazan.*

We have to identify with both sides, how they both stand. We have to maintain neutrality. All is demagoguery; the government lies. There is no solution for us, the poor. It is we who are suffering.

The civilian [government] authorities attend to us, but behind them there is the military doing other things. For us, there is no democracy. They really have the people humiliated. We are all dwellers of the same earth. We are Salvadorans, too. I wish the government could understand this.

*Dolores Vigil is a spinster in her fifties with long, graying tresses of hair. She lives on a coffee farm on the edge of Perquín, in northern Morazan. Vigil has lived in Perquín continuously since the war began, the sole resident of the town to do so. She is an outspoken community leader, a member of its "civilian directorate."*

We'd like to be legalized to live in our zone, as Salvadorans that we are. There are constant bombings in this area. Sometimes, you can't work or leave the home for them. We are all witnesses of the bombings and the machine-gunnings. The problem is we don't have anywhere else to go, or to work. The employment problem makes it so that we stay where we have our little farm.

The army has told us many times they don't want us living here, but here we don't have to buy the firewood or the water. The people who have taken refuge in other places suffer. They are spied on and there is no water or firewood there. We stay here. We just want to be respected and not to be afraid.

The planes come and kill, the people say. It is true, because we have seen the planes kill. And when the militaries come on an operation, they take our boys with them to carry their equipment and they make them walk in front!

The army has never come to give out food here. Sometimes the small plane which talks [psychological warfare broadcasts] comes, but you can't always hear it. Sometimes we think it is going to throw bombs and then we see the pieces of paper fall down like swallows.

We don't want to leave the town, because, if we do, they'll destroy it. We have always suffered, before and after the war began. As poor, we have always suffered. This is a [FMLN] liberated zone, but we are civilians. Our crime is that we are poor and we live in the liberated zone.

*A Revolutionary People's Army (ERP) guerrilla officer in northern Morazan, on the steps of a recently bombed peasant's home.*

Actually, the government is really stupid to bomb here. For one thing, they never hit us, just the civilians.

In La Tejera, they dropped a bomb; it didn't explode, so the comrades retrieved it and took it to the workshop. It will make about eight hundred mines for us! The same day, they dropped more bombs and the comrades found five more which didn't explode. So just that day, they gave us enough mines for about a year!

*Augusto Crespin, 30, is a self-possessed painter who sports a sparse goatee. The interview changes locale, from a gallery where he has a dozen paintings on exhibit, to an empty restaurant on a noisy boulevard near his home in San Salvador.*

I was born on the flanks of San Salvador Volcano. Immediately upon being born, one is aware of the problem of the farmer in El Salvador—that is, the necessity of having land but to not possess it, no? So, naturally, you go down to the city, you begin to study, no? Since I was small I studied art, drawing and painting. I was about thirteen years old. I consider myself a professional painter, a painter of society. One might think that to develop one's social conscience one has to, in El Salvador, form part of a political organization. For many, yes, but for others, in my case, it's not necessary. It only requires sensitivity to be able to advertise the problem. I never formed part of a political organization; it's enough just to be a pedestrian in this city to be able to understand the social problem. We live in a country at war, and for a painter or a maker of words, it is important, this life, because he paints his experience. If he lives in a country at peace, he has to paint its peace. If he lives in a country of violence, he paints its violence, no? It is my source of inspiration at this moment.

In one painting, you can see perforations, a deformation of what is a sensual face, with sensuous lips which become . . . plaited. Because, behind this face there is a deterioration. Because I believe that Salvadoran society has tended to deteriorate in recent years, from the moment that the death squads were formed.

The next series, "Birds of this Paradise Dream with Serpents," was to deal with the rural reality of El Salvador through the dragonflies which fly every day through its villages and amongst its people. The dragonflies are seen discharging, apparently symbolically, but they are helicopters dropping bombs, bombing the people.

The truth is that painting, or art, doesn't present solutions for a sociopolitical process of a country. Rather, it is a way of signaling things; it can't affect things enormously. And I think that painters are necessary in a country, so that a certain period can be witnessed. So I think it would be an abuse to "touch" an intellectual; even more, a painter. Because in the future, I think this, the art, is what is going to remain.

Undoubtedly, the years of war in this country, this class conflict . . . has affected everyone. From the moment of just hearing seven helicopters passing over my roof . . . You know the destination of those helicopters and you realize that this city isn't the same one as your childhood. Walking through its streets, I can see that this city isn't the same anymore. You know that the other people, other Salvadorans—although you don't know them personally—are dying. Just so with the army; it also loses people, people who don't have a lot to do with it but just follow orders and, of course, in the end are cannon fodder. So this affects you, that now you can't smile quite the same . . . you don't smile the same.

I am an urban guy. I grew up in San Salvador, so I know these streets, I know this city, I have seen it change . . . I have seen it fall down, from bombs, no? So in this way I have seen . . . The demonstration when Monsignor Romero died, it was an enormous multitude in the streets of San Salvador. And to see this multitude and to hear the gunshots and see all those scenes, it touches you, it hits you, no? You realize that the painting you did, which I did, in earlier years, didn't respond to the moment being lived. So to see all this pain, all this desperation, I realized that in my painting I had to vary, to change, because I consider that painters have to be present with their epoch. If not, what will the future say, when they look and see the work, the results of an author, if he didn't paint his period?

Right now, I am painting a series. I'm not totally satisfied with it, but it's called "The End of This Universe." Of nudes. But I've painted seven or eight so far and I see myself as having gone outside my earlier intentions, so you could say that I am being false. I'm thinking I may leave it as is, inconclusive. The female anatomy is by nature poetic so my paintings are turning out too poetic . . . so I'm not satisfied with this poetry, you know?

There is one of very beautiful buttocks, perforated, no? It is the buttocks of a woman, extremely beautiful, but they are shot through with a gunshot. This is beauty and this is violence, but I still don't feel satisfied. . . .

So I have thought of an alternative, leaving behind the nudes and doing a series focusing on Salvadoran children. And it will be of the world of children, like their toys, no? All that infantile world mixed into a violent reality, that of El Salvador.

*Julio Pinto, 36, is a successful* mojado *(wetback) who has returned from the United States to his home village of La Reina, a grimy spot on a back road in northern Chalatenango department. A dark, muscular man, he wears black pants, boots, a straw hat, and a yellow T-shirt from Benny Asuza's Liquors that instructs: "In case of emergency, buy me a drink."*

I thought I'd live my whole life in the United States. I was a foreman in a plastic pearl factory; started out as a machine operator. I thank God and the people of the United States who gave me an opportunity to make some money.

In Reno, I was a busboy and later a waiter. When I went, I was sixteen years old; went illegally. I just decided to go. I dreamed all the time I'd live in the United States, since I was a little boy. I tried to get a visa, but they denied me; I was very poor. I never got a green card, but I got permission to live in the United States and they gave me social security. After four years, I came back here and married my wife and took her back in the United States illegally, through Mexico. Both my mother and father I brought there illegally; now they have alien [resident] status. The whole family's there now; they're okay. I got a good record in the States. I never got arrested.

I worked very hard to get my money and then I got my properties here. I got my first property five years ago and my next property a year ago. It was a couple of years ago I thought about coming back to enjoy my real life. I was working in the MGM hotel in Reno and was making a hundred, hundred forty dollars a night in tips.

But I don't miss the money. I got my hammock here. I've got a very good 26-inch color with remote control. I got three stereos. I just sold my four-by-four truck—the guerrillas bothered me too much for it—and my 750 motorcycle. It was nice, but it was too big for here.

I decided to run for mayor, because I really wanted my town in other conditions. In summertime, we have very hard troubles with the water. Second reason: the streets around the park are okay, but everywhere else they're very bad. And the road in, it's terrible. This town needs enthusiastic people with good insights into the future.

I learned a lot in the States. I learned how to live and how to spend money. I learned better conditions, regarding health. I wanted to show these people proper, for example, how to make a bathroom inside or in the back of the house, but not just on the floor like that. But we need water and we need "black waters," too, for sewage.

So I decided to run for [ultrarightist] ARENA party. I lost by about 138 votes out of two thousand. I prefer ARENA one hundred percent. It's very curious to see how the PDC [Christian Democratic Party] is working with the leftists; for example, before the elections, there were a lot of ARENA candidates dying by guerrillas but none from PDC.

The guerrillas . . . some are friendly with me. Before I took the decision to become a candidate I talked to them. They told me, "We won't touch you; you're a good guy." I give them food and so on, so I don't have problems with them.

I'm building my dream house right now. Three bedroom with yard and Ping-Pong. Kitchen, dining salon, bathroom. I will have it finished in three months. Brick and cement. It'll be like any house here, but inside it's gonna be beautiful. It's my dream house.

But I want to go back to the States to see my mother soon. I miss her very much. I keep good feelings for people from the United States. I'm a good soccer player and I worked out at the European Health Spa there. I was a member. I had a MasterCard, good until September '85.

*Simon Arguello, 26, is a former member of an FMLN musical group that toured in Europe and Latin America. It is not his real name. He has a boyish, chubby face and is full of enthusiasm. In the band, he sang, and played the guitar and a bongo.*

I was born here in San Salvador. My family was, up to a certain point, normal. My mother was a teacher in a public school and my father was a Honduran. When I was little, my parents separated; my father went to live in Honduras, and so we lived all our lives with our mama. In El Salvador, the teaching profession is really badly paid, and so we endured some economic stages that were really hard. It was difficult to get shoes, to pay for school, everything—the norm of the majority of the Salvadorans. Despite all this, we had our house, and so we lived, more or less . . . we weren't really part of the people who were really fucked up, but we did go through plenty of bad moments.

I left for different reasons than my brother. We were part of a revolutionary mass organization and my brother left on orders of the organization to carry out international tasks, while I left for purely personal reasons. I left for twenty days, because there was a really strong security situation with my family. They captured a guy who had extremely close access to our house—he was almost family—and he gave declarations up to the . . . When my mother was operated on, he had given blood, he was almost family. But then they captured him and he spilled all he had, and what he didn't know he invented. Many people were captured at that time—it was in '80.

So I left to see my brother for twenty days in Mexico and, after, I was going to return. But things got complicated and I had to stay more time there, and there I assumed a post with the revolutionary movement. It was in these circumstances that I left [El Salvador]. The same as my brother; he left for Panama for four days and was gone six years! He took clothes for four days and was gone six years!

I returned to El Salvador for family reasons. My mother died, so I needed to return. I came, and it was a tremendous shock; I had been outside almost five years. One has a mountain of fears because of the information you get. "Ah no," they told us, "if you put a foot in the airport, they'll cut it off; if you go out in San Salvador, there's a whole bunch of squealers who'll kill you . . ."

And to come on one's own—if one goes as part of the organization, it directs you, it takes you from here to there, it knows how to operate and all that—but to come on "your own pistol" is another problem, and all you've heard and been told begins to play an important role—the fears you have, the repression which you imagine is exaggeratedly strong. But you arrive in San Salvador and you don't see it! It really is a strong shock! You don't see the repression.

When I left, if you went out on the street, you found five, six, seven people dead and you had to look and see that it wasn't your brother or your friends. You left your house to go to school or to see your brothers and they could consciously kill you, whether because they were looking for you or because you walked into a shootout. And that reality is not as palpable as before. Before, you walked over the dead.

Another thing that really hit me. Here there's a park where I've played basketball since I was little. And in that park I always met up with a guy who studied in my class, every day at four P.M. without fail. When I came back here, one day I went to the park, just to see it, because it holds an important part of my memories. And at four P.M., the guy was there, playing basketball! It gave me great happiness to see him, but I said to myself, "This boy has been coming here continuously to play basketball all the years I was abroad." For him, that was reality; the war didn't touch him. And like him, there are many people the war hasn't touched. The war passed by San Salvador, and many people didn't live it. There's also an ice cream man who always passes by the home at a certain time, and he continued coming by. In '80, when you went out on the street there was a danger they would kill you, but these people went on with their lives.

I have friends who have been here the whole time, ex-school companions, people who never got involved, counterrevolutionaries, antisubversives to the teeth. For me, it's important to talk with them, to become their friends anew, to know what happened. I am trying to widen the world of people I know. There are also people around who are sound, really progressive, but who were never in agreement with the revolution; they, too, can tell one how they lived those five years. Many of my dear ex-companions are now dead. There are many of my friends who are dead today because they were judged by the revolution. There is an ex-companion of mine with whom I used to get along really well. They tell me that he became a torturer. He got out of the military school and was one of the biggest killers there was. And they broke him, they killed him, people from the revolutionary organizations. The people who were progressives became militants and those who weren't became reactionaries and even murderers.

I came back to San Salvador with two hundred dollars in my pocket, with my bicycle and my guitar. And the house I lived in, the bank was about to take it because it was my mother's mortgage, so there came the problem of eating first. I went the first two months striking out, looking for work everywhere. Two months without a nickel's income. In the end, I got a job with a friend selling Chiclets on the streets.

To return to San Salvador in these circumstances is to return and begin from zero, at every level. If you don't know how to handle the situation, you can get enormously frustrated. The fact of quitting an organization to which you've dedicated part of your life is a serious frustration. You've also got to consider all the psychic problems that you've created during your militancy and face the fact that all your efforts didn't really count for much. Another thing that affected me was that most of my friends are dead. And on finding out how they died, who murdered them, this really hit me . . . and the fact that they [their deaths] didn't serve much purpose. . . . These elements hit you.

After returning here, I went out walking a lot in the city. And the state has really been intelligent; many things have changed in San Salvador, and it has won a social base. The fact that you don't see soldiers in the streets. This to me, to a certain point, gives you confidence that you can walk in the streets without them killing you. But this is part of the policy of the state, to create extreme confidence in the people and in the least expected moment—*boof!* They get you like they get a lot of people.

So for me, when I just came back, each night was hard for the fear that does exist. The first two months were torture. A total torture, a psychic torture that one does to himself. Any sound on the street wakes you up. The psychosis of the war is there. . . . And then, little by little, this changed.

Since I came back, I think it's the best decision I could have taken. Because El Salvador is changing. The reality of the people has changed in these years and even now, I still feel a little left out of the changes there have been, culturally and politically. I am also undergoing a change, and I want to change, not with the people of Spain or the United States; I want to change with my own people.

One thing that I have experienced that has been very positive for me is, before I had written songs, but it was about one a year and these even I myself didn't like. Now, in El Salvador for one year, and I've written more than twenty-five songs and many of them I like. Why is this? I think I'm going through a different emotional stability. I'm finding out each day which way to focus my life. That's what I learned in those five years and which won't be erased. My decision is to gamble up to my skin for my convictions, and those convictions I'm going to maintain.

Also, the music and the songs are a way of expressing the sentiments that one represses in El Salvador. This permits me to do work with the mountains of other people who also write and hide their songs in a box.

There is an emptiness, though, because for me to sing a song on a stage, more than just an artistic thing, it was my political function. What I miss is that function.

Right now I'm making songs and all, but I have the need to get on a stage. Why? To return to transmitting a work, to have a function. In music there is a space in El Salvador; we can sing whatever we want. They let you sing. This is one instrument that the state is allowing us. I have the need to go out on the streets and find more people who work as I do, who make their songs and then put them in a box.

*Jorge Blanco is a 33-year-old farmer in La Laguna in northern Morazan.*

The only thing the guerrillas give is talks—that they are winning the war and that the revolution is advancing. But the war hasn't changed the poverty. What most tires one is the combat, because afterwards come the bombings and the mortarings, and that has killed a lot of people. What they [the guerrillas] tell us in the talks is that this is because of the North American aid, so we ask that there be no more aid so there won't be more bombings, because that costs money and is what makes us suffer. That there be peace, come how it comes, because we can't take much more of this.

# Uganda: Easy Death

In Uganda's tropical heartland of the Luwero Triangle, piles of bleached human skulls are made into roadside displays. Beside them, friends talk, children play, and villagers sell their fruits. In many cases, the remains, some whole, others shattered by machete blows and bullets, belong to their relatives.

The skulls represent a small number of the estimated three hundred thousand people slaughtered in this area by marauding government soldiers between 1981 and 1986. The Triangle, formerly home to as many as a million members of the Baganda tribe, is today a doomsday mosaic of war. Behind ruined homes, their windows and doors borne away by looters, the untilled fields are choked with jungle growth. The Luwero survivors, barefoot and clad in patches of dirty rags, stumble along the dirt roads, like survivors of a nuclear war crawling from their warrens. At the sight of a car, they stop, move to the edge of the trees, and stare, a haunting mix of wonder and fright in their wide eyes.

The keepers of Luwero's skulls speak of them possessively; the skulls belong to and are an integral part of the new society being rebuilt here. In this tormented place, they symbolize an angry, impassive demand for reckoning by the victims' families. The skulls gape at the buses and cars that trundle the pitted roads of the Triangle, reminders that a vast, five-year horror occurred here while the people of the capital, Kampala, just ten miles away, did nothing to stop it.

The political value of the skulls has not been lost on the current regime, which fought its way to power at the cost of Luwero's dead. It was in the Triangle that guerrilla leader Yoweri Museveni began a bush war against the government of President Apollo Milton Obote in 1981, and it was here that he recruited his National Resistance Army (NRA). As Obote's army reacted by killing Luwero's civilians on sight, the NRA ranks swelled with vengeful orphans. As Museveni's child army grew stronger, Obote's rule became more inept, his army more vicious. "Easy death" reached Kampala as soldiers robbed cars at roadblocks, looted at will, and killed civilians at random. It was the climax of state-sanctioned chaos that had been building for decades.

In Kampala, the effects of the years of misrule are apparent everywhere. Great, scraggly maribou storks fly and caw over a decayed city. On the rusting cranes of abandoned building sites, the grotesque birds line the iron spans like pallbearers at a funeral. The city's streets are pocked and pitted and run red with Uganda's fertile earth. Without maintenance, the overflowing mud has crept into the city and the roads are bare etchings of their original form. Nothing has been built, painted, or repaired here for a very long time. Normal life stopped for fifteen years as terror took over. Today, the unrelenting fear that lived here for so long has subsided, but it is still there, waiting to resurge.

It has been a terror where ideology hasn't played a role; it has been a slaughter caused partly by tribalism, partly by religion, and partly by personalities, in a place where all three elements overlap. Since 1971, it has taken as many as a million lives, or eight percent of the population.

Some of Uganda's problems can be traced to its former colonial master, Great Britain. Attracted by its location at the edge of Lake Victoria, the source of the Nile, and its rich soil, ideal for coffee and cotton, Britain created the colony of Uganda, carving its borders out of a dozen tribal kingdoms. The Bantu tribes of the south and west were the farmers, the fishermen, and, eventually, the civil servants. The northern Nilotic tribes, such as the Acholi and Langi, traditionally cattle-grazing nomads and warriors, became the soldiers, the *askaris,* of the British colony. The British used the tribal kingdoms as pawns in an elaborate chess game of divide-and-rule. They also brought in Protestant missionaries to convert the natives and wean them away from the Catholicism established by rival Western powers.

The British controlled Uganda, with the tribal kingdoms intact but held in rein, until independence was granted in 1962. Apollo Milton Obote, a Langi, became president. In 1966, he abolished the tribal monarchies and exiled the most powerful of them, King Freddy Mutesa of the southern Baganda tribe. In one swift move, the tenuous political glue that had held the nation together was gone and government became a score-settling vehicle for tribal rivalries.

Obote's attempt to consolidate his power base achieved exactly the opposite. To shore up his increasingly unpopular rule, he turned to the army for support, giving it a strength and ambition it couldn't have aspired to alone. In 1971, Idi Amin, Uganda's heavyweight boxing champ and its army chief, seized power while Obote was out of the country.

Initially, the new leader, a Muslim from a minority tribe of the West Nile District, was greeted as a savior. Britain and Israel proffered economic and military aid. To the average Ugandan, Amin was seen as the man who would halt the slide into fractious misrule. But the soldier had grander plans, to "liberate" the country from its political and economic colonialist legacy. Amin declared himself Field Marshal and Conqueror of the British Empire. He threw out Uganda's seventy thousand Asians, the backbone of the nation's economy, and his troops robbed them as they fled. Their confiscated businesses succumbed to the neglect of their new Amin-chosen proprietors.

When guerrillas, led by both former president Obote and Yoweri Museveni, then a Tanzanian university lecturer, infiltrated Uganda, Amin reacted with brutality, staging public executions and giving his secret police, the State Research Bureau, a free hand in ferreting out any opposition. Countless thousands died at their hands over the succeeding years.

But Amin murdered with style. A dissident facing a firing squad was chained beneath an advertisement for batteries promising "longer life." In 1977, the nation's Anglican archbishop was killed in a "car accident" arranged by Amin. The Field Marshal was a man who could find enjoyment in playing Santa Claus to a cluster of delighted children, as well as, by all accounts, presiding over the torture and execution of prisoners.

For all Amin's perversity, however, the world viewed him not as a butcher but as a buffoon, an African Mussolini. In the West, his antics and bombastic comments found frequent media coverage as light, humorous asides. Fellow Africans admired his penchant of thumbing his nose at the white "imperialists"; Uganda's current president Museveni bitterly notes that the proceedings of an Amin-era Organization of African Unity conference in Kampala were taken up with denunciations of the racist regime of South Africa, while less than a mile away Ugandans were being beaten to death with sledgehammers.

The end finally came in 1979, when Tanzanian troops invaded Uganda and Amin fled into exile. He lives today in Saudi Arabia with his numerous wives and children, periodically threatening to return and "liberate" his homeland.

After a succession of weak, Tanzanian-sponsored interim governments, elections were held in 1980 and Milton Obote returned to office the next year. One of Obote's first acts was to carry out a punitive expedition against the West Nile province where Amin loyalists continued to resist. Hundreds of thousands fled into neighboring Sudan and Zaire and untold thousands more died in massacres by the government troops.

Obote soon had a bigger problem than Amin's remnants. Yoweri Museveni, who had run against Obote in the 1980 elections, claimed the elections were fraudulent and took to the bush of the Luwero Triangle. There he began the guerrilla war that would cost so many civilian lives before bringing him to power.

In July 1985, Obote's own army overthrew him. The military junta, headed by Generals Tito Okello and Basilio Olara Okello, held negotiations with Museveni and, while the war in Luwero continued and spread beyond, signed a peace treaty. In January 1986, Museveni broke the treaty and marched into Kampala, sending the forces of the short-lived junta fleeing in disarray to the northern border with Sudan. There, the routed army regrouped with Obote loyalists, and yesterday's soldiers are today's rebels.

Museveni, Uganda's "revolutionary savior," swore himself in as president and promised elections in four years. Until then, he is establishing his own power base and, as part of that campaign, has urged Luwero's survivors to place the skulls and bones of their relatives by roadsides, to "show the world what happened." His child army polices Uganda's streets and stops cars at roadblocks. Some as young as seven and eight, the boys saunter along Kampala's sidewalks, weighted down with machine guns or rocket launchers bigger than they. They cruise the city in Mercedeses, clad in Ray-Bans and inexpertly smoking cigarettes. They are to be found dining in the once-opulent restaurant of the Fairway Hotel staring sullenly at other patrons, with their weapons placed handily on the carpet by their chairs. They are, everyone remarks, unusually well-behaved, but still people are nervous; they are used to the very worst from governments and their troops in Uganda.

Meanwhile, Museveni's guerrilla government is intent on consolidating power through revolutionary indoctrination and by arming loyal cadres of its grass-roots "resistance committees." This campaign operates with the unofficial slogan of "a gun for everyone."

While the regime pursues its revolutionary course, foreign governments and relief agencies are trying to rehabilitate Uganda. Their task is an enormous one. New wells are being dug in Luwero to replace those destroyed in the fighting. Mobile inoculation units are roaming areas where once-suppressed diseases— malaria, typhoid, measles—have come back with vigor. Hundreds of thousands of refugees are waiting to be repatriated, or searching for family members who disappeared in the war. Theirs is the task of restoring an economy that has reverted to subsistence farming and barter and, most pressing of all, combatting the spread of AIDS, which has already infected an estimated 30 percent of the Ugandan people.

Then there is the war, today's war. It is no longer in Luwero; the skulls and gun-toting orphans are all that remain of that one. Now the conflict is in the north, where Obote's and Okello's renegade troops have teamed up with primitive cattle-raiding Karamajong warriors. Together they are cutting a murderous swath through the villages of the north and east, stealing cattle, killing peasants, and assaulting aid convoys, missionary outposts, and government garrisons. An obscure, undeclared war without an ideology, it is simply a conflict in which people are killing and dying, as if by long habit.

*Uganda's expatriate community plays a vital role in the nation twenty-five years after independence. Mostly Britons but including a smattering of Greeks and Asians, they are a clannish, privileged elite. Ranging from aid specialists and missionaries to businessmen, they have a unique, and callous, view of what has taken place.*

*Some of them have also conspired in the tragedies of Uganda: still legend in the community is the infamous Robert Astles, Idi Amin's security adviser. Today, in a more benign role, British journalist William Pike serves as the Museveni government's paid propagandist.*

*The anecdotes in this chapter were gathered from a number of expatriates in conversations that took place throughout Uganda.*

*Expatriate:*

This business about Amin eating people, I never believed that; that was just some concoction of his enemies. There are so many stories floating around here, you can't believe a half of them.

But there was this case about the oldest son, Amin's oldest boy, Moses. And a nice boy he was, too. I knew him. My children were in school with him. He was a really nice, quiet boy, very friendly, and we do think that Amin ate his liver.

You see, Amin didn't do anything without consulting his witch doctor first, and this witch doctor told him that if he killed his son and ate the liver he would have great wisdom. So that's apparently what happened because, all of a sudden, we didn't see Moses around anymore. Some of us started to ask questions, and finally Amin said the boy was off visiting his grandparents in the north. But it was found out he didn't have any grandparents in the north and he has never been seen or heard of since.

So that much is probably true, that Amin killed Moses and ate his liver. But as far as him eating bodies, I think that was probably greatly exaggerated.

*Rhoda Kalema, a graying, handsome woman in her fifties, is one of Uganda's small but powerful group of businesswomen. While raising four children, she took over her husband's surveying business after his disappearance and murder in 1972. A graduate of Kampala's Makerere University, once considered to be East Africa's finest, she worked for the Ministry of Culture and Community Development from 1958 to 1966.*

It will be fifteen years in January since my husband was kidnapped, and I suppose he was the first victim around Kampala to suffer in that way. It was a very trying period because for some time we thought he might be detained at such and such a detention center. But as time went by, after months of looking . . . I remember the radio; the government announced, responding to some journalists who had asked where Peter was, the government announced, "It is understood he went to an unknown place." That's all that government said. So that, to the family, to me, made it clear that the government knew he was a dead man.

Within a week, I began to suspect the government had been involved. When the government would not come out with any action or any results—the government did not show any concern, either—it was easy to realize the government knew something about it.

I can't tell you why they took my husband. It's delicate but, in general, it was for political reasons. It was done during Amin's time, but that doesn't really mean that Amin took the move against my husband. I know Amin gradually became more

. . . anxious and ferocious, but I hate blaming it all on Amin, all the kidnappings, murders, horrible things during his reign. I can't blame him directly. There could have been forces outside Amin's government, but it's possible that anyone could have used personnel in the government. But perhaps it was not Amin; I can't pin down Amin on all this.

At the time, my children were in two groups, the older group and a younger group. The older group were lucky because they had had enough of their father, so it was easier for them to accept it. And it happened at a time when they were bigger and their minds were full of studies. For the younger ones, number four who was just eleven . . . that one had big problems. It did not show any effect on him in that year of 1972, but after two years he became very unhappy and frustrated. And it took time to realize it wasn't just ordinary adolescent stubbornness. He started to become very, very unhappy. His studies began to suffer. And I realized it was the loss of his father. He had been just eleven.

The people who stayed here, from what I can see, are people who have gone with the deterioration. You know, something can survive, but surviving and deteriorating for a long time; the Ugandans have survived, but they are not healthy. Just survived. Someone who has just survived can do very little for himself; he can do nothing for another person.

So that is how I look at Ugandans who have been in this country for fifteen years, or for ten or for five. For me, I've been here nonstop for the last fifteen years. But I feel that if only people could be more encouraging, I think it would bring a lot of those people who left back here to the country, and those people would instill in us who are here new morale, new strength, new hope.

I would like to add one last thing. I thank the Lord for giving me this life, for I've been able to go free. I don't think I would have been able to go free, alone, without some power, some spiritual power. And that is why I believe in Lord, who has looked after me, taken care of me, so well in this country. And I've been detained twice, in Amin's time for one day and during Obote's government for six weeks, and in both cases I came out without torture and I stayed here and I've been . . . I've been well. So I really am thankful that He has been so good to take care of me and my family.

*Expatriate:*

Bob was a good bloke, a damn good bloke. But it all went to his head, fell in with a fast crowd. I mean, he was making money hand over fist with Amin and he just couldn't stop. You've seen the pictures of the white men carrying Amin around in that chair? Well, Bob was one of those. He wasn't forced to do it; he volunteered! To show his loyalty to Amin!

It was a bad situation, and all of us could see it coming. I used to go over to Bob's for a beer—he lived just up the road here—and every time he'd have a new car, a new television set, money stacked around. And he'd say to me, "Come on in with me; you'll be set up for life." And I'd say, "That may be, but if I don't come in, my life might last a lot longer."

Apparently, he crossed somebody in the inner circle. There was some bad business about some [contraband] coffee going across the border to Kenya or something—maybe it was some cars, Bob was deep into everything. And the next thing we know, Bob's gone. His wife—a lovely woman—is calling everybody, asking, "Have you seen Bob?" but that was the end of him.

We heard they took him up to Lubiri and tortured him for three weeks and then took him outside and poured petrol over him and set him on fire. Some others said they heard he was chopped into little bits. Never will know the true story, the exact circumstances. Anyway, it was a real shame, because Bob was a good man.

And it wasn't just Bob. Oh Lord, the number of people [in the expatriate community] who were in with Amin! If the truth were ever to be told!

*Aboki is from the Batoro tribe of western Uganda. With ten children, he exists on a primary schoolteacher's salary of fifteen thousand shillings ($1.80) a month.*

Our country was shining like other countries, like your country. We had enough food. We had everything. But now we have nothing but decline. All these things have resulted because of war.

SA: Since Amin?

Aboki: No. Amin is considered a powerful president here. In fact, he made us think about money. We never had any use for money before. When he talked about the importance of money, he made people believe it. He encouraged us to get a lot of it, so I think Amin made Uganda shine. He made people have these hopes.

SA: Was there a time when people started to not like him so much?

Aboki: An ordinary man would not hate him. It was only top officials. Amin was good.

SA: And with Obote?

Aboki: Only his party liked him, the UPC [Uganda People's Congress]. The rest of the people never liked him. I was not happy. We thought he came to milk the nation. Some people were killed; some people run away. His henchmen, the UPC men, just hurt us people so much so that we were afraid.

SA: What about you personally?

Aboki: I was a parish chief, and they made me stop. They wanted to harass me. Some men I was working with were killed. So I went running. Or else I would have been killed. Some of my family were killed. Our sons were killed—the family sons, about six or seven. Almost the whole family of my brother.

I'm telling the truth, the nation has lost gallant sons, gallant daughters, so much that when I tell you this I'm almost lamenting. Because all of our relatives, brothers, fathers, have really gone. When I say that we have lost sons and daughters here, we have lost a lot of lives, so we feel embarrassed by what that president [Obote] did.

You can even experience it now. We are here thinking, every time thinking, shall I reach tomorrow? Shall I reach next week? So our state of mind is not stable. Any time; we don't know.

*Expatriate:*

Amin was just like a big kid, you know. He'd come and play with the children and all. And at first his soldiers were gentlemen, real gentlemen. But later they got real tough, real bad.

When they made the Asians leave, an awful lot of them killed themselves. They was given ninety days and then they weren't allowed to take anything. Their belongings, all their little things, were thrown along the road, broken open. You could see their whole lives there. . . . Oh, it was terrible! We thought we'd be next, that Amin would give the Europeans twenty-five days to pack up. But it never happened; someone must've brought him to his senses.

*Dr. Yona Okoth, 60, is the archbishop of the Anglican Church of Uganda, the nation's largest denomination. He is a hulking man, with a wide, expressive face.*

As a Christian, this conflict has strengthened my Christian faith very much, because through suffering many people tend to turn to God. And also, during that time of hardship, it made many people put their trust to God. And, of course, people suffered. They have lost their relatives. Many people died. In such a way, when there is nowhere to run to, the only way to run is to God, who is the Provider of our protection and life.

It is a pity that such a thing could happen, because wherever there is war there is no peace. And if there is no peace, you don't expect anything, no progress, no development. People were just thinking how they could survive, how they could be alive. So, for me, it was an unfortunate thing to happen.

The story was very bad during Amin's time, and I don't think that you will ever experience such a life, because it reached such a time when you do not know whether you will wake up alive or dead. And before you take your journey, you never know whether you come back or not.

I escaped death four times during Amin's time; I will tell you one of them.

On the fifth of February, 1977, I was a bishop of Bukedi. I did not sleep in the residence in Tororo, but I went back to my farm, which is fifteen miles east of Tororo. So it was about ten P.M. when I had a knock at the door and my aunt told me there are two large cars outside. And she told me that there were people coming out of them with long sticks—she did not know whether it was guns, but later on we discovered they were guns.

So when she told me that, I changed into my sleeping jacket and went to my living room. As soon as I entered it, I met this giant man! Tall! Black! With—well armed!—but in plainclothes. So one of their leader asked me, "Are you Bishop Okoth?" I said, "Yes." He said, "Why do you sleep here?" I said, "This is my home." And then he said, "You are under arrest," and I asked him, "What have I done," and he said, "I understand you have got some arms here," and I said, "Where are they?"

So by then they had already searched all over the house; they couldn't find any gun. So while they were getting outside through the back door, the one who had taken cover came running and said, "Oh, there's a lot of guerrillas here." I said, "Where are they?" So I asked one of my childs to bring the lamp and I gave him [soldier] a lamp. "Would you take us where these guerrillas are?" So when we went there, we found cows were just abreathing. And I said, "Are these the cows which you say are the guerrillas?"

So they were stuck, couldn't answer, but one of them—might have been a Christian—he said, "Bishop, we do respect you as our spiritual father, but Amin, our president, wants you in Kampala!" So, when I heard that, I knew for sure that my time has come to be killed, because during that time I had already buried many Christians—they go like that and you never see them again.

So I said, "Fair enough! If death, it is the gateway to Heaven; if life, God will spare me." And my wife was not with me, so I left a message that if my wife comes, tell her that if she will not see me here in this world she know where we will meet. So I entered in one of their Land Rovers.

So we were traveling from that place to Kampala during night. And I was not sure whether I would reach there or not. On the way, they were pointing me with a gun, like this. Six of them! 'Cause I was in the middle. At first I thought I was very strong, I would not fear death, but as they continue facing me with a gun, and looking at the gun, the fear of death just surrounded me. I started trembling. But in the midst of that trembling, I remembered Psalm Twenty-three, "God is my Shepherd. . . ." So I went on reciting that psalm. All of a sudden, the fear of death just disappeared! And I was relieved! And I was ready to face death!

During that time, we were crossing the River Nile, the bridge between Basoga and Buganda [tribal boundaries]. I saw the first car stop there, and my car also stopped there. And this was actually the place where they used to shoot people and throw their dead body in the water. But I was not there; I was with the Lord!

So I saw the other driver coming to talk with this man in our car, and they said, "Oh, we don't have enough gas!" And this man also said, "Mine is showing red! So we won't be able to reach Kampala!"

So what they did was to reverse, and we went to Jinja. So, to me, God passed through the gas! So when we went to Jinja, they went to one of the Palestinians' houses—because Palestinians were one of the people working as intelligence for Amin—so I was put in the kitchen where I was locked in the kitchen. But there I was dead in prayer for a period of two hours. Later on, I saw them opening the door, and it surprised me to see that they were bringing me a cup of tea.

So they told me that they had already communicated to Amin and he told them that they must return me back to Tororo. Again, the car they had already brought— a Benz, a black Benz—filled with petrol. So they took me back to Tororo, and when they reached my official residence, they searched. They read all my correspondence because they accuse that the Church were the agent of the imperialists. But they couldn't find anything to fault, so they said, "You are now a free man. But don't tell anybody."

That was on the sixth, so you could imagine what sort of life we were leading like that. But I was lucky, because they couldn't kill me. But many people did not have the chance of surviving! The archbishop was killed a few days later, on the sixteenth. It was actually Amin who shot him himself. In his mouth.

You see, Amin wanted to implicate us, because he had found some arms and he was accusing the Church of Uganda that we were the people who were concerned. That I, because I was near the border, that I used to bring these guns from Kenya. He just wanted to kill us. The reason was, at that time he was murdering many, many of our Christians, so we, the bishops, wrote a very strong letter opposing him. That is why. He did not like any criticism.

*The editor of* The Star *newspaper in Kampala is Drake Sekeba, age 42. A youthful, spare man, Sekeba studied mass communication and journalism in England before returning to Uganda to found* The Star. *In 1984, he spent four months in prison for an article he published calling for the Obote government to investigate official corruption. During the interview in Sekeba's office, three different messengers enter with briefcases and withdraw six-inch stacks of bundled money. They represent part of the daily receipts of a newspaper that sells for three thousand shillings per copy.*

During the time of independence, everything was perfect. Everything was going on very well. People were happy. . . . There were no miseries, no wars, no scarceness of commodities. There was no insecurity . . . you know, it was really lovely. And everyone trusted others.

Then, in 1966, in May, when the former prime minister of Uganda, Milton Obote, abrogated the constitution, abolished the hereditary rulers, things started to go bad from that moment. Since then, this country has never had any peace.

When Amin came to power in 1971, there was a regain of hope in the first year. People thought they had a deliverer, someone who had come to deliver them from their problems. But this changed gradually as Amin turned out to be differently from what the people expected. People started being killed. The situation got worse, up until when he was removed.

SA: And then Obote came back and, by all accounts, he was even worse than Amin.

Drake: You see, it is very difficult to make a comparison, to say, as many people say, that Obote was worse. People have been saying that there were so many deaths during Obote's time, but definitely it cannot be considered the same way people died during Amin. I think we had more people dying during Amin than Obote, but we take Obote to have been more sensible, more understanding, than Amin. But generally neither regime has been good.

SA: And the present regime?

Drake: You see . . . it has come at a time when we really wanted to have a change. The same way Amin came. It's very difficult to say right now where these people are taking us. I only hope they don't change from what they've stated, because what spoils some of these leaders, they start very well, and people have hopes they are going to be delivered, but eventually as these people continue being in power, they change. They don't want to be told off. They don't want to listen to the people. What they say is democracy you start seeing is no longer democracy. I hope this government does not go in those footsteps.

SA: Some feel it already has.

Drake: Yes, there have been some signs . . . but many people don't want this government to fail.

SA: What effects do you see this turmoil having had on the Ugandan people?

Drake: You make people get fed up with their lives. The life becomes meaningless to people, because they know each and every day that comes is the end. You know, you never know what will come up tomorrow, so why should I bother working? So it affects your— Suppose you have had a very close friend, he's dead and the reasons for his death are just . . . you know, it does not make sense to you. Your life, it's— You become miserable.

Some of the families have been torn apart. Because you find they have been displaced, scattered, and you can't find them anymore! And we used to, in the good old days, we used to have *tabus,* family gatherings, where you find the units of families coming together maybe once a year or once in three months and there you get to know each other. Those things have had to collapse. Because, you see, in the past, when you used to meet, more than twenty or thirty people in a home, then the government agents would come and destroy you and say that you are plotting to overthrow the government. You know, stupid notions.

So you find that the families are no longer one. What we have now is just the small unit, families like you find in your country—you know, five or six people. Which we used not to have. We used to have very large families; it's a tremendous loss.

SA: Are there circumstances under which you would leave Uganda?

Drake: Yes. This time, when things get worse, I think I'll have to go. Because I don't think there will be any future for Uganda after the next time.

*Joseph Byaruhunga, 30, was born in the village of Butiti in western Uganda and is of the Batoro tribe. A mechanic, he now lives in the city of Fort Portal, not far from his birthplace.*

Obote was doing detentions and killing people here and killing people there, so people hated Obote. So when Amin came in, everyone was very happy. He was not known, but we were happy because Obote was gone.

Amin didn't bother small people. We were small people, so Amin was not a problem for us. He went for some of the big people and for some of Obote's people. Later, he became worse. In the last years, he was killing more and more. So when the Tanzanians came, we were very happy. They were so kind! And we were so happy. Then, everything in Uganda was up, up. And we had big hopes.

But then, in the elections [of 1980], Obote came back. That night, we all stayed by the radio all night, but then the results were suspended . . . and then Obote was named winner. At first, his soldiers used intimidation. They had guns and that was their power. It was when Museveni was starting to win that Obote's people became very bad. They killed many people, many of my neighbors.

It was a terrible time. You did not live. You only waited from one day to the next to die. You waited for the *toc toc toc* on the window and for the soldiers to come in and take you away. Maybe they would kill you then or maybe they would take you to the barracks and make you tell lies about your whole family so they are taken, too. You just waited. You didn't talk to your friends, because you think, "Maybe they will inform." You didn't talk to anyone. You were alone, and you just waited to die.

Because when a bad man is in power, everyone becomes bad. When the bad one in power says to kill, the soldiers will kill and kill. I have lived all my life with soldiers about me and, I must say, I was always afraid. But now, with Museveni in power, that is . . . easing off. When Museveni came to power we were all very, very happy.

*Charles Kabuto Kabuye, 48, is a short, dapper poet and playwright who makes his living as the vice chairman of the British-American Insurance Company. His office is filled with grisly paintings and posters depicting the events in Uganda of the past fifteen years. Originally from the town of Masaka in western Uganda, Kabuye is of the Baganda tribe.*

Some people think we have become more hard-hearted. I don't think so. We have tasted suffering. A people which has not tasted a bit of suffering would not grow up.

Let me compare it with a child. Here we have the disease of measles. We in our tribe don't consider a child grown up unless he has actually suffered measles. So I think that Ugandans, through the testing, the tasting, of suffering, have known what it means to grow up. That is a bit of change.

Secondly, I think after this period of suffering we possibly know more about the value of life. Life becomes much more valuable when you see it being squandered, being wasted. You appreciate it more when you see it all the time at the risk of being lost. Because I remember in some of those years, especially this last period, you'd spend all the hours of the day just trying to find out ways in which you are going to keep your life alive and also your people's lives alive. Just to think about that, even without thinking about food. Just how you will escape these people who ambush you or shoot you. And in this process, one values life, because then you carry it like you carry a baby, holding it, all the time.

As you know, we Baganda people are born in a region where we had an organized kingship. And this was not just on the top; it was organized right from the top throughout all the strata of society, down to the family level. But in '66, there was this change, and a change that was not very amicable. It was done out of sheer malice, somebody [Obote] wanting to destroy a people.

Now, this gradual change for the bad became worse when Amin took over as an Army man. Meaning in life, especially for people who normally sought meaning in the social system, became such a really painful experience. Even now I still feel a lot of anger. I still feel the anger, because I feel if this had not happened, this country would be a different country altogether. So this pain is what I'm trying to portray to you.

For me, it has come out in a lot of my writings. Previously, before I went to Europe—that is, '61, '62—when I look at what I was writing, it is more peaceful. Much more in harmony. The turbulence sets in when I came back, when I really saw what was on my doorstep, when I saw it setting in, just really getting hold of you. So my writing became more violent, in a way; in some cases, possibly more . . . questionable by the authorities. Especially the period after '77. The period became worse, seriously worse! It was then we saw that any time was dying time.

And then Obote came back, and he was much worse than Amin. I feel that Obote is somebody who had a specific plan. In that way, he was more deliberate than Amin. As one got to know Obote, one could see him as really a very malicious man, somebody who sees a child playing with toys and comes and destroys them. That kind of person.

Of course, I am one of the persons who joined the struggle against Obote in one way or another. I believed we had to join the struggle. The struggle really meant a fight for one's freedom and survival, and this meant coming out, not only in writing but as a public speaker, to speak out.

I joined the resistance mainly by encouraging the young people. After being in contact with the organizers of the freedom movement, the NRA [National Resistance Army], one had direct contact with people who were involved within the bush. And one was helping the young men to get information, to get into contact so that those who decided to go [to the bush] could go without fearing they were going to be arrested. And, of course, in some cases negotiating their way to the right places. Very, very secretly, of course. Then, when the struggle came to the crux, we organized how people moved with their guns into Kampala and into other towns.

I feel that human history can never be accidental. I think the seeds of any revolution are sown at the beginning of a certain phase of history. I feel that what has happened in this past fifteen years is something that was sown many, many years ago, even before independence. I wouldn't like to blame the British only. I would even blame my ancestors—and someone coming from another tribe should also blame his ancestors—because I think what they did in those years, both before and after independence, lies the seed of what has happened. This over-complacency, that a system once set up will continue even if you don't care, this has been a very bad seed, and many of our people have bought it. That is what is happening now. They are complacent. I feel that all of us have contributed to what has gone wrong.

Now, the Museveni government is still trying to find its way. The water is seeking its level. Some of us are trying to convince others who are not yet convinced, give it a chance! If you gave Obote eight years and he messed up— every day we were saying, "Oh, maybe tomorrow he'll change, maybe tomorrow he'll be good"—he didn't change. Okay . . . '71, Amin came in with a full-fledged military regime. You gave him a chance. "Oh, he will change." He doesn't change; he gets worse. Eight years he tyrannizes you. You gave him a chance. Give Museveni a chance.

I don't know if you've read much of Museveni's ideas about the gun, the future of this country vis-à-vis the gun, and comparing that mentality to what Obote and Amin had in mind. Museveni thinks that a gun can be held peacefully to defend one's rights, to defend one's freedoms. And this is what he is struggling to instill among the Ugandans. He thinks you can hold a gun in your house with a license and only use it when it is absolutely necessary. The future of this country is that we must learn to hold the gun properly and peacefully.

If this time it cannot be managed, this country is going to face the worst civil war that has ever been thought of. Because this time the chance came after slightly more reflection. The chance came when people had been warned. A lot of things have been uprooted and brought to the surface. Now, if they cannot be patched together again and people continue disagreeing, then I can see the anger of the people really flowing up. For me, if I see this is going to work up like this, I will either join direct freedom fighting or I will go into exile forever (laughs).

*Expatriate:*
This place is going. I can feel it; the house servants let you know. I give it another

month. Museveni promised things, and nothing has happened. There's cars being stolen. Shots at night. It's one of the signs.

*The Crested Towers is an eighteen-story high rise in central Kampala that once headquartered the now-defunct East African community of Kenya, Uganda, and Tanzania. Today, water lies in pools in the halls and many of the windows and wall panels are missing, stolen or destroyed in fighting. Nevertheless, the Towers is the seat of most government offices, and daily crowds troop up the stairs or squeeze into the one operating elevator to seek a favor or obtain a permit.*

*From her Spartan office on the sixteenth floor, Joyce Mpanga, deputy chairwoman of the Uganda Public Service Commission, looks out over the flowery hills of east Kampala. A heavyset widow in her late thirties, Mpanga has a tired and vaguely mournful expression, at odds with her infectious giggle. On the wall behind her desk is a portrait of President Yoweri Museveni in combat fatigues.*

Civil war is difficult because you know people on both sides. Government troops are killed; some of them are your relatives, your friends. What was called the insurgents then, if they were killed, it was also . . . it's people you know on each side. It is fear. There is terror. Things happen which . . . Like my mother's house was taken over by soldiers. In normal times, in my position I would have just gone to the Ministry and said, "Look, take them out." But because I feared it may risk her life or my life, I kept quiet. I took her quietly into my home; she stayed there for four years. Last year, I managed to maneuver, because of my position in government, and got the house back. But I would not risk her life being there, so she still stayed with me. She only went back two months ago (laughs). You know, war is a terrible thing. . . .

It is usually forgotten, but women have been affected a lot. First of all, let's take Amin's period. They used to take off [kill] men more than women; it meant the women were left as widows, with their orphans. And until they enacted a law to change insurance policy regarding missing persons, you had no evidence your husband was dead, so you could not manage his estate legally. And many of them were not even able to do so, because they have no experience. So that way they suffered.

But it heartens you when you talk to them. They are determined to start, to restart life—many of them—if only they can get help; it needs a lot of determination.

But I don't think the war has just affected women; I think it has affected all forms of life here.

If people will let us get on, I think we will have a bright future. We are hardworking people, and we have learned from our experience, bitter experience. I think if we could contain the peace . . . We are lucky; our country is fertile and can get many crops a year, and I think this is the only reason why people like Amin could rule for such a long time. Because once people could not get supplies from anywhere else, they resorted to subsistence farming. I've had land, three hundred acres which I've never done anything with, but when it came to a crunch I started subsistence farming and eventually I made it into a farm.

It has taught almost everybody to go back to the land. This place . . . you stand here, you look over into the town, you will see banana trees growing. Those used to be just green gardens and flowers, but when it came to a crunch, people said, "Why don't I put a banana tree here?" because you could no longer afford to buy it. It has taught us to improvise.

*Alice Nanyonga, 34, is a shopkeeper in the war-shattered town of Nakeseke in the Luwero Triangle. She returned to Luwero in 1986.*

We have been away from this place. Since 1981. All of our properties were taken. We run for some months, run into the bush. There we lived. For all those years, we have been away from this place.

Before, we were many, many people. As you see, all the houses and shops, the owners, most of them, are dead. The houses were full of people. We were many people in this place, but most of them are dead. They were killed by the soldiers of Obote.

At first, we are here, everyone working. We heard that there are soldiers coming this way to take the guerrillas. We heard that story, but we were very surprised. We don't see the guerrillas. Where are the guerrillas? They told us that there are guerrillas in this place.

But one day—it was Friday—we heard that there are some lorries bringing soldiers—full of them—and they come here in the morning. Some of the people started to run with their property, but for us we said, "Let us wait and see." The commanding officer came in the morning and gathered the meeting: "Don't run. We have come for a certain reason. We want to take guerrillas here."

We remained in our houses, but the next morning the soldiers started to rape the young children, to steal everything. They slapped people, and we started to run from our houses and leave the properties there for them. They started to carry everything. They steal everything. They brought in another group. They started to stay in our houses. We had nothing to do. We went into the bush. And our friends who remained in this place, they started to kill them. But we who went away, we save ourselves.

We left very quickly. We left the town and went into the villages. But when the soldiers finished their things here, they also came into the villages and we were running away from the villages up to the main road and went away.

SA: You went with your children?

Alice: Yes. I had seven. Three of them died. Now I have only four.

SA: And your husband?

Alice: The husband, the father of those children, was also killed. When he was riding in his vehicle, he runned on a land mine. And he died there. And I went with my children.

JLA: And your children that died?

Alice: They died when we are in the village. I had no medicine. There was no medicine, no help, no good food. We had nothing there at all. And the children started to . . . they started vomiting and diarrhea. They died. It was 1982 when my children died, when I was in the village. But in November 1982, I tried my best in reaching Kampala. There I found my friends.

JLA: And you had this store before?

Alice: I had a store with my dead husband. It was very large. But now I have started this one, a new one. Because in this area, there is nothing to—to live, to get the home. . . . To live, you have to do something to live.

*Grace Wagwa is a 22-year-old Baganda layworker in the Anglican Church of Uganda. He has been sent to assist in restarting the church school in Nakeseke, Alice Nanyonga's town. Wagwa has a handsome, open face, but his eyes, which do not blink, are disturbing.*

I am teaching the children of Nakeseke. I find it quite difficult for the top three classes—five, six and seven—as they cannot perform well. It is only the infantile group that we can train now. We cannot know exactly where each one of the older ones has stopped their schooling. Most of them want to join class according to their size, not their standard. They claim to have stopped at a time when they really didn't. It will be a great problem.

Then, there is the problem of discipline. They cannot respect elders at all. We have two cases where the children are confronting the staff, they are torturing the staff, they are assaulting the staff. In public! Because they are now mature enough, you can get that atmosphere. They don't want to be directed. They want to come any time they want. They are lazy, in short form. So they don't have qualities for being students at all.

JLA: So your students have been affected by the war. What about you?

Grace: Even my father was killed in town [Kampala]. He was killed. He was shot dead. You see, the government had a disorder within, and we never knew who did such. Except that we got the body and we could not find out who did it. He was a businessman. That was the second of September, 1982.

Fortunately, I have been gifted; I am not interested in politics, because of what I have seen, because of these rough politics which have brought the death of my father. According to what I have seen, each party has got a special manifesto, but when they come to power, when they come to practice, they don't practice what they have put forth. They do quite opposite things, adverse things, immoral things, forcing other people to believe what they want to.

I have witnessed this on several cases. First, when I was in secondary school. We were forced to say what we had not seen, to give witness to what we have not seen. There was a case, some of the workers there—even some of the teachers—were killed. We were asked to give witness, written witness, statements that we had seen them collaborating with the bandits. Yet we had not even seen!

I personally am not interested in politics. I feel what I have seen is enough to choose what I should do.

JLA:  And you've chosen God over man?

Grace:  Yes.


*Expatriate:*

There was this boy who brought us our food. And one day he came with onions that were really overpriced, and I told him, "That's the last time you come here; you don't work for us anymore."

Anyway, a few weeks later, it was during the coup and he was in a truck with the looting soldiers going from house to house in our neighborhood. He was pointin' out the places for the soldiers to loot. Down the hill, the people saw him. He was away from the soldiers for the minute and they stoned him to death. People hate thieves here. He paid for it badly . . . but he was a little bastard. He was just lucky they didn't pour petrol over him and burn him alive.


*A correspondent for the leftist* Telecast *newspaper in Kampala, Jackie Aber, 24, is a statuesque, confident woman from the Acholi tribe of northern Uganda. Curiously, her idol is former U.S. secretary of state Alexander Haig; she carries his autobiography with her and has memorized key passages.*

I went into exile in 1977 with my parents. My father was being hunted by Amin. He was the director of the duty-free shop at that time and the chairman of the Ugandan Advisory Board of Trade. So we went to exile, first to Kenya, then on to Zambia. He came back in '79 hoping for a better Uganda, but he was in for a big shock. I came back in '83.

I was quite surprised the way the NRA came into Kampala. There was no looting. They were very nice to people, and we said, "Oh, my God." I mean, the change! And I said to my friends, "Do the southerners have a different way of looking at life, or is there some trick of a kind somewhere?" I mean, these people were so nice, despite what had happened. So even when they went up to the north, everything was okay according to the people coming from there. But all of a sudden, after about two, three months, hell broke loose.

A lot of problems usually comes from the center of Uganda. The Baganda were

# NORTHERN IRELAND

Burnt-out Protestant church in Londonderry.

"Supergrass" wives: Mary McCrossan, Evelina Sayers, and Ruth Hewitt, on the Shankill Road.

*Left:* Protestant zealot, George Seawright, at Belfast City Hall. In November 1987, he was shot in the head by Republican gunmen, and died two weeks later. *Below:* Maggie Darragh, peace activist.

Republican leader, Danny Morrison, in Sinn Fein's Falls Road office.

John McMichael, Loyalist para-military strongman. In December 1987, he was killed in a car bomb blast.

# EL SALVADOR

Dead guerrillas in coffee grove outside Jucuapa.

National Guard Lieutenant Sebastian Alvarado after fending off guerrilla attack on Jucuapa garrison.

Ana Francisca Corea, mother of boy killed in mine blast, Jucuapa.

*Left:* The man who painted Chalatenango white: Colonel Jesus Natividad Caceres. *Above:* Indian leader Adrian Esquina Lisco with mandolin-playing friend.

War refugee Marta Julia Coreas in her squatter home.

# UGANDA

Vinandi Wawire beside the grave for his brother, killed in a rebel raid.

Alice Nanyonga in her Nakaseke shop.

Eliphaz Kivumbi in the ruins of his coffee mill.

*Left:* Anglican Archbishop Yona Okoth. *Right:* Rebel leader Basilio Olara Okello in the garden of his exile home in Sudan.

Lawrence Mukasa with the remains of his friends and neighbors.

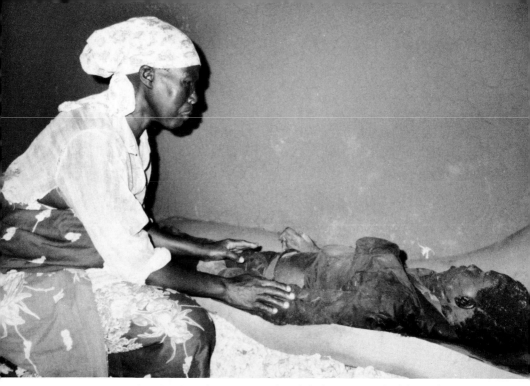

After the Gweri attack, Martin Ajalo is mourned by his mother.

Theresa Nansikombi with Robert, "the monkey boy," in Kampala.

# SRI LANKA

Youthful Tamil Tigers in their guerrilla camp outside Batticaloa.

*Top Left:* Ex-Prime Minister Siri-mavo Bandaranaike in the sitting room of her Colombo mansion. *Top Right:* Tiger "theoretician" Anton Balasingham, in India.

*Above:* Buddhist Venerables Piyadassi and Pannasiha at their Colombo temple. *Right:* Somalata, with her maimed son at her lotus-blossom stall.

*Left:* G.G. Piyaratna displaying his military vigilance. *Right:* The youngest Tiger, twelve year-old Shankar, cradling his weapon.

Executioner and victim: Kumarappa and Athuma in the Tiger camp. Within days, both would be dead.

# ISRAEL

Muhammad Musallem and his wife, Amni, in front of their tent-home in the Gaza Strip. The photographs they hold are of their two sons, imprisoned as terrorists.

Batya Medad at her home in the Shilloh settlement.

*Above:* Fathi Al Najii in the Jabaliya refugee camp in Gaza. *Right:* Surica Braverman at the perimeter fence of Kibbutz Shamir.

*Right:* Nathan Nathanson, one of the men who bombed Bassam Shaka'a, in his Jerusalem office.

*Above:* Bassam Shaka'a, former mayor of Nablus, in his wheelchair.

*Right:* Jewish housewife Galia Tamam, holding photograph of her son, who was murdered by Palestinians.

the first to get civilized—well, not really civilized; the schools started there but, in fact, not even the majority of them are educated. In fact, the majority of the people who are educated are the westerners and then the northerners. And, um, in both places, if you get someone, he's really educated. The Baganda have taken over business; education I don't think really mattered very much to them.

They believe they should rule. So long as they are not ruling, war is imminent. As long as they can't rule, there will always be trouble. And one thing I think a leader in Uganda should realize, you don't need the whole of Baganda support to rule, just a sensible fraction of them. That's all that matters. Because they're always there to create a lot of trouble.

I don't believe that all the killing in the Luwero was done by the northerners, because I went around with an army officer in the Luwero after Museveni took over. Now, we get to an area where the road is bad. He says, "This is where we blew up three lorries." Beside there are skulls. Now I ask, "All these skulls belong to only the villagers, or are some actually belonging to soldiers?" Because, at war, I don't think anybody had time to bury or even carry away corpses.

About three or four months ago, I was in Luwero. I found a fresh body—not really fresh; it was decomposing. And this gentleman, I don't know what group he belonged to. Anyway, the Luwero Triangle . . . You see, in 1982, they [Museveni's NRA] blew up so many buses. Where did all those people go?

One time I was very annoyed because someone came to me and said, "Obote was a murderer. Obote didn't know how to do what. Obote is a stupid man." But they don't have any right to say that! To me, I think Obote was a great man. I think in the history of the world very few leaders have gone to exile and come back. It doesn't matter what ways they use. And I still don't believe the [1980] elections were rigged.

The situation in Uganda, the way it develops day and night, worries me. The boy soldiers are very brutal. You give them an order, they do it. They don't question, they don't look back, they don't think. Who are these guys? Just who the hell are they? We do all the donkey work, and they just sit there and say, "Do this, do that!" So one of these days, I don't know how long it will take . . .

*Hilary Mubiru is a soft-spoken 65-year-old. A retired civil servant, he now works in the administration of the Catholic-run Child Welfare and Adoption Society of Nsambiya in Kampala. Mubiru has close-cut gray hair and wears spectacles.*

JLA: You used to be a civil servant; what made you decide to move into this voluntary work?

Mubiru: Well, I have a love for children, and I wanted to help in this department, which I thought would be something good for me to have in my last

years. Trying to help the disabled children, the orphaned children . . . We didn't
have very many people thinking about them, you know?

We had a war that swept so wide as to make people homeless, tearing up
families. The mother runs her own way, the father runs his own way and leaves the
children and spends years—ranging from one to five—without knowing where
his own children are. Some are killed, others are still alive, but parents do not
know, even up to now, where their children are. Quite often, quite often—even up
to now—we still get these people coming in to inquire whether his or her child has
been picked up and kept here. . . .

JLA: What has all this meant to you personally?

Mubiru: Me? (laughs) What has it meant to me? It's meant quite a lot, because I
have been displaced from my own home, from my own house, which I have
personally built for my family. Even now, I am homeless, I am just hiring a house
somewheres . . . and I won't be able to return to my own plot, to my own area, to
my own land, until I have a lot of money to rebuild a house, a house sufficient for
my family. So that is something I take as extraordinary, you know, happening in
my . . . whole life. And this has happened to a number of Ugandans.

JLA: Where was your home?

Mubiru: It was about fourteen miles west of Kampala, at the corner of the
Luwero Triangle. We have— My family and I ran away when the soldiers arrived.
They were killing people throughout the village . . . and we dispersed. My wife
went west, I went north, so . . . The children went their own way and we did not
come together until after nearly two years, when my wife returned from the
western side that she had run to.

JLA: Were you afraid that they had been killed?

Mubiru: Oh yes, I was. Except that . . . they were big enough. They could,
you know, also run. I lost a brother in this run. He was shot, just on the village, also
running, and he was shot dead. But my wife was out. I didn't know exactly where
she was for eighteen months—that's a year and a half. She didn't know . . . where
I was. She felt that either I was . . . killed, or I was . . . what? But she didn't know
exactly where I was, that I was alive or dead. She didn't know.

JLA: And how did you finally meet up?

Mubiru: Really, it was . . . it came to me as a sort of—shall I call it a
miracle?—because . . . I had all along tried to trace her through the Save the
Children Fund, the Red Cross. They did quite a lot of work for us. They used to go
out in these camps and places to try and trace them. But because I didn't know
exactly where she had run to, I couldn't give them any useful information about
her. So it was just one day, she happened to . . . just drop in, like that. I was sitting
here in the office, and one of my children who had also rejoined me from another
angle, came in and said, "Mommy's back." And that . . . surprised me.

JLA: And your other children? What happened to them?

Mubiru:  The others also collected slowly from where they had run to, and we are now all together.

Most of them are now big. I have three who are still schooling. They went with different people. You know, at the time of running away, there was no time for, you know, arranging anything, any order of any kind. Just like that and everybody runs! The three children didn't stay together, but eventually, because they knew I was here in Kampala, when things got better they slowly came in and . . . rejoined me. I am—I am just hiring a small, small, tiny room where we are.

Thank God they were big enough and three of them were in boarding schools. So that saved me a lot of . . . trouble. And my daughter spent three weeks with these people, with these Anya Nyas ["Snake Venom," Sudanese rebels working as mercenaries with Obote's army] in the Luwero, captured. She was only seventeen, sixteen, and she was taken for a wife. . . . Three weeks! But . . .

JLA:  Who were the Anya Nya?

Mubiru:  The Anya Nya are these *askaris* [soldiers] that we had, the soldiers in the recent regime. We don't know what they were, but many of them were not Ugandans. They are the people whom we hated looking at because they were killers, weren't they? Going about killing people . . . Anya Nyas . . . Anyway, if you speak of Anya Nya we all understand what you are talking about.

*Vincent Nsiiro Bukenya, 38, has recently returned to his hometown of Kapeka in the Luwero Triangle. Shoeless and wearing tattered pants and shirt, he has the wide-eyed, vacant stare of a man in shock. The interview is in front of one of Kapeka's few remaining shacks. Fifty feet away is one of Luwero's ubiquitous skull mounds.*

JLA:  What happened here?

Vincent:  It was during Obote's regime when we lived here. All the town was brought down.

JLA:  Were you here when the soldiers came?

Vincent:  No, I had escaped. That was in 1982.

JLA:  And your family? Did they stay?

Vincent:  I have my mother only. My father died during the war. The soldiers killed him.

SA:  And your wife and children?

Vincent:  I don't know where they are now. I don't know if they're still alive. I run my way and they run theirs. I don't know what happened to them. I still don't. My mother only.

SA:  When you escaped, where did you go?

Vincent:  I went as far as Malaba [Kenyan border], because I was very much in fear of Obote. Because Obote hated me so much. He suspected me as a guerrilla.

SA: How many children did you have?

Vincent: I had about six.

SA: How have you gone about looking for them?

Vincent: I have just come back from Malaba, and now I am trying to get some sort of income so that I will go and start looking for them.

JLA: How many people live here now?

Vincent: I don't know the exact number, but very few.

JLA: And before?

Vincent: We were many here. All this place was surrounded by people. But, as you see, it's now a little place.

JLA: Before Obote, what was life like here?

Vincent: No problems here. It was Obote only. I wish he had better come back here and we can ask him about what he did.

SA: What do you think about the new government?

Vincent: I don't know, but, for me, I wish him well if he does good for us. But if he doesn't, we have to revenge.

I didn't use to look like this. And how do you picture me then?

JLA: Before you had a house?

Vincent: Yes.

JLA: You had shoes?

Vincent: Yes, that's it.

JLA: Everything is gone now?

Vincent: It's gone.

*Expatriate:*

Nobody, but nobody, not even Museveni himself, knows what's going to happen here from day to day. Because I've been here for thirty-five years, and more or less ever since they got independence in 1962 I never really felt secure. Back under the British, the police and all were nearly all Irish. And the advocates were all Irish or Scots and the judges were Irish and Scots, so you couldn't go wrong. It was a free country at that time. Marvelous place, and we stayed on because we liked it so much. I mean, the best bottle of whiskey you could possibly buy then was seven shillings! Seven shillings!

*One of the few Ugandans who wishes to remain anonymous, "Father Oswald" is a pudgy, middle-aged Catholic priest wearing Western boots under his soutane. The interview, in a side office at Kampala's hilltop Rubaga Cathedral, is interrupted occasionally by whispering nuns. Throughout, the lounging Father Oswald wears a careless expression, his voice somewhat disdainful.*

What has happened for the last fifteen years has been rather unfortunate. And, if

I may say so, a bit absurd, due to the fact that we have had wars, conflicts, frictions—political and military—which essentially should not have taken place.

For me, it has meant confusion. And when I ask myself why, for the last fifteen years so many people have died, for what cause, I don't see myself answering it. Because they didn't have a political belief or a particular leader . . . and that's the whole reason why they died. And those that killed them did it for power, and that's the end of the story. I don't think it warranted their deaths, and probably even those who have been killing them now regret having done it. But still, it is done.

The amazing thing, as a priest . . . people have suffered, you know, and when there's a lot of suffering, people turn to God much more than when they are having no problems. And the past fifteen years have caused much more people to come to church.

JLA: How did the Church deal with the fact that tens of thousands of people were being massacred not very far from here in the last several years? Many were Catholics, correct?

Oswald: I wouldn't be able to tell you because . . . I mean, even in my own village when, at one time, they were ambushed by soldiers they were never asking about religion. If there was a trouble in the area, they would come and kill everybody, irrespective of religion.

JLA: Nonetheless, the Luwero Triangle, where many of these massacres took place, is an area where the Catholic Church is very influential.

Oswald: Yes. Well, as a matter of fact, the bishop here, whenever he heard of a matter, he contacted the authorities. There was nothing more he could do, other than talk to the government and, whenever possible, go and save the lives of some by evacuating them from these areas and giving them some assistance, food and water, blankets. . . . Apart from that, he couldn't do much more.

During this time, Kampala was relatively safer than staying in the villages. There was some sort of . . . Yes, they were killing people, but not so much as in the villages. There were so many roadblocks and they used to check everybody, priests and nonpriests alike. They treated you like everybody else. But I always had my proper documents. I never had any harassment. But . . . it was not very pleasant. . . .

JLA: How has this time affected you?

Oswald: I don't know. One who saw me before this time would be able to tell me. I wouldn't know.

JLA: But surely a lot of a priest's life, or so I'm given to understand, is spent in reflection?

Oswald: This time of trouble has made us very close to our people. More close, closer to them than ever before, even through their suffering.

JLA: What do you see for the future of this country?

Oswald: I wouldn't tell you . . . because it's very difficult to predict.

JLA: I'm not asking you to look in a crystal ball. What is your sense about the way things are moving?

Oswald: For the whole country, I wouldn't tell you.

JLA: For here?

Oswald: And for here, it is difficult to tell. I wouldn't be able to commit myself in any way.

JLA: What would you call the mood here right now?

Oswald: At the moment it is quiet.

JLA: Is it an uncertain mood?

Oswald: It's just a quiet mood; I wouldn't say it is uncertain. You see, it's very difficult . . . all I can notice is that at the moment. It's a quiet situation at the moment.

Except now . . . last night there were gunshots. I don't know what happened. . . .

*Expatriate:*

Hope the cannon fire didn't keep you awake last night. That was a bit unusual. Oh, we get a lot of little stuff—the AK-47s—over here, but it's been a while since I've heard the artillery.

Sounded like it was coming from across at the prison. Probably an attempted breakout; they like to use artillery on those.

But we're pretty well situated here. If anyone does manage to get out of the prison, they'll take out over that far hill. They won't come this way, because that whole area you see down below there is full of mines. And it's a swamp and supposed to be full of all sorts of poisonous snakes. They'd be mad to come this way.

I do wonder what all the shooting was about, though. Of course, we'll never find out; you never do find out about these things.

I wonder how many they got. They'll bring the bodies out around six in the evening and bury them just there on the ridge. Last time there were six or seven. It's really quite awful, I guess, but I suppose they bring it on themselves.

*The Reverend Christopher Ssempa, 58, is the outgoing Anglican pastor of the community of Namulonge, twenty miles northeast of Kampala on a dirt road. The site of a large agricultural research station, Namulonge today is all but deserted after the soldiers of the last regimes occupied it and, in a four-year killing spree, steadily exterminated the local people.*

*Ssempa, a gracious man who appears fifteen years younger than his age, remained in Namulonge throughout the slaughter. Part of the interview is conducted on a tour of the blood-drenched rooms of the agricultural college where the soldiers tortured and killed their victims. Throughout, Ssempa moves in an incredulous trance, as if he is seeing the horrors for the first time.*

JLA: Soon you will be leaving this place. Are you happy or sad to be leaving?

Ssempa: Very, very happy.

JLA: Why?

Ssempa: I'm tired of this place; I'm tired of it. Because I've seen a lot, and I am saddened by what I see.

JLA: Do you feel changed by what you've seen?

Ssempa: I already found change, because I am saved. That's how the world goes. When I read in the Bible, I see that very little has changed. By saying that, I don't mean that these people were right to do this, but what I see I've read about it. It surprised me a little, because these people who died, they died for nothing. But in general, this is what is happening in the world. So many people are dying everywhere, everywhere. So when I see these things happening, I only get strong in my belief that God created people in different thoughts, so everyone has to prepare his way. Try to do good in this world, because nothing you can get from this world. Nothing you can get. So that gives me strength in my belief, to see that whatever we do, whatever we see, has got an end.

JLA: And what did happen here?

Ssempa: Those people arrived here on the eleventh of August, 1982. They said they had come to protect us for security in this area. And then after a week, they started capturing people and killing them. Some of them were taken from the bush, some were taken from their homes. So they started killing people daily, daily. . . .

JLA: Did they threaten you?

Ssempa: Yes. Six times. They just came and beat me. They even pushed me with the *panga* [machete] here. It [the scar] was very big. They beat me the whole part of my body. I count six times they came here and beating me. One child was beaten, and my wife also.

JLA: Why do you think they did this?

Ssempa: I don't really know what their intention was, but their intention was coming from the top, because they were sent by the top men, the president and so on. Their intention was to kill all Baganda here.

Before, the life was not bad. People were settled down in peace. There was no trouble before they came, because I had been here for seven months before.

JLA: Did you ever ask them why they persecuted?

Ssempa: Yes, I did, and they said it was their job and that is what they were sent for.

When they came, many of the people run away. Except myself and very few. Four people were left here. There was a time when I was just left here alone.

JLA: During this time, did you ever go to your archbishop and tell what was happening?

Ssempa: I went to my bishop and told him so many times. I don't know what he did, but he said he was reporting to those who beat me and to the president and so forth. I didn't see any change.

JLA:  Did this make you resentful?

Ssempa:  No. I was still strong. I remained strong in Jesus. So I remained here, because I knew that when death comes there is not any resistance.

JLA:  Were you angry that your superiors were not helping you more?

Ssempa:  I didn't think about that very much. I thought that's how the world goes, and I knew that even Jesus Christ was persecuted.

(before a pile of skulls)

Ssempa:  We place them here so that people who are passing by will know what happened here.

JLA:  Was this requested by the government?

Ssempa:  No. It was done by individuals, so people could understand how life was spent here. These are very few skulls because some were taken, but those who are unidentified were left here. Because you cannot identify that one, or say this one was so-and-so.

JLA:  How were they killed?

Ssempa:  By all types. This one you can see is by beating . . . this here they used a panga . . . this one they cut by knives . . . some were burnt. It was terrible here, my friend. A hammer here that they used . . . this one here was killed by a hammer. . . .

(points to a house beside the skull pile)

Ssempa:  They lived here. This was the barracks. This is the place where the roadblock was.

(walks across the agricultural research center grounds and enters one of the houses. The cement floor and walls are stained with bloodstains, and there is the stink of death. Above the doorway, still-visible graffiti warns, "He who enters this room meets death," and, "Here the panga falls easily.")

Ssempa:  This was the killing room. . . . When we were collecting bodies, many of them had no heads. We could not find the heads.

JLA:  How many bodies did you find after the soldiers left?

Ssempa:  Over one hundred.

(at the edge of the field behind the killing room)

Ssempa:  The bodies were put here. This was the place they put them. Dead bodies were lying here, so many you could not count. There were very, very many. You know, they started from '82 up to '85, killing daily! I don't think that there was a day in which they didn't kill. Daily. At six P.M.; they used to kill at six P.M. Especially I knew it because I was here. They [victims] used to go on crying, "Why are you taking me? I've done nothing, don't kill me, let me go, don't make me suffer."

JLA:  And what would the soldiers say?

Ssempa:  Ach, nothing . . . (gazes over the field for a long moment) It's terrible here. . . .

JLA: Why did you stay here with all this going on?

Ssempa: Because I was sent here just to do good work, and when I thought of going I thought, "Where shall I go where these people will not find me?" So I said, "Let me stay here until I come to my end, perhaps in that way." I said, "Let me to be here."

And . . . you can't know that you will be killed tomorrow, today. You can't know you're dying tomorrow. You don't know your date.

Because, first of all, we had done nothing wrong. So when you have done nothing, you don't expect to be affected with such a thing. That's why some people stayed, because they had done nothing. They said, "Why should I go, what have I done?" Those who were unlucky were picked up and brought here. Those who were lucky stayed, remain.

But what is funny . . . I mean, dead bodies were here and the soldiers were living here. All these houses were full of people, dancing, doing whatnot—the soldiers. The smell didn't bother them. That's what I was wondering; perhaps they used to even eat them. They couldn't even think about smelling, and the smelling was terrible. By the time they had gone, you could smell the smell from far away. The heap was higher than this fence. So high . . .

JLA: As a Christian, how do you feel about not burying the bones?

Ssempa: That would be good, but if that had been done what would you see now? We left this for other people to see. As you see, we have a museum in the country, to show people what has happened.

JLA: Have you prayed for those people? Have you blessed the bodies?

Sssempa: I'm sorry, I haven't done that. . . . I haven't . . . and I feel conflicted about that. I haven't done that. I haven't done that. . . .

*Expatriate:*

There's a great trade in skulls around here, you know. Ones with hair on 'em go for more money. Sell 'em to tourists, so I hear. Not long ago, a lorry tipped over with a load of 'em in Jinja. That's how they discovered it, so I hear. The fresh ones get the best price. Foreign tourists buy 'em, so I hear.

*After his timely escape to Kenya in 1977, Bishop Yona Okoth went into exile in the United States. He returned to Uganda in 1979 with the invading Tanzanian "liberation force" that toppled Idi Amin. Since his return, Okoth has been ordained Archbishop of the Church of Uganda.*

*Okoth is accompanied in this interview by his chaplain, the diffident John Waramoya, and the dour Reverend Charles Obaikol, his provincial secretary. All three men are from northern or eastern tribes.*

*During the period of Obote's rule, Okoth came to be seen as a crony of the regime by many Ugandans. Many criticize him and the Church of Uganda for not decrying the Luwero slaughter while it was occurring. It was to this church that the Reverend Christopher Ssempa (preceding interview) was making his reports about the massacres in Namulonge.*

I was the first bishop to come back. At first, we came back with a great hope that now maybe we could work together but, unfortunately, it has not worked like that way. There has been a lot of fighting. So this has been the problem.

JLA: There was also a great deal of killing between '80 and '85, especially in the Luwero Triangle.

Okoth: Yes. There were a lot of fighting groups. I did not know that until Okello took over from Obote and then we came to . . . I was amazed to see all the different groups who had been fighting! But before that, I didn't know! Because they used to have a uniform, you couldn't tell who is who and who is killing who! But when we—when I knew that, after that, after the fall of Obote and I knew . . . there were a lot of people fighting.

JLA: But there were outright massacres of civilians during that period in the Luwero Triangle.

Okoth: Yes! But there were a lot of things fighting. When—when . . . the warfront . . . because with me, I did not know . . . uh—until Okello took over. And about the suffering of Luwero, I used to hear it—until Museveni took over. And, again, I went there and see. We were just amazed!

JLA: It's amazing that so much can go on so close and you don't know.

Okoth: Yes. We couldn't go there! We couldn't believe it! I couldn't believe it, too! I couldn't believe until we went there. We're just ashooking our head. So from that time, I know that the worst enemy of a man is a man. . . .

Obaikol: The main problem with the guerrilla activities is that it is very difficult to identify who is the enemy and who is not. So I think the deaths in Luwero were involving all kinds of people. Those people who died there were all mixed tribes. Some of them were soldiers who had gone there. You see, on the road, trucks have been blown up. Some of those were actually soldiers who were progovernment. Then there were civilians. Then there was also fighting groups. So it's very difficult. We feel bad about it, but, uh . . .

Waramoya: But find it difficult to pinpoint a particular group—"This one was doing the killing." It was so difficult. Because the present government claimed that they were the ones controlling Luwero! Now they turn around, they say it was the previous government killing! Now, if you were the one controlling Luwero, definitely there was some people who oppose you and, definitely, those people are bound to be killed.

Okoth: Well, this has been our task as a church. We are very much concerned about peace and unity and reconciliation, and this is what we have been trying to preach to the people. But, you know, it takes time. We are very much concerned for this unity.

Waramoya: Our society used to be one of the best societies. There was respect for human rights. There was no stealing. There was no murders. But since Amin took over and brought in these corruptions and so on, people actually tend to be . . . Morally, we are corrupt. It is the biggest change we are now experiencing. There is sometimes killing; you don't know who killed who. There is always corruption, so people are not actually as they were.

Okoth: I think the darkness has come.

*Expatriate:*

These are the nicest, the friendliest people you'll find in Africa. I just can't understand why they kill each other. It doesn't make any sense. Uganda is going backward, not forward. Uganda has the best cotton in the world. It used to export it; now it imports it. Seventy years of production and growth has been destroyed in the last fifteen.

This place is going. You can still see what it was once like. God, I'd have loved to have seen this fifteen or twenty years ago; it must've been beautiful.

*Eliphaz S.S. Kivumbi, 46, is a handsome, intensely warm man with soft, rheumy eyes. He built the Seventh Day Adventist Light College in the town of Masuliita, as well as a coffee-processing mill and a large home for his wife and children. Today, Kivumbi's school and coffee mill are in total ruins and he lives in a hut beside the shell of his ravaged home. Throughout the interview, Kivumbi displays an odd habit of punctuating the tale of his misfortunes with a hearty laugh.*

When I left school, I started the Light College, and I was the first headmaster. In 1964, I left teaching, but I remained as the owner of the school. I started this coffee factory.

Now, both of my businesses are in ruins. I can't say how I feel. (laughs) I'm growing old! I don't have any way out, to rehabilitate this place. All the money I had was taken.

So now, how I can start again, I don't know. And my age is now growing old. I was very strong during the last years, but now I'm growing old! I've lost wealth! I wonder, if at all I can get assistance—I still have brains to run this same business—but with money problems, we don't have any chance. The coffee we had in stock was all our wealth. All that money was taken away and we had nothing left in pocket. And now we don't have any coins to buy even one iron sheet. All the iron sheets were taken away.

I'm very, very sad about it. To see how I started this works and now they're all ruined. I'm very sad indeed! If I die today, I die in sorrow. I die in sorrow because, when I started I knew that it would help people who would come after me. But now, it is all finished.

*Peter Oryema is the director of the Uganda Red Cross. A powerfully built, blue-black man from the West Nile District, Oryema has a distinguished air, accentuated by his reflective manner and tailored suits. Among relief workers in Kampala, he is admired for his frequent treks into the Luwero Triangle during the height of the Obote government's pogroms there.*

I was really an accountant. I didn't come into the Red Cross until November 1982. I found myself having to do whatever I could, which, to me, now makes a lot of sense. I have come into direct contact with the various groups of people and I have had the chance to get firsthand the story of the problems.

And especially when I was working in Luwero, the kinds of things I saw to me did not make sense. They tended to mold me into someone quite different, because I had to change my attitude toward life as such. I was a very carefree person. I always thought that life was easy. I never cared about other people until I began to see a number of people—not just ten or twenty, but thousands—being put to endure conditions in which . . . they, you know . . . they had done nothing! At least for a time, each time I went to the camps, I was able to see how these people were suffering, the conditions they were under.

You see, I never thought before about working with any human rights group. To me it was a foreign idea. Being an accountant, I thought of having a nice office and counting figures, not being face-to-face with the problems of humanitarian law and suffering and . . . undue punishment toward individuals.

As I dug deeper and deeper and deeper into the Luwero Triangle, I felt a sense of remorse. At the time the people who were in power were from my part of the country. And I was talking to the soldiers in their language, and what I could not comprehend was how, in one instance, somebody you talk to so nicely would turn to be a murderer. This was my own sense of remorse because I know the people I'm talking about. Generally, they're good people. I don't think you can say "In this country, northerners are this and that." I think all Ugandans generally are good people, but you cannot really comprehend how in a certain set of circumstances people are made to suffer from their own brothers and fellow countrymen. This was the most difficult feeling I had at the time.

Again, there was a feeling of helplessness because you feel you wanted to stop this sort of thing, but there's just no way. I don't know if you can understand the kind of feelings that I have, because you might think about them rather remotely. But having seen some of the people myself, having seen children die of measles, having had to carry dead children—being a father of children myself—to me it was something . . . something quite different. And because I do love my own kids, I do love my own parents, and to see that here were people being treated this kind of way . . . It wasn't nice.

The story [of Luwero] was not told because the people in the villages did not have the power for going out and talking about their plight. They don't know about their rights. These are simple people. They are nice, simple people who are just living their lives on the farmland and that's it.

But almost by pure coincidence, someone stumbled into our office with the idea that maybe we were a group that could help. And he tells us that there are so many thousands of people [being held] in Masuliita, there are so many thousands of people in Wakiso . . . so we took interest when these reports reached us, of starving populations, of people dying of measles at a very bad rate, maybe ten or twenty children every day, so we sent survey teams.

I was one of those people that went and the first place I went to was Endija, which is just a few kilometers close to Bombo town. And I was alarmed to see what I saw. It was something that was not . . . not ordinary. There were thousands— just innocents; I mean, simple people—being crowded in this area.

But we were told it was not just Endija; there were other camps further afield. So we had to find out and, in instances, our teams were actually beaten and tortured because we were told those areas were no-go areas. Of course, we persisted and continued to discover more and more camps, more and more people. So, finally, we sent an appeal to the international [Red Cross] organization, and it was then that the Western media really started to learn about it.

Nobody knew the numbers, but I, for instance, I knew that something ominous was going on. I remember very well that at one stage I was arguing with a number of friends and what we couldn't agree on was how many thousands had been massacred. There were stories of people who had escaped being shot and who had found their way into Kampala, and they would say, "You know, we were sixty and everybody else was killed except me." So it didn't just happen in one camp; the stories were about several places. There were days when my teammates would report to me that they saw a heap of ten dead bodies there, a heap of so many dead bodies in another spot, just by the roadside.

And, of course, there was death from natural causes, death from starvation, measles and, uh . . . One time, I went to a camp. When I arrived in the morning, I was told that because our team had not been able to go there the previous week, over a hundred children had died during that week. And proof of it was the graves, fresh graves. They took me to the graveyard, and I saw that they were all these children. So, in a way, I had known. I knew. But I couldn't talk about it openly. It was not part of my job.

It gives you a sense of being incompetent. You feel guilty. But this was a general feeling we had, that if there was a way to stop all of these deaths, all that had to be done was to stop. But there was no way. I mean, we would go to the camp in the morning and find that in the night several people had been picked up, and we had no power, no control over some of the events. . . . So, anyway, it has that psychological feeling of guilt.

So I don't think it is true that it was only after Museveni [came to power] that the truth was known. I think what the world should blame itself for is that there was some indication that something ominous was happening, but nobody bothered to investigate. Nobody! The eyewitness accounts, they were there!

This has always been my criticism of human rights bodies like Amnesty International. They are so good when a professor of literature somewhere is arrested, but when it comes to ordinary people who are not known in the world, so to speak, this is nothing. This is the saddest part of it, and even today, there are thousands of people in many parts of the world who are dying, but nobody knows them. And because no one knows them, the world does not get to know. Because the conscience of the world is not pricked about ordinary people.


*Moses Kataza, a small wide-eyed boy with a loner's air and hesitant smile, is "about thirteen," say his keepers at the orphanage where he lives. The government-run Naguru Reception Centre is a grassy, downtrodden little place in a working-class subdivision on Kampala's outskirts. From the Luwero Triangle, Moses doesn't speak English; his answers are translated by Daphrose Mbabazi, a smiling 25-year-old Naguru nurse.*


Daphrose: He says he came walking up from Luwero to where they [police] picked him up. They brought him here.

JLA: And why was he walking from Luwero?

Daphrose: He was running away from bullets.

JLA: When was that?

Daphrose: Last year.

JLA: What happened to his family?

Daphrose: They were burnt in the house by bombs. They attacked the family.

JLA: How many brothers and sisters did he have?

Daphrose: He had four sisters, two brothers. He doesn't know where they are.

JLA: What does he remember from that day?

Daphrose: The parents had gone to a certain place for a burial, so they were left with the grandmother to look after them. So this boy was in the house. His parents had gone to bury somebody else. That is where they [soldiers] found the parents and killed them. And then they came to the house where he was staying at his grandmother's. And from there he was hidden somewhere in the kitchen. So they [soldiers] killed the rest and he remained alone. So he ran to that place where they [the parents] have gone for burial. When he reached there, he found everyone dead.

JLA: What does he think about soldiers?

Daphrose: He say he may revenge also.

*Theresa Nansikombi runs the Naguru Reception Centre. A trained nurse and midwife, Nansikombi's maternal feelings for her young wards are immediately evident, as she cuddles children, scolds, and clucks over them. She tells their and her own story in a lovely ringing voice that brims with emotion.*

*One child who stands out is Robert, "the monkey boy," brought to the Centre from Luwero in 1985 by soldiers of the short-lived Okello government. He is "about eight," Nansikombi believes, but he cannot speak or walk. Most of the time, he sits on his own, sobbing or making strange noises. He stops crying when Nansikombi picks him up and cradles him.*

When the children from Luwero, from disturbed places, are admitted here they are really very much depressed. One day, one of those children told me that "Mammy, as you have treated us and we have survived, with my little sister why don't we go to the jungle at Luwero? I remember the place where they have thrown our father, who was bleeding terrible. So I would like you, please, I am asking you, to bring, to go and bring him here and treat him. Perhaps he will get better." And . . . that boy asked me that about two weeks from the date of admission! So it was really terrible to hear. But later on, we heard that the father had died. The mother was badly shot in the leg and she was admitted in Mulago Hospital later. About some months later, she came here and saw the children and then went. Since then, I don't know her whereabouts. And she is also disturbed because of the war, mentally disturbed.

JLA: Will these children grow up to be normal?

Nansikombi: Some of the children are really hot [headed]. Some are always fighting, always playing war. Guns, shooting, beatings, kick—Anyway, I don't know. Anyway, boys are usually rough. Perhaps, sometimes when they grow up, they might become normal children.

JLA: And the girls?

Nansikombi: Some girls are very tough. And there was one girl, but she unfortunately ran away from this place, because we wanted to ask her about her family and we wanted to go visit the place in Luwero and she didn't like it. So that night she run away from us.

JLA: How many children from Luwero have you had here?

Nansikombi: Oh, a big number. During the war, we had about a hundred and fifty children, mostly from Luwero. We had about twenty from other places. Now they are forty-five; about eighteen, twenty are from Luwero now.

JLA: How do they act when they first come?

Nansikombi: They are very quiet, very silent, and they don't talk. But after getting used to the place and getting friendly with us, then they start talking. When we really persuade them, ask them questions, give them some nice things to eat— and perhaps sometimes I have sweets; I can call a little boy and give him about two, three sweets—and I start questioning him and he starts to reveal whatever he knows. . . .

JLA: And Robert, he is from Luwero?

Nansikombi: Robert, yes, he is from Luwero. He came when he was skin and bones. He came when he had a very, very rough skin, like an elephant. The skin was too hard! And when we poured water on him, the water was just running off, as if it's running on a mackintosh! I wonder (laughs) . . . It was terrible! His nails were grown to the maximum. He had both his milk teeth and the permanent teeth, two rows. We had to remove whichever could come out and clean the mouth and give him some antibiotic to prevent sepsis.

JLA: And he had been living with monkeys?

Nansikombi: Most likely, because one of his arm was too squeezed! And I suspected that perhaps there was something, an animal most likely, lifting the boy. How can one arm be so much squeezed? . . . And the mark is there.

And he was running, very fast! With his legs and arms, like a monkey! He couldn't look in a person's eye. Like this? No! He was very, very unfriendly with people. He didn't like us. He didn't like human food. He was eating grass, soil, stones, and he was even eating his clothes. He was eating whichever comes across him, besides human food. And when we really showed him love and . . . so he started slowly to eat human food and to behave like a human. He was sleeping . . . When he squats like this. (mimics Robert and laughs) It was very (laughs) . . . He used to sleep while squatting. Whatever he does, he squats.

Now I am suspecting that his ears are not normal, because when you clap or anything behind his sight, he doesn't respond. Which means that he doesn't hear properly. Perhaps if we can get some aids to help him hear, perhaps he would speak. He only responds when he sees you. Then he can put up his arms to be lifted. He can smile now! This is a very interesting point to me, because he has never smiled before. A year or so, he has never smiled!

JLA: Has it affected you, seeing all of these children, the war orphans?

Nansikombi: Yes, it has affected us because . . . some of the staff members here are coming from Luwero. And the families were all . . . all dismantled, burned, whatnot! Most of their relatives were killed. So it has affected us, so much. . . . Some of our boys were in school during the NRA. . . . Imagine a boy of seven, ten years, moving with a gun! It has affected us so much!

Those boys, haven't you seen the small boys with the guns! Some of those are our children! Even my—my real son, joined the army. We are badly . . . touched. The son, my son was . . . schooling in a certain school in Masaka, and he joined . . . NRA. He was going to school and he was together with his brother and he just run away from the school. He thought that a person who could move from Masaka to Kampala should be a soldier. So he decided to join soldierhood in order to come to Kampala. But when he reached, he refused to give up!

JLA: How old was he?

Nansikombi: He was about . . . twelve. I didn't know until the road was open and we could move to Masaka. I just saw him one day, with a gun! In a combat [uniform]! I was really very shocked! And I started to cry. . . . (begins to weep)

JLA: Is he still a soldier now?

Nansikombi: (nods, still weeping) We are all crying, because of war. We are tired of wars. Since 1966, we are at war! Since 1966 up to now we are in war! We are in a war for twenty years!

JLA: I am sorry if I made you sad. I didn't mean to. . . . Did you ask him to stop being a soldier?

Nansikombi: But he can't! He is all taken. . . . (weeps) I don't know what I can do!

JLA: Can he leave if he wants to?

Nansikombi: To leave being a soldier? I don't think . . . I don't think he will ever reform . . . because he is not at all behaving well. He is now very rough. What I hope is for somebody who can really take him from Uganda, and perhaps he will reform. . . . Now, he's fifteen.

He's moving like that . . . they cannot be controlled in the barracks. As you know, some—these big soldiers are not really . . . they have no parental heart to look after or to advise and uphold, and these small boys are not really controlled. They are not controlled at all. They do whatever they like! What person could he be if he's doing whatever he wants, when he is still a child!

JLA: Have you talked to him about leaving Uganda?

Nansikombi: I didn't talk to him, but I was thinking about it myself. When I have nobody who can take him now, how can I talk to him about it? If there was somebody who can really deal with this boy, then perhaps he could go and grow there. Perhaps he will become somebody!

If some children could be taken out of Uganda, perhaps they will reform. But when they are in Uganda here, I don't think that they will ever reform. . . . Anyway . . . we are always in agony, we are always crying. That is how we live in Uganda.

*Expatriate:*

What's he going to do with all these kids? Is he going to kill them all? All these eight-year-old murderers and murderesses? This has never happened before! This has never happened in history before! Who would use seven- and eight-year-old children to fight a war?! Not even the Russians would do that! Not even the Russians. . . . To me, he's [Museveni] a half-wit. To me he's an idiot. God help Uganda!

A seven-year-old comes for you now, what're you gonna do? A seven-year-old child, just old enough to be baptized for a Christian!

*Lawrence Mukasa, a friendly, thin man in his early thirties, is the Resistance Committee officer in charge of Masuliita, a town in the Luwero Triangle. Of the thirty thousand people in his subcouncil region before 1981, ten thousand are dead or missing. The interview is held while Mukasa conducts a tour of Masuliita and its environs. On a dirt road leading out of Masuliita, over 150 skulls are lined up in tight rows. Behind the skulls are a jumbled pile of bones and, to one side, rotting clothes.*

This is a place where a lot of people were killed. There you can see their clothes . . . skulls. They were killed here. Some of the skulls have disappeared. This is what Obote did. Here, this was from a *panga* [machete] . . . And look at this; this was probably an axe. This was another panga. This one would have been a blade through the top of the head.

We are still finding bodies in the bush. Some are buried, and the other remains are still lying for display. We had over three hundred skulls, but some have disappeared. We don't know how they are taken. Maybe Obote is trying to take them to convince the world that Museveni is killing. This could be the case.

(walking through a war-damaged schoolhouse)

This was a primary school. It used to have good buildings. It got all its property looted, destroyed by these men! At the moment, children takes their lessons in this building (empty shell with water standing on floor). You see, we have nowhere else to teach our children. This is the little furniture we were left with. All desks were used by these men in cooking. So now the children must sit on the floor in here for lessons.

These people were semiliterate. They did not know that education was the foundation of our country. Had they known, I think they would not have done it.

(in the remnants of a graffiti-scrawled building in the center of town)

This was one of the places where Obote staged his men, and it is from where they used to go to those places to terrorize people, loot, kill. And, in fact, his army stayed right here from '81 to '85, when it was liberated by the NRA.

These people took time to write bad words, scandalous words, most of which were used to criticize Museveni. Here it says "Museveni down. You are hopeless. And all your family will get killed. And you, too, will be killed." Some of them wrote in their language, which I cannot understand; they were coming from the north, mostly belonging to the Acholi and Langi people.

SA: What are these lists of people's names?

Mukasa: They are names of people they wanted to kill.

SA: There's ten names there. Eleven there . . . Did you have any personal experiences with the soldiers?

Mukasa: Oh yes, I had my people killed, my family killed. First they were tortured and then they were shot to death.

They claimed that everyone here was a guerrilla. It was very early in the morning, around three o'clock, when they came to the place. To our astonishment, in the morning we were awoken by their knocking on the door. So we came out and were asked a lot of questions. "Where is Museveni?" "Why are you here?" And then, of course, we could not answer to any of their questions, and eventually they started torturing us, kicked, punched. They raped my wife . . . they did a lot of evils.

Eventually, they arrested my parents along with my two children, took them and . . . disappeared.

SA: How old were your children?

Mukasa: One was eleven, the other was five.

SA: Did you stay in Masuliita then?

Mukasa: Of course I had to vanish. I went along with the NRA soldiers, the liberators. I went to the bush and I found them there. I was there for three years. I operated in this area.

SA: What is your job with the Resistance Committee here?

Mukasa: Well, in the first place, we've got to unite the people. We've got to rehabilitate them in all cases, morally and socially. We've got to explain the government policies to the people, because the main organ of this government are the resistance committees. We are differing from previous regimes because before we had chiefs; but this time we have resistance committees.

SA: How do you go about rehabilitating the people morally and socially?

Mukasa: In the first place, we've got to politicize. We want people to know what politics is and what they're bound to do for their country to bring about security and all that. The government provides us with some food, because we don't have food. The process would be quickened up but, the government is—how can I put it?—is in a critical financial position. (laughs)

(walking through a destroyed school outside Masuliita)

It was the most advanced secondary school we had in the place. It had a lot of buildings. It had a lot of students who were taking both primary and secondary education, and some technical courses. Well, all the houses were destroyed by these troops.

SA: Were people killed here as well?

Mukasa: Yes, some people were killed. Some people were killed. Some people were killed. . . . Some people were killed. . . . Some people were killed. . . .

*Expatriate:*

What this place needs is a hundred mercenaries. We could send in a hundred and sort this place out in a couple of weeks, put things in order. That's all it would take, a hundred good men.

*Kagenda Atwoki, 47, is the secretary for information, research, and publications for the Uganda People's Congress (UPC), former President Milton Obote's political party. A short, heavy-set man with a condescending air, Atwoki was a meteorologist before taking up the calling of Uganda's rough-and-tumble politics. During the interview, he frequently slams his fists on the desk and juts his chin to reinforce a point, theatrics that are met with mumbles of approval from the half-dozen party members and bodyguards cloistered in the small room at party headquarters.*

Atwoki: I think the politics of skulls is very sad politics. I think it is sad that we Ugandans devise a form of propaganda that uses skulls. I think it is very bad politics. I think it is bitter politics.

The truth is that there has been a war and the Luwero Triangle was a war zone. The war was between the state army at the time, the UNLA, and a guerrilla force, the NRA. Now, I cannot tell you who shot those people who died in Luwero. I cannot tell you that they were soldiers or civilians. I am damn sure that the majority of the people who died in the Luwero Triangle were soldiers in combat, both from NRA and from UNLA. Now, for anyone to organize those skulls and put them on his side and make them speak for him, it's cheap propaganda, and I think it's very, very sad propaganda.

I witnessed here in Kampala, in January when NRA took over, I saw dead bodies in the streets of Kampala, and there were thousands of dead bodies! As you walk around now you don't see those dead bodies, but there were thousands and thousands of dead bodies on the streets of Kampala! Who died in January [1986]? I hate the day if tomorrow someone will turn up with their skulls and say, "They were my people."

These skulls are the result of war. I think it's very sad politics when a group of people begin to pick skulls and parade them around the world in an effort to prove they are holy.

I don't want to argue also that none of the UNLA soldiers committed atrocities, because I have seen some atrocities. I saw some atrocities with my own eyes! The truth is that there was a war situation, and a war situation, especially involving guerrilla warfare, is an unruly situation. There was no law and order in Luwero during that war. Government found itself in a very tight corner; it found it very difficult to run government services. So I don't know in whose interest it is to apportion blame. But if I were to blame anybody, I would blame those forces which in 1981 refused to follow the legal process after the 1980 elections and chose the military course of action [Museveni's NRA]. I would argue that all those who hold the militarist line in politics, those who believe that only the military solution is the correct solution, are the ones who are the danger to our future.

SA: And what is the UPC policy for the future?

Atwoki: The Uganda People's Congress is maintaining its organization. In fact, the peace that prevails in any part of Uganda now should be credited to the

Uganda People's Congress. Because our membership is disciplined. Our membership has had to bear a lot of hardship. Our members upcountry in the rural areas are
quiet, following the law. They are not retaliating to any hardship. So many of our
people are in jail, so many of our people are in exile, so many in concentration
camps, but our members remain . . . adroit! We are not out to precipitate chaos in
this country. And that is going to remain our strategy until those who are following
the wrong course fail. And they will fail!

SA: Do you fear for your life?

Atwoki: I have only one life.

SA: Do you fear for it?

Atwoki: I have only one life. I have never died. I'm not interested in death.

SA: So you don't worry about your safety?

Atwoki: Why should I worry?

SA: People have a way of getting killed in this country.

Atwoki: They died; (shrugs) I could die as well. But I don't think that those of
us who are alive, we should shirk our responsibilities for fear of death. Because we
can only die once, and we sure shall die! I am going to die, and if somebody pushes
a bullet through my chest now, I will not die any worse than if I died of malaria!

I know members of Uganda People's Congress, the majority, cannot be terrified
by a threat of death! Many of our own members have died! We have seen! We have
buried members of UPC who died because of their belief in the Party! In the
Luwero Triangle! Many of the people who died there are our own youth leaders!
They died in Luwero! We have the register here!

If it was not for a war that was imposed on this country, the future of this country
would have been bright under the leadership of the Uganda People's Congress. I
think the record of the Uganda People's Congress in government, from 1981 to
1985, speaks for itself.


*Steve, a former accountant in his mid-thirties, rents out a portion of a shop to
sell his handmade fishing nets and moonlights as a taxi driver. He is of the Teso
tribe of eastern Uganda.*


Tribalism plays a very small part now. There has been so much intermarriages of
tribes. Acholi come down and marry Bagandas, Bagandas marry Tesos. It is all
mixed in now.

Most of all, it is religion. The struggle is between the Protestants and the
Catholics. The Protestants all belong to UPC and the Catholics to the Democratic
Party. It has been that if you were born a Catholic, you were automatically a DP,
and if you were a Protestant, you were a UPC. Your birth decided your politics. It
was under your skin, inside your blood. It was just as important as your religion,
because it was the same thing, and the churches were very open about which party

they supported. So, while it seems political, you cannot separate religion from the politics.

So I used to be in the UPC. I never went to any of the rallies or anything, but I always voted for UPC; I would never have considered voting DP. But now, after what Obote did, I have no interest in politics anymore. I just want to live my life, and I don't care anything about politics.

There is a belief in Uganda that you can only have power, the authority to have power, through the gun. They believe that you cannot run the government unless you have an army behind you. So if there is a man who is running for president, a democrat, people look at him and laugh and say, "Why do you think you should be president when you don't even have an army, when you haven't even fought for anything?" This is their mentality; this is the Ugandan system.

I plan to buy a lot and build my own house here in Kampala. I won't go back to the countryside. This is what we have learned: in the countryside there is easy death.

*Bearded and tattooed, Manfred Holtzbauer, a 44-year-old Bavarian, is an enigmatic advisor of sorts with the Catholic Diocese of Soroti. A town in eastern Uganda, Soroti has become a point of refuge for peasants fleeing the raids of an odd assortment of characters: Karamajo tribesmen and the renegade UNLA soldiers of the fallen Obote and Okello regimes. Previously, Holtzbauer worked with a German emergency medical team at Nakaseke Hospital in the Luwero Triangle during the worst period. Holtzbauer returned to Uganda in mid-1986 after being imprisoned and finally deported by Obote's government in 1985. He plans to continue working with Uganda's needy for years to come, and eventually retire in the country.*

We tried to protect the hospital, to fence it around. The Obote Special Forces, the military soldiers, especially these youth wingers of Obote's, they have been horrible. They have killed a lot of people in the hospital, just took them out and killed them, just in front of the doors.

They just came in. . . . Once I beat two of them very heavily, and from this time I was suspected. I beat them with a heavy stick because they went into a room to get a patient. He was just operated, just half an hour out of the theater, and they tried to get him out from the room. And I went in and I said, "No, don't touch this man. It is an international law; as long as there is a medical superintendent deciding the patient has to stay in the hospital, nobody can take him out." Then they tried to push me away, and I got very angry and I just stood behind the door and I beat them up heavily. (grins) So from this day on, I was actually suspected.

But we got them out. I have been very tricky in this time. So I filled up the Land Rover and I put a mask in front of my mouth and when we passed a roadblock I say, very heavily, "TB cases, very infectious." So they refused every time to see the identity cards and tax tickets! They were just running away! (laughs) But it happened that they took out some people from cars of colleagues who weren't as clever as me (laughs) and killed them.

Once they took away one of my workers; he was called Johnny. He has an age of about nineteen. He was working with me from the first day. Suddenly, Lieutenant Okello was coming to take him away. I went up to the detachment to get him out, but by the time I got to the detachment they have killed him already.

Killing was a game for them. Sometimes they went up—there was a building about four floors—they went up with the people they suspected, eh? And they say, "Now you see how it is to fly," and they were shooting as he was falling, like a game, so . . .

Then, in '85, I went up to Moroto and I slept in a Moroto hotel. And the [local army] chief of staff has been there also, drinking his beer, and he was just sitting opposite me—chief of staff of the Karamoja barracks—and he was asking me about my opinion. At first I didn't say anything. I said, "Come, let me drink my beer and let me be." He said, "No, I want to know your opinion." And I said, just exactly, "For me he's [Obote] a killer, what I have seen. Your soldiers of Obote, what I have seen is enough for me for the next hundred years."

So the next day, the Special Branch took me—this has been a part of political police during Obote's time—arrested me in Moroto. Then they brought me to central police station in Kampala, and I think only because of the protection of Uganda police in this time I survived. Because most of these policemens have been against the regime at this time, and they never gave me out again to the army.

So they deported me, after six and a half months, to Germany. So I got back to Germany, and you know my health was actually spoilt. And this time I got a heavily heart attack and spent a long time in hospital.

Of course, in the barracks it was not nice. You had to expect all the time to be killed. It was sometimes they took somebody out from the room—it was just a house—and then you heard just some meters away the noise of shooting and then you've never seen them again. Or they brought him out to investigate. They would put fire on a plastic jerry can and drip it on his back to get informations from him, to martyr him. They did very heavily cruels. Most of the people never survived. They castrated them and everything! Blinded them and so on . . . It was a time, it was really a . . . I haven't seen such cruels . . . I have never seen such cruels like I have seen in this time . . .

*Brigadier General Basilio Olara Okello, 59, was the army commander in the Luwero Triangle for a period during Obote's regime. He was the principal leader of the July 1985 coup that installed General Okello Luttwa (no relation) as president. Basilio Okello was the commander-in-chief of the Ugandan army in that short-lived government, which was toppled by Yoweri Museveni and his NRA guerrillas in January 1986. Okello is now in exile in neighboring Sudan and is a driving force behind the guerrillas currently launching raids in northern Uganda.*

*The interview is held in the yard of Okello's large, peeling mansion on the banks of the Nile in Khartoum, the Sudanese capital. Okello, an imposing, gray-haired man with his two lower front teeth missing, is gracious but wary. Bare-chested, his arms and stomach are pocked with large round scars of unknown origin. He frequently defers questions to his younger and wilier aide, Dr. Anthony Oringa, a former brigade doctor and army major. Both men are members of the Acholi tribe from northern Uganda.*

JLA: Do you reject the charge that as many as three hundred thousand people were killed by the troops during Obote's regime? Or did it happen?

Okello: I would not agree with that at all. It was Museveni who carried out the activities of a guerrilla fighting Uganda. If there was no guerrilla activity, there would have been no war. What was the cause of Obote killing people? You've got to consider that. Why would there be killing in a country with no war? Because all of Uganda's problems were compounded by Museveni, who went to the bush.

Oringa: I want to add to that. This is where I think the world goes wrong, because the world does not know who is responsible. If the world would know that Museveni is to blame . . . and he started the war, huh? Fighting, fighting war until hundreds and hundreds of people were dying. And the world say, "Oh, it is Obote who is killing," "Oh, it is Basilio [Okello] who is killing." They do not even say one bad thing about Museveni doing that. Now, Museveni jumps to the bush, huh? Museveni assists the Baganda, "Let us fight these people; they are bad people. They don't like us, the Bantu." Using ethnism. After he has deceived these people, the very people who went along with him and he deceived, are now the people he has pushed in the prison.

Okello: The world has kept quiet. They have said nothing about it. Now, let me ask you one question, this question of Obote. You are the leaders of the country, and someone went to the bush. And they have laid an ambush in the road, where people are dead, military are dead, civilian are dead. And then the personalities there who fired on the vehicle are there inside the bush. What action are you going to take? Are you suggesting these people have the right to do things like that?

JLA: No. But the reports were that there were civilian massacres.

Okello: Yeah, civilians were massacred, but—

Oringa: And I would like to add that guerrillas have no uniforms.

Okello: There are no uniforms.

Oringa: How are you going to go into a guerrilla area and say this is a guerrilla and this is not a guerrilla? I'd like to hear. Museveni has got children in his army, this tall (gestures)! How are you going to leave a child and you are sure he is not a guerrilla also? You will have to tell me! Museveni put children in his army, mothers, young girls. These people, if you met them in a troubled area, what would you do with them?

JLA: I don't know. What would you do?

Oringa: If you met them in a troubled area, an area with a land mine, what would you do?

Okello: And he had a gun.

Oringa: And they have no uniforms.

JLA: I suppose you're expecting me to say you would have to shoot them.

Okello: Are you going to arrest a gunman?

JLA: Let me turn the question back to you, since you are a military person. Say this is a village and there's a nine-year-old kid there with a gun. What would you do?

Okello: Let me answer you. I may watch his activities. If he stands like that, I warn him to drop the gun down. And I go to pick up the gun to ask him how he gets it. If he's hiding in the cover, I will shoot him before he shoots me. I think that's obvious.

JLA: OK, but were there situations where troops came to a village and thought it was a Museveni village so they just wiped it out?

Okello: Not that I remember.


*The offices of the leftist daily* Telecast *are reached by a climb up a grimy back-alley stairwell; the approach is clogged with garbage and mud. Paul Kyesitalo, thin and gaunt, is one of the paper's editors. He has watery eyes and his hacking cough seems contagious. His younger colleague, Alfred Okware, 25, is quiet, healthy and dogmatic. At one point the interview in the dingy, paper-strewn office is interrupted by a Soviet correspondent for* Novosti. *He invites them to a Soviet embassy book exhibit and hands them a news bulletin for use in their paper.*


Kyesitalo: Well, all I can say is that we are a little bit luckier that the new president of this country has at least managed to make the biggest number of tribes rally behind him. Those who have rejected to rally behind him are those who identify themselves with those fascist groups of Basilio [Okello's], and those are the ones who are trying to fight desperately in the north.

Okware: The NRM [National Resistance Movement] government has got one thing the others haven't, its ability to maintain discipline with the soldiers. People of this country have been tortured, they have been killed, by undisciplined armies. But I believe that before we can attain a unified nation, this country will maybe have to go through some fifty or so years of turmoil.

Kyesitalo: Yeah! Turmoil is on the way. It hasn't ended.

Okware: Stability may set in temporarily, but instability is the norm. Instability. I think in the growth of a nation, instability is more permanent than stability.

JLA: They say as many as three hundred thousand may have died in the Luwero Triangle. Did those deaths merit this change in government?

Kyesitalo: Of course. Even one million people would have died in this struggle for the government to be changed. We expected it to be more than that, because these were governments which had deeply entrenched themselves.

What happened in the Triangle is now what is happening in the north, because these people have also removed uniforms. They are running through the bush with guns and they come and ambush the government troops and they run away. Now, how will the government troops handle such a situation?

JLA: Through massacres?

Kyesitalo: No, we don't expect that—

Okware: But we can't rule out the possibility, if war and the fight there escalate. But the tendency is less likely, because this army is not based on tribal grounds, so it is not likely to kill because of tribal animosity. But, like everybody when it is faced with a threat, they have to use maximum military force.

JLA: If it comes to that and massive numbers of people are killed, will you continue to support this government?

Kyesitalo: Of course!

JLA: Even if three hundred thousand are killed?

Kyesitalo: Of course!

Okware: How the people are being killed is the question. . . .

*Expatriate:*

I'm due to leave soon for two, three years, and then . . . I don't know if I'll come back. . . . I'll be sixty-five and . . . oh yes, if there was peace and security, of course. If it was peaceful, there'd be no problem. The country would go up . . . it's so fertile, you know. But, oh, I don't know. . . .

It's the people. They have changed. I think it's a legacy of Amin, the shortages and material things. The other day when there was raiders, the boys at the college here ran, left their things. And when they came back—nothing. It was all gone. And it was the people! It wasn't the raiders who took their things! It's become a way of life. . . .

Now, when I'm driving, I don't pick the people up. They say, "Oh, but you're a missionary; you're supposed to help me." And I tell them, "No, I've been here too long, and you people have taught me your customs."

*The remote northeastern corner of Uganda is the Karamoja, the desert home of the primitive Karamajong tribe whose young warriors sally forth every year during the "raiding season" to rustle the cattle of neighboring tribes. The area has also become the sanctuary for Uganda's defeated armies.*

*In late 1986, the Karamajong's raids began to extend far beyond their previous limit and included assaults on large towns and government garrisons. This new pattern, marked also by an unaccustomed brutality, has caused many to believe that rebel soldiers, led by such exiles as Brigadier General Basilio Olara Okello, have teamed up with the Karamajong and that the attacks signal the beginning of a new round of civil war.*

*Its dangers were made frighteningly plain to us en route to the area. Just past the small town of Mukura we were caught in a brief but vicious crossfire between NRA soldiers and a raiding party.*

*In the heartland of the raiders' expanded target area is the rambling community of Gweri. It lies only a few miles from the Teso District capital of Soroti, where the government mans an army garrison.*

*The interview with the Gweri parish chief, 31-year-old John Benson Okodel, takes place hours after raiders have hit the primitive village of rounded mud huts. Like other survivors, Okodel has just emerged, sweating and nervous, from hiding in the nearby swamp. Nearby, an old naked woman, called simply Salima, lies dying in the sun. Neighbors, who seem afraid to touch her, say the raiders beat her and threw her there. Dehydrated and delirious, Salima will die in a matter of hours. Inside one of the huts at a family compound, women are keening over two young men lying dead on bloody straw mats. Okodel translates for the mourning family.*

JLA:  Who are these dead people?

Okodel:  Vincent Oterega, twenty-five years old.

JLA:  And this boy here?

Okodel:  He is Martin Ajalo, about twenty years.

JLA:  How were they killed?

Okodel:  By gunshot. They were killed by gun—you can see there.

(walking on through village path with Chief Okodel)

JLA:  You have lost cows, as well?

Okodel:  Yes. They have taken! My father's also they have taken. Saucepans, clothes, nets, beds, what! Everything of the households!

JLA:  Do you think it's the Karamajong or other people doing this?

Okodel:  They are together! They speak different languages. And I understand, according to the rumors, they say that the *askaris* [soldiers] captured one Turkana [Kenyan tribesman].

(Further along the track is Michael Begu, 24, the local schoolteacher. He is the grandson of Salima, the old dying woman, and a cousin of the two dead men. At first, he is frightened at the sight of strangers.)

JLA:  What happened here exactly?

Begu:  These Karamojas came. We also . . . ran away. They got that old woman around [Salima], then they started beating her! And even killed two of our own brothers!

JLA:  Did they kill other people?

Begu: Yeah. They killed in some others places, even in Mugenya [nearby hamlet]. They killed a number of people.

JLA: Did they say things when they were looting and killing?

Begu: They never mention anything! The moment they come, they tell us, "You give us what we want! Where are animals? After, if you don't produce animals, we are killing you. . . . But if you don't produce animals, give us clothes and money if you have!" Plus saucepans and every so . . .

JLA: And afterwards you remained hiding?

Begu: I remained hiding somewhere, to move away from Gweri. Then I went to hide around the swamp there.

JLA: Why did they let you go?

Begu: They will only let you go if you produce something! When they hit you and you give them money and clothes, then they will allow you to go away. Or if you take them where there are cows, that is when they will leave you.

JLA: What were they dressed in?

Begu: There are some of them dressed in these sheets. Some of them come in shorts, just very poor shorts, and some come with coats, just coats!

JLA: How were they armed?

Begu: They had this G-3 [assault rifle] and Ensillah [Kalashnikov] and then spears and axes. Some of them are even in combat [uniform]! Especially those ones who are armed, they come in combat! The first group is always that one who is carrying arms! Then the second group will come with spears, axes—plus women who are to come and carry anything they get in your home. And young kids . . . Those who come for saucepans, plate, and money, most of them tie just pieces of cloth around their waist. They are women mostly.

(Entering Olelai village, an extension of Gweri. Here, one hut is burned to the ground, and in another a man, Christopher Gulo, lies dead. His family is fearful and silent. They pull back the sackcloth covering the body. His skin has melted. Behind the hut, some of his brothers are digging his grave.)

Okodel: They came and found that man. Then they shot him! After shooting, then they collected grass and burnt him! This is (motions to assembled people) his father and family. . . .

JLA: (to one of the men) Are you his brother?

Man: (steps forward) Yes. I am Vinandi Wawire.

JLA: What happened?

Wawire: These Karamajongo, they came at night where we went to sleep. They reach here, they started to take these cows (points to an empty cattle stockade made of thornbushes). They go to asking people, "Where's the cows, where's the cows?", and they start to beat people to take off their clothes. Some of the women also, they take their clothes and money, money is also taken! They have broken everything in my house there (points to a hut).

JLA: What did you lose?

Wawire: Twenty, twenty cows. And . . . my clothes, also taken!

JLA: (to Chief Okodel) How many raiders did they see?

Okodel: They came in abundance! Two groups they came. This one (gestures to another brother of Gulo) say four wanted to at least shoot him, but then he survived. They wanted to shoot him, but then he fell down. That's how he survived, or otherwise . . . with his child there . . . so they caught his wife and they started beating the wife and then they started with them . . . butt of the gun at the back [of the neck] and all is gone of his! Clothes, everything—money! Three hundred thousand shilling [about forty dollars]! All his radios!

(Further on, in Mugenya village, another dead body lies bloating in a hut. Two male relatives are standing guard.)

JLA: What is this dead man's name?

Okodel: Agiripinyo Odekenya. They (points to relatives) say that they all ran away, but on their way back to this place that is when they kill him. They shot him in the backbone here and then the blood got out from him.

*At an army roadblock on the outskirts of Soroti, the strutting, 22-year-old sergeant in command, resplendent in mirrored sunglasses, gold braid, and swagger stick, is gossiping with Jimmy, our young driver from Kampala, who listens to the soldier in rapt admiration. They are leaning against a car in the front yard of a British missionary. The 13-year-old son of the missionary's houseboy stands barefoot nearby, listening. Just the day before, raiders from the Karamoja struck several communities and missions around Soroti, killing people and rustling hundreds of cattle. The soldier is turning back all vehicles attempting to leave Soroti to the east; the raiders, in retreat, are engaged in combat with the NRA an hour down the road.*

Soldier: Let them come to us, rather than harming people. For us, we are ready to work with the Karamajongos. But most of them disturbing people are from the remote, remote areas. They are still like animals. Barefooted, moving naked. They come through the bush like animals. . . . and how can you make such a life?

Jimmy: They don't have house?

Soldier: They don't have house! They put up in the bush.

Jimmy: Like animals!

Soldier: Yes! (look of disgust) They don't mind the water, rain, or what and what. They depend on blood and milk!

Jimmy: Blood of cows!?

Soldier: Yes!

Boy: (softly) They are just nomads.

Soldier: You will find that these people are collaborating with other people somewhere, spotting the cows, somewhere abroad. You can't know. Moving cows, travelling with other things which I can't understand . . . Human beings staying in the bush!

Boy: And they drink blood instead of water, of cows.

Jimmy: They don't drink water!?

Boy: They drink water, but they are not interested in drinking water. But they drink blood.

Jimmy: Instead of water!?

Boy: Yes.

Soldier: The fresh one!?

Boy: (nods) The fresh one.

Soldier: Have you ever seen them?

Boy: Yes, I've seen.

Soldier: (suspiciously)Whereabouts?

Boy: We lived there before, in the north.

Soldier: They are making the banditry, a sort of banditry, but they are wasting their time! Because this is not a good place to make banditry. Nowhere they can escape.

Jimmy: No place! Nowhere! Ah!

Soldier: They are wasting their time! Here we have arrested so many, removing guns from them! So many! Huh!

Boy: They come sometimes with the camels, for carrying their things.

Jimmy: The Karamoja have got camels!?

Boy: Yes.

Jimmy: Where did they get it!?

Boy: We don't know where.

Jimmy: These are not people!

Boy: It used to be a sort of a game, but now it is dangerous.

Jimmy: It is dangerous!

Boy: They have guns now. But that time when they are using spears . . .

Soldier: Even in the earlier regime the Karamajongos were disturbing people. For us, we are trying to bring them to us so that we work together.

Boy: You should take them something—*posho* and bean—because Moroto is a dry area; if you leave them, the population will just continue coming this way because they have nowhere to grow. That is the most important reason why they come and fight, because they don't have anything to eat.

(Soldier, looking displeased, turns away and walks over to his men at the nearby roadblock.)

*"Amos" is the pseudonym of a young merchant in a town near Soroti, in the eastern Teso district bordering Karamoja. The day before, Amos's roadside town was hit by raiders. He and many other local Teso tribesmen are suspicious of the current Ugandan government and believe it may actually be carrying out*

*the attacks in their homeland. The interview is in the dusty back room of Amos's*
*shop. Most of the rest of the townspeople are fleeing due to rumors that the raiders*
*are preparing a second attack. He wishes, for his own security, to remain*
*anonymous.*

JLA:  You think it's the government soldiers who are actually doing the raiding?

Amos:  We think so. We think so. Because people who have seen these people
who raid, they have seen them in uniform. And this uniform is the military uniform
of this government.

JLA:  And why would they do this?

Amos:  Oh, we don't understand it. It could be a political reason.

JLA:  What political reason?

Amos:  Um . . . this place we are in, which is the eastern region, was an area of
strong support of the ex-president Milton Obote, and of that party, UPC. So I think,
since the government's aware of this, they believe the tribe of the Iteso can possibly
give aid to the ex-president to come back. So, for that reason, the government
knows the Iteso has got one strength, and that is the animals [cattle], and if the
animals are removed from them, they become weaker. That is the belief we have.

We have also heard that the westerners, which is where the president [Museveni]
comes from, would like us also to suffer, like the Luwero Triangle some time back.
I know how bad the situation was there, so they would like it to happen here. They
believe that the tribe of the Itesos have never suffered. We have been enjoying all
throughout. . . . That is what we hear. . . .

JLA:  Is there a difference between these raids and the traditional Karamajong
raids?

Amos:  There is a big difference. Because from Karamoja up to here is about
130 miles. Can you believe that a raider can go as far as 130 miles on foot and reach
to this area? It's impossible! They used to raid the area that was next to them,
twenty-mile radius. But now they have extended to two districts, Soroti and Kumi.
It means this man must be sure of his power! He must be sure of his position!

Also, this is not the traditional raiding. The traditional raiding, it used to be by
spears. You could expect a few local-made guns by the Karamajong, but the guns
that are being used now are guns that are being used by the government as well. So
we are wondering as to how these people have managed to take these guns. . . .

JLA:  What is life like here normally? What was it like during the previous
regimes?

Amos:  Life has been quite very good indeed. Because in the past we have been
free! Secondly, we have been having enough peace! You could travel anywhere
without any difficulty. We used to be free! We used to have plenty of commodities
and everything. But now we live under fear! You can't travel for long distances,
because you feel something will happen and you get you far away from your
family.

JLA: All along the road from Soroti to here I saw people fleeing. Why today?

Amos: They still believe the raiders will come back, as usual. Because once these people have come, they will have to repeat! By all means they will come. By all means it will come even worse than this! It's the first time that they come to this area. If they are going to come for a second time, it will be worse! Because they will be hungry. They did not get the cows; people have tried to drive some animals away. So they will be angry about it and perhaps even kill people. So people are fleeing away because of that fear.

JLA: But are you planning to stay?

Amos: I don't plan to stay. I am trying to find a way out where I can go live somewhere also, at least until things go down.

JLA: This place was raided yesterday. Was your home or shop raided?

Amos: It was not raided. At this time they were not after commodities or things around, they were particularly after animals. But I understand it's during the second raid that they come and look for things like clothes, what have you, like that. That would be the second raid coming up. That is what I fear.

JLA: What do you hope will happen now?

Amos: Right now, we are so blind, we don't understand, we don't know what to do. We ask whether we shall get any peace or we shan't get any peace at all!

JLA: If the people of this area believe it is the government raiding and killing them, will they rise up?

Amos: They will. They will definitely.

JLA: But they are not armed.

Amos: No. We are looking for any external help that we can receive, because we are getting weaker and weaker all the time. We are getting helpless. We really have no hope. We are just hopeless. There is no progress that we see. The price of things are going higher and higher day by day. The common man is not happy. He's not having any good experience. Life . . . life's just too, too sad. So, as far as the eastern region is concerned, we are looking for external help so that we can be relieved of this problems. Otherwise, we shall remain hopeless for a very long time.

*Expatriate:*

You get all these rumors. I mean, like yesterday, the rumor was there was an absolute bloodbath, there had been a big battle upcountry, up in Moroto area between the Karamajong and the NRA. And the NRA was getting the worse of it until they moved some helicopters and machine guns in from Mbale. And they used this on the Karamajong, and this is something new to them. I mean, a spear, they're not scared of that, but a helicopter . . . well, they were massacred.

Now, Norman—you know Norman, don't you?—well, all his place was completely flattened. And all the guys that worked up there, local people up there, they've all died. Because when the Karamajong were coming in or something, the NRA led these people out into the front lines and then, of course, the helicopters came over and so . . . He said villages and everything were wiped out there. They have cleaned villages off the face of the earth! There's just piles of Karamajong up there!

Maybe it's a good thing you didn't get up there today, because, I'll tell you, I think things are bloody bad enough in Kampala. The stories we hear of the amount of . . . Somebody was stopped at the roadblock last night, maybe two nights ago, and they asked "What have you got in this great big box in back?" and he says, "I don't know. They made me take this box." And they lifted it down and it seems it was packed—if you can believe; as I say, if you believe half of what you hear—but it was packed to the top with men's penises, women's breasts, and what have you. Packed!

And they were going to shoot him and he said, "I had nothing to do with it. They made me take it." But you see, you hear, and there must be something in it, because they've got buggers in the army and they've got buggers in the government.

*William Mubiri, 41, is the stocky colleague of Charles Kabuye at the British-American Insurance Company in downtown Kampala. An accountant, Mubiru is also the secretary for the resistance committee in his home village just outside Kampala.*

My role in the community is to teach these people to know their rights. I try my best to teach them to realize that they are the holders of the power. And this is the first time they are having that experience; they can decide on matters affecting them, which has never before been the case.

My role as one of the leaders is to encourage them to bring in as many ideas as possible. At the same time, if they see anything wrong, they should point it out, because this will be for their own good and this is how they will improve their area. If the village is okay, then the councils will be okay. So this is where the resistance committees draw their power, being backed up by the masses who elected them. I think it is a very good idea.

The eventual plan could be to give everyone guns. They will start with the resistance committees. That man will be taken for training, and then he knows definitely that the gun is not something to be used for violence but as a means of protection. Then after they have been politicized with these political schools, under the guidance of the Museveni government, a few young men will be taken and given this knowledge, how to handle a gun, how to use it for the defense of the village, and eventually it will go on spreading until perhaps everyone will have guns.

Once the resistance committees are really effective, they are supposed to be the eyes of the government, right from the grassroots. No evildoer will be able to rise, because he will be among us and we will notice. He won't be able to hide there, because we know him.

*The office of the Uganda Human Rights Activists [UHRA] is a building on a residential street in central Kampala. On the walls of the reception room are posters: "Love One Another For Peace," "We Want Peace, Not War." On one wall is a horrific doomsday painting of soldiers shooting villagers, and screaming people. In the center of the painting is a face, half man, half skull. The painting itself is framed by two human skulls set atop a bookshelf. One of them has a deep straight gash, apparently from a* panga *[machete] blow.*

*In his dark office, Sera Mwanga, a beefy, mustachioed man in his early thirties, sits on a tattered, lumpy couch. The Secretary General of the UHRA, Mwanga fled Uganda in 1973 after his prominent brother was murdered by Amin's troops. He was an early supporter of Museveni and worked secretly for his cause while in exile in Sweden, before returning to Uganda in 1986.*

If somebody doesn't know his rights, he can't even claim them. And if he doesn't know how to claim them, he's bound to use violence, because it comes out of instincts. And these instincts, if they are not trained, they always end up in a mess.

You take these infant soldiers. I don't know what future they have. These kids have been exposed to killings. They themselves have taken part in killings, and I wonder if they can ever depart from that. It will remain part of their life.

It has made the precedence that to achieve something you want, you have to use violence, that the barrel of the gun can even lead to leadership. Then people come to realize that in leadership is where you become well-off. I've seen people driving very expensive vehicles, having nice homes, and traveling abroad, and that through being in power.

I think for us [of the UHRA office], we have taken some courage even to operate. I know that we should be grateful to this government for allowing us to work, but at the same time they have committed this country to a human rights declaration. That means they are wishful for human rights, and that means, of course, they must allow a countercheck of their activities.

But, as you know, at times it is so difficult to accept criticisms or accusations. We know they are faced with their problems and, by the way, I can say that there have been a lot of improvement, but . . . shortcomings started slowly and slowly until now we are approaching a wider gap. There are human-rights abuses today. Some people ask me to what level, and I say, "Well, it is too early to say that." But there are violations, oh yes.

The violence in the beginning, that came as revenge. One could give an allowance of a new regime coming in—you know, you can't control all of your people. So they really carried out a lot of revenges here and there, but we could give that allowance, really, for two or three months when one is not in full control. You can say it's all right. But after that, the violations must be seen as part of a plan. Those attacks is what we condemn. Because the same methods we were accusing Obote to have applied in Luwero area, Museveni has chosen to use. We feel it will just put us back in the vicious circle.

What is happening now is a matter of rotation. Now it is in the north. Next, the north is going to go after the west. Those people are going to revenge. They are going to clean! Because it is their turn now, their turn in power, their turn to revenge.

This is going to happen in the north. If you come back after some years you will see the same wars, simply because it has been a change, a short change, a change maybe . . . of the wind. Those people there are suffering. In the Luwero they suffered, their relatives died, but what about those dying now today? It's the same thing.

Unless a solution comes about, it's not worth even giving any sympathy to us Ugandans. It is not worth it, because it's too early. It's better you wait until the whole thing will be over, and then you can come back and say, "Oh, my goodness, look what happened here."

*In February 1987, Sera Mwanga was arrested by the Museveni government. As of November 1987, he was still being held without charge.*

*Brigadier General Basilio Olara Okello is one of the leaders of the rebel forces fighting the Museveni government.*

SA: So will the bloodbath continue?
Okello: That one I cannot answer. That depends on the people of Uganda—how they have suffered, how they enjoy it, how their peace will come—not myself. If it was myself, it shall continue until we attain democracy.

# Sri Lanka:
# Burying the Future

The women of Batticaloa clutch photographs of their missing sons, tears falling from tired, bloodshot eyes. In small groups they cluster outside the offices of the Catholic bishop or the local human rights group awaiting a turn to tell of their loss, prostrating themselves before the feet of anyone they think might help them. Others seem to recognize the futility of these gestures: they kneel on the long expanse of green grass before the cathedral and hold aloft the photographs of their loved ones, softly crying to God for intervention. But there is no intervention; the men of Batticaloa are disappearing, and no one can do more than watch and keep record of their passing.

The war that has wrenched Sri Lanka since 1983 has been felt throughout this island, but most harshly in areas like Batticaloa, where the Tamils, the nation's largest minority, are concentrated. In the northern and eastern provinces, where Tamil militants are fighting for independence, the Sri Lankan government has launched a terrifying "antiterrorist" campaign. The result is a civilian population under siege from both sides.

Once an important fishing community on a coastal lagoon of eastern Sri Lanka, Batticaloa today is desolate and eerie. Police stations have been transformed into bunkers, ringed with barbed wire, sandbags, and high walls. The heavily armed Special Task Force commandos patrol the streets from the relative safety of armored trucks. After dusk, Batticaloa is deserted; there is no official curfew, but the curfew of fear—of drawing the fire of jumpy commandos, of being detained and tortured as a suspected "terrorist"—is just as effective.

The villagers in the countryside fare worse. When the police commandos raid a village, a thousand Tamils will be picked up for interrogation. While most are released within a day or two, many end up in prison camps without charges. Still others are "disappeared," executed by the police, their bodies burnt. Since 1983, over seven hundred Tamil men have disappeared in the Batticaloa area.

But the people can hardly turn to the Tamil guerrillas for salvation. Based in a hidden camp ten miles away, the local detachment of the Liberation Tigers of Tamil Eelam, now the dominant Tamil separatist group, has degenerated into banditry. The Tigers appear to devote much of their energies inflicting suffering on those they claim to represent; they demand "taxes" from Tamil civilians, kidnap and ransom Tamil businessmen, and execute others they suspect of being spies.

The young men of the area must choose between terrible alternatives. They can stay in their villages and endure the roundups of the security forces. Or they can join the guerrillas and risk death in battle. Or they can run. Many have taken this last option, fleeing across the Palk Straits to India in small boats, braving the guns of Sri Lankan patrol boats. The result of it all is the virtual destruction of a Tamil generation.

If there is such a thing as a logical war zone, Sri Lanka surely isn't it. Set in the warm waters of the Indian Ocean, its palm-lined beaches of white sand are a vacationer's dream. The fertile flatlands have been terraced into rubber plantations and rice paddies, rising to the tea plantations of the mountainous central highlands. Everywhere are reminders of the confluence of civilizations and religions. Colossal brick pagodas, built in the third century B.C. by the Buddhist kings, soar above dense foliage. Ornate Hindu *kovils*, ornamented with Vishnu and Ganesh, the Elephant God, are found alongside mosques and Christian churches. The island of fifteen million people is a mélange of ethnic groups, Sinhalese, Tamil, Arabic, and Dutch, practicing Buddhism, Hinduism, Christianity, and Islam. This ethnic and religious pluralism is the root of both Sri Lanka's vitality and its violence.

The island of Ceylon is the homeland of the Sinhalese, an ethnic group quite different from the Tamils of neighboring southern India. In the third century B.C., the Sinhalese wholeheartedly embraced the "new" religion of Buddhism and a great Buddhist culture flourished. Symbolic of the strength of that faith is the sacred Bo Tree in Anuradhapura, a seedling from the original tree under which Buddha meditated, lovingly tended by monks for two thousand years.

Periodic invasions by the expansionist Hindu Tamils of India pushed the Sinhalese farther south on the island. While the invaders were eventually defeated and sent back across the Palk Straits to India, some Tamils stayed and settled in the arid north and junglelike east. The modern descendants of those settlers are Sri Lanka's three million "northern" Tamils, and, to many Sinhalese, the war today represents but another thinly disguised Indian invasion. Here is the deadly riddle of the nation: the Tamils feel a persecuted minority on an island of Sinhalese, and the Sinhalese feel a persecuted minority within the larger geographical context.

With the arrival of colonialism, first by the Portuguese and Dutch and then by the British, the ethnic divisions were heightened. When the British discovered that the cool central highlands of the island were ideal for growing tea, they imported tens of thousands of new Indian Tamils to work on the plantations, as the Sinhalese, living in a fertile and abundant land, were not overly attracted to the slave wages being offered. In time, these Plantation Tamils grew to number nearly a million, further fueling the Sinhalese fears of Tamil absorption. Ultimately even more contentious was Britain's divide-and-rule policy, through which the northern Tamil minority became the prime beneficiaries of education and government employment opportunities while the majority Sinhalese lagged behind.

With independence in 1948, the Sinhalese prime ministers, as representatives of the island's seventy-five percent majority, sought to quickly rectify the legacy of Tamil favoritism; the Tamils trace the onset of Sinhalese discrimination from that date.

First, the proportional imbalances in education and government jobs had to be corrected. Laws were enacted to ensure that Sinhalese had greater access to land, schools, and employment. Many of the Plantation Tamils were either repatriated to India or made stateless by the first government of independent Ceylon. Quotas were established for university admission examinations according to ethnic ratio; through this policy of "standardization," Tamils needed to score higher marks than their Sinhalese counterparts to gain entry. Thousands of Sinhalese settlers, sponsored by the government, moved into and occupied vast tracts of land in the predominantly-Tamil Eastern Province, diluting Tamil authority and political power. Perhaps most galling to the Tamils was the Sinhala Only Act, a decree born of fevered nationalism that made Sinhala the official language, replacing English.

The disenfranchised Tamils sought redress through their opposition political parties and in public demonstrations modeled on Mahatma Gandhi's nonviolent principles. On several occasions, these peaceful protests were broken up by the force of the Sinhalese army or police force. At other times, Sinhalese mobs went on rampages in which Tamil enclaves were looted and destroyed and Tamils beaten or hacked to death.

In the 1970s, radical Tamil youths, incensed over the legislated double standards and contemptuous of the Tamil political parties' vain attempts to obtain reforms from within the system, turned to violence. Inspired by a variety of Marxist and national liberation movements, the militants began to organize and to receive military training and weapons from abroad. Some of the first Tamil "cadres" were trained by Palestinian guerrillas in Lebanon, while thousands more were drilled in camps in southern India. The struggle for these disparate and fractious groups was no longer to seek redress but a separatist war to establish a new nation, Tamil Eelam.

The war truly began in July 1983, when the Liberation Tigers of Tamil Eelam killed thirteen soldiers in a land-mine explosion. The ambush sparked off three days of wild anti-Tamil rioting throughout the island. Sinhalese mobs pillaged and burned entire Tamil neighborhoods, killing any Tamil they could find. Throughout, the government remained curiously inactive; when it was finally galvanized into action, at least four hundred Tamils had been slaughtered.

The 1983 riots spawned an enormous population shift on the island, with thousands of Tamils fleeing towns in the south and west, where they had lived for generations, to take refuge among their own kind in the north and east. Since then, the violence has led to a massive Tamil exodus from the island itself; as many as three hundred thousand have fled abroad as refugees.

The bloodletting, and the government's perceived complicity in it, gave the

Tamil militants a popular support they had previously lacked, as well as the impetus to embark on a full-scale guerrilla war. Operating out of training and supply bases in south India, the separatists attacked with a viciousness. With stunning speed, the Tigers, the strongest of the groups, came to have virtual control of the northern Jaffna peninsula, home of nearly a million Tamils.

But the Tigers have spent nearly as much time fighting fellow Tamils as they have the government. Wrapping themselves in the cloth of a socialist national liberation movement, the Tigers have liquidated two rival Tamil groups, murdered several moderate Tamil politicians, and waged a campaign of "lamppost killings" in which suspected spies or government sympathizers are tied to lampposts and executed.

The Tigers appear to be as rigid with themselves as they are with others; their fighters are made to carry cyanide capsules attached to a thong around their necks, to be bitten into in case of capture. Once dead, the loyal cadres enter their own roster of martyrdom, immortalized on wall posters and graffiti.

When they are not ambushing fellow guerrillas and government soldiers, the Tigers frequently carry out "retaliatory punishment" for army atrocities by massacring Sinhalese civilians. On one morning in May 1985, a Tiger unit killed over one hundred and fifty civilians in the sacred Buddhist city of Anuradhapura. In February 1986, they attacked two Sinhalese villages in eastern Amparai district, killing forty-three men, women, and children by hacking them to death with knives, axes, and swords. An allied group, EROS, is better known for placing bombs in public places. In June 1986, it blasted Colombo's main post office, killing a number of civilians. The same day, it set off a bomb aboard an Air Lanka passenger plane, killing a score of foreign tourists. The actions of these groups have caused many, including Tamils, to agree with the government's definition of them as "terrorists."

The government, however, has itself reacted brutally and, often, murderously. Led by an octogenarian president, J.R. Jayewardene, who has ruled Sri Lanka since 1977, the government has quintupled the size of the military, contracted foreign mercenaries and introduced repressive emergency laws under which anyone suspected of terrorist involvement can be detained for eighteen months without charges or a trial. As many as three thousand Tamils are held in Boosa, a prison camp in the south. For many of those picked up in the sweeps of the specially created paramilitary Special Task Force, torture is almost a certainty.

Today, there is at least hope for an end to a war that has taken at least seven thousand lives. Jayewardene's government has held round-table peace talks with most Tamil groups, mediated by the Indian government of Rajiv Gandhi. Facing an often restive Tamil population of fifty million of his own, Gandhi is eager for a negotiated settlement.

Even if peace comes soon, the effect of the war on this once-idyllic island will be felt for decades. Tourism, the nation's third-largest foreign earner five years ago, has virtually vanished. The huge expenditures for the military have diverted money from social welfare projects and energized a resurgence of leftist activism among the Sinhalese. The cost to the Tamil minority, however, has been the highest. A generation is being lost, to the government detention camps, to the guns of the security forces and Tamil militants, and to the diaspora of India and Europe.

For all Sri Lankans, their society has been riven in two, and for the neighbors who found they couldn't get along anymore, there is no going back.

*The senior Sri Lankan government official, in his fifties, is relaxing with a bottle of arrack coconut whiskey on a hot afternoon.*

Nobody sees our problem. We are just a few Sinhalese, but the Tamils are millions, here and in South India. We have nowhere else to go. But they! They can go wherever they want! They can go to India—where are so many—they can go all over the world—to England, to West Germany, to Sweden! Everyone will take the Tamils.

But if something happens here, will anyone take the Sinhalese? This is the only place we are! We don't have people all over the world, like the Tamils do. We don't have a mother country like India! We only have this little island! Who will take me, a Sinhalese? I must live and die on this island! No one else will save the Sinhalese. Where can I go?

Everybody listens to the Tamils' problems, but does no one see that for us, the Sinhalese Buddhists, it is a problem of survival? It is the perishing of a race. . . . If we wanted to, we could wipe out the Tamils in an hour or two. But we haven't done that, because we are Buddhists. We are patient, and, maybe it's bad, but we have this thing we believe in . . . karma, that this is the way things are destined to be, but the Tamils don't.

So this is why many people, many Sinhalese, are angry with the government, because in '83 they didn't let them finish off the Tamils. If we had, there would be no problem today. We are seventy-six percent; they are seventeen! In one, two hours, the problem would be over. But no; the government said anyone found doing this would be shot. So you can imagine the anger; the Sinhalese know the Tamils want to finish them off, and their own government will kill them if they defend themselves!

Don't you see? It's not just the country, it's the survival of a race, our history, our culture. This is what is at stake. But nobody sees this.

*Gunewardene is a Sinhalese civil engineer from Colombo.*

I don't blame anybody. It's a misunderstanding, a misunderstanding between two communities. What happened in '83, the mob violence, that was a problem of the government; that is what I believe. How could that have happened in the biggest city of Sri Lanka, the most secure place? You have the police, national security, air force, army, navy, everything is there! But they did nothing for three days!

JLA: Did it shock you, as a Sinhala, to see other Sinhalese turn to mob violence?

Gunewardene: It did, sir! It did! I was out of Colombo, but came in that next morning. It was not the city I knew; hate filled the city! There was a lot of looting. People had robbed the Tamils' shops and were going through our neighborhood selling what they had stolen. A person came to our door with a bolt of cloth and wanted to sell it for a fraction of its cost. And I told my wife, "No! You are not buying it! Nothing that has been stolen will be allowed into my house!"

What I will always regret in my life is that our honor, our country, our religion, what I hold important in life, was disgraced. I had a friend; he was from Jaffna, a Tamil. He was a builder, doing very well, highly educated, accomplished, lived in a very nice house and all that. They went to his house and took him and his four sisters and killed them. Burned their bodies. I cannot forgive the Sinhalese for that. He was a good friend of mine and he was a nice man.

*The raucous city of Madras is capital of the south Indian state of Tamil Nadu, with a population of fifty million ethnic Tamils. Here also live tens of thousands of Sri Lankan Tamil refugees. Cramped together in rented homes in Madras's back streets, ghettos, and in refugee camps, these victims of the Sri Lankan conflict flow into India by the hundreds weekly. Some of the lucky have found refuge in other countries, notably West Germany, Canada, and Sweden, but the torrent is so great that most have now closed their doors to Sri Lankans.*

*A cottage industry of "travel agents" has sprung up around the lucrative refugee trade. In return for mortgaged land, pawned valuables, and cash, they recruit prospective emigrants and install them in crowded Madras transit houses, covering their minimal expenses with a food stipend they must pay back, and obtain visas and passports, often stolen or forged, for them to travel. Some of the refugees eventually reach a foreign country, where they then work to pay back the patron agents' loans. But others are caught with the false documents and are deported back to the hopelessness of India. Many are swindled by the more disreputable agents, and never leave Madras.*

*One of the refugee houses, on a working-class Madras street, is run by a surly, drunken landlord. It is eight in the morning, and in the front room fifteen Tamil men and boys wait to leave. They have already been waiting for three months. Balachandra, 43, a wizened fisherman from Jaffna, is one of them.*

There became a strain in our country because the armed forces they are coming and searching us, they are catching, they are giving us problems. They came with the bombers bombing and they come shooting, by the land they are coming.

Before, I was a seaman. Now we are never to do this. Because the Navy has put in the sea, they've put along the sea, so nobody gets to catch the fish. When we push the boat, they'll come and shoot us. Now there are so many problems there, so we can't stay in our country. So we came here. I came recently; seven months.

SA: What do you hope to do now?

Balachandra: Now, I am going to go to Germany or Canada.

JLA: And your wife and children?

Balachandra: They are still there [in Sri Lanka]. When I go to any job I find, after six months or one year has passed, I will take my wife and children.

SA: How will you get to Germany?

Balachandra: I am waiting for the ticket to Germany. I am waiting.

SA: If the situation gets better, will you return to Sri Lanka?

Balachandra: When the peace comes, I can go back to Jaffna. If the army is not there, we can go back to our country. I don't want to spend my life in Germany. If peace comes, there is no bombing and no helicopters shooting, there is not nothing and everything is okay, then we can go back to our country.

SA: What do you think of the Sinhalese?

Balachandra: We can't live with them, because they don't represent the God.

*Kala is a large, smiling Tamil woman dressed in a violet sari. She lives in Batticaloa, a coastal city in eastern Sri Lanka.*

On principle, I won't leave the country. If those who can afford it leave the country, only the illiterate and the poor people will remain. So our integrity is lost. The Tamil race will be looked down on as laborers, because illiterate people will remain and the poor people will remain and the educated and wealthy people will migrate . . . and most of them are leaving now.

*He lounges majestically on the threadbare golden sofa, the gold brocade curtains behind him completing the effect of a throne room. Appapillai Amirthalingam, 59, is a husky, bespectacled man wearing a white dhoti, matching shirt, and gold watch. The balding head and sturdy, rotund figure give him the appearance of a mirthful Buddha.*

*The room is spacious, with chairs arrayed against the walls and toys in the corner for visiting grandchildren. On the peeling veranda of this "state guest house" in Madras, where Amirthalingam lives on invitation of the Indian state government, a sentry is poised with an old Lee-Enfield repeating rifle. Amirthalingam's wife moves through the room occasionally with a cordless phone;*

*her husband receives many calls in his role as the paterfamilias to Sri Lanka's Tamil exiles.*

*Amirthalingam was once the chief of the main Tamil political party in Sri Lanka, the Tamil United Liberation Front (TULF). While historically it sought to bring about reform within the existing political framework, in 1977 the TULF campaigned on a proindependence platform, winning a majority in the Tamil areas, but also inviting the anger and suspicion of the government. In the wake of the 1983 anti-Tamil riots, the government demanded a loyalty pledge; the TULF members refused and consequently were stripped of their parliamentary seats. Today, most TULF leaders are in exile, leaving the Tamils without any elected representation in Sri Lanka. Now the Sri Lankan government is reestablishing links to the Tamil moderates; Amirthalingam plays an important role in the negotiations between the Tamil separatists and the governments of Sri Lanka and India.*

I came here to Madras as a result of the '83 riots. You see, most of our houses were attacked and destroyed. In fact, I was leader of the opposition of the Sri Lanka Parliament, and my official residence in Colombo was attacked and, though it was a government house, the hoodlums attacked it and plundered everything—all my documents, my clothes, (chuckles) personal belongings. All were looted.

When the riots actually broke out in Colombo, we were having the annual convention of the TULF in Mannar, the northern city. In fact, in Mannar itself we would have been killed by the mobs, if not for some Tamil police officers who happened to be there who saved us and took us to a remote village about fifty miles away, to a place of hiding.

I wanted to come across to India, to meet Mrs. Gandhi and get India's support to put an end to the genocidal attacks that were going on against our people. So, actually (grins), I managed to get to Colombo under disguise and took a plane and came over to India in August '83.

To go to Colombo I had to go in disguise, or I might have been attacked on the way. I had to pass through Sinhala territory and, you know, I am easily identified— they all know me, having seen me on the television and my photograph in the newspapers and all that. I covered my bald head with a *toupee*, (laughs) and some of my friends helped me and took me across.

Now I am the guest of the government of Tamil Nadu state. This is the state guest house, and they have provided security and all facilities for me. Right from that time, I have been enjoying their hospitality. You would have noticed the sentry outside (laughs) and the security officers and all that, because they feel that there is a danger to me even here. They have provided that security, not that I asked for it.

The danger is also from the [Tamil] militants. In fact, that is some . . . a matter of . . . recent development; during the last year that situation came up. You see, newspapers published reports that there was a pending agreement between us and the Sri Lanka government on some solution. That provided an occasion for . . . some groups—for one particular group—to attack two of my colleagues and kill them in Jaffna. Two of my former Members of Parliament were killed on the second of September, '85. So, since that time, there is the danger . . .

Now, I think we have reached a stage when we have to finally decide whether a negotiated settlement is going to come through or we'll be thrown back to a protracted armed struggle. The longer this thing gets protracted, the more radicalized the youth are becoming. And also, frustration is leading to quite a number of our youth leaving the country. From four to five hundred thousand Tamils have left the shores of Sri Lanka. They are living as refugees in India and all over the world. In Western Europe, I am sure we must be having about a hundred thousand by now! And every day the youth are leaving. I do not know where they are going! Because judging from the number of young men who come to see me, to get letters that they may use for claiming to be refugees, I can see that every day, one hundred, two hundred young men are coming here to see me, to get letters from me! So if every day there is an exodus . . . this can't go on indefinitely!

My own son is a political exile. My eldest son. You see, he was one of those who . . . one of the pioneers in the militant youth movement at a time when I was a moderate parliamentary politician.

What happened was, in 1974 he was a student here in Madras, just seventeen years old at that time. There was a World Tamil Research Conference held at Jaffna; Tamil scholars from all over the world had come and participated. At the final meeting, where about fifty thousand people were assembled, the Sinhala police ran amok and nine Tamils were killed. That was when Mrs. Bandaranaike was prime minister, so when she came to Madras, my son, along with three other young men, got together and they bombed the deputy high commission, and he was arrested and prosecuted. But, of course, there was a general sympathy here; he pleaded guilty straightaway and some [minor] punishment was imposed.

But when he came back to Sri Lanka, the police started hunting him down. You see, the mayor of Jaffna, a Tamil gentleman but who was thought to have had some connection with the police and had played a part in that [1974] attack on the crowd, was shot and killed by the youth. The police thought my son was responsible for it and they made him the first accused in the case. But they could never arrest him. They came and surrounded my house with eighty-four truckloads of army, navy, and police personnel! Fortunately, my son was not there at that time. So he managed to get across illicitly to India, and some friend had sent a ticket so he went to UK [Great Britain] and claimed political asylum.

That was in '76. So he has been living there ever since. He can't go back to Sri Lanka. In fact, even in '79 when they published a list of thirty-two wanted militants, my son's picture was also published, though he had been living in London for three years.

He has now become a more moderate person; he is working with a TULF branch in London. As for me, my position has always remained the same. I don't believe in an armed struggle. I don't think that under the circumstances . . . Of course, our youth were forced to take arms.

You see, for nearly twenty-five years we struggled in a nonviolent way for our rights. From 1949 until 1976, we were agitating for a federal form of government and nonviolently we were educating. No one can say there was any element of violence; we adopted purely Gandhian methods.

In 1956, they introduced a law in Parliament making Sinhala the only language, in violation of an earlier agreement that both Sinhala and Tamil would be official languages. I had been elected to Parliament in 1956, and we protested nonviolently against that by having a sit-in opposite Parliament. With the prime minister Bandaranaike looking on from the balcony of Parliament, a crowd of about three, four thousand attacked us. My head was cracked in two places and I walked into Parliament with a handkerchief tied round my head and with my dress blood-stained. Bandaranaike tried to make a joke of it. He said, "Honorable wounds of war." (laughs)

That was the beginning of mob violence against Tamils. On that day, Tamils all over Colombo were pulled out of their vehicles and beaten up. And in the Eastern Province, where Sinhalese had been settling in the Tamil area, Tamil villagers were attacked by the new Sinhala settlers that night thirty years ago.

But still we continued our struggle in a nonviolent way. We had marches. We had civil-disobedience campaigns. In fact, I have been arrested and put in jail many times during the last thirty years of our nonviolent struggle. In 1961, we had a nonviolent campaign wherein we blocked all the government offices in the Northern and Eastern provinces and for fifty-seven days we paralyzed the entire administration in a nonviolent way. Ultimately, they brought out the army, beat up the people, and arrested all of us and locked us up in the army camp in Colombo. For six months, all the leaders were locked up, including my wife. And army violence was unleashed on our people.

So, whenever we agitated nonviolently, the Sinhala people and the armed forces reacted with violence. So the cumulative resentment that built up among the Tamil youth, the younger generation that grew up in this atmosphere, decided that they had to meet violence with violence. And the last straw that broke the camel's back was this World Tamil Research Conference in 1974 and the attack on the purely peaceful cultural meeting of Tamils by the Sinhala police. And then, of course, the youth, once they started taking to arms, they started attacking the policemen who were responsible for it. Tamils who had cooperated with these policemen were attacked. And the police retaliated by arresting young men at random and torturing them. This snowballed, and during the last twelve years it has grown to this position.

I don't believe in violence as a method of solving political problems—it creates more problems than it solves. That is what I think, but, (laughs) of course, under certain circumstances it may . . . in our case, it was purely defensive action. . . . But, nevertheless, it is bound to lead to other consequences, and today we are getting to a scale where our whole younger generation is getting more and more brutalized, which is revolting to our whole culture.

*The two bald-headed monks sit forward and talk easily and intensely, shifting the folds of their loose saffron robes occasionally. They nod peremptorily and are not distracted by acolytes who come edging by and prostrate themselves briefly on the concrete veranda before their feet. Birds sing and a cool breeze rustles the coconut palms in the swept garden of the Vairarama Temple in Colombo.*

*The Venerable Madihe Pannasiha is the chief prelate of Sri Lanka's Amarapura, or Burmese, sect of Buddhism. He is 73 and frail. He is accompanied by the Venerable Thera Piyadassi, a youthful, energetic 72, with a high, clear voice.*

Piyadassi: In Sri Lanka, we have four out of the five world religions. We have Buddhism, Hinduism, Christianity, Islam, not Judaism. There is religious harmony, all right. . . . They enjoy the religious freedom here very much. Very much. And our country's a very democratic country and our president and the prime minister are . . . Absolute freedom for all religions!

Now, what is happening in the north is nothing to do with religion, you see. It is political, hundred percent political. They tried to create trouble by saying, "A fight between Hindus and Buddhists."

And, you know, many Tamils, they are in the south. Plenty. They move about, you know? They are quite free and no trouble for them, and they are living a very harmonious life here. But no Sri Lankan–Sinhalese can go there to north now. You see?

But when you think of the Tamils, they also say, "We don't want the separation. We are living peacefully and harmoniously, and we don't want the separation." There's a few who do but, as you know, it is connected with South India, Tamil Nadu state. Their bases are there, they are trained there.

We all want peace, we are always calling for peace, you know. Colossal damage, you see? The destructions and the . . . you know, more than a million rupees for the military, government has to spend. All this from our progress . . . wastage of money and energy. It's a question of time and energy and destruction, colossal destruction, you see. In Jaffna! And this is well-known everywhere. They [Tamil militants] break bridges and they destroy our trains and engines . . . it's colossal damage! Colossal!

But definitely we are against separation. Definitely! All are against separation. And even the Tamils, they say, "We don't want separation." And some Tamils say, "We can't do anything in the north now." And they are losing, you see?

Our people, they are restless because they feel that they can't move about. We are here in the south, they say, but they don't know . . . at any moment, anything can happen. There could be a bomb. That happens. And really, in fear they live! When they go to the offices and institutions where they'll put a bomb or hand grenade, you see? This . . . is working in them. And they are threatened, you see?

And see, we don't want this . . . but you can't have the separation! This is a small country! How can you cut from this palm? (gestures with his own out-stretched hand) You can't cut the palm, you see? It's like a palm here! (laughs) Everything is upset, you see. No peace, really! No harmony!

JLA: Do you think they hate Buddhism?

Piyadassi: No, it's not a case of religion!

SA: You don't think it's religion, but there have been cases where Buddhist monks have been chosen as victims.

Piyadassi: In the north, yes. Because in that part of the country a monk has a say with the people, you know? When there is a temple and a monk, he has the say. Many people are obedient to him. So if they get rid of the monks, it's easy for them. When they remove the head person, then others are helpless.

Pannasiha: The trouble really started in 1957, in Jaffna.

The first lie that the Tamils said—that they were not being treated properly and that we were very unjust towards them, and that we had not done our duties towards them—that is the number-one lie they said. Because, at that time, the Chief Justice was Tamil. Attorney General was Tamil. Police Chief was Tamil, you see? Many people in government were Tamil. So it was very wrong to say that they have been ill-treated. This is number one, that we should make clear, that what they were saying was wrong.

To say that they have been ill-treated is a lie, and we have the statistics to prove that! We have statistics to say this is all wrong!

I suggest that there should not be a separation of the two, Sinhala and Tamil. They must mix! Already, the Tamils are living in this part of the country, no problem at all. They are moving about, you see, unharmed. So what I suggest is that Sinhalese also should go and mix up there, in the north. Otherwise, you separate, then start all conflicts. Even slowly, we have to do this: otherwise this quarrel, this struggle, will go on forever. Unless they mix up. With separation, enmity comes. It's now too late, but they must make an effort to speak to the Tamils and make them understand, and they must, because . . . Tamils are moving about everywhere, you see? Without any problem. You know, the idea they come with is always separation and . . . struggling.

You know, the tolerance and the patience of the Sinhalese is so strong because, from the start they [Tamils] have been destroying 276 temples and monasteries in the north. And recently, they have destroyed in Jaffna City twenty-one Buddhist temples and monasteries and only some remains of one or two. Even the stones, they are removed! It is complete destruction! So you can imagine the patience and the tolerance of the Sinhala Buddhists. Still they are tolerating . . .

JLA: Is it difficult to maintain this tolerance?

Piyadassi: Of course!

Pannasiha: You know, if you see the history of Sri Lanka, all the struggles we had in the past, none have been caused by the Sinhala Buddhists. If you study the history of the country, all the struggles were started not by the Sinhala Buddhists.

JLA: By?

Piyadassi: By them! Tamils!

Pannasiha: This is the country of the "Hilas." Hila means Sinhala. But always, they [Tamils] came from south India and created trouble. But this is really the country of the Sinhalas. All the trouble came from South India. You cannot deny that, because it is recorded.

*Ratika Kumarasame is a Jaffna Tamil with the Centre for Ethnic Studies, a liberal research institute in Colombo. A vivacious, plump woman in her thirties, she studied law at Columbia and Harvard universities.*

I came back after the sixties in America, and I was going to change the world. (laughs) Brought up not only on Mahatma Gandhi, but the sixties, Vietnam, and America and university life there. With very set categories of right and wrong and how racism and how conflicts manifested themselves, certain moral assumptions about how everything worked . . . and that shattered. (laughs) Having to really put away my categories after the reality of Sri Lanka, which fundamentally has shaken me emotionally, intellectually.

Now when I go back and speak to many of my friends, both Indian and American, there is an emotional gap. Even though I share the same values, unless you have actually been a target of ethnic riots—like the Tamils—you can't understand the insecurity.

Most fundamentally, and what the Sinhalese statistics don't show, is this lack of physical security. It is that violence, with its emotional residue, that makes the Tamil cause popular. It is not the land, economic, education issues—all that can be negotiated—but when people feel physically threatened, as a community.

I don't come from the same background as the Tigers. My grandfather was a senator, my father was an adviser to the president . . . and someone like me, from that elite, to feel that after '83, when you know what it's like to be the possible victim of arbitrary violence, that insecurity is something very deep with us. Arbitrary violence. You can just be wandering down the street and something,

some incident has taken place in Anuradhapura and you don't know it and you will
be subject to attack, that sort of insecurity. That fear is something you can't explain
to your Sinhalese friends. I mean, they can show you statistics which show that the
civil service in 1948 was forty percent Tamil, but how do you explain to them you
fear for your life?

After '83, I remember going to the refugee camps and staring at these refugees,
and you're so used to—you know, a refugee is cast in the class concept, the
wretched refuse (laughs)—but you were looking at your mirror when you went
into these camps. There were people from your class. There were boys from
Trinity College and Royal College there.

Nothing has happened since '83, but the emotional fear remains to a great
extent. If the Sinhalese were ashamed, I don't think the Tamils would be
demanding a separate state. Instead, there is a sense that it was justified: "These
Tamils are too much." A belief that a good thrashing would teach the Tamils a
lesson. Instead, it turned a guerrilla movement that was about a hundred people
into one of two thousand armed and ten thousand on call.

*"Naranja" is a thin, quiet man of 26, shy and a little nervous at seeing strangers
as he enters the priest's office. Despite his schoolboy demeanor, Naranja is a
recruiter and "fund-raiser" for the Liberation Tigers of Tamil Eelam. The priest
convinces the Tiger cadre to speak about his involvement.*

SA: Why did you join the movement?

Naranja: I am denied a fair opportunity for employment in this country; the
unjust employment problem is part of it. And these race riots that started coming to
the country, all the way back to 1957—each time, the Tamil were on the receiving
end and treated like rubbish.

JLA: What do you hope to win out of the struggle?

Naranja: Political forces have not been effective for the past thirty years.
Gradually one felt that the rights were taken away, rather than more rights coming
in. Gradually one felt that there was no use being a Tamil in this country. That's
why we had to go to an armed struggle.

JLA: Are you willing to die for it?

Naranja: I am willing to give up my life for the cause.

SA: (to priest) How is he able to move about in a high-security risk area like
this?

Priest: (smiles) They see him, but they don't know who he is. Probably they
have his name. In a roundup, if they catch him and they look at the identity cards,
probably they will know. But he comes from a different place; he's a well-dressed
young man. They won't suspect him. They would suspect a very unkempt boy
with a sarong and shirt, looking suspicious, looking furtive.

These young men, you know, every day you bump into them. You can guess. So I won't go and ask who he is; I don't care to ask who he is. He comes here for a job; I help him out. Or he wants a little money, I give him. Many young people come to my office. I know where they come from, but we don't care to ask—even dare to ask—who they are.

JLA: What kind of help do they ask for usually?

Priest: You know, "Father, can I telephone somewhere?" Or "Can you make a telephone call?" Or "Can you give some certain people some financial help?"

*In May 1985, a group of Tamil separatists dressed as government soldiers entered Anuradhapura, Sri Lanka's ancient and sacred capital, and embarked on a killing spree. Shooting civilians at a bus station, then at the venerated Bodhi (or Bo) Tree shrine, and on through town as they escaped, they killed at least one hundred and fifty people in less than an hour.*

*G.G. Tilak is a tall, slender Sinhalese 21-year-old in Anuradhapura. He has long black hair cut like a European rock star's. The interview is mobile, held while bicycling along paths under the towering pagodas and rain trees of the parklike Sacred City. Pedaling along, Tilak speaks of that day in May.*

That time I was in the town. So the terrorists come in one bus, and I thought they were soldiers, you know? They were in uniform, same uniform as soldier. They came in the bus to the bus stand. I also in the bus stand at that time. People were waiting for the bus and then they shoot the people.

They never talked to the people, never say anything; they just shoot the people. Then we thought, "Ah, this terrorists, Tamils," you know? Then we run away, like that. We run to the lake and people jumped in. Then they [the gunmen] get in the bus and they go quick to templeside. Then I heard them shoot everybody there at sacred Bo Tree.

I had another friend. We get the bicycle, then we going to look what happen. Dead people, dead body, many, at the bus stand. About hundred seventy. Then on the way, more people—some had died—on the road.

Then, Sinhalese people attack the Tamil people [after the attack.] The Tamil people they have shops here, so Sinhalese people came and burned all the shops. I also get angry. I want also to attack, you know? Then after . . . I think and I understand why they did it . . . because first, Sinhalese soldier went there [to Tamil areas] and shoot—that's why they come to here and shoot Sinhalese people like this.

SA: Why do you think all this is happening?

Tilak: I think the Tamil, they want half of Sri Lanka, no?

JLA: What do you think of Tamils now?

Tilak: I have never got any problem with the Tamil people. I am a Sinhalese, but

I also have Tamil friends. They are very good people. I am really friendly with the Tamil, you know?

But I don't want to live anymore in Sri Lanka. I want to live in another country. I like to go somewhere in Europe, find work. Problems here meaning no work, because difficult to find a job here. Before, I work big hotel, no? So there are many [tour] groups coming. Then after problem, I am out, eh? No job. Then . . . I work in small guesthouse now. . . .

Now, many young peoples going into military, you know? Many young people are going to be a soldier.

*G.G. Piyaratna, 39, is a member of Anuradhapura's paramilitary Home Guards. Thin and mustachioed, Piyaratna is a Sinhalese and the father of four children. He lives in a simple home on a street overhung with trees in which bearded monkeys scamper. His spare parlor is dominated by family photographs and pictures of Lord Buddha. His Home Guard badge and regulation shotgun are sources of great pride.*

I am the leader. Under me there are thirty-five Home Guards. My area is the Sacred City. We have shotguns.

On the day of the May 14 massacre, we were not yet formed, so none of us were on duty. Before the attack, some people known as Home Guards associated themselves together in the village, and they went walking, sometimes at night, taking sticks and . . . like that. But we didn't have any experience or training, so it was just walking with the gang. These were the village Home Guards. Then the government formed us after May 14 and issued weapons and so on, and we received police and army training.

I wanted to be a Home Guard because, since the police and army were fighting against the enemies during that time, as villagers we must look after the villages from any invaders or anything. Looking after the streets, roads and temples, public places . . . The terrorists are attacking our country, Ceylon. He wants to take it, but it's our country. . . .

I like being a Home Guard. I like helping the army and police to make our country go forward. We have to protect our country. The terrorists want to make another country, but this is our country.

*K. Alvis, 34, and E.A. Somalata, 28, are the parents of three children in the city of Anuradhapura. They operate a small kiosk outside the gates to the sacred Bo Tree, where they sell coconut milk and lotus blossoms to the pilgrims. They were at the kiosk on the morning of May 14, 1985, when Tamil militants attacked.*

*Alvis is a handsome, heavily tattooed man with a long, deep scar running across the top of his back. Somalata is a short, smiling woman who stays in the*

*background. The interview is in their home, an earth-floored, two-room hovel in a*
*slum near the Sacred City. Both are wearing sarongs.*

Somalata: We have a small kiosk, selling flowers and things to the pilgrims,
just outside of the Bo Tree. There is a park there, and we have a kiosk under a
tamarind tree.

Alvis: So that day, we were there. At about seven o'clock on that morning, all of
us were there. Under the tree, the tamarind tree, outside the wall of the Bo Tree.

As the first pilgrims came, we heard the noise of the firing of the terrorists from
the bus halt. After a little time, a few seconds, one bus came over [the causeway]
and stopped at the park. Three persons with weapons got out. We didn't know if
they were terrorists, because they were dressed as army soldiers; we thought they
were us because of the putting-on of the uniform.

Then they were shooting some people right around the bus. We stood under the
tree. We thought then that they were not soldiers of Sri Lanka, because they don't
want to hurt the people, our people; we thought that they were terrorists, so we ran.

One man with a gun came after me. Walking. Came by foot. At a normal walk.
A normal walk. Then he looked at me and he held a weapon up like this [close to
the hip] and I was shot. Then all the other persons under that tamarind tree were
shot. They fell down. All fallen down. And this man was shooting them.

JLA: And what do you remember?

Somalata: So I was shot in the leg and he [her husband] was shot in the back and
he was bleeding and I gave the baby to him and I told him to run. Then I was falling
down. I was lying on my back. Then I was shot again while I was on the ground.

SA: Did you see the man who shot you again?

Somalata: Yes. He was black. He looked angry. He said nothing; he just stood
there and shot. Just shot. And he shot the other people like that.

JLA: What are your feelings about being victims for no reasons?

Alvis: I don't know. The terrorists, they are usually killing the normal people.

JLA: Does it make you want to take revenge?

Alvis: No. Because we don't know who are the people who make the killings. I
have nothing to make any revenge. Because this is not in me.

SA: Does it make you feel differently about Tamils?

Alvis: Because of the shooting, we don't like those Tamils; otherwise, normal.

SA: Do you have any permanent damage?

Alvis: I have pain sometimes. I had five bullets.

SA: (to Somalata) Do you have any problems now?

Somalata: I am falling sometimes. When I want to carry a pot of water,
sometimes I fall.

Alvis: The worst is my son. My little boy was shot. Five years old. Now one leg
is shorter than the other one. Four inches.

(Alvis holds up the little boy's shoes. One has a large, orthopedic sole. Somalata bursts into tears, backs against the far wall and covers her face, sobbing.)

Alvis: We don't have any support. I had some money in the bank . . . all finished. It all went to hospital. My boy was in hospital ten months, I was in for two months, my wife four months.

SA: What should happen to the people who shot you?

Alvis: We want to see them punished.

Somalata: We feel saddened. They killed many, many people like this. Innocent people. That is not good.

Alvis: We don't make any mistakes to the terrorists. We didn't make any mistakes to the Tamils. We didn't deserve like that. We have just been living, a small family. Not even a mistake to the terrorists. Nothing wrong!

*The Venerable Nanaratana, 75, is the custodian of the sacred Bodhi (or Bo) Tree of Anuradhapura. He sits on a divan, framed by two enormous elephant tusks, and gazes from behind horn-rimmed glasses. In the display case behind him are dozens of Buddha statues from around the world, religious trinkets, and a half-dozen clocks. Small songbirds, their nests in the ceiling rafters, flit about the ornate room.*

*Nanaratana was abroad when the Bo Tree massacre took place.*

I was very worried that perhaps some of our monks and workers had been hurt, but I was able to find out that those killed by the Bo Tree were just beggars and pilgrims, the people who are always around. And, of course, I was thankful that none of the sacred objects had been damaged.

People think that we have only suffered at the hands of the Tamil terrorists for a few years. They forget that we have been the victims of their terrorism for over two thousand years.

*Karu, a former military policeman, lives in Anuradhapura. He is Sinhalese and a devout Buddhist.*

I was at the Bo Tree. I saw it happen. On that day, I was writing a letter. Normally, if I want to write a letter, I write a draft in my home of the important things to be included. Then I will come to the Bo Tree. Morning. And pray. Then I will start to write. Under that tree.

I had arrived there, written about two or three sentences. . . . About seven o'clock. I was there. And I heard a sound from the old bus station. Crack, crack, crack. It was a sound very familiar to my ear because from my time in the army, so I knew it was shooting. Then I saw some people from the railroad down there running, fleeing up toward the Bo Tree. Then I decided to take my bike, but the key failed me: I was trying to open the lock, but it wouldn't open. So I went away on foot. Then after, I came back to get my bike, and I have seen some bodies . . . under the Bo Tree. I felt like crying. . . .

Then, I am walking out and my brother, he meets me at the Bo Tree and he tells me, "Our brother-in-law has been killed on the road."

JLA: What do you feel about the conflict after what you've seen here?

Karu: (long pause) Very sad. To come to the Bo Tree, loved by the people, for them to come and kill the people, it is very sad. But they said they came to kill because up in Jaffna the army had attacked a Tamil *kovil* [temple] and killed many people. So I guess what they did here is understandable. It was . . . revenge.

SA: So, because the army attacked a Tamil kovil and killed people, it makes the massacre here understandable?

Karu: Yes.

JLA: Justified?

Karu: Justified, indeed! Because the army was killing people who didn't have anything to do with the conflict, but they killed them because they were there.

SA: But Anuradhapura is a sacred site to Sinhalese Buddhists. How can a military attack against a religious site be justified?

Karu: They didn't attack Anuradhapura as a religious place; they only attacked it because they knew it was very important to the Sinhalese people. They didn't destroy any of the sacred spots. They killed people with their heads down, under the Bo Tree, but they didn't damage the Bo Tree. Killing the people was bad, but killing the Bo Tree would have been more bad. Because we have two important sacred things for the Sinhalese in Sri Lanka, the Bo Tree and the Tooth Temple. More important than ourselves.

JLA: More important than human life?

Karu: More important . . . because those who were killed under the Tree were killed on sacred ground . . .

SA: Did the attack change your feelings about the problem?

Karu: I want to fight again. I have applied for the army again. If they want me . . . but they haven't replied. I would like to join again. I suppose . . . because these people go around killing young people . . . Already, my two brothers were killed by the terrorists. Both were in the army. Both killed. One brother on the way to Trincomalee. There was a blast, a land mine . . . no more brothers now. My eldest brother is twenty-eight years old; my youngest brother is twenty-one—I mean was, he was twenty-one.

Now is completed two years after the death—March thirty-first—of my eldest brother. And my second brother, it is one year in December.

JLA: And because of this, you want to go back and fight?

Karu: Yes, I suppose.

JLA: For revenge?

Karu: No . . . sometimes . . . yes. Can you blame me, sir? These people come to kill our nation! We should be allowed to defend our home.

SA: Do you feel bitter toward Tamils?

Karu: (very long pause) Yes. I have hate. Because they are doing evil things. Crippling, breaking lives, killing many soldiers . . . a lot of dying. I think Sri Lankan people, we have hate in us.

SA: Some Sinhalese say the Tamils should be sent back to India. Would you agree with that?

Karu: No. No, I don't agree. They were born here. They live here. Like we do.

*A devoutly Catholic Tamil lawyer, "George" only agreed to speak if he could remain anonymous.*

The incident that took place in Anuradhapura brought home to the Sinhalese their vulnerability. For the first time they realized that if this fighting went on, this could happen to them, too. And if the Tigers had not stopped when they did, but many more Sinhalese had been massacred, there would be a settlement now. Just as the Hiroshima and Nagasaki bombs, though they wiped a large percentage of the Japanese population, it was necessary because it made the war end quicker; if not for that, more people would have died.

It is true that a few died in Anuradhapura, a few died in Colombo, but I think it was not enough. If more had died, the government would have taken a more . . . shall I say, a practical stance, and this would have ended and a greater number of killings would have been avoided.

JLA: But back-and-forth massacres only cause more hate.

George: That's right. It polarizes—true—but the thing is this: what is happening now is there is a massacre on only one side. As far as the Sinhala population is concerned, they seem to think that nothing can happen to them. They think they are safe. As long as they think they are safe they are not going to act to end this. The only two things that can stop this are, one, heavy massacres of Sinhalese and, two, heavy financial losses as far as they are concerned. If the government is brought down to its knees financially, maybe they'll settle.

Even today, I believe if five hundred Sinhalese had died in Anuradhapura it would have brought it home to the government that this has to end. It is necessary. This is why I think the need for massacre is inevitable. You see, there are only two times when there is a reaction from the government, when something happens to Sinhalese or just before an aid conference, when donor countries are about to meet and decide what aid they're going to give Ceylon.

SA: But surely, if you go out and kill five hundred Sinhalese you are going to have another situation like '83, when hundreds of Tamils were killed?

George: That cannot happen for this reason: there are no Tamils in any part of the south except in Colombo and in the hill country. In the hill country, they are able to defend themselves.

SA: And in Colombo?

George: After '83, many of those Tamils went to the north. Those that remained made that decision to stay, to live among the Sinhalese. If the '83 situation returns, they will have to defend themselves as best they can. . . .

You know, I think if you added up all the Sinhalese civilians killed since this began, I don't think you would have five hundred victims. That's the really alarming situation.

*Karu's brother-in-law was one of the people gunned down in Anuradhapura. At the dead man's modest roadside home and shop at the outskirts of town, his widow, R.N. Kamarawathi, 39, describes what happened. Her four sons, ranging in age from five to twenty, listen.*

The terrorists were here at twenty minutes past eight o'clock in the morning. We heard the terrorists firing up the highway, at the junction. We thought that it must be a punched tire of a vehicle, that noise. When we heard the noise, my husband, he was eating breakfast. After he finished breakfast, he went into the [adjoining] shop. Two of our boys were there. They told him, "There are some terrorists firing," and I followed my husband when he went out front to look.

They came by feet from the junction, in front of the bus which they traveled by. They were just walking; there was one who was walking in front. They stopped the bus before the shop. Two more men jumped down from the bus and they were chasing the people away on the other side of the road. Then one came around in front, just there, in front of the shop. So my husband thought that the person is from the army, so he started to raise his arms above his head. They talked something in Tamil to us, but I cannot understand what it was. He said something in Tamil, but I couldn't understand Tamil. . . .

One shot. Then two more. He is not dead. Still standing. Then he pointed the gun to the chest of my husband . . . close, very close, and shot again. Twice. And then I ran away.

JLA: Before this happened, did you have any feeling about the terrorists?

Kamarawathi: It was totally a shock for me, because I didn't know about terrorism before my husband is dead. I had heard about the terrorism in Jaffna from the radio and newspaper and things like that, but my husband's murder has explained to me the activity of the terrorist.

SA: What do you feel about the Tamil people now?

Kamarawathi: I hate Tamils. This one also [points to littlest son], he says, "I will kill Tamils because they killed my father." He was three years then.

*Her coquettish smile contrasts with the harsh words, delivered in a deep, wheezy voice, of Madame Sirimavo Bandaranaike. The world's first elected woman head of state, she was elected prime minister in 1960 after her husband, Prime Minister S.W.R.D. Bandaranaike, was assassinated by a Buddhist monk.*

*In her two terms in office, Madame Bandaranaike changed the nation's name from Ceylon to Sri Lanka, led it into economic chaos, and, according to many, aggravated tensions between Sinhalese and Tamils. Often compared to Indira Gandhi, another iron-willed contemporary who brooked little dissent, Bandaranaike strengthened her hand by repeatedly invoking emergency powers. A leftist rebellion in 1971 was crushed by her troops, resulting in the deaths of thousands. In 1977, her Freedom Party was resoundingly defeated in elections. Today, undeterred by a decade of enforced retirement, Bandaranaike is planning to run for president in 1989.*

*The interview is held in her enormous, colonial-style house on a leafy street of Colombo's exclusive Cinnamon Gardens neighborhood. In the octagonal sitting room is a large bust of her late husband, along with signed photographs of world leaders, Dwight D. Eisenhower and Richard Nixon among them. In the passage-way outside, a burly bodyguard stands watch.*

Now, I'm not boasting, but I was prime minister for twelve years in this country, and not one day was there a racial riot in my time. I didn't have it. They tried in the north; I stopped it. I managed to clinch it there. Problems spread to other areas, and I suppose I had to take the leaders into custody. I didn't hesitate to do that. All of them! The leaders were taken, and all this nonsense stopped! They were kept quiet and safe in Colombo, given all the facilities, whatever they wanted, but they were kept quiet until the whole thing settled down, and then they were allowed to go.

This man [Prime Minister], Jayewardene, cannot act. He could have taken steps, he could have done these things. That's the complaint of everybody, even his own supporters today. I don't know why, whether he was betrayed, or . . . what he's thinking on—it's very difficult—but anyway, the fact remains that certain things could have been controlled at the beginning. It could have been nipped in the bud; he did nothing. I'm not criticizing him because he's my opponent, but it's a fact; you ask anybody, they will say that.

If I was PM, the situation would not be there. (laughs) Talk to anybody they'll say that. I wouldn't allow it to come to this. During my time, they may have discussed these things privately, but my government wouldn't allow it to spread.

SA: Specifically, what would you do to stop the conflict if you were to assume office today?

Bandaranaike: It's going to be violent. The situation is so bad, it's gotten so protracted, it's not going to be very easy. Certainly not. I won't say it's an easy task.

It could have been stopped, but it wasn't. You see, in a situation like this, you must not tell the people everything. There are certain things you have to keep quiet. When I was PM, I remember one incident just before the '76 elections. It was a very unfortunate incident. Mr. Sivanayagam, the Tamil leader, died, and they brought his ashes from Jaffna to Trinco[malee]. They brought it there, and some of the Tamils viewed the body and went to a Sinhalese village and tried to create some trouble. There was a clash, and some Sinhalese and Tamils died there.

I received the news, and I wanted to somehow control these riots, so I sent the army commander to Trincomalee and ordered, "Somehow, contain this; don't let it spread." And I called all the newspapers and said, "You are not to put this in the papers. I'll bring censorship rules. You're not to publish this in the papers, because the rest of the country must not know what has happened there." And we controlled it! And the problem did not recur! So that is how one has to act! There are times when you can't tell the country everything, in the interests of peace. . . . But this government didn't know that, I'm sorry to say. They didn't because, I suppose, for some reason they didn't want to.

Now, in the '83 riots, it was not the Sinhalese people who really rioted; it was a group of people—Sinhala or not—but all supporters of the government. It's known! Ask any Tamil and they'll tell you that. They got workers from the trade unions, and they're the ones who did it. They went around in government vehicles, marking Tamil houses to be set fire. It was not done by the Sinhalese; they were Sinhalese, but it was not the Sinhalese feeling. It was just orders, and the president kept quiet.

But still, no decent Sinhalese joined in that, and a lot of Tamils were coming to my house—I had ten Tamils living here for three or four days; I gave them protection because they were afraid that their houses would be attacked. So a lot of Sinhalese, decent Sinhalese, protected Tamils. Decent Sinhalese. It was just a set of . . . thugs who did that. Really, the mischief-makers were these thugs behind the government, I'm sorry to say. That's well known; talk to any of the Tamils.

JLA: So you don't think the riots were symptomatic of any deeper division between the two ethnic groups?

Bandaranaike: Now there is strong feeling between the two. Of course, the tension between the Sinhalese and the Tamils has been in conflict for generations, but we lived as one nation. Unfortunately, this last riot made the Tamils very angry, because it was the innocent Tamils that suffered. They were living happily here, doing business, making all their money—because all the lawyers here, all the doctors, the top ones are Tamils. And my lawyer is a Tamil. (laughs) He was a good lawyer, a clever lawyer, so we went to him; we didn't say he was a Tamil so, therefore, why should we support him? Now, Tamil always goes to Tamil, but we don't do that; Sinhalese are not so communal-minded. . . . So they lived quite happily here.

SA: How do you think history will judge your term as PM?

Bandaranaike: I ruled for twelve years, and there was never a day of racial riots in my time. There was a riot in '57, during my husband's time. Very unfortunate. That, again, was a set of people, not the normal Sinhalese people. After that, since '57, there were no racial riots in this country, not during my two periods.

During our time, people could go to Jaffna. We were able to move freely, right from the north to the east, without any problem. There was no problem; Sinhalas and Tamils, they had grievances, bitternesses, but they lived happily. They lived together. Not like now.

*Subramanian Sivanayagam is a chain-smoking, dapper man in a Madras shirt who repeatedly lights incense, the scent of it pervading his small office. A Tamil, he was a lawyer and magazine editor before going into exile in India; he fled by boat in 1983 upon learning the Sri Lankan government planned to detain him. Today, Sivanayagam runs the Tamil Information Center in Madras.*

Nineteen fifty-six was the year in which, for the first time, the Tamils were subject to Sinhala violence.

On that day I was in Jaffna and, unfortunately for me, I had decided to travel to Colombo; I was doing my law studies, and for us Tamils the job opportunities were in Colombo. When the train reached the next large station after Jaffna, I found a large crowd waiting to board the train but not getting in. I called one of them and asked, "Why are these people not getting into the train?" and he said, "It seems there is some trouble in Colombo."

Mind you, at that time we never knew about problems; we never had attacks, we never had any case of this kind. Anyway, most of these people decided to stay back.

On that day, we reached a town about twenty miles north of Colombo at eight o'clock in the morning. As the train started moving, I heard some commotion in the next compartment. I looked out and saw people's belongings, suitcases and pillows, all getting thrown out, and then I realized there was some problem. And then this gang of about twenty people came rushing in and asked, "Are there any Tamils here?" Well, I was the only Tamil in my section of the compartment—all the others were Sinhala people—so I was in the corner seat and wondering what is going to happen. Then one man saw my suitcase and my pillow and he knew I had to be a Tamil coming [overnight] from Jaffna, so that fellow pointed out that I am one. So they came for me. They pulled me out—even then I was wearing glasses—somebody socked me and the glasses fell off.

Of course, there were some Sinhala people protesting about this—"Why do you want to harm him?" "What has he done to you?," "Leave him alone!"—in Sinhala. But these thugs, they managed to put me out of the compartment, and the whole idea was to push me out from the moving train. I resisted to the last. Fortunately for me, at that moment a guy who was in the corridor blocked the way.

In this situation I ran to the next compartment and then went as far as I could go, almost to the guard's van, and there I had to stop. Fortunately, when the train slowed down for the next station, these guys all jumped off, but until we reached Colombo Fort station I was still nervous.

When I got down, there was a police van in the station itself. So then I became aware that Colombo already had this problem. Anyway, they said, "You get into the van. We must convey you." And they took me to the Fort [police] station. Even on the way the mobs were gathering, because they could see me all surrounded by the policemen, so they thought there was a Tamil inside and they started to push the van. Anyway, we managed to go to the police station, and in another three, four hours they took me back to my home.

But that was my first taste of . . . I realized that, as a Tamil, I don't have to hold any particular view, I don't have to be critical of the government, I don't have to do anything to fall in as an enemy of the Sinhala, but the simple fact that I am a Tamil meant that they could put an attack on me. It could cost my life. That—that shattered all the illusions I had.

*Bernadine Silva is a middle-aged social activist. A left-wing Sinhalese Catholic, whose name comes from her ancestral Portuguese blood, Silva works out of the Centre for Society and Religion in Colombo.*

What has happened is that you find you are thinking in terms—when you talk to a person or when a person is rude to you—you think, "Oh he's rude because he's a Tamil. They are angry with us." Now I hear people who say, "You know, this chap knocked my car and he was very rude to me. He must be angry because we are Sinhalese and he's a Tamil." I mean, that kind of ethnic interpretation is given! That has happened today, which is very sad for me! You know, "He's a good chap even though he's a Tamil," that kind of thing. And I think even among the Tamils, they do not trust the Sinhalese. Even their close friends, they are not sure what will happen if it comes to conflict.

So you see this manifesting itself like that with people's attitudes and prejudices, though they may not physically attack now. They have not been reacting like they reacted in July '83 as such, but they manifest it through prejudices, not wanting to employ Tamil people in firms and things. Sometimes the excuse is, "We might have trouble. We don't know whether he's a terrorist or what contact he has with the terrorists, because they are all related to each other," and that kind of thing. And of course, that is the excuse. There is fear, no doubt, but the prejudice is there.

Now I don't feel the prejudice. It's not a kind of boast, but I really don't feel it. I don't feel that "this person is a Muslim or a Tamil"; I don't think in those terms. I don't know the reason why. As a result, I sometimes find it very uncomfortable even in my own family and my friends . . . because they sort of talk sometimes in those terms. And I used to always have arguments and quarrels, and many of them have made statements like, "You are always for the Tamil." So I tell them, "It's not a question of Tamils, it's a question of justice!" I'm not saying that the Tamils are always right, so I now tend to remain a bit silent as such. They think that I fight a cause and that I don't see the problems that will arise with the Tamils trying to take over Sri Lanka, and things like that. So sometimes I make a joke: "We can be under the British, Portuguese, and Dutch, why not under (laughs) the Tamils?" That makes them very angry! (laughs)

*The enigmatic "theoretician" of the Liberation Tigers of Tamil Eelam (LTTE) coyly shrugs off suggestions that he is its real powerbroker, but he seems clearly that. Anton Balasingham, 48, is a ruggedly handsome man with deep-brown skin, a resonant actor's voice, and piercing eyes.*

*In an upstairs conference room at the Tigers' Madras office, Balasingham, freshly bathed and relaxed in a white dhoti and cotton shirt, elegantly smokes a British brand of cigarettes. A young Tiger disciple at the end of the table listens raptly.*

*On the wood-paneled wall there is an early photograph of Fidel Castro, a pro-Palestinian poster, and, prominently, a framed photograph of a "martyred" Tiger commander.*

*His building is both an office and a home. At one point, Balasingham's Australian wife, wearing a colorful Indian dress, comes to take out the pudgy yellow dog that lies at her husband's feet.*

Our organization was formed in 1972 to fight back the ever-mounting state repression against our people. From the beginning, the Tigers were an armed organization. Of course, the movement emulates Marxism and Leninism, but we have . . . charted our political program not on orthodox Marxist principles. It is a combination of nationalism and socialism, intermixed together to mobilize people. Our objective is to liberate not only our repressed Tamil people from state repression but also to create a socialist society where there should be economic equality, and so on and so forth.

From 1976 onwards, we have expanded gradually our military activities. First, against the state intelligence in Tamil areas. We . . . assassinated political traitors who colluded with the Sinhala government. We killed police agents who were rounding up our members. And finally, we eliminated the police secret service in Tamil areas. Then we launched attacks on police stations, hmm? And, in the meantime, the Sri Lankan [government] sent its military forces to the north and east and we had to confront the armed forces.

July '83 marked a turning point in the history of our struggle. There was a massive racial violence, as you know, in which hundreds of Tamil people were massacred. This gave a new momentum to the struggle. It led hundreds and thousands of young men to join the liberation organizations, and it also gave birth to other liberation groups of different ideological perspectives.

And the cycle of violence, or rather the cycle of repression and resistance . . . was aggravated. The Tamil political parties became defunct, their leaders sought refuge in Madras, and there are no political, democratic institutions, as you would put it, but rather . . . national liberation movements with socialist ideologies emerged and, among us, contradictions emerged.

You would have heard about conflicts between our organizations and how we were . . . compelled to take action against certain groups who turned against the public. . . . Finally, the Tigers emerged as the dominant military organization.

Apart from the armed trained guerrillas we have, you find supporters, sympathizers, carriers, people doing various sorts of work. And also, vast, vast numbers of the civilian masses are also involved in the struggle now, hmm? We are constantly recruiting, strengthening ourselves, mobilizing, because of the fact that the Sri Lankan Army is constantly expanding, strengthening its forces. We know the struggle is going to expand and we have to fight a very long battle, a long war.

It's not a question of numbers; it's a question of commitment, courage, dedication. You know, our fighters carry cyanide pills. When they're cornered or about to die, they swallow the pill. That signifies the commitment of our fighters, that they are prepared to die for a cause. Whereas the Sri Lankan soldiers are paid servants of the state; they fight for wages. And when they see a few casualties, they withdraw to the camps. That's the situation. So even though they are large in number and are using highly sophisticated weaponry, they cannot match an iron-disciplined organization like ours.

JLA: So the peasants were repressed. But you don't seem to be a man of peasant origin. What happened to you to bring you where you are today, in exile, involved in an armed group?

Balasingham: I come from a very poor family in Jaffna and, of course, we were subjected to various forms of repression. It was extremely difficult for a man like me to enter universities there or study. We are self-made people.

But my generation of Tamils are lucky, in the sense that we didn't experience the horrors of state violence as the present generation of young people are. They have no access to education; their lives are threatened. They have two choices: either to join a liberation movement or to go to Western Europe as refugees. There is no other way for a Tamil youth. If they are rounded up by the military, they are put into camps, tortured, and sometimes put to death. There are nearly three thousand innocent Tamil youths kept in army camps. So that is why you find large numbers of youth joining the liberation struggle. And, of course, we have to politically guide them, channel the revolution, liberate the people so that the older generation, like me, are also involved.

JLA: So you went from being in a poor family to being here, but what happened in the interim? You say it was difficult for you to get into university, but you did get in, didn't you?

Balasingham: (sighs) I had a long, complex personal history, but, uh . . . it's not that important. I went to foreign countries, studied, and then came back in 1978. But I can tell you one thing. I . . . at the early stage, I was a journalist, a writer, so I had an acute perception of the complex realities of the struggle. And . . . yes, I had a perception of a life that is entirely different, and a background that was different, but, spiritually, I am with my people.

I came to Madras in 1978, met Prabakaran [Tiger leader] and . . . became their political advisor, theoretician, and the spokesman of the movement. And, since July '83, I gave up everything and came to Madras, and since then I am permanently working for the movement.

Sri Lanka is carrying out a campaign, that they are confronted with terrorism, instead of characterizing our struggle as an ethnic problem. They are simply reducing the whole complexity of the ethnic problem into a phenomenon of terrorism. And they say, "These Tamils are Marxists and they want to destroy the state and bring about a communist regime here."

We are trying to put across our case, that we are not terrorists, but patriots defending . . . involved in a defensive struggle for our people. And our objective is to find freedom, security for our people, and if a viable alternative political solution is offered, we are prepared to reconsider our struggle for secession.

JLA: What about the bloody clashes between the Tigers and other Tamil groups, like the EPRLF [Eelam People's Revolutionary Liberation Front]?

Balasingham: It's a struggle for supremacy. They want to destroy us politically and, to our shock, we found, uncovered, some documents from an EPRLF comrade, that there was a plan, a plot was worked out, in which they were planning to launch a sudden, unexpected attack on the Tigers. And all the details of the plan we have got. So what happened was . . . we had no other alternative but to take immediate action, because otherwise they would launch an attack on us. We decided to strike back. For self-defense. Now we have taken control. We have arrested almost all the EPRLF; most of them have surrendered without much resistance in the north and east. There are pockets of resistance here and there, but these will . . . fizzle out.

So, as a consequence, the Tigers have emerged as the sole politico-military organization in Tamil Eelam. And all the other tiny groups, like EROS [Eelam Revolutionary Organization Struggle], are falling in line with us. EROS doesn't want to have any conflict with the Tigers. They are more mature politically, and militarily very wise. (chuckles) Now, they have accepted our leadership and (uproarious laugh) we have built up a very cordial relation.

Say, for example, there are four or five groups, each imposing various taxes, getting money. Somebody will come and ask you for money and you give money to the Tigers, and then EPRLF will come and demand money, then the other organizations will demand—then you will get frustrated. What the people here want is a single movement, committed to the struggle. That is the general opinion among the Tamils.

So now, a single movement has come. The fight is over. It is true it is unfortunate—it's a tragedy—that we had to fight, but it is inevitable and unavoidable in our situation.

*Longanathan Ketheeswaran is a skinny pockmarked man in his thirties with shiny black hair parted in the middle. He has a thick mustache and Coke-bottle glasses, and his long fingers play relentlessly with a small pair of scissors and a paperweight. Behind his desk there is a red flag with a yellow star and several portraits of Lenin in heroic poses.*

*Ketheeswaran is the Madras-based spokesman for the Eelam People's Revolutionary Liberation Front (EPRLF), a communist Tamil guerrilla group. As the interview takes place, the Liberation Tigers of Tamil Eelam (LTTE), a rival Tamil group, is launching an all-out attack on the EPRLF's bases in Sri Lanka to wipe it out militarily.*

What has happened is that because the LTTE sees us as a threat to its hegemony, it has attacked us. So we now have to face two fronts, Sri Lankan armed forces and LTTE. The LTTE has to face two fronts, Sri Lankan armed forces and EPRLF. But the Sri Lankan state also knows that if it makes any move now, we will be able to iron out these fratricidal clashes. In fact, they will be doing us a favor (smiles) by launching an attack. That's why they aren't doing anything right now. But we are hoping they will do something! (laughs)*

*"Kumar" is a middle-aged Tamil businessman who has lived all his life in Batticaloa. He is closely aware of the goings-on in his area and has contacts with both the guerrillas and the security forces.*

The Tigers believe they are mature enough to judge others, which is not correct. You see, there are certain things which young people do when they are emotionally carried away. The heat of the moment can make you take wrong decisions. That is why in any movement in the world, even where there is militancy, you must have mature minds which are brought to bear on the problem. Unfortunately, in our

*According to the exultant Tigers, Ketheeswaran's comrades in the field had already been 'crushed' at the time of the interview in December 1986. The EPRLF claimed it had held out. What is certain is that scores of guerrillas died in the pitched internecine battles on both sides. Fighting continued in different areas between the rivals well into 1987, with the LTTE coming out on top.

movements here they are all youths and they seem to have taken the idea that the older generation cannot understand.

That is why the people are concerned: what will happen when there is a settlement? The people certainly are not going to accept these young people as the correct people to run the country. They will want mature minds, and when that happens there is going to be a conflict. Of course, as long as they have their weapons they may be able to dictate terms.

These people have been in the bush for years. They have lost contact. With fighters it is essential to be in a position where you discuss. You can't be in an isolated position, just giving orders.

The citizens are totally in fear. The Tigers are good fighters; they may win the battles, but they will lose the war because they are not in touch with reality. They are trying to instill fear in everybody. This will not work.

The Tigers have no ideology whatsoever. They have not said up to date what type of government they would form; they merely want a dictatorship of one-party rule, of their people only. This certainly is not going to work.

JLA: So what happens to those Tamils who have been trying to bring about democratic change?

Kumar: What happens is this: if there is going to be a peaceful solution, the militants will have to give up their arms. Whichever government is in power will take those weapons away.

JLA: And what will happen to the militants?

Kumar: That's their problem.

SA: Do you think they'll ever give up their arms?

Kumar: Not willingly, but they will be forced to.

JLA: There is a degree of extortion in the Tamil community by the guerrillas, isn't there?

Kumar: All the groups have been involved in extortion. . . . Let's put it this way, they come to a Tamil who they think has money. They say, "We want money to run the movement." Somebody, one group, might come to me and ask for five thousand rupees. So I pay those five thousand. If I don't pay it, they might decide I have to pay ten thousand rupees. So that is what has been going on all these days.

But recently they have made very large demands. They make an excuse. For instance, in January a government minister came to open up a new post office. So all the rich [Tamil] people who went to that particular function were kidnapped. One of those chaps was killed and very heavy demands made on the others—five hundred thousand, six hundred thousand. This was by the LTTE. Through fear they paid.

Subsequently, they went to shop owners. They kidnapped three and kept them hostage and demanded five hundred thousand or one million rupees each and, again through fear, they paid. They were all Tamil, people that have been helping them in the past, but their argument is, "We are fighting the Tamil cause, and you, as Tamils, have to pay for it."

As this war went on and on, people who gave willingly, some of them are no more and others can't afford to give. So the militants are finding other avenues. In Jaffna, they have taxes; even here they have a tax on timber. Anybody transporting timber, they have to give compensation.

They're going about it the wrong way. Because the Tigers are strong now they're able to carry on, but I think they're going to get killed. The moment the other groups are strong enough, I think the Tigers will find that everybody has turned against them, even their own people. The LTTE became too strong too fast, and I think they're the wrong type of people to come up.

*Balraj's unruly black hair, mended shirt, and worn sarong give him the appearance of an ordinary Tamil peasant. Actually, he is a member of the Central Committee of the Eelam Revolutionary Organization Struggle (EROS), a Tamil guerrilla faction. EROS, whose trademark is bombings, operates today in an uneasy alliance with the powerful Tigers. Balraj is interviewed in Batticaloa.*

JLA: Your group is allied with the Tigers; one of the things that characterizes the Tigers is their killing members of other Tamil groups and executing Tamil civilians. Do you have any problems with these tactics?

Balraj: I accept that it is creating a negative impact. I accept that it has caused a lot of resentment among the Tamils. It has done a lot of damage to the cause, and I have also personally known that a lot of innocent people have been executed for various reasons. But we, as one group, cannot take up the responsibility to change the situation. But we do object to all this, and it has even begun creating dissent and resentment within the Tigers themselves.

In certain instances, the killings of civilians or combatants is inevitably necessitated. That I accept. But beyond that stage, when people get killed and people continue to get killed, that has caused me to spend many, many sleepless nights and great despair.

SA: Does the situation cause you to question your group's affiliation with the Tigers?

Balraj: This is something we expected right from the beginning from a group like the Tigers. So we worked with them, but were always prepared for this kind of eventuality. So we aren't surprised.

SA: What were your personal reasons for getting involved in the struggle?

Balraj: I started as an ordinary social worker. I started with helping people through religion, because that's mainly how the whole thing operates in a traditional society. From there, you get involved socially, giving people facilities, building up libraries, and so on. And in trying to give more facilities to the people, you realize that through this government system you cannot, that the needs of the people are not what the government will give them. And if the people are to be liberated and get more facilities, then the present system doesn't work. That is where I changed.

JLA: What do you feel about the attacks which are not directed against the military, but against civilians?

Balraj: Except in the Central Telegraph office blast, where about six civilians were killed, all our other targets were very carefully chosen to cause minimum civilian damage. If we had wanted to kill civilians, we could have put bombs where hundreds and thousands of people move and we could have created quick chaos. So it's only tactical targets, and it is not with the aim of creating civilian targets.

All the massacres, in Trinco[malee] where the Sinhalese civilians were killed, similarly in Anuradhapura, we have totally condemned these massacres of Sinhalese civilians [by the Tigers]. But in certain places, in certain instances, when we choose the targets, because of circumstances even if my mother happens to be there, in the large interest of the cause and the community, I may have to sacrifice my mother. It is the incident and the place that matters, and not, in that context—even if I have to lose my mother—not the person.

JLA: How can Eelam be helped by putting a bomb in a telegraph office?

Balraj: As for the blast in the Central Telegraph office, what is important for the government is communication. The government communication facilities are used for false propaganda totally against the Tamil community. So, in terms of that, and since the whole communications facilities were concentrated there, it was very important for us to show our protest and destroy as much as possible, and to make the government realize the threat to their communication. So it is in those terms that we placed the bomb. It has definitely had a political impact.

In a conflict situation, it is not purely the combatants that matter. It's mostly destroying the economy of the enemy so that he is unable to function. If the government is paying overtime and fuel and so on to the military, the best way would be to create a situation where they would be unable to supply fuel and they would be so bankrupt that they cannot pay their salary. So that is why our group has mostly economic targets, and all our military tactics have that basis in mind, where the economy is severely disrupted, where the government will be unable to function tactically.*

Now, for instance, look at the bomb blast at Hotel Lanka Oberoi. In direct loss, it would be may be a couple of thousands [of dollars], but the impact it had on the economy, the third-largest foreign-exchange earner—tourism—could not even be the fifth-biggest earner now. So that is a direct impact; all that is just gone. These are the kind of activities that are best.

---

*The next day, the Sri Lankan government discovered an EROS explosive charge in the main fuel depot near Batticaloa. At the same time, police were searching for EROS operatives in Colombo in connection with a plot to bomb the Presidential Palace.

SA: But surely, when you wage a campaign of economic warfare, the people it most hurts are the Sinhalese and Tamil civilians. Is the hardship it causes the civilians justified?

Balraj: Proportionately economic warfare doesn't affect the people. The effect on the people is relatively less and more felt by the other side, the government.

SA: But you can't deny that it affects the people. If they're laid off work because the tea or rubber plantations are closed, it affects the people.

Balraj: The balance is between life and the quality of living. What matters is whether the loss of life can be reduced in terms of the larger community. So many valuable brains have been lost. So much suffering has been caused to the people. So many people have been killed. So, in order to prevent all this, if people could make material sacrifices, that is justified.

SA: But a state will always find money to buy weapons, even if they have to close hospitals or schools.

Balraj: If hospitals and schools are closed, then the people feel the impact of the government and people begin to take decisions.

SA: What about you? How has being involved in the movement changed the way you live?

Balraj: The past has almost been forgotten. I will never disrespect my past. I continue to relish the past in my own way, but that past has almost been pushed to the side, and my priority is not me and my past but the cause that I have taken up. That is what I enjoy the most.

SA: How long are you prepared to keep fighting?

Balraj: As long as the need exists.

SA: So forever, possibly.

Balraj: Yes.

JLA: You mentioned earlier that you would sacrifice your mother for the cause. Have you told her that?

Balraj: My mother realizes my commitment and all that, for a greater cause, even if she has to be sacrificed, she will do it. This is not something that I need to tell her or that she needs to be told. She realizes my commitment and she has . . . stomached it. She has to stomach it.

SA: Is your family proud of your commitment?

Balraj: Initially, there was a lot of opposition and there was a lot of resentment. I have lost regular contact with my family, but through the messages I get from people who meet the family, they seem to think that I have taken up a worthy cause and they are happy about it. Though they are sad . . . for the reasons . . .

When I came to talk to you, I did not want to talk personally about me, because that would only reflect badly on me. . . . But I would like to tell this, to say how I have changed:

Earlier, when I was small, we had a cow and that cow was sick. He wouldn't eat the grass or straw. So I stole eggs from my house, sold the eggs, bought some biscuits and gave them to the cow so it could eat something. I was very sympathetic and . . . soft-minded. As a child, I was very softhearted and kind.

SA: And you don't think you are now?

Balraj: This whole thing has to be viewed scientifically. The killing, the necessary killing, cannot be stopped because of sheer sentimentality. It could cause a lot of damage eventually, or it could retard a lot of things from happening in the future.

And so, over this period of time, the experiences which have been given me have made me more mature. It is a maturity and not so much a hardening. To be viewed objectively, in the larger interests.

SA: And if you saw a sick cow today?

Balraj: If a cow is found with a broken leg, I would certainly feel sympathetic and I wouldn't pass without taking the fellow aside and treating it. But the fact is, there are various levels of responsibility. . . . Then it was a child's behavior, and now it is a grown-up man with a larger responsibility. But that doesn't mean I have lost my compassion.

*Tall and hale, Gamini Gunewardene is the deputy inspector general of police for the country surrounding the city of Kandy. He has embarked on an elaborate "hearts and minds" campaign, forming police-supervised "peace committees" among the so-called Plantation Tamils and their Sinhalese neighbors.*

*The Plantation Tamils, descendants of the Tamils imported from India by the British in the nineteenth century to work on their tea plantations, number about a million people today and are concentrated in this cool, hilly Sri Lankan heartland. Because of their traditional poverty and political alienation, the government now fears their infection with the secessionist fervor of their Tamil cousins in the north and east.*

I have seen a lot of violent situations, mass violent situations, and, you know, whatever can be done must be done before something happens. Once it goes into action, there is very little that police can do to control it. It's like the floodgates being opened. It's mass hysteria. And I think in any country police are assailed, their morale is affected, when there is large-scale violence taking place. The concept of policing throughout the world is policing by consent. If, at some time, reason leaves people and they resort to mass violence, what can the police do?

Now, in upcountry [riots], none of the police opened fire. I had to open fire myself. Because the policeman in the street, face-to-face with the people, he finds it difficult to act! They did not fire.

This was upcountry, last year. Maybe ten thousand people came into a town and started setting fires. I found that the police were unable to pull their guns. I don't know what the reason was, whether they didn't want to fire or they were scared to fire, thinking that the whole mob might attack them . . . but it happened that I had to open fire from my position. Luckily for me, they did not know from where the shots came.

After some time, that stopped them, but, by then, they had done the damage. So I don't know if they stopped because of my shooting or because they thought they had had enough. That time, it so happened that Sinhalese were setting fire to the Tamil shops and they were also attacking poor human beings—Tamil laborers—who came by their way.

I must tell you, I felt quite mixed up after that death. After the whole thing was over, two or three days later, it disturbed me more. Not because I killed a person of my own nationality, but because I had killed a person . . . because, as a Buddhist . . . we have been trained not to kill, not to harm.

I have been in the battlefield in the north. That time I had no regrets. That was battle; this was different.

*Tim, a deeply tanned Briton with predatory eyes, is a mercenary pilot fighting with the Sri Lankan Army in the southern reaches of the Jaffna Peninsula.*

I just don't think the Sinhalese have it in them. The Tamils are a more . . . vigorous people—I guess that's the right word. You know, the Sinhalese have this whole Buddhism and karma thing. . . .

They fight a gentleman's war. They've carried over all the worst characteristics from the old British Army. They'll go out, fire a few bullets, and be home in time for tea. They have a . . . lack of enthusiasm.

We were out on a patrol and drew fire from some coconuts [trees] near this village. They wouldn't return fire: "Too close to the village, might hit some civilians!" I mean, they practically won't let you shoot unless you actually see the bloke standing there with the gun in his hand. All the boys over from South Africa and Rhodesia, this was a joke to them. They got totally fucked off with it; most of 'em packed up and left. Went to Nicaragua.

I just think these boys don't know how to fight. And don't want to fight. They just want to hold back and wait for a settlement. I tell you, it's bloody frustrating. Can't tell you how many times I've gone to the colonel and cussed out the whole lot of 'em.

*Nassim is a tiny, cheerful Muslim in his fifties. He lives in a town near Kandy.*

Tigers are making a lot of troubles! Killing innocent people and all. When they kill innocent, the Army people also kill—as a reaction, you know, to the terrorists.

But another thing, the Tigers kill their own people. (laughs) To lampposts they put people. They write a letter saying, "You are our enemy," and they tie to the person on the post and then they shoot. Now, guys are supposed to join, no? So the Tigers might call them two or three times. If they refuse—boys, youngsters all!—they tie them and shoot them! So these people are losing, no? So these innocent people, sometimes they come from north to Colombo. They say, "I don't want to make any war and get into trouble." They just want to spend their life, their very few years, and die. (laughs)

They want to divide the country. That is the problem, no? Now, this is a small island; if they divide this country, then when I go to the north I will need a passport, (laughs) a passport to cross this small island!

The Indian Tamils on the tea estates, they don't like the Tigers. But these Tigers are interesting them to fight. These are the guys creating all these troubles; it is not the Tamil people. Very few. Only one man is controlling it—Prabakaran, the Tiger leader. It is him and his people. Now, they are educated, no? These people know how to incite the poor ones. So that is how it is done, because they are educated! So many people he has killed, even Muslims.

Now, even we Muslims have been killed by the terrorists, because they say, "We also aim to get the Muslims." So we don't want to suffer anymore. We want peace, that's all. The Muslims don't want anything.

You know, in the east, Muslims and Tamils are having some problems. Some Sinhalese murdered some Tamils, so the Tigers come and shoot the Muslims! So because of all this, people think . . . I don't know, people just want it to stop, to end.

People get used to it. Murder is nothing, you know? Killing and murder. In Sri Lanka, if I saw a dog [in the road] I would try to escape it, no? Now, people don't care about any others. It doesn't matter. Murder is nothing now. Before, if there was a murder, we would go three, four, five years without another one. But now, it is nothing.

People are losing now. (laughs)

*In the tea estate community of Norwood, Assistant Superintendent of Police Herath, an imposing man with sharp eyes, presides over a meeting of the local peace committee. About two dozen members are huddled together in one room of the police station. They have been assembled by the police and, in addition to Herath, there are always at least two policemen in the room during the meeting. Two committee members do most of the talking: Rasih, 34, the Tamil school principal; and a Tamil labor foreman, or* talava, *from a nearby tea estate. Herath prompts the conversation at times.*

Rasih: I am the principal of the Tamil school with fourteen hundred children. We are Tamils who immigrated from India and settled down in the plantations. We have our own differences and grievances also, but in this area, by tradition, we are peace-loving people.

But there's not much understanding among the people in these places, so small, small incidents create problems. And we think that forming these committees, with the help of the police, we can create an opportunity to spare more communities and to live together as we lived in the past. In this Norwood division we have not had very much problems like in other parts of the island, and we hope we can continue this same situation through these committees.*

We Tamils think that this is our nation to be lived in and we have got our privileges as citizens of Sri Lanka, and we also try to live as the Sinhalese. Therefore, we also expect the same rights as the Sinhalese have. There were misguidings through the politicians and things like that . . . and, of course, we Tamils are really peace-loving people. In some incident, there may be misguidance, and there are some influences from other labor organizations . . . so, when these youths are misled, people like us, literate people, try to point the correct path.

SA: Do you see youths here that want to be a part of an independent Tamil state?

Rasih: Uh, not to the extent . . . uh, there may be some individuals who give their support, their moral support. But not the community; they think that the problem in the north and east is quite different from what they face here.

JLA: Do you consider yourself different from the Tamils in the north?

Rasih: There are common features, as far as religion and the language we talk, but politically and economically there is a vast difference from the north and we Indian Tamils. They have more advantages than us. They have more advantages than the Sinhalese!

SA: When there is a problem in the community, does the peace committee handle it, or do they turn it over to the police?

Talava: (uneasily) The peace committee give their moral support to the police to maintain law and order.

SA: Just moral support? Say you know something that the police doesn't about an individual. Would you give the police that information?

(silence)

Assistant Superintendent Herath: Yeah, they do give that.

Talava: Whenever there are problems on the estate, I am the first person to handle it there. If I think I can tackle the matter—I know everyone on the estate—I try my best to tackle it on my own. If I fail, I get police assistance.

SA: What about in the Tamil school? Are the children more ethnically conscious than in the past?

Rasih: As teachers, we know the current situation. Though we [Tamils] are a majority in this area, we are a minority island-wide, so we think we must live among this community. Every day, we hoist the national flag, we impress on the

*On the same day of the Norwood peace committee meeting, mob violence broke out on a nearby plantation. Police opened fire and killed two. In the following week, police reported they were searching the area for Tamil guerrillas who had been recruiting Plantation Tamils.

children this is the country where they live, so they must appreciate our leaders and our resources. This is our nation, and the children must follow full-step. If they are studying Tamil, they must also be able to read and write Sinhala, which is essential for them if they go out of this area.

JLA: Once the conflict here is settled, should the peace committees end, or should they continue?

Talava: Once this problem is settled, whatever human beings survive, there will be problems. So we need these committees to remain.

*The Government Agent in Kandy, S.M. Tennakoon, a 51-year-old political appointee with a freshly scrubbed demeanor, sits in a large office festooned with the portraits of his bearded, British colonial predecessors. His job is to coordinate all civilian government agencies throughout Kandy district, the hub of Sri Lanka's central hill-country and its famous tea plantations.*

*The interview is interrupted several times while Tennakoon deals with the morning's most urgent matter: authorizing an underling to ferry government medicines to Raja, the nationally revered temple elephant injured by a car several days before. Tennakoon speaks on the telephone with the custodian of Kandy's Buddhist Temple of the Tooth, to which the beloved "tusker" is attached; medicines on their way, the Government Agent resumes the interview.*

I have been associating with all the communities in Matale [a nearby town] where I was Government Agent for seven years before coming here. I know personally that all of these people—the Sinhalese, the Tamils, the Muslims—are very friendly. They have absolutely no problems. The Sinhalese go to the shops owned by the Tamils. The Tamils go to Sinhalese shops. The Muslims go to Sinhalese shops. Sinhalese go to Muslim shops. If you go through these town areas, you can identify the names of those Tamil people; go there and you will see they are very friendly. Go to the kovil, their religious place; a lot of Sinhalese people are there. On Fridays, and even on other days, our Sinhalese people attend the kovil because, from a religious point of view, there is very much in common among our religions.

Even in the estate areas, the tea estates, the Sinhalese work there together with the Tamils. Even in town areas and other places, they are together. Except in the north and east. But every other place they are friends!

JLA: Yet in 1983, this was one of the worst scenes of anti-Tamil rioting—

Tennakoon: Yeah. Kandy and Matale . . . No, I can tell you, because at that time I was named the Coordinating Officer for Matale District. I was there in '83, doing all the coordination, so I had a lot of experience, taking people to the refugee camps and settling . . . Now, this started as a backlash, you know? About fourteen Army people were blasted and killed, the tension all of a sudden developed. Some undesirable elements—maybe some thugs, maybe some useless people—got together and started attacking these Tamils. This was not planned or anything, as far as I know. This, you know, tension all of a sudden . . . people get ideas and . . . they start looting and . . . lot of damages were done by these people. Number of houses and boutiques. Some people, Sinhalese people, went to the extent of saving all these [Tamil] people. And we were able to control it. In two days, we were able to control them. We took them to camps and then . . . it settled down. And some of these Sinhalese people provided meals. They brought meals to the camps. This is my experience, I'm telling you.

SA: The undesirable elements you speak of, how many were arrested?

Tennakoon: Yes. In Matale, we arrested nearly, say . . . six hundred.

JLA: But you don't think that under the surface there is some basic antagonism between the two communities?

Tennakoon: No, no, no, no. No. Not for me, not even the general people. The common people are not that way. They can't see any difference at all. The same, all people, the same friendship, the same association, will continue and still continues. We don't feel that there is anything, although they fight in the north and east. People here, they don't feel that. This is . . . all of a sudden, erupted, and this created a . . . division, unfortunately.

JLA: So you don't see it happening again?

Tennakoon: I don't, because they are friendly! They are very friendly. They help each other. During the problem, most of these people were staying in Sinhalese homes! They didn't go to [refugee] camps, even! Some of these poor creatures went to the camps, but some of them were accommodated in Sinhala houses. They are friends! Even in my house, (laughs) there were about twenty families! It happened everywhere, all the friends accommodated.

All the people realize that '83 was a very . . . unfortunate incident. But, you see, now there can't be any problems. Even now, people are very friendly. They get together during their wedding festivals and so forth.

Kandy cannot be affected, because this is a very, very safe area. All the communities live in harmony, close relationship. There are no threats, nothing, up to now. The security measures have been taken. No problems . . . although there are certain . . . these estate people are . . . there are a lot of Tamil people. . . . But, absolutely, we have no problem! They are very friendly with each other! So, for tourists, it is very, very safe. There was a big drop of tourists three, four years ago, but now it's going back up, and I hope next year—I am sure—we will have a lot of tourists.

*"Tony" is a middle-aged civil servant in the embattled Eastern Province which is under military rule. He is in a particularly delicate position: a Tamil senior administrator working with the predominantly Sinhalese government in an area claimed by Tamil separatists.*

We have nothing to do with security. When people come and complain to us of harassment, detentions, and so on, I go to the CO [police Coordinating Officer] and help them sort it out. But as for security matters, there are really two separate administrations here, and the security forces normally don't consult us. We are seen as security risks, so we try to keep out of security matters.

The militants understand our position. As long as we don't interfere with them, we are all right. If they think someone's giving information against them, there's a problem. But they generally don't interfere with the civilian administration. They might think the alternative would be worse, and the government might think there's no one else to replace us with to run the life here. A Sinhalese couldn't do this job, not in this area. He'd have to depend on the security forces.

My personal opinion on the security forces is that there are occasions where they overreact. They shoot at random. If someone runs, they shoot. They do roundups in villages, and it's very humiliating to the people. They round up three hundred, five hundred people. And maybe they release ninety percent that evening, but they've spent the day in the sun and been abused, so the damage is done. If I see cases of overreaction, I can bring it to the attention of the CO. Or Colombo. But I would rather try to do it at this level first. Last week, though, we had to call Colombo, and it had an impact. The occasion was that they had wanted to set up a camp and, in their words, "clear the area and put fright into the civilians."

Now, fifty percent or more of my work is related to the war. I feel I'm a member of this community, so I have to share in its problems. I see a lot of people; I give a lot of letters for people seeking missing or detained relatives, if only for consolation. I am telling you the truth. It may be a little damaging, but that is the truth!

I have daughters. As I have, I'd like my daughters to grow up and be a part of the community and experience its problems so that they *know*. I sent my daughters to school in Jaffna, because that is what all the others here do. I didn't want to send them to Colombo, because I would have lost confidence with the [Tamil] people here. And that's why I haven't sent them abroad for studies either. Even if I could afford it, how would that look?

*There is no longer any reason to maintain "Tony's" anonymity; his real name was Marianpillai Anthonimuthu, and he was the Government Agent in Batticaloa. In October 1987, he was killed in a land mine explosion set by the Tigers.*

*Christopher Romesh, 30, is a thin, frail Tamil with haunted eyes and a severe stutter. A Christian, his left arm bears burn scars in the shape of a cross, made by torturers' cigarettes. From Batticaloa in the Eastern Province, Christopher now*

*lives in Madras, India, but hopes to be sent to a hospital in Europe to obtain*
*physical and psychological therapy..*

Batticaloa police caught me under suspicion of railway robbery. They caught me on February 6, 1982. I was in prison for one year and three months. When I was in the police station, they tortured me very badly. After that, I was suffering from asthma.

They used to say me, "Lie on the bench," and they gave me leg belt. They used to hammer with a big, big pole everywhere. After, they put on me chili powder. This was in the police station; then they took me to Batticaloa Prison. They released me in May '83.

Then, February '85, I was caught in Batticaloa by police commandos. They used to take boys [as informants], and they would go by the roads. So they ask the boys who is who, like that. If they do like this (nods head), the police take us. This way they caught me. And I was wearing a T-shirt and trousers. So they took my T-shirt and tied my eyes and they put the handcuff like this and they put me inside the van and I was lying down. So they took me to police commandos camp.

So five days, my eyes were tied. Sixth day, they took me and they said, "Will you tell anything?" I said I don't know anything So they said, "We are going to give you helicopter training." Helicopter training means to tie your hands like that [behind back], and they used to hang you like that . . . So I was ha-ha-hanging-like . . . for nearly five hours. I was in the, uh . . . while—and they were ha-ha-hammering also. They were hammering with the poles and the strong pipe with cement inside.

They asked me whether I was in the movement, or "Do you know anyone who is in the movement." I say I don't know anything. And they were putting chilis—this was the worst—they put in the eyes, nose, mouth, everywhere, all over our body.

Then after five hours, they put me down. My hands were paralyzed. I couldn't move my hands or anything. I was inside a very small cell; there were about ten boys. So I couldn't go to the toilet or anything. I couldn't eat. I couldn't move my hand at all. So boys used to help me. They used to feed me, take me to toilet and everything. But they didn't do the helicopter again.

When I was in the camp, about fifty boys were dying. Sometimes they hammered, struck on head. Sometimes they used to bury and sometimes they used to burn. After killing them, they would say [to the families], "We didn't have him." Once we saw two bodies in the hall, and another one, he escaped and ran, so this one they shot. And they came in and showed me: "If anybody escapes, we will do like this."

I know Sinhalese also. I can talk Sinhalese. I used to talk with the police commandos. They used to come and talk with me, but they say, "We can't help this. It's a hard time for you, but we can't help you."

They kept me two months, and my mother went to the MP for [the town of] Galle in order to pursue my thing. After that, they moved me to Colombo hospital. They gave me physical therapy. In hospital, I was in for fifty days. After forty days, little by little I got my feeling in hands back. Then I came home. For two months after I didn't speak anything. I was shocked. I thought I'm going to die like that [mute].

I was staying at home, but I not go out because I knew I would have problems. I was staying for a while, and then, in November '85, there was a case, some militants put a land mine and police jeep went over it and some police were injured. So police commandos came and they took about fifty boys and they shot thirteen boys on the incident. So, because of that, my parents were scared to keep me, so I came here on November twenty-fifth, '85.

My friends are helping, so I stay here. But it's very hard to pass the time; I just read books. Because I have suffered enough. I just want to go somewhere.

Actually, I like Sinhalese. I know it is just for politics that they do things like this. It is unnatural. Just like us, they are human beings. So we Tamils must fight and we must kill persons, no? But I have no guts for that thing. I am very softhearted.

*With his eagle face and unruly tuft of silvering hair, Bobby Wickremasinghe hardly looks like the deputy commissioner of prisons. A Westernized Sinhalese, he speaks with the cynical, world-weary slang of a man who has spent years outside his own country. Wickremasinghe is inspecting the program at the rehabilitation "transit camp" at Pelawatta, a prison for Tamils detained under the Prevention of Terrorism Act.*

The concept behind this center is to bring about an understanding between the inmate—that's the Tamil terrorist suspect—and the Sinhalese. All the officers are Sinhalese, except for the occasional Muslim, and we believe that we wield a certain rapport between . . . They understand us and we understand them. I mean, we would like harmony and peace in the country, and when they leave this place we would like them to go, not only trained in some kind of vocation, but also with an understanding about the Sinhalese people. Because we lived very harmoniously in the past, and now it is . . . a little away from that.

This is more of a transit camp, really, than a prison. They are borderline cases who . . . those who may or may not be indicted will be brought here. We started this camp only in October [1986]. This is the first such institution. It is really . . . a rehabilitation center, you might even call it. The inmates have been picked up from an army camp, at Boosa. We will be getting more as time goes on, but this is still an experiment. The length of stay will be decided by the attorney general. I mean, he will go through the papers and see whether they are to be indicted or if there is a case against them, and then he'll decide as to . . . how long they're going to stay. But . . . hopefully, a number will be let out.

You see, these are categories where they are really on the borderline. They have not committed a very serious offense, and there may be cases where we, the state, may think they are not so involved in this business of terrorism. There may be cases like that.

The situation has not yet arisen where a single inmate has been very vociferous about terrorist activities. They have not . . . spoken! You see, from what I can see, I have a feeling they're not interested! They want to get back to their homes, get back to their work. They want their fields, their families, to educate the children. They don't seem to be . . . that violent, you know!

And they are not being kept illegally. There is the Terrorist Act, and also the emergency regulations. So they are kept in . . . really, you might even say legal custody.


*Pelawatta's 125 inmates are housed in two dormitory-style cell blocks with an adjoining courtyard. The youngest inmate is 15, the eldest 67. They receive their foreign visitors suspiciously, delegating their leader, a dark, bearded, hulking man with a scarred face, to ask questions of them first. A Muslim, Tamil-speaking guard is their interpreter. Finally, the inmates agree that a few of them will tell their stories.*

*Wearing sarongs and sandals, they assemble eagerly on the bare cement floor of one of the dormitories while the prison guards stand nervously at the edges. At one point, the guard-interpreter, unusually candid and sympathetic, whispers, "All these people here, they have no charges against them at all; they are all innocent."*

*Chandra Kumash, 26, is intense and has a firm, determined voice. He is from a farming family in Trincomalee.*


On the sixteenth of December of 1985, I was arrested when the army rounded up my city. After that we were taken in a gunboat and we were even burned! We were assaulted and we were burned! And from there, we were handed over to the Navy officers, who transferred us to the Boosa camp. There we were injured [tortured] until they found that we were innocent.

They said after three months we will be discharged, and there was an order that when we are discharged we had to go back to our same villages and stay there for at least three months afterwards. We signed letters agreeing to that; I was released to my village with this letter. There I was employed as a laborer, and I had to maintain my elderly mother, who is sixty years old.

Then, in the same month, we were re-arrested when the army rounded up our village! And after we were arrested, we were told that we would be produced before their big boss and then we'll be released. So I produced my letter to them. That letter was destroyed by the army officials! And we were asked to eat that letter! We were fed, were—by force—asked to eat that letter! It was destroyed and torn, and we were asked to eat it! And that letter was signed by the national security minister!

We were loaded into a vehicle and taken to Trincomalee army fort. There we were kept for about one month and statements were recorded. There I told the superiors that I was arrested earlier and released and this is the second time. I was told that I would be kept three months in Boosa and then released.

So far, they have not done anything about my release. Now my father is dead. My stepfather was looking after me; when I was here, he, too, died. I could not go for the funeral. He was a government servant. After my stepfather's death, my mother and my sister are all suffering. They don't have a house to stay in now. I am the only person who has to maintain that family. Now I am suffering inside here, and I have no outside assistance.

Here you can see people just shedding tears. Now, nearly for two years, I have been suffering in this custody. I don't know how I will go out and live. If I think of my future here, I don't know what will happen to me.

SA: Are you worried that, even if you are released, you will be arrested again?

Guard: (interrupting) I think so. Even for the third time. When the army rounds up the villages, if they get that chap he will be re-arrested again!

SA: So what can a person like you do?

Chandra: What we can do is run, die, or commit suicide. That's the only things we can do. If we run, they will shoot us. Inside the house they will arrest us. So what can we do? When we run, they say that we are terrorists and they shoot us. So I think running is the best thing, so they may shoot us. That is what has happened to most of the people. There's no remedy.

*Marimuttu Shanmugan, 27, a small, almost-black Tamil from Trincomalee, rises to speak amid laughter from the crowd. As a low-caste laborer, he is the object of apparently good-natured derision. Apologetically, he waits until the hoots die down to begin.*

I am from a low-caste family. We are the people who fill the roads and drains and that type of thing.

On eighteen November, 1985, I was there in the Sinhalese [detention] camp. The army officers came there. They selected fourteen among us. Took us to the fort, army fort. There they injured us. They said that after injuries we will be released. After ten days, we were all put into a lorry and brought to the Boosa camp. Up to date we are not released.

My wife has already written that she doesn't have any sort of income even to stitch a frock. I don't have parents, and her position is also that. My child was born, and after five months only, I was arrested. So far, I have not seen my child or wife. If you can—I can't even talk Tamil properly, I have not studied—if you can, please help me. I am not in a position to talk beyond that.

*Every morning, the anguished women appear on his doorstep, their thin, peasant bodies wrapped in loose saris. They are the wraiths of Batticaloa, the growing throng of women whose sons and husbands have disappeared, been detained or shot by the government's antiterrorist Special Task Force (STF). Sam Thambimuttu, a bearish Tamil lawyer turned shrimp farmer, documents their cases. He is the secretary of the ad hoc Batticaloa Citizen's Committee, formed in the absence of any local political representatives since Batticaloa is under martial rule.*

You must first understand the attitude of the STF. They are all young chaps in their teens. If you watch them going out on their vehicles, they go like you would expect a person going on a safari to go. When you go on a safari, big-game hunting, you get on top of the hood with guns pointed out. Here, this has become a safari for the young fellows, but the game are human beings. They go around the streets; if they see somebody running, they fire at him! The only provocation is that a man is running!

Now, there was a land-mine incident just down the road. Following that, the STF indiscriminately opened fire everywhere. Thirteen persons were officially reported killed. About twenty-eight persons were missing subsequently; we don't know what happened to them, but we know, we have evidence, that some of them were killed and their bodies taken away. Here, once the Force shoots a person the body is taken away, old tires are heaped, and the body burned. Thereafter, there is absolutely no evidence that that person ever existed! It's very easy for the state to turn around and say, "X, who is missing from his home, has become a terrorist. He is hiding in England or he is hiding in Germany."

They must have learnt the lesson after the last [world] war. Germany made the mistake of leaving skeletons behind (smiles); in concentration camps, you found millions of skeletons. So these people are not going to leave any evidence behind. That's why they burn all the bodies. Here, they are legally entitled to burn the bodies in their camp. They are allowed to; it's not written into a law, but, under the emergency regulations, the Coordinating Officer is permitted to dispose of the body however he thinks fit.

What we do is, when a person comes to us and tells us that so-and-so has been arrested by the forces, we do not take any step immediately; we wait for three days, because a large number of persons who have been arrested are released subsequently. But after three days, if he is not released, we immediately write to the Coordinating Officer.

We have a system with the CO. . . . You see, when a person is arrested and taken to these camps, the state does not provide him with any clothes whatsoever. So, even if he is kept there for one or two years, he has only the clothes that he has been wearing, nothing else. So we request that the next of kin be permitted to give them clothes. So, after about three days, the next of kin take a change of clothes to

the camp and they hand over the clothes, and if they accept the clothes, we know that the person is alive and in the camp. But if somebody comes back and tells us, "I went to the camp; they refused to accept his clothes," then we know that something is wrong and immediately we write to the CO asking for his where-abouts. Invariably, the reply comes in that he has not been arrested.
(Thambimuttu opens a loose-leaf binder.)

In all these cases, we have affidavits by persons who saw the person being taken away by the STF. We prepared this list in May of '86, of persons arrested by the STF forces whose whereabouts are not known. This list gives the name of the person, his address, age, place where he was arrested, and by whom he was arrested. We sent this list to the Coordinating Officer. I sent 359 names and asked him for the whereabouts of these persons. I received a letter from him in September 1986; I have it here. It says there is only one person who had been sent to Boosa [detention camp]. The reply to everybody else was, "not arrested." That means they have killed them. Now, the number of people who have disappeared in this district is roughly about seven hundred.

According to the Prevention of Terrorism Act, any person can be taken into custody on suspicion of being a terrorist; it says, "any person." But it is not merely a person who is being taken into custody; they are taking entire villages! Which certainly is not the intention of the law, but there is nothing we can do about it.

Say in one of their cordon-and-search operations, they round up a thousand people. They are kept there, and people like government servants and old people are released, and so maybe five hundred will be taken to the camp. There, they pass before a hooded informant. If he nods his head, it means that person stays in the camp and goes through the full range of torture. The others are released. This takes a period of three, four days. Along the way, a few chaps may get bumped off. Or there at the camp, in the "helicopter training" [torture], one or two may die. These are the cases that become "missing."

This maltreatment is virtually throwing the local people into the militants' camps, because if they join the militants they are safe. If they remain at home, they are invariably caught and taken and killed or sent to Boosa. So, the only way to escape is to join the militants, and once you do, you know how to avoid these chaps!

Now, the biggest problem we have here is that about thirty-five hundred breadwinners of families have been either arrested, are in detention camps, or in Boosa, or missing, or are dead. These thirty-five hundred families are destitute, with absolutely no means of sustenance. We are also worried whenever an advanced-level or university student is picked up; invariably, they never come back.

You know, this area is essentially an agricultural and fishing area, but because of constant raids and constant harassing, these people now refuse to go into the fields.

So much so that [rice] paddy cultivation in this area has decreased by as much as forty percent. This has been going on for the past three years. Batticaloa was a surplus rice-producing area, but now we have to get our rice down from elsewhere. This affects others, too; you see, the entire community exists on the income of paddy. You have the paddy miller, you have the paddy trader, you have the man who pounds the paddy and sells the rice. So the throwback, as far as employment is concerned, is vast.

In Batticaloa, we live for the evening, not even the next day. Life has become so uncertain. Everything is so uncertain that in the morning you only think of the evening and nothing beyond that. All our actions are based on the immediate necessities, rather than on thinking of the morrow.

We don't go out after six. You see, in Batticaloa, by six o'clock, life is over. There's absolutely no social contact between people. This is also affecting children. You see, if you hear a noise, you immediately think that there is a blast somewhere. If you're on the streets and you hear a sound, you think there's a blast and you're running for shelter somewhere.

Now, every parent who can afford to, sends his child out of the country . . . You know, one fear that we have is, if this goes on, we may lose the flower of our youth! That may be the end of the community. I suppose that is what the government wants also.

*(The interview is halted as a group of women appear at the edge of Thambimuttu's veranda. One woman, who is crying, holds out an identity card. It belongs to her teenage son, taken by the STF from their home that morning.)*

Woman: My son was home and he was sleeping inside the house. He was arrested and taken to the STF camp. I went there about ten o'clock, and when I inquired for my son, I was told that they had shot him. So I asked them, "Why did you shoot him? After all, he's a baker. What has he done?" And they just said, "We shot him."

*Another woman who is listening squats suddenly on the ground by Thambimuttu's feet and begins to wail, her arms outstretched, beseeching. Her son has been missing for a year, "which means he's dead," Sam explains.*

*After consoling the keening woman, Thambimuttu turns his attention back to the mother whose son has just been shot. He leads her to his office, where his aides will take down details of the case.*

*The baker's mother was refused the body of her son for burial. An item in the newspaper reported that the STF had killed a "terrorist" in a shootout, the government version of the baker's death.*

*Father Chandra, 44, is a Tamil Catholic priest in the city of Batticaloa. He is a beefy, powerful man with jaded eyes. Crowding the open doorway of his office next to St. Thomas' Cathedral is a cluster of women waiting to speak with him. They are the wives and mothers of Tamil men who have been picked up by the security forces. The priest's office is one of the stops they make on their daily rounds, seeking help and information.*

You know the problem we have in the Church today? The Church in the south doesn't know what's really happening in the north and east. They have not come and seen. We want them to come and see with their own eyes what is happening here and talk to the people who have been affected. And let them go and see the camps and how the young men are treated there. They have never come. And when we go and tell them, they don't believe all this is happening here. The Church is divided. We are completely separate now. The Tamil bishops of the north and east are one, the rest of the bishops are another. The Sinhala bishops condemn the bishops of the north and east. They don't say anything, just keep quiet.

Even the Sinhala people don't know what is really happening here. The policemen can come and kill anyone on the road, and they'll not give the body and they'll bury them and tell them, "I have killed ten terrorists." There's no postmortem, no inquiry, nothing.

Even at night, they go and knock at the door and rape the girls and women, and break their houses, steal their gold, jewelry, and arrest people. They have killed so many people. Here, today, no young man can live. Because between the age of, say, fifteen and forty, every man has been arrested from time to time. Even last night, they opened fire at five people who had dinner here. They were shot at, and they arrested two and released them in the morning.

They killed a sixty-three-year-old man who looked after this church and took the body. They never returned the body. Sixty-three years old. In September. He was the watchman of my church. For no reason. They just came and shot him and took the body. We saw them do it, but they said, "No. That incident did not take place." Where's the body? Nobody knows.

We have no one to complain to. There's no civil authorities here. We have no Members of Parliament. So who can you complain to?

The upper ranks of the Special Task Force are very nice people. You will find the CO [Coordinating Officer] a very nice man. But the lower ranks, the ordinary police, are very bad. They go and arrest some people and come back and tell him, "We arrested so many people." He has to believe. He says, "I have to believe my own men."

I told the CO one day. "You believe your men's story, but one day you will know what the truth really is." At least before God, he will have to answer one day and give an account of what happened.

You know, they were sent here, specially trained men to fight against terrorism.

And to fight against terrorism, you have to win the hearts and minds of the people. But they are not winning the hearts and minds of the people; they know only the hatred.

SA: So can you understand why some of the Tamils have turned to violence?

Chandra: Yes. We were taking up nonviolent struggle from 1956 to 1983. We were nonviolent; we were beaten up, arrested. And the number of communal riots we experienced . . . So they found, the young men, that nonviolence is something which cannot bring you anything. So they've taken up to arms.

SA: But the Church advocates nonviolence. If a militant came to you, would you counsel him to lay down his weapons?

Chandra: (pause) What about defending our own land, our own men? I have to see that also. Now, today, so many villages and so many people are defended only by them; otherwise, the whole family there would have been destroyed. If I advise them to put down their arms, who is going to protect the Tamils? I cannot be one-sided, because I am born and bred here, I live among my own men. In this situation, I can't but support the young men here who are armed.

SA: Does it cause a conflict within you to go against the dictates of the Church in order to follow your conscience?

Chandra: Actually, I can't preach violence in public. I can't because of the teaching of the Church.

JLA: So what can you preach to the young men here?

Chandra: (long pause) Here, most priests will tell them to pray, pray, pray. Make sacrifices. Most all the priests are asking the people to pray. That theory can be popular. In some places, every Sunday, the people come and make a day of fasting. Actually, most of our people who are churchgoers are emotionally and sentimentally of that nature.

Actually, the work of the Church today is the work of the Red Cross. It doesn't prevent, but it helps the people who have suffered, but the important work . . . It's the Church all over the world; it cares for the affected people but never tries to solve the problem. Every time, all over the world, the Church plays a very safe game. It won't decide. You will never see the Church standing up. The Church keeps quiet. They don't make statements here among a majority of Buddhists, because the Church doesn't want any problems.

SA: But, as a priest, how do you feel being put in a position where you are condoning violence?

Chandra: (smiles archly) First lesson, the Church doesn't support violence. Of course, you find in the Bible, even the history of the Church—you know the crusaders?—you've heard how they were against the Muslims, and the Church supported the killing of the Muslims? Through the history of the Church, you will find so many examples. But the Church doesn't support violence; the Church is against violence. . . .

But I am working here. They are my people. Their problems are my problems, so I have to work for them. All over the world, so many priests are taking up arms to help the people. I am for the people, so I stand with them in this.

JLA: Has it changed the way you look at your religion?

Chandra: Sometimes you go around about the existence of God, and you look at all these things, your own people who have worked for you and are killed and we could do nothing. Even last year, people were killed inside the Church, on the nineteenth of January last year. Three young men were working inside the Church; they were killed inside the Church. Even the bishop didn't ask why they have done this.

Sometimes you wonder whether God exists.

*In the lagoons around Batticaloa, the only means of transportation are small canoe "ferries" that shuttle the local people to and from their villages. It is also the means of travel for the guerrillas who exercise a certain control over some of the outlying areas. As a result, it is a perilous journey for everyone if the security forces decide to lay an ambush.*

*Yesterday, the STF police commandos attacked a nearby ferry crossing. According to the Tigers and local Tamil civilians, the three men they killed were a bus driver, a schoolteacher, and a 17-year-old student, none of them militants. Sellathamby Kamalanathan, the mother of the slain student, appears in the rectory of St. Thomas' Cathedral in Batticaloa, with a delegation of her friends and neighbors, seeking help. Amid tears and wailing, she tells what happened through an English-speaking schoolteacher who is present.*

Teacher: The circumstances were this: they do not have toilets in most of these villages, so these people go to the bushes for relieving themselves. Her son was relieving himself like this when they shot him.

Mother: He goes in the morning to relieve himself and he comes back and has a bath and goes to school. He is studying his pre-university examinations this year. So, as he was coming after relieving himself, he was shot. When I heard gunshots, I went out and saw my son bleeding.

SA: You saw the soldiers?

Mother: Yes, they were all over the village. I saw my son lying on the sand and I thought he must be lying down flat to escape the firing. And then I lifted him. I took the boy into my arms. He died. And two soldiers told me not to take the body and started firing to the air. So I ran back to my house.

JLA: And what happened to the body?

Mother: After, I went and prostrated before the soldier and begged for the body. "Even if you shoot, I don't mind, but give me my son's body." They said, "It's there in the bushes where we shot him; you can go and collect it." But when I went there, I found only a piece of bone, a part of the head, and a small cloth and some blood.

Teacher:  When they fired into the air and she ran into the house, they must have dragged the body away to the camp.

JLA:  How old was he?

Teacher:  He was seventeen years old. Name, Silvathamby Kalamanadam.

(Mother offers her son's identity card with his photograph.)

SA:  (Looking at identity card) His birthday is tomorrow.

Mother:  Yes, tomorrow is his birthday.


*The rendezvous is at noon, two hundred yards from the fortified Batticaloa police station. The two men on motorcycles approach, swerve, and motion us aboard. We roar off; a quick turn down an alley avoids an STF truck idling in an intersection. The rest of the trip out of the city is at breakneck speed. At one point, a third cyclist comes alongside and the young men exchange words. The "spotter" points to the road behind, and the motorcycles speed up.*

*Finally in the countryside, we stop at the edge of a lagoon. The cycles are placed in fiberglass outrigger canoes and, with the riders, are paddled to the junglelike opposite shore by old, sun-blackened men in turbans. The trip continues on the other side, down a narrow road that cuts through a shrimp farm, to a Methodist church, its yard filled with youths bearing weapons. As the cycles pull up, one of the armed men speaks into a walkie-talkie. An hour later, a jeep arrives to take us the final leg of the journey to the Eastern Province headquarters of the Liberation Tigers of Tamil Eelam.*

*The rustic base camp is surrounded by verdant rice paddies on Kokkadichola Peninsula, ten miles west of Batticaloa. The placidness of the setting is deceptive; the rutted track to the tree-ringed encampment is guarded by jumpy Tiger guerrilla sentries armed with Kalashnikovs and rocket-propelled grenades. In the camp itself, the forty-odd cadres are swathed in weapons. The visit by outsiders has been prepared for with careful, intimidating ceremony; the fighters pose around the camp, their fingers on triggers.*

*Kumarappa, 27, is the Tiger commander for the Eastern Province. A heavy man with a drooping mustache and cold, brown eyes, he is wearing khaki pants and a white shirt, with a revolver tucked into his belt. Wicker chairs are arranged in a half-circle in a thatched hut; Kumarappa sits and waves for the questions to begin. His men crowd into the hut to watch and listen, and one Tiger with a camera snaps photos throughout the meeting.*


SA:  Why did you join the Tigers?

Kumarappa:  Me? Because I am also part of these people. I am losing my freedom. Because when I was studying, you know, advanced level, when I was doing my exams, I had to get more and more marks than the Sinhalese people. Because I was a Tamil, you know? If you want to enter any university, you had to get more marks. For example, in education, in everything education-wise, and agriculture-wise, and job-wise, everything, the government . . . it's, you know, at the price of the Tamils. Actually, you know, it turned into genocide.

SA: What's the average day like for a Tiger?

Kumarappa: Our soldiers, every day when they get up, they do some exercises first of all. Then they have to get out and guard. Then, every day, they have to do some duty, politically, economically—you know, some intellect training. Everything, you know.

JLA: What are the rules about being a Tiger?

Kumarappa: You mean discipline? You know, no drinks first. Smokes, yeah, we accept—if they want, they can smoke. But no connection with a woman. They can feel with them, you know; I mean, they can love any woman, they can love, but nothing physical. They can't make love.

JLA: For how long?

Kumarappa: That depends on the length of the war. To a girl, I will say, "If you want to marry me, you have to wait for me until we get our freedom." I mean, that's the rule, you know. Because, in the situation in here, in the movement, we believe we can't survive with women. Afterward, okay, everybody, if they like, they can marry. After some period, maybe three or four years, then the Tiger can marry. In the early days, no . . . too much weakness.

JLA: It looks like a static situation, with the STF over in Batticaloa and you here. Is there even any confrontation?

Kumarappa: We face a lot of direct confrontation. At this moment, we are taking the rest in here. But our soldiers, every day they are searching for commandos. Some direct confrontation in Batticaloa town and some other places, around STF commando camps. Every day. At this moment, we face a confrontation against EPRLF [rival Tamil guerrilla force]. At this moment, they're almost finished, EPRLF. We captured their arms and ammunitions and everything. A lot of them have surrendered.

JLA: Why the confrontation with the EPRLF?

Kumarappa: Because, you know, every day EPRLF was doing antisocial activities. Especially here in Batticaloa. We have Tamils and Muslims together here, you know, and they are actually imposing on the Muslim people. We accept the EPRLF, their self-determination and their rights, but they're looting the Muslim shops and lorries. They're making antisocial activities every day, day by day. Lots of times we warned them, but they persisted. That is the main reason. Because we are fighting for the liberation, the dedicated fight against the government here. Because we are, deep down, soldiers, you know, politically. That's why.

SA: Do you find it difficult, as a Tamil, to take the life of a fellow Tamil?

Kumarappa: No. Because we're fighting for a cause, you know. I mean, we're dedicated to a fight, to give our lives. And the EPRLF are doing antisocial activities. We should try to cleanse them. "Okay, if you surrender, you can keep your life; we want only your arms and ammunition." We got a lot of arms from the EPRLF.

JLA: What kind of country do you see for Eelam?

Kumarappa: (long pause) Oh yeah, socialist. A socialist country, yeah. Because in here, sixty percent of the people are poor; only ten percent are very rich. Corruption, you know? We have to develop our country. New socialism.

JLA: Two countries, Sri Lanka and Eelam?

Kumarappa: Yeah. A separate state.

SA: Will the Tigers accept anything less than a separate state?

Kumarappa: No. We will fight, you know. We want it, the Tamils. And to get Eelam we will fight.

JLA: So you don't think negotiations will work?

Kumarappa: I think that's a failure. Better to fight. My opinion, and of all the Tigers who have been here in this situation. Because every day, the STF commandos kill innocent people and loot our properties, destroy our economic schemes. Every day.

SA: All your soldiers carry cyanide capsules, is that correct?

Kumarappa: Yes, and, you know, the cyanide, no other army in the world goes into a fight with it. I think the cyanide helps our morale, you know? Especially, it increases our morale . . . and people have to keep our secrets.

JLA: Have any of your men had to use it?

Kumarappa: A lot of them. Time to time, since '83. Sometimes men are captured by STF commandos. They take this, and that's it.

JLA: What if he doesn't take the cyanide. Say, he gets caught and is afraid?

Kumarappa: He must have to take it. That's our rules. A Tiger, he will. Sometimes there's no opportunity. For example, two or three of our Tiger soldiers, they didn't have any cyanide capsules. They were caught, but they fight with the STF so they would shoot them. It's a good death. . . .

JLA: To make them shoot you?

Kumarappa: Yeah, it's a good death. Our soldiers did that. It's a very brave death. . . . I'm not afraid to die, you know?

SA: Is this a fight between the Tigers and the government, or between the Tamils and the Sinhalese?

Kumarappa: The government and the Tigers. We love the Sinhalese people, you know, we love them. They are also innocent. But we are trying to gain the power. When they support the government, they don't accept our homeland and our self-determination. We are a separate culture—everything, you know, separate religion, separate language. Everything.

JLA: When the STF goes berserk after an attack by you and kills civilians, does that make you feel partly responsible?

Kumarappa: Yeah, but that's a very uncontrolled army, you know, uncontrolled troops. Especially here, the STF commandos react to the civilians. Every day they're doing that here. Today, one incident, the STF commandos opened fire on the ferry, people that were passing on the river. Two of them killed, two civilians.

Sometimes we also feel like doing that, you know. Actually, we don't like that, but sometimes, you know, we don't have any alternatives. Sometimes we have to do that job, too. We have to kill them also.

JLA: Do you feel you have popular support?

Kumarappa: Yeah. We have the popular support. You know, some government intelligence service, they moderate the people by money and they are getting a lot of information about us. The government intelligence is getting the messages every day. We can show you one spy that we have caught.

JLA: You have a spy here?

Kumarappa: Yeah, a spy here. Government-backed, I think MOSSAD-backed, you know? She's a thirty-six-year-old woman. She infiltrated our area and was getting the message and giving it to the commando camp. We've captured a lot of spies.

JLA: But she's a Tamil?

Kumarappa: Yeah, she's a Tamil.

SA: When did you find her?

Kumarappa: We knew about her two months ago, but day before yesterday, we captured her. Now there is an inquiry.

JLA: What will happen to her if you find she is guilty?

Kumarappa: Sentence her to death. That's her final punishment. That's the way it has to be, you know? They can't survive.

SA: And how are they executed?

Kumarappa: Sometime we put them on the lamppost, sometime, you know, we have the Cordex explosive wire—just around her body and then we detonate it. This is our maximum punishment. We do it sometimes. Two or three times we've done it. . . .

*The woman "spy," Kangaratnam Athuma Kirikith, is brought into the hut. She is a tiny woman with wild, unkempt hair. Her eyes are unfocused; she seems to be in a state of shock. Athuma limps badly and is made to sit in the chair next to Kumarappa.*

SA: How did you catch her?

Kumarappa: In Mandur, some ten miles from here. The officer in charge of Vellaveli police station operated her. All the time, if she wanted to pass a message, she would go the Vellaveli police station commandos.

SA: Has she confesssed?

Kumarappa: Uh . . . yeah. She passed information through other sources, sometimes direct.

SA: But she's admitted doing that?

Kumarappa: Yeah.

SA: She's confessed?

Kumarappa: Yeah! Without any torturing, she accepts everything. Now, she asks me for her life now.

JLA: Has she said why she did it?

Kumarappa: Because of money. She's suffering in poverty, you know.

JLA: It's not because the STF leaned on her, are holding her husband or brother or something like that?

Kumarappa: I think now they are holding her brother.

SA: When will you decide what to do with her?

Kumarappa: We have to keep her alive for a little bit, because we need to have some other persons for the inquiry. So you have to keep them alive.

JLA: But it also happens, doesn't it, that the STF captures Tamil civilians, holds them, and then maybe goes to the relatives and says, "If you want your son back you must bring us information." Doesn't that happen?

Kumarappa: Yeah, that's also happening here. A lot of cases of that.

JLA: (to Athuma) Do you have children?

Athuma: (in English) Seven children. One boy. He's six.

JLA: Did you think this would happen to you?

Athuma: (answers in Tamil)

Kumarappa: She know one day it will happen.

JLA: If you knew it was going to happen, why did you do it?

Athuma: (a long, breathless passage in Tamil, her voice barely above a whisper, her eyes fixed on the tape recorder)

Kumarappa: I think she's bluffing, yeah? She's saying her family—you know, the children—are suffering. She says she had two children, and an officer in the Batticaloa police station, his sister took those children—because of the poverty, you know. Sergeant Dissanayake said, "Okay, we keep your children; you give us the information." She accepted to give the two children, and they are now in Colombo with this sergeant's sister.

(Athuma now mumbles continuously in Tamil in a low, hysterical voice.)

Kumarappa: She said the first incident to meet Mr. Dissanayake was the time she went to get her passport. Normally, you have to go to Colombo—very difficult to get a passport. But somebody said, "Okay, no problem. If you go see Sergeant Dissanayake, you can get your passport." Then she went to the Batticaloa police station and talked with Sergeant Dissanayake, so he made her do this way [inform].

JLA: What happened to her husband?

K: She says the STF commandos, they beat her husband. He didn't do anything. After, he couldn't do anything—I mean, he couldn't do any business or any work. Now he's in the house.

SA: What does she think is going to happen to her?

(Athuma answers softly)

Kumarappa: She knows very well the final decision. She knows we're going to kill her.

(Athuma begins another long monologue, repeated over and over until Kumarappa interrupts)

Kumarappa: She says, you know . . . I mean, she's pleading, "They're going to take my life."

JLA: Did people die as a result of her information?

Kumarappa: No.

JLA: Then why can't you forgive her?

Kumarappa: (sighs) Because, you know . . . she made a big mistake.

(Athuma is led out by several armed guerillas and returns to the hut that is her cell)

*Shankar, a 12-year-old Tiger, is beckoned forward. He sits on an older comrade's lap, gripping his Chinese AK-47 assault rifle. A cute, shy boy, he is the youngest "cadre" in Kumarappa's band. He speaks in Tamil; Kumarappa translates. Throughout, the comrade strokes Shankar's back and shoulders fondly.*

JLA: When did you become a Tiger?

Kumarappa: One and a half years ago.

SA: Has he seen action yet?

Kumarappa: Yeah, he's been in action a few times. He went for military training and he joined the assault group. About six miles from here he participated in an ambush against the STF commandos. He's very brave in fighting. He's a sniper.

JLA: He's got a Chinese AK.

Kumarappa: Yeah, good gun, but he does better with an M-16; lightweight, you know?

JLA: Ask him, why did he join the Tigers?

Kumarappa: He says, I'm also a Tamil.

SA: Is your family proud that you joined the Tigers?

Kumarappa: He says, yes. He's a local child, but he lives here in the camp.

JLA: What does he want to be later on, when there's an Eelam?

Kumarappa: He would like to join the military.

SA: Do you like living in the camp?

Kumarappa: He says yes.

SA: You don't miss school?

Kumarappa: No, because he's dedicated to fight, you know?

SA: You don't miss your schoolfriends?

Kumarappa: He says he wants to get freedom. So to get freedom, he doesn't miss anything.

*It can be assumed that Athuma was executed within a few days of the interview. Attempts to intercede on her behalf with Tiger supporters in Batticaloa were futile.*

*Eleven days later, the STF launched a massive raid on Kumarappa's base. In the battle, at least twenty-one of the Tigers were reported killed, including Kumarappa. The Batticaloa Citizen's Committee, however, charged the STF with executing twenty-seven people at the nearby shrimp hatchery and estimated the attack's overall death toll at nearly two hundred, mostly civilians.*

*The khaki-clad Coordinating Officer of Batticaloa District, Sumith Silva, is a huge, brawny man, his affability and personal civility at odds with the reputation of the forces under his command. The interview is at the Special Task Force (STF) headquarters, a heavily fortified complex several miles outside of Batticaloa. The base also doubles as an interrogation and detention center for Tamil terrorist suspects. Also seated in Silva's office is a younger officer in jogging gear who won't identify himself.*

When violence is taken, any state has to take action to counter that violence. This whole problem can be sorted out; if the terrorists lay down their arms, the army packs up and goes. But the terrorists continue their acts of violence.

JLA: They continue theirs and, according to an overwhelming number of people in Batticaloa, you continue yours.

Silva: We don't. Now, suppose we act in self-defense: it is not an act of violence. In every action in Batticaloa, the first act of violence has always been committed by the terrorists. This is how it happens: We go out on a patrol. The first shot is fired by a terrorist. Our counterattack begins in defense, obviously in defense — we have to shoot to save ourselves, you see? In the process, there may be some . . . innocents [hit], but that is provided for by the law. In a situation where someone is trying to shoot me and I shoot back, but hit the wrong man, that is self-defense, provided for by the law. This law is not our law; it is faithfully reproduced from the British law.

SA: But we're not talking about people killed in cross fires. There are dozens of women wandering around Batticaloa looking for their sons, their fathers, and they can't find them.

Silva: Can't find them? You know, I think that's an exaggeration. What happens is this—I've talked about this over and over again but—in 1981, they started their training camps in India. The little youths in Jaffna were brainwashed, were regimented, and they left their homes on their own free will without their parents' consent. Parents didn't know where they were. They've all gone across the Palk Straits to the training camps. Today, I think ninety-five percent of the so-called disappearances are in training camps.

JLA: But some of these disappearances have happened this morning. We've been to places and had the women coming up crying—

Silva: But why do you believe what you see?

JLA: Come on. The women are falling on the ground and crying.

Silva: How do you know what the truth is? That can be arranged, can't it? The women come here also.

JLA: Are you saying they're professional grievers?

Silva: (laughs) I've been here in instances when they came here and said, "So-and-so died." But we have no reason to deny it, you know, if we have shot this boy in action, killed him in action. I won't hide anything from you.

Anonymous Officer: For instance, yesterday, the security forces arrested 110 men after a shootout with the terrorists. Killed three terrorists—LTTE—and then the village was surrounded and we have taken 110 persons into custody. This morning we released 102, 105.

JLA: We were told that the three killed yesterday, one was a boy who was urinating in his garden—

Silva: (laughs) Oh no, no, no.

JLA: —and the other two were crossing the lagoon on a boat.

Silva: (laughs) What can I say? I have perfect proof, but I cannot show it to you. Perfect proof, that would be accepted in any court of law anywhere in the world, that they were terrorists. I'm assuring you of that. Only, I can't show it to you.

JLA: One was a government servant.

Silva: Government servants can also be terrorists.

JLA: It was a shoot-out and they were shooting back at your forces?

Anonymous Officer: (pause) Yes. Across the lagoon. A helicopter was shot [at].

Silva: (opens a ledger book) Here is the incident—we record everything. Here is the history, brief history. Everything is documented. (on the top page of the book are a couple of handwritten sentences; he begins to read them aloud)

On sixteenth January, security forces conducted search at Kullamanam. Boat was seen in lagoon. The people in the boat suddenly attacked; the STF returned fire, killing three terrorists. (closes ledger)

Now, everyone says they are innocent, but we know they are terrorists. We have it from very top authority. The authority I cannot quote to you, because I would be divulging my source of information; I can't do that, because I couldn't go and get information again from these sources. (laughs) We have people who tell us these things. That is because we have perfect rapport with the large majority of the people here.

Anonymous Officer: So far, they [Tamil Tigers] have killed 118 innocent Tamil people tied to lampposts in Batticaloa. One hundred and eighteen. Women and men both, up to last Thursday. Tied to lampposts.

Silva: We don't do that.

JLA: We don't dispute the atrocities of the militants, but we're talking about something different. It wouldn't seem that you're exactly welcomed by the populace here, judging by the way your camp is fortified. Your people don't smile at the local people—

Anonymous Officer: If we smiled at you, you would be against a lamppost tomorrow morning. Women, children, it doesn't matter.

Silva: Look, the terrorists' very existence is against the law. Their presence here is obviously for the purpose of dividing Sri Lanka, which is against the constitution, which is treason, punishable by death in Sri Lanka.

JLA: What about torture? Everyone says you use it widely.

Silva: Sometimes, if they resist arrest, force must be used to restrain them, but once they are brought to the camps they are not tortured.

JLA: How can that be? Literally everyone you've picked up has either been tortured himself or seen someone else undergo it. There are very specific details on how the torture is carried out. There is the "helicopter training," the beating, the chili powder—

Silva: (laughs) Those are just figments of their imagination.

JLA: Really?

Silva: Well, there may be cases here and there, but a microminority.

JLA: But surely your forces must feel frustrated here, among a people whose language they don't speak, fighting an invisible enemy—

Silva: There's no frustration amongst the forces, but there may be a few instances where they may be guilty of excesses. But such actions are very few, and such instances, when they do occur, we view very, very sternly.

JLA: How sternly?

Silva: Such as dismissal, for example.

JLA: What kinds of crimes merit dismissal from the forces?

Silva: Unwarranted torture, rape of women, unwarranted use of force. . . . They'll be dismissed forthwith!

JLA: What about unwarranted murder?

Silva: As yet we've had no cases of officers, of any ranks, accused of murder, because there have been no cases proved. In the three months I've been here in Batticaloa there has been no allegations of murder made with justification. I can't speak about before.

JLA: Do you, personally, have any problems with the way the war is being waged?

Silva: Killing is inevitable, as far as the terrorists are concerned, so we are totally within our rights to fire back.

If a murderer is hiding somewhere, I'm duty-bound to go and arrest him. Murder is an offense punishable by death. And when I go there, if he opens fire at me, I'm perfectly justified in defending myself. You know, this isn't a conventional war yet; they are still of this country, so whatever they do is illegal and punishable by the laws of the country. The STF never opens fire first. I can truthfully say that!

Anonymous Officer: A Tamil terrorist—there are none from Batticaloa to begin with; they all come from Jaffna—they have not been welcomed by the population. The people are sick of them. About three months ago, they abducted eight Tamils—Tamils!—and they raised twelve million rupees, just to raise money!

Silva: They are ruthless, ruthless murderers who are brainwashed and can't see a democratic solution to anything.

SA: Is it true you have a place here in the camp where you burn the bodies of those killed by your troops?

Silva: No, no, no. Who told you that?

SA: Well, we've talked to many people, including the mothers of men who have been killed in the last few days, and they say you don't give the bodies back to them for burial but burn them in the camp. Is it true you don't give the families their bodies?

Silva: (long pause, looks out window) Sometimes . . . we don't give the bodies back, because it's . . . they're . . . because, sometimes, they'll use it for propaganda purposes, the terrorists. For security concerns the law allows us to not give them to their owners. But we don't burn them. We have a place, a cemetery adjoining the camp. They are, however, perfectly able to come to do the last rites—

JLA: Oh, so each has a grave. You have a graveyard?

Silva: (stares) No. There is a common grave.

SA: But the families are allowed to come and perform last rites?

Silva: Well, not in large numbers, of course. But yes, we allow them.

*A few days later, an official of the National Security Ministry in Colombo ridiculed the suggestion that bodies were being buried in the Batticaloa STF base. "Whoever told you that must be a terrorist or a terrorist sympathizer."*

*In October 1987, Sumith Silva was travelling with the Batticaloa Government Agent Anthonimuthu when their vehicle was destroyed by a Tiger land mine. Silva was killed instantly.*

*S.M. Lena, 79, is a wizened, white-haired man whose fiery temperament is moderated by his diminutive size and round spectacles. A retired high school teacher, he now devotes his energies to the Batticaloa Citizen's Committee.*

You see, here we were colonized by the British, and one thing they gave us was a trust in others. So when independence came, we trusted in the political parties. We trusted them! We wanted a political settlement. But they didn't keep their promises.

JLA: What do you think caused the change?

Lena: They have gone back on the promises they made to the Tamil community. They've gone back! Because they feel they must enslave us forever!

I got involved because it's my duty, for my community and my people. It's my duty. We elder people saw the way, and the younger people came. They are liberating us. They have been a great service to us! We don't call them terrorists; they're freedom fighters. They're fighting for a cause. I'm an old man, but I want a new country!

Look at this moment. You see the children on their way to school. They are not safe. There is shooting at random. In the school, they are not safe. On the way they are not safe. In the market they are not safe. In the churches they are not safe! They are martyring our children!

You must have so much sympathy for us. That is the thing that we want you to know. Go back to your country and tell them how much we suffer, how much we suffer, how much of the victims are our children, how much of our future generation are going to be affected by this situation here. Please, for God's sake!

(Overwhelmed with emotion, the old man stops talking as he tries to stifle the tears that have appeared in his eyes.)

# Israel:
# The Unsettled Land

A unit of Israeli soldiers are walking down a dirt street in Gaza as a car, driven by a Palestinian woman, approaches. To warn the soldier in the center of the road, she honks her horn. The soldier wheels on her, face red with anger, and brings the muzzle of his gun against the window.

"Who do you think you are," he screams repeatedly at her, "an Israeli?"

The furious question was partly a taunt and partly an accusation, for the soldier fully knew the woman was not an Israeli and had no intention of ever being one.

For the soldier, as with all Israelis, the dramatic attainment of a Jewish state in the land of their forebears was an ideal realized at the tragic cost of moral compromise: the occupation and dispersion of another people, the Palestinians. Theirs is the insecurity and moral quandary of a man who has built his home on the ruins of another. That insecurity is most apparent on the West Bank.

The hilltop community of Qaddim looks out over a rich valley of olive orchards and fields of farmland, dotted here and there by whitewashed villages. But the residents of Qaddim peer at this pastoral scene from behind barbed wire. Their compound is guarded by Army reservists equipped with walkie-talkies and assault rifles. The beauty below doesn't evoke calm or reflection in them, but unease and a sense of siege, for the people of Qaddim are Jewish settlers and the land below is that of the Arabs.

The war of nerves in Qaddim is repeated throughout the West Bank of the Jordan River, that slice of land that Israel seized from Jordan in the 1967 war and continues to occupy. The ancient scene has not been destroyed; the goatherds and their shepherds remain, as do the mosques with their slender minarets and the men in the *kaffiyes* smoking tobacco from waterpipes in small cafés. Rather, details have been grafted onto it, the gleaming new Jewish settlements on the hilltops, their homes huddled close together behind fences, the Israeli Army foot patrols moving warily through the streets.

To the Palestinian Arabs, those settlements and patrols are reminders that they are an occupied people and that their conquerors are settling on their land. To the Jews, those Arab villages and farmland are reminders that they are an isolated minority, surrounded by a hostile people here in their Promised Land. In one of the oldest lands in the world, the West Bank is the ironic new frontier and the settlements in Judea and Samaria are its most critical symbol. They are the symbol of the Jews' will to return to their land after two thousand years of exile; they are the Palestinians' symbol that their land is no longer theirs. Most of all, the settlements are a symbol of this conflict's contradictions, simultaneously outposts for maintaining security and roadblocks thwarting peace. It is but one more paradox in a place where the contradictions—of culture, history, religion—have created a virtual paralysis.

In Israel, history and religion are inextricably combined. For the Jews, their Judaism centers on a specific place, and that place is Israel. This is their Promised Land, the irreplaceable heart of their religion from which they were twice cast. Left scattered throughout the Middle East and Europe in the Diaspora, the Jews kept alive their dream of returning to their native land for two thousand years, in folklore, prayers, even in everyday greetings.

In the nineteenth century, European Jews began organizing a return to "Zion ." While some Zionists saw this as their religious "manifest destiny," others were driven by political considerations, that it was only when the Jews returned to their homeland that the cycle of persecution and pogroms that had haunted their life in exile would end. Whatever their reasons for wanting to emigrate, most of the early settlers were unified in the new ideology of socialism that would bring about the birth of the Jewish "New Man." Beginning in the 1870s, European Jews began emigrating to Palestine.

But in many ways, their new life in the Promised Land was little better than what they had left behind. Palestine was now ruled by the Ottoman Empire and populated by Moslem Arabs. While grudgingly accepted, the returning Jews were largely shut out of the political life and were the victims of periodic riots and massacres. The existence itself was hard; the early Zionists had to fight malaria and other diseases to scratch out a living on the land.

With the defeat of the Ottoman Empire in World War I, the victorious British ruled Palestine by Mandate. The British, however, eager to keep ethnic tensions contained, put severe restrictions on more Jews entering. Even as Hitler tightened his hold in Germany and his anti-Semitic rantings grew deadly, the European Jews were prevented from what was now an escape to Palestine; instead, they were left to be exterminated in the Holocaust.

After World War II, the few Jews who had survived the genocide were implacable in their desire to return to the Promised Land, British Mandate or not. Illegal emigration was organized in Europe, with old, overloaded ships arriving on the Palestine shore. The British authorities seized the ships and placed the Jews in detention camps. In reaction, the Jewish underground armies, the Haganah and Palmach, began preparing for war against the British, while more radical groups, like the Irgun and the Stern gang, turned to outright terrorism, assassinating British officials and exploding bombs.

In 1947, the newly formed United Nations worked out an ersatz settlement of the worsening Palestine problem—the division of the territory between the Jews and Arabs and the withdrawal of the British. The Zionist leaders agreed to the plan, but the Arabs did not; to the surprise of no one, open civil war broke out the instant Britain withdrew in 1948. Egypt, Iraq, Syria, Lebanon, and Jordan invaded to support the Arab Palestinians, but the tiny Jewish nation prevailed and consolidated the new state of Israel.

Along with creating Israel, the 1948 war also created hundreds of thousands of Palestinian refugees. While some had fled from their homes for safety in the fighting, others were forced out by the victorious Israelis. The end result was an enormous refugee population that still dwells in "temporary" camps throughout the Middle East.

As the state of Israel prospered and grew, taking in a flood of new "Oriental" Jews expelled from Moslem countries, the surrounding Arab nations continued their militant opposition to the Jewish state. In 1956, Israel and Egypt briefly went to war in the Sinai Peninsula. Palestinians in exile formed revolutionary organizations like the Palestine Liberation Organization (PLO) to fight the "Zionist imperialists." In 1967, the tensions erupted into war again as Egypt, Jordan, and Syria simultaneously attacked; with stunning efficiency, Israel annihilated the invading armies in just six days.

The Six-Day War ended with Israel annexing the strategic massif of the Golan Heights from Syria and occupying the Egyptian-held Gaza Strip and Jordan's West Bank, including the Old City of Jerusalem. While Israel may have gained strategic advantages with these acquisitions, it also inherited over a million new Palestinians violently opposed to its rule, and won the continuing enmity of its neighbors. The Arab world, never a cohesive bloc, found in the Palestinian cause a rallying point, as well as a useful pawn. If the pawn could be manipulated, it could also be squashed when necessary; in the Black September uprising of 1970, thousands of Palestinians were killed by Jordanian soldiers.

Still, with its increased funding and training, groups like the PLO were able to execute dramatic acts of terrorism, like the 1972 Munich Olympics massacre in which eleven Israeli athletes were killed, to remind the world that the Palestinian problem had not gone away. Combined with its violence, the PLO won widespread diplomatic recognition throughout the world under the leadership of its chairman, Yassir Arafat. The support resulted in several UN declarations in the 1970s censuring Israel and equating Zionism with racism.

When Egypt again attacked in 1973, Israel was caught off guard on Yom Kippur, the Jewish Day of Atonement. The Israelis suffered heavy casualties before finally gaining the offensive and driving deep into Egyptian territory. After a cease-fire, the United Nations established peace-keeping forces in the Sinai to serve as a buffer between the warring nations.

With the election of Menachem Begin as Israel's prime minister in 1976, the situation in the Middle East seemed to improve and deteriorate at the same time. The former leader of the Irgun terrorist group, Begin wholeheartedly endorsed the establishment of Jewish settlements on the occupied West Bank and Sinai Peninsula, even though this land had not been annexed as part of Israel. At the same time, Begin responded to the peace overtures of Egypt's Anwar Sadat, resulting in the Camp David accord of 1978, which established an official peace between the two mortal enemies and the gradual withdrawal of Israel from the Sinai. For many, it symbolized the beginning of a new path to peace and an end to the cycle of war. While traces of this optimism still exist, they were greatly diminished by the assassination of Sadat in 1981 by Moslem fundamentalists.

For the Palestinians, however, Camp David did little to further their aspirations for a homeland. Palestinian guerrilla and terrorist attacks continued, and Jewish towns in northern Israel were periodically shelled from their bases in southern Lebanon. Purportedly in retaliation for these attacks, the Israeli Army invaded southern Lebanon in 1982, but what was supposed to be a simple buffer-creating incursion didn't stop until the Israeli Army was at the outskirts of Beirut. While the Israeli bombardment of Beirut did result in the PLO evacuation of the city, in the process Israel had been pulled into the Lebanon morass, hundreds of soldiers had been killed, and a massive polarization had been created within Israel as the purpose of the war was debated.

Today, the Arab-Israeli conflict is marked by deadlock. Because of the fractious political climate, it is difficult if not impossible for an Israeli prime minister to build a consensus toward a peace initiative. Conversely, it is difficult for a Palestinian moderate leader to make an overture and risk the wrath of his more militant comrades. Both sides feel they must maintain the state of war, while gingerly testing the waters of negotiation through third parties.

Israel's alternately ruthless and enlightened attempts to deal with the Palestinians exemplify the contradictions; after driving out hundreds of thousands of Palestinians from their homeland in 1948, it allowed two hundred thousand to stay, bestowing upon them a kind of second-class citizenship. It has built universities for Palestinians on the West Bank, yet it frequently arrests the students for their allegiance to the idealized state of Palestine; those who persist in this allegiance are deported, cast into a Palestinian diaspora. A Palestinian convicted of a terrorist offense is not executed, no matter how heinous the act; he is imprisoned and his home is dynamited. The policies seem aimed at increasing the Palestinians' own sense of insecurity, as though by striking them where they hurt most, their sense of homelessness, they can be subjected and pacified.

The contradictions are reflected in the Israeli people. While most Jews realize some concession has to be made to the Palestinians, they are fearful of giving them the only thing that the Palestinians will ever accept: an independent state. The

Israeli dilemma over how to achieve peace while maintaining its security has spawned radically opposing factions. On one side are the doves, who advocate open negotiations with the PLO and a relinquishing of the Occupied Territories. On the other is the rabid anti-Arab dogma of Rabbi Meir Kahane and his followers, who include Jewish zealots who have carried out vigilante "justice" against Palestinians. Both tendencies have brought to the surface long-standing conflicts in the Israeli "melting pot."

For their part, the Palestinians suffer from no such inner contradictions— virtually all of them reject living under Israeli authority and are unanimous in wanting a homeland—but translating that into action is problematic. Closely monitored within Israel and without political rights, they are dependent on the often-fickle whims and intrigues of their Arab-nation benefactors. For all their bravado and dramatic pronouncements, they are among the most powerless of peoples.

The babble of discontent is a clamor for precedence on the biblical land. It is ironic that here, in the birthplace of Judaism and Christianity, the people continue to wage a bloody struggle for existence and identity. Yet it is so. It is that fear, of forever losing an identity, that has spawned the world's most unrelenting conflict.

*A Jewish teenager living in a religious settlement on the West Bank:*

It's not a problem of the land, or that they want Israel or anything like that; the problem is just that we hate each other.

*Ibrahim is a 26 year-old Palestinian Communist. He works in Israel as a farmworker, but lives with his wife and baby son in his parents' home in the Rafiah refugee camp in the Gaza Strip.*

Why should I leave? It's normal that we will stay, because it's our land. The abnormal is that the Jews come! Jewish itself is just a religion, no more, no less than Islamic, Christian, or anything else! I am Palestinian, not because I am Islamic, but because I live in Palestine. So he is Jewish, but he lives in America! His identity card is an American one! And the same you can say in all the European countries! So why did they come here? It's not their land; it's our land. They get it by force! They feel, with blood, that they are the best, the super in all the world! Yes!

*Adaya Barkay was born in Jerusalem and comes from seven generations of Jews born in Palestine. An athletic, alert woman in her late forties, Barkay rises at five-thirty each morning to commute the sixty miles from her Tel Aviv apartment to Nazareth, the base for her job as the district medical officer for northern Israel.*

*She has a deep fondness for classical music, which she plays throughout the interview.*

The war of independence didn't start just like that. There was an overture, you know, a big preparation towards it. There was this tension. Although I myself never felt there was any imminent danger—I never looked around my back—we were brought up to be very cautious. I can't imagine, actually, a childhood without this *basso ostinato*—you know, this background. All the time the tension . . .

Now in spite of that, the Arab wasn't the enemy; there were just some bad Arabs. We never said the word *terrorist*; the word was *klufiot*, mob. It wasn't the Arabs, because we lived with the Arabs, we had a daily interaction with them. Still, one had to be very careful. We were told not to go very far in the forest alone.

Personally, my family was affected by this war by a terrorist act. But this is, of course, a personal . . . thing and it doesn't reflect, surely doesn't reflect on the independence war. . . . It's a private thing. . . .

Well, what happened was that there were acts of pure terrorism, like what now happens so often in Beirut. They used to put these explosions in cars. . . . We lived in Talpiyyot, just outside of Jerusalem, and by December [1947], one could actually not go to Jerusalem and back again because it was really dangerous. From time to time, they shot the bus and there were casualties.

Finally my mother said, "We are not staying here anymore." She was a working woman, working in a bank, and she said, "Because I must be at work at half past seven and you have to be in school over there and your father has to be over there and we're all linked to the center of town and life should continue and we can't afford to be late just because the bus doesn't come or somebody shoots here or there, so we have to live in the center of town because I can't stand it anymore!" (laughs)

So we moved to the middle of Jerusalem and we went to do our jobs and . . . till there was this terrorist attack on the twenty-second of February 1948 in the Ben Yehuda Street. And they blew the street up. My mother was killed there. My father was injured; he survived. And I was . . . there and am still here. And this, and what went with it . . . wasn't a simple thing. Not at all.

Well, she wasn't the only one to be killed there. There were about fifty people. But, as I say, this is a personal tragedy.

Now, one of the things . . . it was never proved that Arabs put this explosive. On the contrary, we have many evidence that these were English soldiers who did it. I don't think it was important whether it was Arab or English people, because I never believed that such acts of terrorism—this is naive—but I never believed that these were actions that were really decided upon by responsible people. I always thought that these were sort of vandalisms. When the Israeli terrorists did such things in the King David [Hotel], I also thought, you know, two or three minority people would do such things. I could never accept that a group of responsible people would choose to fight this way.

Are you interested in what I'm saying? Because I feel it's such a minor thing. I feel that every Israeli has such stories. . . .

Well, what I wanted to tell you about this explosion was that this was 6:20 in the morning. It was February; it was cold . . . but we heard—and this is what I'm trying to tell you, how tense we were—we were supposed to be asleep in the morning but we were on the alert all the time, because I remember that we heard *bong*, a shot. And I remember my mother saying to my father, "What is it?" And my father said, "Nothing, it's a car going down Ben Yehuda"—you know, the muffler. So she said, "No, it's not the exhaust; I'm going to look what it is." And she goes up. And it's cold. And I'm under the covers, and I'm not looking so I don't see, but I hear her walking to the balcony over the street. And we hear a car going away. We hear a car going away. So she said to my father, "But why are the English laughing?" And I hear, "Ha, ha, ha." And there was this . . . it was not an explosion, it wasn't noisy, just a feeling, and so . . .

Well, what shall I tell you? That I was without pajamas so I collected a fur coat. Well, things were not there, and apparently I washed and . . . well, things of shock.

You know, I didn't know where to go. I went to school. I simply went to school. I came late. This was six-twenty and then I saw that my father will be taken to hospital, and then what? What? There was nothing left. I've thought of this so often; where does a person go to? I simply went to school. And I didn't know how I looked. Only afterward I found out that I was covered in dust, the sort of dust that I had under my skin. I didn't know all that. And the fur coat is full of dust. It was February; it was very cold. I found this fur coat of my mother's. And I went to school. I went into my class! And I said, "I'm sorry I'm late." And when I saw the face (laughs) of the teacher, then I understood. So I told her what happened and she said, "What are you going to do?" and I said, "Well, I don't know. I came to school,"—sort of a traumatic, you know, thing. . . .

And when I entered the class, I said, "Well, I'm sorry, but I came now from the Ben Yehuda." And they looked and I remember until today . . . So I said, "Well, everything is okay." I said, "My mother is killed and my father is living in hospital and I am here." And they began to cry, a collective hysteria. So I said to myself, "I can't remain here; they're crying like mad! I'm the cause; I should go away."

Why am I telling all this?

Then my father went out of hospital and we rented a small room and . . . we had nothing. We simply had nothing. We had no clothes and, especially, nothing that people have in their own residences, because most of our things just exploded. I was a refugee in my own hometown.

If I can say something about the independence war, I was extremely hungry. And this was very illuminating for a spoiled, unique child from the Rothschild School for Girls with my British accent then. I wasn't an orphan. I wasn't a poor Israeli. I was hungry, hungry for food. We didn't have anything. We didn't have anything, and I was just a child. . . .

We were told we had to assist in hospital. It wasn't really hospital, but where they had Jewish people hospitalized and wounded soldiers. And we had all sorts of jobs to do. There was such shortage of things because of the siege that they used to wash the bandages, and we had to roll them again. This wasn't very interesting, so I said, "Let me do something with the injured people." So I had to help wounded soldiers to eat. . . .

I was so hungry. I was so hungry. I didn't know how hungry I was until I saw what they had to eat. So I chose to feed soldiers who couldn't see, and I simply stole some of their food. And this is not the ugliest thing I have to tell you; this was not even very humiliating. I said to myself, "He surely has enough; it's too much for him"—you know, perhaps the last two spoons of the porridge. Or if he left things, I would never insist, "Do you want more?"; I said, "You finished?!" and I would finish with the same spoon.

In the meantime, there was fighting in Jerusalem, and the Arabs, the richer Arabs from the neighborhood of Katamon, fled away. They brought us there and we had to make sandbags, and we did that and then we were allowed to go into an empty house—this is the ugliest episode—because there I could see for the first what it meant, and get a deep understanding of the horror of war. Because nothing was touched! People just fled away! Like we left our neighborhood, like us, the Arabs left! I don't understand why!

And I went into this house. I remember it very well; I was very sensitive toward a real home, because I didn't have a home. I think that, like a real orphan, which I was, I looked at every room and I saw what it meant to break a place. But there I remember very well that I saw pictures, photographs . . . that people left behind when they ran away. I remember very well looking at these photographs and saying, "They are people like ourselves." A child. A man. A woman. I think that what I felt was very guilty, even though I didn't even know what was happening in Israel; I just knew that I was there and the Arabs lived there and that they left. No enemy. Arabs like ourselves. Not the bad ones, the usual ones. . . .

Jews bury people without any clothes on, but people who are killed in accidents or wars, they bury them like they are. I don't know why; Jewish laws are very . . . special. So it took me some time to imagine, because my mother when she was killed wore a . . . nightgown. And it was blue. And because it was blue, I myself found her; otherwise, I would not have been able to find her amongst all the . . . these things. I tell you it was very dusty! Everything was white, but something that was blue . . . You know, when you looked for her you saw something blue. So I remember very well this blue . . . thing with which I found her, and then I had to imagine this blue thing . . . So this has to do with . . . death. Death. War and death.

This is the war of independence for me. I think this was an avoidable war.

*Fathi Al Najii is a sharp-eyed young man who lives in Gaza's Jabaliya refugee camp and travels into Israel every day to work. A self-described Leninist, he supports the PLO and belongs to a worker's committee to aid Gazan workers in Israel, a task he sees as one part of the "liberation struggle." When we ask if he has considered joining the PLO, Fathi refuses to answer.*

The Israelis don't like us. They are our enemy. They like to deal with us only because they want something from us. One time I went to Sawafir, to my [ancestral] land, to eat something from my parents' trees, and the Israeli civilians hit me and quarrelled with me. They said, "Why are you eating from this tree? This is Israeli land, not your land!"

Once, I was walking in the street in Israel and a little girl—about five years old—saw me in the street and she pointed to me and yelled, "He's an Arab!" This is how they look to the Palestinians, even the children. . . .

*Beth is a young Israeli woman born on a kibbutz not far from Gaza.*

The Arabs may be very nice, but you can't turn your back on them. One day I was working in the fields and there were some Arabs working there, too—we always worked together—and I happened to turn around and I saw the face of one looking at me. In the eyes were pure hate! I was so frightened, and I have never forgotten that moment. They can be nice to you, to your face, but inside they feel something else.

*Mary Khass is a dynamic Palestinian Christian in her mid-fifties. She is the director of the Quaker's American Friends Service Committee's assistance projects in the Gaza Strip, where she lives. She and her Moslem husband, Mohamed Khass, a newspaper editor, are both scions of Gazan society, as well as vocal opponents of the Israeli occupation.*

I'm a mother. I'm a preschool educator. I definitely have some humanity in me, and I'm supposed to be very sensitive to the suffering of children. So when I pass by and I see soldiers beating little children, it really hurts. It hurts a lot. And especially when there is nothing I can do. I can talk, yes, I can talk to the soldiers, but the minute I start talking I'm threatened with the gun, and it's happened a few times to me. They threaten: "It's not your business." But it is my business! It's everybody's business! They've made it so impossible for the people even to help each other! The knowledge—that your neighbor, when his son is arrested for one reason or another, their house will be demolished within days—the knowledge that there is nothing you can do to help those neighbors.

The intention is to make the population submit and accept. But really, my assumption is that it doesn't. On the contrary, it makes people more angry. Especially the youngsters. I would like you to imagine when you were young, high school or university. You're more excited and more concerned about rights and wrongs and this is normal (chuckles). The young's reaction is much stronger to humiliation and oppression. This is something the Israelis do not want to realize. They ought to.

Before the Camp David initiative, the Strip youngsters, after graduating from high school, would go to university in Egypt. My eldest son graduated from high school and then went to the university. And they always came back at the beginning of summer for the holidays, but unfortunately, one summer, fifty-two percent of the students, including my son, were arrested when they returned.

He came out from prison very sick. He was beaten; they were interrogated fiercely, accusing them that they had been active with the PLO, and many of them confessed simply to get rid of the beating. Really, many of them were not guilty. Luckily, I have a very strong son—he's two meters, point-something tall (laughs), and he was able to . . . He explained to me later; he said, "Mama, it caught on my tongue like a record: 'I don't know, I don't know.' I was being beaten, beaten, and after an hour it is much easier; you can hold up."

His head, lots of bumps on it. And all his gums were swollen. He told me horrible things . . . but he had to go back to Egypt to study. I think, though, I thought I heard him whisper—I thought I did—"Mama, I'm sorry, but I won't be back." But I thought I was wrong. I asked Mohamed, "Do you think he said that?" "Don't be silly; he's a strong fellow, don't worry!"

Next year, which was 1975, he volunteered [with the PLO] and he went to Lebanon instead of coming here. He went to fight in Lebanon against the Syrians and the Phalange. We're lucky that he's alive. But, finally, he was arrested by the Syrians; then he realized what it means to be arrested by the Syrians. He lived on bad bread and dirty water for fifteen days until they took them to Damascus. He was wounded and he swore to me that worms were coming out of his wound.

Four months later, there was this peacemaking between Assad and Arafat and they exchanged prisoners and he went back to Beirut. And that's when we received a letter from him. And he had sworn to stay fighting. . . .

In 1978, our other son, who was eighteen, died here. . . . A wire, an electrical wire—electricity here is so safe! He was walking with his friends, coming out of the football match, seven o'clock in the evening. There was a minor storm and a . . . wire fell on him and he died.

I decided our eldest son should not . . . I was worried, of course. I went to Beirut and I told them [the PLO] what had happened. They said, "We know already," and the fellow said, "Don't worry, we will not take an only son. We will release your son." So they released him and he went back to his studies in Alexandria but, of course, he's not allowed to come back here. Apparently—I didn't know that, but that's the law of the PLO—they wouldn't take an only son.

There isn't a godsent occupation; we all know that occupation is bad. But . . . I don't want to use the word racism, because this is a very big word to use and it rubs the Israelis the wrong way, because they have been subjected to racism. Unfortunately, maybe that anger is being let out on us now. I'm rather sure of that, I'm sorry to say. (laughs) Their suffering, I understand that suffering—more so now that me and my people are going through those sufferings! In my understanding, the Jews are the ones who should understand what we are going through!

And I want to tell you something; it's not an easy thing not to have an identity. You always hear the Palestinians talking about identity. It's unbelievable for you because you don't live that way, you haven't experienced it—maybe your parents haven't experienced it. To be a human being . . . Let me share with you my experience.

I travel abroad and I'm normal, a normal human being wherever I go. On my way back, I'm a normal human being, until I reach the airport. But the minute I reach that hideous desk and I submit my travel documents, I am not a human being anymore! Because two policemen come and I go into a certain room, where I'm searched, where I'm humiliated, where I'm asked questions about what I was doing, why did I go to the States, et cetera. . . .

And that happens to each one of us; it's not a special treatment to Mary Khass! It's everybody! We're not human anymore. That's what it means not to have an identity.

It doesn't bother the Israelis a damn bit, as long as the youngsters don't touch what they call "the security," you know, the magic word. In the name of security, our land is being confiscated. The Strip, as small as it is—yet!—we are still subjected to confiscation of land. And if you go to court, you're told the magic word, "for security reasons." That's it. That's the end. Many things come in the name of security. The fact that when I travel in my car, because it has a Gaza number any Israeli person—not an official, not a soldier, not a policeman, but any Israeli has the right to stop me and search me! Any Israeli has that bloody right! Read the law, you'll find out that I'm right! There is—

(A gunshot rings out nearby; Khass becomes subdued.)

That was a bullet.

My family came from the Galilee. I was born in Haifa, but my ancestors and my parents' parents were born in a small town up in the hills, twenty-five minutes' drive from Haifa. We used to go in the summer to Shefar'am because my grandparents had a beautiful home and we used to camp there, up on the hills. It was confiscated; the last bit of land that my family owned was confiscated.

I remember '48. Very much so. I was eighteen. We were living in Haifa and we had a very nice house. It was nice. We were what you call a middle-class family and . . . in '48, we were thrown out of the house because they had to collect all the Arabs into one area. So they gave us other quarters in another area. My mother, her brother, all her cousins and uncles and my own uncle lived there. We had four rooms and a hall and a kitchen.

So we lived there, and in December 1948, settlers—they called them settlers, and this happened many, many times, not only with us; I must say we're not the only ones who suffered (laughs)—one day, all of a sudden, our house was raided. Two soldiers and a young woman with a baby came and threw our furniture from two rooms and the kitchen—threw them out. And she opened—I remember—a camping bed and put her baby on it and started feeding the baby and let the soldiers do the job. My mother was expecting a baby, and she was beaten. She was in the sixth month. She was beaten so badly that she lost the baby and she was in a coma for many days.

And finally, we had to . . . let go of one room, and that woman and her husband lived in it. It was taken from us. But it happened to so many others. . . .

It really affected me. Until that age, I had never seen a baby born. (laughs) I had to be my mother's nurse and I had to be the witness of the baby being born and dying in front of my eyes. And . . . I was very frightened because I didn't know what to do with my mother, where to take her.

We had no income. We didn't have anything! I started working. I started working selling soda (laughs) in the evening.

But you see, I'm really thankful. It made me realize the sufferings of the Jewish people, because of our suffering, because I saw my people suffering, always, all the time. What I think really helped me understand and become more concerned as a human being was the very first experience, that all of us, all of these Palestinians—workers, educated people, petit bourgeois, feudalists, everybody, every member of the community—we were in one quarter, equal to each other, starting from zero! It helped me get rid of lots of my snobbishness, and that's how I became a fighter for peace, for equality, and that was a very good lesson.

*Eugene Sockut, 52, is a robust, silver-haired American-born Jew with a mischievous gleam to his eye. An aide to Rabbi Meir Kahane and his ultrarightist Kach party, Sockut lives in Bet Neqofa, in the hills below Jerusalem. Prominently filling one corner of the warm living room is an enormous Torah on a stand.*

I made *aliya,* which means to ascend. For a Jew to return to the Holy Land and to Jerusalem was to ascend.

People asked me why I was coming, and I said, "Did you ever read Jack London's *Call of the Wild*?" I said, "There is a genetic time clock and I am just pulled to Israel. I'll never be happy living any other place." I didn't think it was religious at the time—I don't know, call it tribal nationalism or something—but now I realize it was a religious feeling. It was the continuation of Jewish history, and I was brought back because it was time to return.

The Jewish people are a unique people. You just have to read the Bible and it says so. I wonder how many people really read it and really see what God is really saying. What is God saying? He's saying that Jewish people are a priestly people who are supposed to be apart from the rest of the human race. That these people are supposed to be a light unto the rest of the human race, a light unto the Gentiles. That we have obligations as a people, not only to God and to ourselves, but to the rest of the human race.

The land of Israel itself is a part of the package, the contract made by Moses on Mount Sinai, and it's also part of the original verbal contract made with Abraham almost four thousand years ago. So we're not like another religion. Protestants (chuckles) don't have to have a particular geographic locality, but Judaism is based on the Holy Land. The land was given to the Jewish people. Forever. And it's not ours to give away.

Back in the States, people would ask me, "Why is Israel doing this? Why doesn't Israel give this piece to the Arabs?" and I would say to them, "Look, if you have any gripes I suggest you stop attacking me and start talking to The Man Upstairs, because it says in the Bible it belongs to the Jewish people, that it was given to us! And you can't tell me you believe in the Bible, that you believe in God, and then start telling me to do things against it, because it's clearly written!"

I want Israel to be a special country. Because the human race needs it. It needs the best; it doesn't need us to be a Hebrew-speaking Puerto Rico.

JLA:  But what about the Arabs living here?

Sockut:  It says in Judaism, "You remember that you were a slave in Egypt and you will be good to the stranger that dwells in your midst." Now, what does that mean? It means that this land was given to the Jewish people by God—you got a complaint, go to Him. Second, Jewish people are to control this land one hundred percent, not ninety-nine percent, because to do anything else is to insult God.

Now, a stranger living in your midst means that if you, as Christians, want to live in Israel, you are allowed to. But as resident strangers. You cannot control the land; it is against the Bible. You cannot have control. The Bible is very clear; people living here who are not Jewish, who are not from the seed of Abraham, these people cannot control us. That means no ownership of land, they don't have rights as overseers of Jews, they have no sovereign rights, they have no political rights. You have rights; you have lots of civil rights, but not political.

It's irrelevant whether you came here when the Jews were dispersed, and it's irrelevant how long you've been here. If you accept the conditions of resident stranger, you're welcome to stay. If you do not accept these conditions, you will be compensated, but you have to go. There are twenty-two Arab countries in the world. There's a 150 million Arabs! Don't tell us that your little . . . persecuted, tiny, little minority has nowhere to go, because that's a lot of nonsense!

You cannot have a concept of a Jewish state and a Western democracy; they are contradictions. Equal rights is against the Bible. If the Arabs say they want equal rights as resident strangers, all right, that's acceptable, but to say you want equal political rights? There are fourteen Knesset members who are Arab! That's madness! They don't want to have a Jewish state, and we know it! It's not that I tell you. *They'll* tell you! You find me an Arab anywhere that says that he wants to live in a Jewish state, well, he's a very strange Arab!

An Arab is a man of honor. He doesn't bargain for what is his. He believes this land is his, just like I believe the land is mine. But I have a contract, the best contract in the world. Not just from all the people in other countries that recognize us. Not just because we drained the swamps and planted trees. We have a contract with the Almighty. You [Arabs] say you're religious people? Well, then read the Bible. If you don't like what the Bible says, then stop fooling around and saying how religious you are and how much you believe in God, because obviously you don't!

So that's the situation, and it's very hard to explain to people because they say, "But that isn't a democracy." Well, you cannot have a democracy and a Jewish state; it won't work. It's a total contradiction against reality. We're not going to hurt the Arabs, we're going to compensate them, but they can't stay here.

JLA: But they aren't going to go peacefully, so you're talking about war. How, then, can you live by the Ten Commandments, one of which is "Thou shall not kill"?

Sockut: First thing, the Ten Commandments says, "Thou shalt not murder"; it doesn't say, "Thou shall not kill." That's a mistranslation from the original Hebrew. God never told people not to kill; it says in the Bible to the Jewish people, "If someone comes to murder you, get up and kill him first." Meaning that self-defense is not evil in Judaism. It's very clear. So self-defense and destroying enemies that come to kill you *is*, on the contrary, a Commandment.

SA: Do you feel that people hold Israel to a double standard?

Sockut: They should! They do and they should. God told Abraham, "You now are the father of a great nation, a nation that is a blessing on the human race, and that nation is Palestine." Why was it set up like this? I don't know. I only know this is the way it is.

You see, the one thing we have is intelligence. Jews are, as a whole, a highly intelligent people. It's a fact. There's no point in being modest and saying it's not true. It is true! The average IQ of the average Jew is 113 to 116. That's an average; it's unbelievable! The average IQ of the average Japanese is 102 to 106. Unfortunately, in many other parts of the world the average IQ is much lower.

Civilizations grow, flower, blossom, peak out, degenerate, and collapse. But not the Jews. The Jews are an unbelievable thing in human history! People say we're a living fossil, something that shouldn't be, but here we are. The genetic seed of Abraham has been preserved.

*Intense and defiantly confident, 18-year-old Rula Abu Duhou is a student at Bethlehem University on the West Bank. The university was established by Israel in 1973, but is periodically shut down in retaliation for Palestinian student unrest. A plump, curly-haired woman, Rula is majoring in social work and social psychology.*

As I am in the student senate, the [Israeli] Intelligence comes to my house, (laughs) and sometimes I have to wait the night in my uncle's house or my friend's house so they won't be able to catch me. They come and try to threaten my mother: "She has to come and we want to see her in the military offices," or whatever. It's really affected me. Sometimes I'm confused. I can't think, I can't do nothing. If I'm sleeping in my friend's house, I spend the night thinking what if they came to my mother, what they did to her, that maybe they arrested her. . . . It's really . . .

JLA: Have they arrested you?

Rula: No, they could not. I always run. (laughs)

JLA: You were born under Occupation, so you don't know what life was like before, do you?

Rula: No, but by stories, history books, yes!

I remember once when I was exactly seven years old in the school. One day the older girls made a strike and they threw stones on the soldiers. And there were gas bombs and . . . shooting, and it was . . . like the war. And the soldiers came into the school and in the schoolyard they just took a girl—she was very pretty, she had long hair—and they took her by her long hair, and they start pulling her around. Well, that affected me. She did not do nothing! She had the right to say, "No for the Occupation." We are Palestinians and this is *our* country; we have to say, "no"!

It's as if we were under sin or something because we are Palestinians. We want to say, "No." We want to say, "No!" It's our right! They can't just come into the school and for nothing try to shoot us with gas bombs and hit us with their sticks. They don't have the right! It really comes . . . I was seven years and now I'm eighteen. To have eleven years passed and I still remember it like it was yesterday. How do you expect a child, who is supposed to watch Superman instead of (laughs) watching this, to live like?

I feel bitter. I feel . . . hatred. I feel . . . any kind of feeling, bad feeling for them (laughs). But you have to make a difference between feeling bitter for the Israeleans, the military, the Zionist, and toward the Jewish. It's a really big difference.

JLA: How do you see the difference?

Rula: Well, there's a difference between a man who's raising a gun toward you and a man who's living next to you. Like, for example, a professor from Tel Aviv University, he's a friend of my sister, came to visit us in the house. It was the first time he speaks with a Palestinian family; he did not even know what Palestine means! (laughs) So there's a big difference between him and the soldier that stands a Palestinian person against the wall.

SA: But if it comes to another war, that professor will take up arms—

Rula: And I'll take up arms. War is war. In war you don't make differentiations! You don't make nothing. It's a matter of living. Either you prove you want to live, you want your freedom or you want to die, you want to be a slave for the rest of your life. It's war. And when you decide to take a part of it, you have to take it all. You just don't make a difference: "Oh, he's my friend, he's not my friend! I used to know him . . ." No! He's the enemy, and I have to fight him. It's a matter of living.

SA: Does it bother you to think you may have to fight one day?

Rula: No! See, for us, we just don't care. We want our freedom and freedom costs lots. So, if you want to live, you have to fight. In whatever; there's many ways you can fight. By guns, by anything. We are under occupation, we are in a revolutionary situation, and we have to live in it. Otherwise, we will accept what is happening and shut up and stay home!

JLA: So when you finish college you plan to stay and work in the Occupied Territories?

Rula: Yeah, sure. I had the opportunity to study in the States, but I refused. I wanted to stay here. I don't want to leave, even just to study.

Anything could happen here, but one thing for sure, we're gonna get our freedom and Palestine will come back, one day. We'll fight for it till the day will come—and fight everything—when one of two things will happen: Israel stays, or the Palestinians. Nothing else. One will have and nobody else! Might happen tomorrow, next year, after ten years, or maybe after one hundred years, but one thing for sure, we're gonna have it.

JLA: What about the Occupied Territories becoming Palestine and the rest being Israel—

Rula: No! Palestine is Palestine! It's one piece, it can't be separated. We want it all. And Gaza Strip, of course!

JLA: So what about the three million Jews?

Rula: What? What about them? If they want to live under Palestinian rule, well—welcome! If they don't want, (laughs) they can leave!

*Lieutenant Colonel Alexander Sella is a chubby, jovial man of 40 with a walrus mustache. A Ukrainian-born Jew who lost most of his family in the Holocaust, Sella has spent the past ten years in the Israeli Defence Force and will soon retire. His current post is as liaison officer to the commander of the South Lebanon Army, Israel's surrogate force in its "security zone" in southern Lebanon.*

The Palestinians don't have problems of their life. If they live normally, they can live fifty, a hundred years. If they fight, it's another problem. But it's normal; if I am a young Palestinian, I would fight, too—and maybe (laughs) do it better! I don't blame them. It's not a question of wrong and right; it's a matter of power.

The Palestinians are not a problem for us. The problem for the Palestinians is that they can't fight inside Israel. There's only place left from where the Palestinians can carry their revolution now, and that is Lebanon. Without it, they're finished. They can't fight from Yemen or Libya.

Now, the Palestinians are finished in Lebanon. After '82, no one will come to help them. The Palestinians will become like ASALA [an Armenian revolutionary group], small, terror. From time to time you will have a fight, but that's it—you can live with that for a long time, two thousand years.

In my ten years in the army I've learned one thing. To be right, you have to be strong. If you're strong, you're right. Everyone wants us to be supermoral, but Arabs kill Arabs every day. If Jews kill an Arab, it's a big deal.

My family is from Babi Yar [site in Soviet Union where the Nazis massacred Ukrainian Jews]. Only my mother survived that. So from when I was very young I understand that my life is nothing, and I knew I needed a place of my own. And so here, if I want my child to be secure, my country has to be. I am very sorry, but my generation is the one that must fight to give security so that maybe my children can live here in peace. But to be realistic, that's also what my father said in '45 when he fought against the Nazis. And now I have fought six wars with the Arabs, so I must be realistic.

It's a matter of life. I'm very afraid that the younger generation will come and say this isn't a battle of life and death; if they do, at this point, Israel is finished, because the Arabs will never stop. I have no trouble fighting the Palestinians, because after what happened to me in Europe I know what life is like.

*Attalah Mansour, who bears an uncanny resemblance to Teddy Roosevelt, is an Israeli Arab, one of some seven hundred thousand Palestinians who have Israeli citizenship. A Greek Catholic who lives in Nazareth, he is the author of* Waiting for the Dawn, *an autobiography, and writes a column for the Israeli newspaper* Ha'aretz. *Mansour has a take-charge personality; the few times his wife tries to speak, he rebukes her into silence.*

Since '48 there is the conflict which I describe as a hate explosion. And ever since we live under the radioactivity of this hatred. And this explosion came from earlier; this was from Treblinka and Dachau . . . this hate, this anti-Jewish, anti-Semitic hate was responsible for the fact that Israel was established. Without that explosion, without Treblinka and the rest of the anti-Jewish, barbaric Nazi activities, the Jews will not come here. Without the shame complex of Europe, there will be no support of both America and the USSR of the partition of Palestine in '47. And then, without that war, there would be no Palestinian refugees. Without these refugees being in refugee camps for the last forty years, there would be no hijacking of planes and terror and American hostages and Sabra and Shatila and Palestinians starving in refugee camps in Beirut today. So this living of ours today, in these conditions, is a kind of living under the effects of the radioactivity of hate.

So, if you ask me how this affected my life, more than half of my family were driven out of this country by the war. And they managed, most of them—not all of them, yet—to go to California. These people are ex-Palestinian refugees who managed during these forty years to go away. My parents stayed. My two sisters also stayed here. But my uncle and my first cousins moved to Lebanon when the Jews came.

The Israelis, during 1948, I think were not behaving always in a coherent manner. Some Jewish military units would come to one place and drive people away. Some units would say, as in the case of my village, "You Christians stay here, you Muslims go away." And I don't think that was any Israeli policy, that they preferred Christians to Muslims; I think this was just simply the commander of that unit who came to this village decided he would tolerate Christians. He would not tolerate Muslims! In other places, they behaved in other ways.

The village of my birth is Jish, near the Lebanese border. The Jews tolerated our village, which was mostly Christian, but ordered the Christians in the neighboring Christian village to go away. Some of them came to live with us, some of them crossed the border to Beirut and to Lebanon. And if you want to read propaganda, you will see that the Arab side says that the Jews pushed away all the refugees. If you want to read Israeli propaganda, you will find they say, "The Arabs were always going away when we arrived," something like that—which is not true! Both are telling what suits them! Of course, there are no refugees in history who left their homes because they were seeking pleasure somewhere else.

That was real misery! (chuckles) For some twenty years, between '48 until '66, we lived under Israeli military rule. Any Arab in this country who would try to travel from one village to another village needed a written permit from the Israeli government. I would, my father would, queue for hours outside an office to come to the Israeli corporal and say, "I travel to Haifa for a day or two." And he may say yes or no. And I have no way to try and change his decision. We lived under this rule until '66.

JLA: Have you ever had any second thoughts about having Israeli citizenship?

Mansour: There are people with bank accounts in Switzerland who are free to choose where to go, to Miami or to Shanghai. But we, those Arabs who remained in Israel, were on the whole poor farmers who had no choice. I mean, across the border, the Arab countries took us as traitors and enemies. So we were unable to cross the border to the Arab countries, unless we would say to ourselves in advance, "I am going there, so they will arrest me for a few months, subject me to real harsh investigation to find out that I am not coming to spy or something, and after they are convinced that I am not a spy they will make me one. They will push me back across the border to be a spy in Israel for the Arabs." And that was a choice that very few did.

Of course, there were a few who managed to go to the U.S., or to France or whatever, but a very tiny minority. And we were, as a matter of fact, a kind of prisoners. Of course, we could always console ourselves that we are prisoners at home, that we are visiting the cemeteries of our forefathers, or that we are going to visit our neighbors, and that we are living under our sun and that this is our land. . . .

JLA: Let's say the West Bank and Gaza Strip were to become Palestine tomorrow, not to replace Israel but to become a separate Palestine. Would you remain an Israeli?

Mansour: Oh yes. I'm an Israeli citizen, and what is good for Israel is good for me as well. But I am also an Arab, so what is good for the Arabs is good for me as well. So what is good for me is good for both the Arabs and the Israelis.

Israel is like a pond. This is a closed water, quite often rotting water. (laughs) I mean, unless God himself sends a lot of rain, it dries and is dirty and full of mosquitoes, so it depends so much on God and rain. That's Israel.

*Yosi, 20, was five when his parents emigrated to Israel from the United States. Bespectacled and husky, he lounges on the cot in his room at the West Bank settlement of Shilloh. There, he and other youths are attending Shilloh's* yeshiva, *a Jewish religious school, in a special five-year program combining Talmudic studies with military service. He carries a .45 automatic in his belt and plans to become an accountant.*

*Benjy Goldstein, 19, another* yeshiva *student, comes from New York and is deciding whether or not to make* aliya.

*Shilloh, built in 1981 on the hilltop above an Arab village, is the home of about one hundred Jewish settler families. It has been a focal point of Arab-settler tension, and several Shilloh residents were members of Jewish terrorist groups implicated in anti-Arab car bombings in the early 1980s. Residents of the fenced-in community point to a nearby mound, the remains of the ancient Jewish town of Shilloh, as one of their chief justifications for building their settlement here.*

JLA: What is it like living here surrounded by Arab villages?

Yosi: I guess you get used to it. It's always a little dangerous here. They throw stones and you have to do night duty; even during the day, there's always someone with a rifle, an M-16. Everyone has a gun in his room. And most guys at the yeshiva classes have their own pistols they carry. You have to be careful, but . . .

recently there was no problems. Here and there's an incident, but there's no real conflict or whatever.

JLA: What do you think about being in the Occupied Territories?

Yosi: The way I look at it is, we believe that all of Israel belongs to us, the whole country, so I have no problem with that. But even if I didn't have a belief in the Bible and all that, I mean, there was a war which the Jordanians started and they lost the territory. I mean, any country in the world, when they lose a war they lose their territory.

JLA: What do you think about the Arabs here?

Yosi: At some point it's going to be a serious problem. They're growing faster than we are. Per family they have more kids, so there will be a more serious conflict than there is today at some point, I believe. Right now, what we should be doing with them is letting them feel that we're in control. That doesn't mean you have to be mean to them or go over and doin' all kinds of bad things—but the second they do any problems . . . Say a soldier's on patrol and he asks a guy to give him his paper or whatever—he doesn't have to do it nasty, like scream at him or hit him—he should ask nice, just to show his paper. Then if he's okay, let him go. He must show the Arab who is in control and that he deserves respect. If he doesn't, then Israel won't have a chance. Because you have a million Arabs, you'll have more and more and they'll be able to take over in no time.

JLA: What's the best way for a soldier to show an Arab he deserves respect?

Yosi: They know, the Arabs. I believe they know it. If you ask them nicely and they show you [their identity papers], all you have to do is say, "Thank you." But if he starts giving you stories, or asking you questions, and he's trying to show you, to back you down from that power you have, you have be very tough, whatever the law lets you do. You could arrest him, you could take away his . . . There's all kinds of laws, you know, to show him. . . .

This I know from Arabs who work here, and we have very good relations with them. And they tell me themselves, I mean, that first of all, this is a war. Obviously they'll go for their brother's side, and I don't blame them, they'll go for the Arab side. So already you have to be careful, you know? You can never really trust them.

They're not scared. They're not scared of telling you. There's a guy who worked here, he was building a wall and he put the stones in a certain way and they told him to put it this way, and he said, "Anyway, soon there's gonna be a war, I'm taking over this territory, it's gonna be mine so I want it to be the way I want it." You know? No, they're not scared. They speak very freely. And . . . I mean, it's obvious, every Arab family I'm sure has someone who was killed in some war, in '48, in '73, in '67, so there must be some hatred, y'know, towards us. Must be. And everybody's gotta be careful. But on the other hand, I won't go round not treating them as human beings, because, right now, they are human beings.

The Arabs, they tell you themselves, are totally different from us. The way they

think is totally different. They . . . respect someone who has power. It's not like a
normal human being, where if you're nice to them they'll be nice to you. Arabs
themselves say you have to be tough. Like when Jordan was in control of this area,
if there was any problem, they'd knock down a whole row of houses, and they'd
keep quiet for a few years. So they respect that kind of power.

JLA: What do you think about a guy like Kahane and his ideas?

(Yosi and Benjy look at each other and smile)

Benjy: (chuckles) It's a sensitive issue.

JLA: Why?

Benjy: He's right, but he's not a diplomat.

Yosi: He's not a diplomat at all. But basically all the things he says is right. But
you don't just go and say, "We have to kick them all out." There's ways you have to
do it—

Benjy: He doesn't speak nicely, he . . . compares them to rodents. And to . . .
to an extent, he's right. Like in South Africa today, if suddenly they let everybody
loose, and they didn't keep anybody in hand, there'd be a mass rebellion there.
Here it's the same story. There's eight hundred thousand Arabs here in Judea and
Samaria, and if they let 'em do whatever they want, hell'd break loose.

Yosi: It's not that Israel's making them laws that they can't keep. I think Israel's
giving them a very fair chance to live comfortably without giving any problems. If
they just did what the law tells 'em to do, they wouldn't have any problems.

Benjy: They actually live better than most Israelis do. There are no taxes, no
army, no nothing. They're allowed to do whatever they want. Actually they have it
a lot better now than when Jordan was here; there's roads, schools we built them.

Yosi: It gives them lots of jobs. In this yeshiva, there must be twenty, thirty
Arabs at work every day. Could be one per family, so that's supporting thirty
families. If you ask a local Arab if he's happy that Israel's here, I think he'd say
yes.

JLA: Benjy, have you ever gone into an Arab city?

Benjy: (pained expression) I went in once. I mean . . .

JLA: How did you feel?

Benjy: I felt . . . annoyed. That they are complaining and this and that. I mean,
were you in Ramallah? They live very well there. I mean, there's no one here in this
place that lives like that. Yet there's always complaining, they're always throwing
stones at the bus and . . . it gets me very annoyed. . . .

You see kids standing there by the bus, as soon as the bus goes right by—
smash—the windows are gone, the bus is dented. It's very, very annoying . . . I
don't like them. They—they've killed people I know in the wars, and, but . . .
they annoy me very much. I mean, I see somebody in the street that is thinking "I
wish he was dead."

I wish they wouldn't be here. It'd make life a lot easier here. But they're here (sighs) and you have to live with it. The thing is to . . . you know, they talk about peace all the time. I believe it's impossible, it's never gonna happen. It's like saying peace in South Africa. It's an impossibility. Two conflicts that aren't based on money, they're not based on schools and education, they're based on . . . they don't want you here and you don't want them there. And it's an everlasting conflict. And we're never gonna finish it. It's never gonna happen. You can always hope but . . . I wish they weren't here. It would make life so much easier.

*Feisal Huseini operates the Arab Studies Society, a Palestinian research and documentation center. A former PLO commander who spent a year in Israeli prison for possession of explosives, he is now a prominent Arab activist in Israeli-annexed East Jerusalem and is the son of the late Abd El Khader Huseini, a famous Palestinian guerrilla leader killed in the 1948 war. Huseini was released from five years of home and town arrest on state security charges one week before the interview.*

This occupation is different from others. They are seeking not only to rule us, or to use our raw materials and the land for a while, but they are trying to place another people in our land. They are trying not only to take our land from us and rule us, but also they are anxious that one day they can find this land without us.

I look to Jerusalem as the capital of Palestine. My grandfather was the mayor of Jerusalem. His father was mayor of Jerusalem. His father's father was the mayor of Jerusalem. And we have another six or seven of the family who have been mayors of Jerusalem. And now we are treated by, in the municipality and in the police station, by the Section of Minorities. So the main pain is that they are dealing with me as a minority.

But at the same time, I can say that before 1967, when I was thinking about the Israelis I was thinking about the army, the enemy, the tanks, the airplanes, the military machine, about the people who threw my people outside of their land, and looked at all of them as fighters and as enemies. In 1967, when I came back here and started traveling and walking in the streets of Jerusalem, I started to see the Israelis as a people, as a common people. I saw the old man, the old woman. I saw the child, the strong one, the rich one, the poor one, the weak one, all kinds of people, good and bad. And I start thinking, if at any time we will conquer Israel, what are we going to do with these people? Are we going to throw them outside the country? Me, as a Palestinian who experienced—at that time, twenty years— being a refugee, of being without land, really I wouldn't like anyone else to feel this feeling, even the ones who caused that for me. So from 1967, I started to think that we must find a solution which will finish this suffering of the Palestinian people, but without moving it to any other people.

We would like to have one state for all of us, a democratic secular state for Jews,

Muslims, and Christians. So I have this feeling, not the feeling of hatred, but the feeling of trying to understand them and let them understand me more. This doesn't mean that if there will be a battle I will not be a part of it—I will be a part of it, for sure, because I am a Palestinian—but what I am looking for is to live together. I would call it the Palestinian dream.

JLA: Do you think you'll live to see a Palestine?

Huseini: (pause) Yes! Yes. I'll tell you why; I believe that occupation, ruling another people, it doesn't destroy only the people who are under occupation, it is destroying also the morality of the occupiers themselves. That if they are going on and on in this occupation, they are paying a higher price for their morality, their principles, that if they are going in this policy, they will find themselves in the Germany of 1936 or '39. When Hitler started, he was no more than Kahane today, and everyone was saying he was nothing!

The occupation corrupts people; it doesn't corrupt only individuals. It will go deep into Israeli society. And the only solution for that, and to reach a real peace, is to give the Palestinians the right for self-determination and to create their own state. Logically.

*Neomika Zion is a pretty woman of 27, active in the leftist Kibbutz Haartzi movement. She lives where she was born, on Kibbutz Reshafim, in the Yizreel valley near the Jordan border. A Bruce Springsteen tape plays in the background during the interview in her small, comfortable flat. Her parents are veteran kibbutzniks who came to Palestine before Independence, her mother from Austria and her father from Bulgaria; they were among the founders of Reshafim after the war of '48. Zion is preparing to leave Reshafim to join a small group of other young kibbutzniks in a socialist experiment to form an urban kibbutz in a town in the Negev Desert. For now, she continues performing her duties at Reshafim, which include working in the dairy farm.*

I think that we have to find a solution to finish with the Occupation, because it destroys us, and I think that's very clear, yes?

Look, when you send a teenager, a boy of eighteen or twenty years, into the occupation army, and he has to spend two years in Jenin or in Shekhem [Hebrew name for Arab city of Nablus], and he has to rule and control other people—and we know that he doesn't do it in a . . . nice way (laughs)—you have a system how to control other people! So it's a different game. You play a different game. And when you're back home, some of this becomes something of you, yes? They take people to the prison in the middle of the night, or when you have to hit them and— we know many stories about what happens there—and it becomes part of your life with your family and everywhere that you go, in work, with the people that you work with, and you don't think about it, you don't notice, but it works slowly on people, you know what I mean?

I will tell you something about the kibbutzniks. We belong to the left, and we support the ideas of living together in peace and that we have to give back the West Bank. But when you talk to the kibbutznik from the high schools—and we arrange every year a seminar with Jewish teenager kibbutzniks and children of the Arabs, Israeli Arabs, mixed together for three or four days to talk together about our problems—there are so many stereotypes. And many times you see that our children, boys and girls, can give many solutions in the classroom—they are very intellectual—but when they have to meet the Arab teenagers face-to-face and speak with them and maybe to sleep with them in the same house, many of them can't do it! It's so deep, the image that you have of the Arab people! And we can't . . . run away from this. It's our problem, too. In our deep feelings, we are not different; we think the same things about the Arabs, that they are primitive. Most of the people are thinking this way even if they say another thing.

Most of our lives in the kibbutz we don't meet the Arab people. We talk about the problems sometimes, but we don't meet them and we don't talk with them.

JLA: Do remember the first time you talked with an Arab?

Zion: . . . I don't know. I think I am a very open woman, and I talked, always I talked—many times—with the people who were building our house. It's sad to say, but today the Arab people are building the Jewish buildings, building the country! And the kibbutzim are the same! And we have some kibbutzim that decided that the Arab workers don't eat in the dining room, for example. There is a meaning to this. . . .

SA: Have you ever thought about leaving Israel?

Zion: No! I am Jewish and I am Israeli and I have no problem with this definition. It's very clear to me that I have to live here! I believe in Zionism. I think that I have to live here . . . because I have no other country, and I think here I have to struggle for a different society, okay? More . . . socialistic, yes?

Before the '67 war, the country was so small and we didn't believe in our power like today. But now we think that we're an empire!

SA: What do you remember of the '67 war?

Zion: I was seven years old. And . . . we believed that the Arabs were going to throw the Jews to the sea. That's what they said, yes? And that's what I remember. . . . I can say I was afraid . . . and our parents, too, not only the children. The whole atmosphere was that they were going to win the war. And we sat in the shelters most of time. . . . And, it was a big surprise when we won.

And I remember when we got Jerusalem, occupied it. This moment I remember very good, because I was with my mother and another woman in a room and they said it in the radio, and my mother told me to remember this moment for all my life! (laughs) That we were back to Jerusalem! And everybody started to cry, and this I remember! This moment, that we were back again to Jerusalem, this I remember. Seven years old. It was a very . . . it was a moment with a lot of meaning to everybody, even if they were not religious. Jerusalem was something special for everybody! This is what I remember. . . .

JLA: And '82?

Zion: Yes . . . (laughs) this is the worst. I think . . . most of the people on this kibbutz didn't agree with this war—yes, maybe with the first forty kilometers— but our education is that when the army calls you have to go! It's so deep! And to break the democratic rule, it's very a complicated decision. If I was a man, I don't know what I would do, I don't know. It was very convenient to be a woman (laughs) in this war!

In the kibbutz, it's difficult for them not to go to war, because if one of the guys refuses to go, he has a problem. When he comes back, it's a problem for him to live on the kibbutz afterwards. Because it's something for a kibbutznik; most of them are officers, so if you have to go, you go and you have to be the best in the war. So it was a real problem not to go to this war.

I remember that when the war was begun, I went to the station and I asked the men not to go (laughs)! I! I go to the bus station and I asked the men not to go. Not to go to this war.

JLA: What did they say?

Zion: Hmmm. They go! (laughs) They went. All of them.

*Avner Shur is a powerfully built man with intense green eyes. Born on a kibbutz in the Negev Desert, he now lives in Tel Aviv with his wife and young daughter. A reserve soldier with special training in military intelligence, Shur belongs to an elite antiterrorist unit and has taken part in numerous special operations, some of them still secret. In the 1973 Yom Kippur War, in which he fought, he lost a brother and, after participating in the 1982 Israeli invasion of Lebanon, he helped form the Soldiers Against Silence, a group opposed to the unpopular war.*

I don't want the leaders here to use my innocence, my desire to defend Israel. I don't want them to use it for other ends that I don't agree with.

We thought that Israel had nothing to do in Lebanon. Maybe, yes, to clean the border twenty kilometers up, not more than that. But the aims of this war were much greater than just to clean up the border. And we didn't agree with these aims. They were dragging the government of Israel, and also the soldiers, to an unjustified war.

I was against it from the first shock of this war. To be there, it was very frustrating. You see, to be in a war that you don't agree with from the first moment, and to have to fight in such a war is very, very frustrating. I think in a way it's a bit similar to the feeling of the American soldier in Vietnam, that you are looking for something very, very far from your country, that you don't know really what you are looking for, that you are asking yourself every moment, you know, "What am I doing here? Why did I come here?"

But anyhow, we know that if there is a war we are soldiers and we belong to Israel and we belong to the army of Israel and if you begin steps to oppose in the middle of the war it would be very, very dangerous to any army, especially to Israel's.

For our good luck, we were on the east side of Lebanon, and there it was the Syrian Army and not Lebanon civilians. So it was better for us; since we had to go inside Lebanon, at least it was to meet the Syrian Army and not the Lebanon civilians.

It's very hard to say, "Let's stop this now," because you are in the middle of it and you don't have time to explain or to stop. You are running day to day, five, six days. On the sixth day we stopped. We stayed at that position for a month and a half and didn't advance, so then there was no reason to argue. It was very hard being there for us. Not physically hard, but mentally, it was very hard.

SA: Even though you disagree with a war, would you ever consider not going to fight?

Avner: It's very, very difficult. Everybody here, even the radical left, knows that if the PLO fights against you, you have to fight back. You have to do certain things to . . . to stay here. And if you ever refused to go, it would be a black mark on you, with your employer, your kibbutz, and friends. So it's very hard not to go.

All the time you are under this. It's hard, you know, you never know when the next war will start, and so you are really very under stress all the time. Every time after a war they say maybe this is the last one, but it never seems to be. It is something very, very frightening.

There's something in the air, and you know that once a year, or every two years, you have to . . . you can't live like a normal life. It's not like in the United States—you work, you have your job, and you have your family, and that is the life and you know that will be for the rest of your life. Here you always have to be ready to fight, to go to war and then another war. If you are here, you are a soldier.

*Raya Harnik, an editor and producer for the Israel Broadcasting Corporation, lives in a Jerusalem apartment overflowing with books. On one wall are two photographs of a young man in uniform; they are of Guni, her eldest son, who was killed in Lebanon in 1982. He was 25 and a major. A widow with three surviving children, Harnik became a leading spokesperson for the burgeoning Israeli antiwar movement that emerged during the war in Lebanon.*

It's very difficult to be compassionate with the whole universe if you're in the middle of the storm yourself.

I can't remember in my life since being a very small girl without living in a state of conflict, without taking sides. Continuously taking sides. Shifting sides sometimes from issue to issue. Never really living in peace. I mean, not personally being under fire, but on the border of a fire zone, certainly an intellectual fire zone. I think for my whole life it has always been with me and part of me and the effect of my son getting killed in the Lebanon war only made it more dramatic.

I was very much opposed to that war from the outset, but on the third day of the war my son was killed, so perhaps I'm not very objective. But I know that even before I was notified that he was killed, I remember that I was standing in the yard of the radio broadcasting station and I was discussing it with people there, and I said to them it was the most silly reason to go to war and what can we possibly gain from this war. Then, after my son was killed the views, what were private views, somehow came out publicly, because a lot of newsmen came here and asked about him and my views, and I was very outspoken about it. So suddenly it became a national issue.

People started calling at all hours and cursing me, and there were constantly letters in the papers about things I said and . . . it wasn't very pleasant. To be out of the consensus is never a pleasant experience.

People could understand on the level that I was a mother who lost a son, but I didn't want them to understand on that level. I mean, I thought this way before he was killed, and I think I would have thought so even if he wouldn't have been in the war.

It's a terrible thing for us to be in a position of having to hold one and a half million Arabs who obviously don't want to be under the rule of Israel. I don't know what they want, but I know they don't want us. And I don't want my children to be patrolling in the streets of Nablus or any other place and having to hit children or being hit by them. I don't see any reason for it. I just don't want to rule or police another nation.

But I'm more pessimistic about the life in Israel than even the threat of war, because I think that the society now is splitting up into so many fragments that life is going to be very difficult. People have to take very extreme stands, even if they don't want to. If you want to be moderate, it's getting more and more difficult because you have to take a stand . . . and I'm very much afraid of this. The same thing is happening with the Arabs. I mean, I'm no more extreme, but the moment they are getting more extreme, I have to be more extreme also. I can't travel now through the Occupied Territories without weapons. I think it's irresponsible to do it. I don't want to do it, but I know that if I have to go from here to Tiberias and I'm going through Jericho—where now they are starting to throw stones—then to go without carrying a weapon is not responsible. I'm not going to fire first, that's for certain, and I'm not going to carry a weapon to fire at anybody, but . . .

This is how it happens.

*Azza Izat Gassem, 24, is a Palestinian feminist activist in the Gaza Strip. She and her family live in a modest but comfortable home on a dirt street in the refugee camp of Beit Hanoun, where she was born. She works with the Norwegian Red Cross and she is a leader of the Palestinian Woman's Committee in Gaza, which runs a sewing center for women and organizes health meetings.*

They try to give the people a bad view of the activist women. The Occupation authorities will spread the rumor that I am not good, a prostitute, and this is very shameful. The aim of this is to prevent me from doing anything for Palestine. They also try to work on my family, not just the neighbors, and they are always sending me orders to come to their center in Beit Hanoun. And the people say about girls who go to the Occupation center that they are raped and won't be virgins anymore, and this is something very difficult to accept in our society.

But I don't care about all of this, because I think the people know me and my behavior well enough. When the Occupation knows the girls are afraid of these reactions, they will keep up their actions against them. If they know we don't care about this, they try to find a new way to deal with us.

Every day I see the suffering of my people and I am part of these people, so I want to do something to relieve this suffering. I want to devote my life to it. There are many problems here, even for my family.

My father was in Egypt in '67, so after the war they wouldn't let him come back. He died there, so we never saw him again.

My older brother was studying in Iraq, and when he came for holidays they arrested him and refused to give him his passport. He was finally able to return to Iraq, but they have refused to let him return to Palestine since then.

The other brother, he was studying in Egypt. He studied for three years and then the Jews refused to let him go again and study there. So he tried to begin his studies again in Bir Zeit University. Then they arrested him for three months prison and six months town arrest in Gaza. He returned to the university, and again they renewed the town arrest. He is studying art; he should have finished in four years, but it has taken him eight years because of the arrests.

My eldest brother was arrested four years ago, just before his wedding day. They came in the night the day before and they took him. He stayed in the prison for twenty days and then they released him.

The smallest one, he was studying at Bir Zeit and he was arrested for seven months—he got out two months ago.

On the first of November '86, they arrested Nehad, my sister, for six months town arrest. So she can't continue her studies at Bir Zeit.

We have lots of problems. (laughs) The smallest sister was studying in the Islamic University here, and she had some troubles with the administration and they expelled her because she is active. So now she is studying at Bir Zeit.

JLA: Why is your family picked out so much?

Azza: It's not just my family, it's all the families. Here in Beit Hanoun most of the boys have these problems, but it's not so usual for the girls, like with us.

SA: So what do you think when you see an Israeli soldier on the street?

Azza: (laughs) The same thing he feels when he sees me.

SA: Which is what?

Azza: Uh . . . he wants to fire at me, to kill! (laughs)

*Hadra Gassem is Azza's mother, but they seem from two different worlds. Hadra, her head covered and robed in a traditional hand-embroidered Palestinian dress, is the depiction of Arab traditionalism, while her daughter wears a Western shirt and fashionable slacks that end at midcalf. As Hadra speaks, in a harsh and vigorous voice, she swells with emotion, causing Azza to giggle.*

JLA: Almost all of your children have been imprisoned or under town arrest. As a mother, what do you think about all of this?

Hadra: What is for you is for you, and what belongs to the others is theirs. The land is ours, and we must try to liberate it, whatever the price. If you die in this, everyone will remember you and know of you.

I don't feel sad when one of my boys or girls are arrested. My son is a son of all the town and all the people, and when I visit to prison to see my sons, I feel as though I go on a Haj [pilgrimage to Mecca], to something beautiful. It's good, because he is in the prison because of Palestine, not because he is a thief. He is a man. A first son without land, he is not a person.

When I sat at home and the Israelis came and asked if he was here in the town, I asked them, "Why are you coming every day? This annoys us." He told me, "Why did you bring them to the world?" I said to him, "As your mother brought you here to this world, I bring my sons," that's all.

I am very glad to see my sons as they are. They want their land and their town and their Palestine.

*Galia Taman, a stocky woman of 45, lives in a dilapidated house in front of some riding stables on the coast north of Netanya. She and her husband, a dour, dark man who is painting over the kitchen wallpaper, are Jews who came from Tunisia in 1956. A big black Schnauzer guards over her rambunctious newborn pups on the concrete porch outside. Sitting at the kitchen table, Galia speaks of Moshe, one of her sons.*

The boy was on leave and had traveled with a girlfriend to Tiberias and then he came back alone to Netanya. The boy was kidnapped by Arabs when he was waiting for a bus at the Haifa–Tel Aviv intersection. They stopped and grabbed him and threw him in the car. After five days we knew he was dead.

Before, I hadn't thought there was anything to worry about. Because it's our country, I didn't think that kind of thing could happen. I never thought that one day an Arab could come and kill him . . . an Arab born and living in Israel doing that. I thought it could come from a car accident, but never something like this. The killers were Israeli Arabs! They come from only five minutes away! We were neighbors! The police found him. It was midnight of the Sabbath that the police came to tell us.

They had put the boy in an Arab village house for two days, and they took him to a quieter place and shot him. They caught them after one and a half years, and now they are in prison for life.

Now I feel like I don't have a life. The family before was good; now, it's not so close anymore. We can't cheer up anymore. Now we live like nothing. I don't do anything anymore, not even cooking, cleaning. When I put something somewhere, I forget where it is after a few minutes. Food has lost its taste.

All Arabs are responsible, not just those four men. Always before I was sympathetic to Arabs, but after the killing all that has changed. The Arabs you can't trust. They can eat with you and everything else, but then they can shoot you in the back. I don't want to live with the Arabs in this country. I don't want peace with the Arabs.

One day my child brought Arabs to eat here. And they used to work on this house and I would feed them. No more! I am afraid of them. Never, ever would I have an Arab in my house again!! When I see an Arab, I think "bad." Arabs are sadistic and thirsty for blood!

All of the people think like me, but they're afraid to say so in this country. Those people who want peace, they are innocents; in the future they'll wake up.

*Bassam Shaka'a lives in a large, sprawling house on a hillside above the West Bank city of Nablus. It is a new home, built three years ago to enable Shaka'a to maneuver in his wheelchair. In 1980, Shaka'a was the mayor of Nablus, when a bomb planted in his car by Jewish terrorists blew off his legs. The same morning, two other Arab mayors were the target of car bombs. The three men who were eventually convicted for the Shaka'a bombing came from the West Bank settlement of Shilloh; they all received light sentences.*

*Shaka'a sits in the airy sun room of his home, a caged songbird chirping in the corner. He is an animated speaker and moves the stumps of his legs, one severed just below the hip, the other just above the knee, when excited.*

*Shaka'a was the last elected mayor of Nablus; since then, the mayors of the Occupied Territories have been appointed by the Israeli government.*

Before I was mayor, maybe I had many things which lent me fear. But after that, the Israelis treated the fear in myself, because there is nothing I feel that I can be afraid for. I haven't any chance. If you haven't a chance, for what are you afraid?

And everybody shall arrive to that point. He who is afraid now loses the respect and his responsibility.

They have a plan to fight against our daily life, against our facts in the Occupied Territories, and to establish their fact. For that they fight against everything, even your thinking, your familial relations, everything! Politically, economically, socially, everything! For that, when they tried to kill me it was not as Bassam Shaka'a; they fight against anyone. They want to control you daily. This is Israel. It is not against me; it is against everyone who has an idea to return or who thinks of improving our life. And if you don't believe this, please follow my incident.

I was the elected mayor of Nablus. After that time, the actions began against me. Not against me alone, but against all the [West Bank] mayors and all the councils. The Israelis wanted us to take orders from their military administration.

The incident happened in 1980. The second of June, 1980. They tried to kill me with another two mayors. In the same way, in the same day. Today, all of those men who did that are free.

I opened the door and I started the machine. When I want to use the gear and clutch, the bomb exploded.

Directly, I feel that my body began to be empty. Fell down. And I know that I am in great danger. I looked to the car with the smoke. I looked at my body and I—no legs—and I believe that I cannot use the car. I open the door and I left the car with my hands. When I arrived to the ground, I saw my . . . situation. But I . . . I didn't lose my consciousness until I left the car. Things began to be quiet and I was sleepy. I hear people. I hear my wife. For a moment and then . . .

And people in my home believe it is from a plane, a sonic boom. My wife thought that and she said to my son, "Don't worry, it's a sonic boom from the planes."

At that time, I want to take my child, who was six years old, to her children's school. She was lucky; she was still on the steps. And she saw . . . she was the only one in my family who saw the . . . incident. For months, she won't accept me. She was afraid when she saw me. She's afraid. And she escaped [ran away from home]. And she don't accept me. To look at my legs directly. And she's scared. And she refused to live in our house for a time.

But now she is better; she has gotten away from that. Now she's very good, very active and . . . she's the first student in her classes.

SA: What do you feel about the men who put the bomb in your car?

Shaka'a: I tell you that from my side I feel it is an official act. Because when it happened, my wife, she can't use the telephone. It is cut.

On the same day, the military governor of Nablus tells my family that they have information on the people who tried to kill me. And they explain many stories and try to hide the real members and to hide the signs. The Israelis made many attempts to hide everything. They arrested some traitors in the prisons and they made their story that "We are fighters from Al Fatah and put this bomb," et cetera.

When they say they discover the terrorist groups, there was no investigation in our community. No one met me or my family or my neighbors to ask them about any information about the attempted murder. Nothing at all!

SA: But they did eventually arrest some members of the Jewish Underground for the bombing. Did you ever see them?

Shaka'a: When they bring one of the criminals to my house to review what happened when he came and put the bomb, they chose a time when I would not be there in the house. And they forbid my son to see, to follow what should happen, and they ordered him to be in the house. He connected me with the telephone, and I returned back quickly. They forbade me to arrive at my house. I left my car and go walking; they forbid me also to continue, and they quickly take the criminal from my house to the car. I said to him, "Look, I know that you are a victim and that you have been used."

JLA: This was one of the settlers from Shilloh?

Shaka'a: Yes. Nathanson.

SA: How do you feel about them being free?

Shaka'a: I feel that it is an incident in the dangerous circumstances of our common cause, our national cause. The criminals that tried to kill me and the others, they killed many children in the streets and many citizens and they shoot at my people, our brothers. They shoot at them daily! They didn't come from Tel Aviv or from Kefar Sava to kill; they came from here, my land! They settled here and they live against my rights, against the international law, against the human rights. From the beginning, lived against the rights and the humanity of others. From the beginning, he is not ashamed if he do any crime! They live by the gun; they live by the crimes. Officially. Because he has permission to live here; they took the lands and give it to him. I believe even the murder, even the crimes, it's an official plan.

JLA: Do you feel hate towards the three men who placed the bomb?

Shaka'a: I have determined to keep myself clean about hatred. It's my . . . decision, to keep myself clean. From the first moment after, I didn't lose my mind and I've been objective and I have my conscience to explain everything. I have my memory. Until now, I keep my determination to be objective.

I didn't feel hate toward those men in that meaning of the word. But he is dirty. He is a criminal. He is a victim in the same way I am!

JLA: When Nathanson was brought to your house, what did you feel when you saw him?

Shaka'a: I said to him, "You are a criminal and you are a victim, a victim!" And they take him quickly. And all of them . . . smile. They push him quickly to the car.

SA: We are going to be interviewing Nathanson this afternoon. Is there anything that you would like us to ask or to tell him?

Shaka'a: I ask for you to succeed, to know him well. (laughs) He is not human! He lives for the crimes, and he still is in the crime line. He lives against the rights of the others! And his future . . . is not good!

*Nathan Nathanson, 30, is a powerful, towering man with a long beard and piercing gray eyes. He was one of the three men who placed the bomb in Bassam Shaka'a's car in 1980. The former head of Gush Emunim (Bloc of the Faithful), the religious Jewish lobby which leads the push for West Bank settlements, he is still its second-in-command, and directs a yeshiva network. Married with four children, Nathanson was released from prison in mid-1986, after serving two years for his role in the Shaka'a bombing. He lives in the settlement of Shilloh.*

JLA: You were in what is called the Jewish Underground. Can you explain why you joined?

Nathanson: First, you must know that there is no group called the Underground. We haven't an Underground. There is some groups that do things. One group does something to Bassam Shaka'a, and a second do something in the same night in Ramallah. I was doing it with Bassam Shaka'a; I know that another group is doing it in Ramallah, but I don't know who. A bomb. There was several things, but I only know and do the Bassam Shaka'a, and I'm not in the organization after this.

Nineteen eighty was not normal. There were six students in Qiryat Arba' who were killed in Hebron at the Tomb of Jacob. At this time, we are seeing that the Arabs are doing everything that they want and that if we want to live we have to do something. There is no other option. And we saw that the Army's hands were tied and they cannot do anything. They wanted to do things, but the government doesn't want anything done because it thinks that Bassam Shaka'a and the others are big in their towns. The officers of the Army saw that they cannot do anything.

So they say to us, "If you want, do it yourself, but we cannot help you." So we haven't another option, and we have to solve the problem. We know who among the Arabs have the power to do what they want. And then we thought about the things that we must do. And it is true that after that bomb the Arabs were very quiet. After we did it, we can see how it is good, how it gave the answer for the big question that the Army cannot give.

Sure, we have a problem with the law, but after we saw that there was not another thing to do, we have to do it and we need to do it. Because if we want to live with our families and neighbors and friends, we have to do something that we would not be doing if the atmosphere was not like this.

JLA: Why did you choose the mayors as your targets?

Nathanson: The mayors are the men that have the power. They're not like mayors in a town in Israel; they work with the political things and the extremist Arabic things. So we saw that they are not just mayors but something else, something that keeps all the town and all the area under their hands, everything they want. There was a very big danger all around, in the settlements, in the yeshivas, everyone that lives in that area was in danger. And the mayors, if they want, they can stop it—it is no problem for them. But they don't want; they want that the danger goes on.

JLA: What was that night like?

Nathanson: What do you want to know? (laughs) I knew that we were going to do something that was not normal, that you don't do every day. We had two problems. On the one hand, it's a bad thing that we go to do someone harm, but on the second hand, I approved because I could see that my bomb will stop all the bad things and atmosphere that was in 1980.

JLA: Was the bomb supposed to kill him?

Nathanson: No. Only harm.

JLA: How could you be sure?

Nathanson: We know where to put the bomb and we know how big the bomb is; if it's bigger it can do more, but when it's small it does little.

SA: Did you think about the possibility that someone else might be in the car, some of his children?

Nathanson: No, we go for two weeks before this night to see, every morning, who goes in his car. Shaka'a had two cars, and we knew who went in his car and who went in his wife's car. And we put the bomb in his car, and we know that he goes to the office in the city alone or with his friend that he picks up on the way. But on the start, he was always alone.

SA: Did you ever have doubts about putting the bomb?

Nathanson: When I saw Bassam Shaka'a after the bomb, it did something to me in the heart. Because it's not easy for a man to see that another man is not good, is feeling not good, cannot go good, because of something I did. That's on one hand. But on the other hand, I saw the danger if I did not do the bomb. We couldn't go to town, I and my wife, my children, my friends, everyone. Because there is not one man in the government of Israel that had the power or the idea to stop the problems and to say that the way is this. They talk and we do. It's a problem of today. Even today the Arabs think that they can do everything that they want.

JLA: If the situation was again like it was in 1980, would you do the bombing again?

Nathanson: I think there cannot be another time like 1980, because the government knows now that we have a deadline, that beyond there is danger and that we will act. Now they understand it and every day they have to remember, to listen to what is the matter in this area, because they don't want the dangers of 1980 to repeat.

Today the government listens to me much more because they know that we have a deadline, too. We don't want that. Surely, we don't want it. But they, the government and the Army, are afraid it will come true, so they do many things to stop the danger before it comes to our deadline.

SA: Do you feel any conflict between your religious work and your action against Shaka'a?

Nathanson: It's not a conflict. If we do the soldier things under the Torah, it's good. We Jews, we have the Law, and in the Law we have the Law of Wars. Our Jewish lives are both war and peace, and we have them together all the time. If, in war, Jews go and fight, it's good; if it's out of the Law, it's a problem. Always we want to go in the Law. In the case of Bassam Shaka'a, it's a problem. Some rabbis said it is good, some rabbis said it's not good, it's out of the Law. I did what the rabbis thought at this time.

SA: You're saying that the rabbis said it was okay to do the bombing?

Nathanson: There was rabbis that said, before the bomb, that this thing is in the Law of the Jews. There was some other rabbis who said that the bombing wasn't in the Law. Some of the group went to ask the rabbis before, and most who we asked said it was in the Law.

SA: So after the rabbis said it was in the Law, you didn't have any problem with doing it?

Nathanson: Yeah.

JLA: How did you get hold of a bomb?

Nathanson: I was in the Army! (laughs incredulously)

JLA: Did you feel you had the support of the Army to do the bomb?

Nathanson: Yeah. Of that I'm sure.

JLA: High-level?

Nathanson: Yes. They said, "We cannot help you in this black war, but you see the danger and do what you want." They wanted the black war to be done, but they can't do it alone.

SA: And after the bombing what happened to you?

Nathanson: I was put in the prison for two years.

SA: Did you feel when you went to prison that the Army had failed you?

Nathanson: Yes. It's not fair. And I have other friends that are even now in prison! One for Shaka'a. And other bombs, in Hebron or under the bus in Jerusalem. There was some friends who are still in jail now!

JLA: Do you fear for your safety now, that the Arabs might try to take revenge?

Nathanson: Maybe, I cannot know. I have many Arab friends. They invite me to their house, no problem. Maybe the friends of Shaka'a, I don't know.

JLA: Do you consider yourself a religious man?

Nathanson: I? Surely I am a religious man. I live by the religious rules.

*Jabaliya refugee camp is a sprawling jumble of shacks at one edge of the city of Gaza. Muhammad Musallem and his wife, Amni, have lived here since 1948, the year they were dispossessed of their original home in what is now Israel. Inside Musallem's improvised fence of oil-drum lids is a large tent and a makeshift tin shack.*

*The tent has been their home for the past six years, since Israeli soldiers, following policy, destroyed their house when their eldest son was imprisoned for life for "making explosions." Musallem's youngest son is also in prison, arrested at sixteen and sentenced to six years for making "tomato can bombs."*

I had a house here with four rooms. In 1980 they took my son and arrested him and soldiers came after three months and blew my home up. They didn't tell me what they were going to do, they just did it. They exploded the house with the furniture in it! They told me to get out of the house, and when Amni tried to go in to take out the furniture, they hit her with their gun and told us they would burn us, not the furniture. And then they blew up the house with explosions. They refuse me to build a new house, forever.

JLA: So what do you feel about the Israelis?

Musallem: I want to kill them! To punish them. The PLO is our sole representative, no one else. . . .

We must live in our land. If we die, our sons will liberate the land. And if all the people die and only one woman survives, her children will liberate the land, surely liberate the land! Because we are Palestinian, even if all of us died and only one Palestinian was in Lebanon, he would liberate the land! No matter where he is, in Lebanon, in Egypt, in Yemen—even in Europe—if he is a Palestinian, he will liberate the land!

*Hashem Mahameed is the harried mayor of Um-el-Fahem, located a few miles from the former Jordanian border on the West Bank, or the Green Line. The Palestinians on the other side of the Green Line live under Israeli occupation; solely by virtue of their location, Mahameed and the twenty-five thousand Palestinian inhabitants of Um-el-Fahem are Israeli citizens, or "Israeli-Arabs."*

I was four years old in 1949 when we were taken by Israel. We were not taken in 1948 by war; we were given to Israel by the Jordan kingdom in 1949.

I remember we lived in a very old-fashioned house, a house of stone and mud, where we had the cows and the animals in the same place. This was the first time I met Jews in my life, and it was my first shock in life because . . . you know, we used to hear, "Jews are coming!" When people wanted to frighten each other they would say that the Jews are coming. And so, not only Jews but soldiers came in, and I remember seeing them with the helmets and . . . on the roof of our house, with the very high [radio] antennas and, of course, guns. And I remember that this gray hair you see here [points to temple] came on that day, which was a Sunday. When I was four years old. Since I was four years old I had gray hair.

Anyway, this was my first contact with the Jews, which I can call, of course, a negative contact. My father took me outside, because I was shaking, to show me. "Don't be so afraid! Look, they are not anything." But while they were stepping on the roof of the house, because it's made of mud and some branches, some of the mud was falling down. . . .

At that time, Um-el-Fahem was about thirty-five hundred people living here. This was a very rich village once, with thousands of *dunams* [plots] of land, with all kinds of orchards and plantations. Most of it, about ninety percent, was confiscated by various rules and laws, so that we became the poorest city in Israel, with twenty-five thousand people possessing only twenty-five thousand dunams.

I finished my elementary school in Um-el-Fahem. Then, the ninth grade, until I finished high school, was in a Jewish town. I made my matriculation exams in Hebrew, as all Jews do, and I was the only Arab in my class. My parents sent me there because there was no high school in Um-el-Fahem. My father was illiterate and he never could read a word, and the same with my mother, but my teachers at school advised my father that I should be sent to a Jewish school, because maybe the standards of studies might be higher than an Arab school.

I won't say it was my best period of life. I was a good student, but I would say I was in a conflict with the majority—of course, Jewish majority—in the school. I had friends, of course, but . . . many times when we played football, students would say to each other, "Don't play like an Arab," okay? Or, "Don't behave like an Arab." It wasn't meant for me exactly but . . . it wasn't nice to hear that. And then there was the Jewish feast, where they made fire and then danced around. I remember going with my class, and then the students danced around the fire singing a song in Arabic, which means, "Mohammed is dead and he left girls behind." Which means Mohammed the Prophet died and didn't leave any men behind. And I felt bad with all this. I'm not religious—never was!—but it wasn't . . . comfortable.

And I had problems with students saying, "What are you doing here? Why don't you go back to Cairo or Amman?" And, of course, the only answer I had was, "My father and grandfather were born here, and you just came, you just landed in this country." I remember the discussions we had together! Of course, some teachers helped me a lot.

So I'm not sorry for studying in a Jewish high school. I think I learned a lot. I understand them more; I can be in their shoes sometimes. When I say I understand them, it doesn't mean I agree with them, but I can understand.

We are Israelis, regardless of our feelings. But personally I would like to feel more Israeli than we are permitted to. When my son goes to school in a very small classroom and goes to see a Jewish school and sees the way they live he comes home with a bitterness in his heart. When he sees their gardens he doesn't feel well. When he sees their roads, and then comes home with the sewage and the dirty water on his roads and he has to step in it.

There is a feeling that you are a hostage, in a way; your state is in a war with your people. You get the feeling that every time something happens, you are looked upon as if you were the enemy, as if you are part of this war. You're looked upon as a dangerous demographic problem. Then comes what the United States exported to Israel, Rabbi Kahane and the rest, and they tell you, "Get out of here, because it's not your land, it's not your homeland." And that's something I cannot say toward Jews; I cannot say, "Well, Jews, you don't have any place here — get out!" Okay? But that can be said to me.

You can never be a boss for a Jew. A Jew is always your boss. He is always the one who is responsible for you; you can't be responsible for him. Even if he doesn't understand you, even if he doesn't speak your language, except for what they call "the Arab mentality." They don't talk to me, they speak to the stereotype of my mentality. They speak to the stereotype they had of my father or grandfather.

You know, until 1966 we were under military government, and you couldn't move without permission from the military governor. The things my father used to say: "Oh, thank you, thank the state of Israel for giving us permission to move." It's very tragic. It's like "Thank you for not shooting me." It's very tragic. Today I don't think you have to thank anybody for anything! I'm not going to follow my father's way of thinking, which was made — which was the result of fear! It's not the result of my father's beliefs! It became part of his beliefs because of fear! So today I don't think I have to thank anybody for me being here, for having these clothes, because I work hard to get them and, besides, it's my right to be in my homeland, so nobody's doing me any favor for anything!

Even if there were a Palestinian state, I am going to stay in Israel to fight for equality, for a political tool, for understanding between the two people. For me, a homeland is not only a symbol, it's also the house, the garden, the stones, the rocks — there are beautiful rocks in my garden, very beautiful rocks — the trees that my father planted, the very, very small things. That's a homeland. A homeland is not a piece on a map. It's a more psychological feeling towards the small things which, all together, make your homeland.

(A muezzin in a nearby mosque begins his call to afternoon prayers; Mahameed turns and slams shut his office window.)

I remember I was in Amsterdam in 1969 and I met some Arabs. They looked at me as a traitor. "Why are you staying in Israel? Why didn't you leave it? Israel is our enemy. What are you doing there?" And I was asked if I have Jewish friends: "Yes." And they said, "Then you are a traitor," and I said, "No, I think I am very loyal to my homeland and I want to stay there." And they couldn't understand, those Arab people, that us staying here wasn't easy, that we sacrificed a lot. And I said, "Do you need more refugees? Do we need more refugees?"

(Mahameed rests back in his chair and points to a flag on the wall. It is of a tree with a gash in the trunk.)

This is the flag of Um-el-Fahem, our symbol. It shows the roots, strong roots of this place. The tree was cut and then another is growing. The tree always grows. Even if it's cut, the roots are still there. You still exist under the ground.

*Gary Cooperberg is a small, bearded man of 41 who made aliya with his family from New York in 1979. Today he lives in Qiryat Arba', a Jewish settlement outside the Arab town of Hebron on the West Bank. Qiryat Arba' was the first settlement to be established in the Occupied Territories and has been a source of Arab-Jewish tensions.*

*Cooperberg, a deeply religious Jew who compares his emigration to Israel with God's test of Abraham, works in public relations for a tiny community of Jewish settlers who are trying to spark a Jewish revival in Arab Hebron. His job before coming to Israel was as an elementary school teacher in the South Bronx.*

*It is mid-March, and today it is snowing heavily in Qiryat Arba'. Cooperberg's apartment is warm. His teenage daughter lies on the rug in front of the potbellied wood heater in the living room listening to her father speak, while her mother rustles in the kitchen.*

Everything I have done since deciding to make aliya was simply out of faith in God and a desire to be as much of a Jew as I can be. As a result of my willingness to lose everything—even my family—by coming here, I have doubled everything! My family is living today right near where Abraham lived, and we're all very happy living a religious Jewish life. And to me that's definite proof of the reality of the faith of Judaism and of the existence of God. Not only faith, I have proof now!

When we came to Qiryat Arba', we set roots and I determined that no way I'm gonna leave this place. I loved it here. For the first time I really felt that I was in what I conceived of as Israel. This is where it began. This is where Abraham lived. This is where Abraham, Isaac and Jacob are buried—all of the early Jewish history is centered around Hebron. And I felt very close to it and very much a part of it and determined that no matter what happens I'm not leaving here.

You see a little tiny settlement on top of a hill; that's the tremendous settlement that's upsetting the Arabs and world opinion, as if we're coming and conquering all these Arabs and making their lives miserable. We're the prisoners, not the Arabs! They go freely wherever they want, they build homes wherever they like. We're afraid to come out of our homes! We have soldiers guarding right in our backyard! That's not normal; that's sick! That upsets me, it really does. I'd like to see that change. I want to live like a normal person in my country. I have no objection to anyone who wants to come here and to live here, if they're willing to accept me as the owner of this land as a citizen of Israel!

There is no compromise. There is no possibility of compromise. Either we win or we lose. And the sooner we face that fact, then we can start dealing with it! But nobody in leadership here has faced that reality yet. They're unwilling to. It's too frightening! It smacks of racism, but it's not racism—self-preservation is what it's called.

Talk to any moderate Arab in this country—they're decent, reasonable people—they will tell you what they really would like is their own state! They want independence. And they don't want independence next to me, they want independence instead of me. That's their goal! Now, I don't feel that I have an obligation to help them achieve that goal, any more than I have an obligation to help a murderer find a weapon to kill me! We are living among our enemies, our blood enemies! Number one, there is no Palestinian people, there never has been! There's never been a nation called Palestine. It never existed!

I am in favor of the policy of expelling the Arabs from my country. There are many places for them to go, and if they are willing to cooperate, I think we should help them financially and physically if we can. If they're not willing to, then we should just dump them someplace, like on the Lebanese border.

SA: What about the Arabs who can say his father and grandfather were born here—say he has a little farm or a store—can't he say he has as much right to be here as you do?

Cooperberg: Forgetting even a biblical point of view, we physically are in control of this country now. We call the shots! If we wanna be nice and allow them to live here, fine! They don't have rights; they have what they're given by the people who are in charge. And that's the rule of all nations. But if Israel becomes another mini-America, the home of the free and the land of the brave, where everybody should live equally, then eventually it won't be a Jewish state anymore.

Again, I can tend to be liberal. If I felt that people are willing to live quietly and accept the authority here, without making plans to destroy me, I have no objection to them living here and keeping their little farms. But I have spoken to a lot of people—a lot of Arabs—and I'm convinced that ninety-nine percent of them are just waiting for the day when they're gonna throw me out. I don't want to make that day come. I don't want to give them the opportunity to do that! That's my point of view.

Two years ago, I think it was, a Jewish soldier was walking through the casbah. He was not provoking Arabs—he was probably windowshopping—when a young Arab boy stuck a knife in his back and killed him! That is the highest act of treason that anyone can express in any country, to cold-bloodedly murder a soldier, just because he's a soldier.

What was the government reaction here? No reaction at all! The fellow was eventually captured and, as the policy is in Israel, his house was destroyed. They broke down his house and they put him in jail for what is termed a life sentence— which I have a funny feeling will come to an end very, very soon, because right now preparations are being made for another prisoner exchange! So what are we supposed to do?

If Arabs, Arab extremists, see that the very worst that's gonna happen should they get caught is they'll go to jail for a while, why shouldn't they do what they do? They're fighting a war of liberation! We're encouraging this war! Any normal country, when you find a traitor, when you find an assassin, you hang him! You make an example of him!

Then there's the kids throwing rocks at us. A rock is a lethal weapon. It kills people. It's just as dangerous as a gun if it's used properly. And yet our soldiers are given strict orders that if somebody throws a rock at you, shoot in the air first. If they don't stop, you can shoot their legs. If they still don't stop, then you can shoot to kill. By then you could be dead. But that's the orders of our army!

JLA: What do you think it should be?

Cooperberg: Somebody picks up a rock, kill 'em! That's what I think. You do that once, they will stop, they won't throw rocks anymore. There's a price to pay! If you're willing to take that step, then you risk your life to do it!

First of all, a terrorist has no right to live. You don't give 'em a second chance! We shouldn't have terrorist prisoners! There should be no such thing! Why was that Arab who murdered a soldier in cold blood not hanged, publicly? Is there a country in the world that wouldn't do a thing like that? That's normal! That's how you do it, and that's how you show them. No, we encourage the violence and the extremism on the part of the Arabs. It's our fault! They're doing what naturally anybody would do; *we're* not doing what's natural.

Any Arab who lives in Israel is a potential terrorist, absolutely. That's natural and that's national pride. That's normal! That's why they have to be taken away!

But I think the troubled times now are more proof than anything that the Messiah is very close. The time has come, very close, the Leader will come. There will be supernatural intervention here! Now, we as a people have an obligation to observe the Torah, to fulfill the command of God. If we fulfill the will of God, our redemption will come and the miracle will be greater than the original miracle in Egypt.

Israel will eventually be the leading country in the world. Because it's God's will, not because I'm greater or better than anybody else. We have a Bible that tells us, and I believe it. I've seen enough evidence in my own life to know it's true, and I will do anything I can to help it along.

*The village of Buq'ata, muddy and exposed, sprawls over a scrubby plateau of the Golan Heights. Above it looms the snowcapped Mount Hermon. Buq'ata is a village of the Druze, a secretive offshoot of Islam, and many of the townsmen still wear the white fez, black cloak, and baggy, white pantaloons of the traditional Druze. They eke a living from the surrounding apple orchards and grape vineyards.*

*Until 1967, Buq'ata was in Syria. After the Six-Day War, Israel occupied and*

*then, in 1981, annexed a large portion of the Golan Heights, including Buq'ata;*
*the current Syrian border lies a mile behind the village.*

*On this day, a group of Druze men have gathered in a Buq'ata home to tell us*
*about living under Israeli rule. Three days before, the people of Buq'ata staged an*
*anti-Israeli demonstration; one woman, Ghalia Farhat, a 45-year-old mother of*
*five, was shot and killed by Israeli soldiers. Yesterday, the funeral of the dead*
*woman, the first person to be killed in civil disturbances on the Golan, provided*
*the arena for a much larger anti-Israeli and pro-Syrian outpouring. Thousands of*
*local Druze attended the funeral, in which Syrian flags draped the coffin and fiery*
*political speeches were given.*

*Before the dialogue begins, there is a lengthy debate in Arabic among the*
*twenty-seven men sprawled on cushions in the bare room. Most finally leave, and*
*four speakers remain: Farhat Issmyil, a high school teacher and the nephew of the*
*slain woman; Ali Abu Awad, a doctor; Shams Sliman, an English teacher, and*
*Najib El Kish, a farmer and the host of our gathering. Throughout the cold, gray*
*afternoon, Najib's daughters and wife lay trays of food and fruit and an endless*
*train of small cups of Turkish coffee before us.*

JLA:  Why did they come and shoot here?

Sliman:  Tell me why there is occupations here! The occupation here is different
from all the other occupations. They want to teach a lesson. They want to put the
law here. When they make the annex law of the Golan Heights, they think—they
hope, of course—that the Golan became an Israeli part. They think so.

Issmyil:  We don't agree. We refuse.

Sliman:  In the past, we are of Syrian government; we are citizens. But now we
are occupation people.

JLA:  And what is that like?

Sliman:  Like any people in war.

Awad:  The truth is we are Syrian, Arabic Syrian people. But they say—Israel
does—we can't go outside. After the occupation in '67, we, the people here,
asked the occupiers to let us make visits to the other side and to let our students
continue to live in Syria. They told us, "If you want to go, go! Leave!"

Sliman:  But don't come back afterward!

Awad:  They want this, they like it! But we know the truth. We are Syrian, and
this is our land here. It's Syrian. The people don't agree to leave from it. This is our
land, our land, our land!

Issmyil:  Our roots here in this area are deeper than the roots of the trees—

Awad:  (shakes fist) We never leave this land! This is our land!

El Kish:  We only care about our land, our houses, our homes. They try to take
us for themselves, but their ideas are like the snow—it falls from our heads.

SA:  Israel has officially annexed the Golan Heights, so they are saying they will
never give this village back to Syria. What is your future to stay here?

Awad: These people are like all the other people in the world. We had the occupation of the Turkish and the French and, like those did, we believe this occupation will go out at the end.

Issmyil: When the French were here, we fought. We went outside the village and we fought outside. It was very hard for the Druze man to leave his home. And we learned in this war that we must stay on our lands. We have here our trees and our farms. The other people have no farms; they have sheep, they have cows and they can go with them! But our trees, our lands, can't go with us. So we must stay. We are farmers and we had our lesson in the past, and the lesson taught us not to leave our lands.

*In the evening, the men in Najib El Kish's home take us to another house down the rutted road. There, the family of Ghalia Farhat, the slain woman, is being feted by friends, as is Druze custom. Dozens of people mill about several rooms of the house, the Druze elders with their walrus mustaches and long beards, women in long dresses preparing and serving food, along with visitors coming and going to pay their respects to the dead woman's family.*

*The rooms are large and bare of furniture, but layered in carpets and pillows. Everyone sits, backs to the walls, legs folded shoeless under them, as a huge feast is laid out, and we all eat before trooping to another room. There, we speak with the dead woman's uncle, a hard-featured man with piercing blue eyes, and her son, Farhat Said, a tall, 30-year-old farmworker wearing a white turban. Despite the killing three days ago, there is a festive, almost congratulatory, air to the gathering.*

SA: Why does no one seem sad here?

Uncle: In our religion, sadness is forbidden for the people. To die in this way is a patriotic thing. When a person dies like this, they are sacrificed for the motherland.

JLA: So it's something to be proud of?

Uncle: Of course. It is even a national duty for us.

*(The room falls silent and everyone stands with the arrival of a neighbor paying his respects. Farhat Said, who has been kneeling silently in the center of the room, rises to greet him. The newcomer speaks with emotion, and his words are embroidered with ritual: "We raise our heads with honor at your mother's death." After, Said places his hands on his friend's head and kisses him four times on the mouth. The ritual over, the man takes his place in the room and Farhat turns to us.)*

I feel the same as anyone when he loses his mother. But I consider myself one of the citizens of the Golan Heights and my mother is the mother of all of us. I don't want to make our children sad with miserable people. It's a patriotic feeling in the Golan Heights! We lose our lives for our motherland and for the Golan Heights. We consider her a martyr forever!

(Another elder stands up to address us in a shout)

Elder: I am from the Golan Heights, the Syrian Heights, and I would like to say that if the Israeli Army kills all Golan peoples, the stones in Golan will still be Syrian afterwards! I would like you to tell all the people—in Israel, in America, in Germany, in the world—to know that we will be Arab Syrians till death!

Farhat: She died, and everybody would like to die like her. For the motherland.

*Irith Tabenkin, her husband Uri, and their four children live on the Ein Zivan kibbutz in the Golan Heights, a stone's throw from the Syrian border and about five miles from the Druze village of Buq'ata. The area is heavily militarized and her kibbutz was one of those established as a strategic frontier outpost, in 1968. Apart from raising a family, Irith is the export manager of Ein Zivan's boot and sandal factory. Her children fill the room, noisily demanding her attention.*

We moved here in December 1974. I was nervous about moving to this place, but not because it is near the border. (smiles) It's cold, it's far away, and it was very young then. And so I came here, I would like to say, as an adventure, and have stayed for the last twelve, thirteen years. But the border didn't make any difference. Almost every place is near the border. I lived in Jerusalem as a child near the border. So . . .

Before '74 it was very hard, quite a tough time for this kibbutz, and they had to live in the Yom Kippur War. Since then, there was one attack of terrorism a little bit south of our place, but actually this is the quiet border.

JLA: The countryside around here is so militarized; there are bunkers everywhere. Do you no longer notice these things?

Irith: No, we do, we do very much notice. I mean, not the bunkers and everything—that you are used to—but when the Army moves in and moves out, for example, you have a . . . bad feeling. You can feel it from time to time. Here they have a very large exercise and you hear it all over and you have the feeling of being bombed yourself! These are not things that you can get used to. I mean, even though it doesn't frighten you terribly, still you have this feeling . . . and you know, always, where you are.

SA: Do you have any contact with the Druze villages around here?

Irith: We do. For example, we tried to have relations between the two schools, ours and theirs. For example, we have a truck driver that is doing jobs for us, who comes from Buq'ata, and people are coming and going in the kibbutz from Buq'ata even though now it's very tense. You can't feel it with those people. The school relations were nice . . . we had an Arabic teacher coming from Buq'ata . . . That was the period when it was more quiet. Very interesting. We went there, and they came here. He taught Arabic to our children, and their children came here, went to the swimming pool in summer.

JLA: Is this still happening?

Irith: No, not the last year. . . . But we have to work at it; it doesn't come spontaneously.

*Batya Medad is a housewife and mother of five children in the West Bank settlement of Shilloh. She and her husband, Israel, emigrated from New York in 1970. She has a kind of blissful glow and speaks with a half-smile. In keeping with religious Jewish dictates, her brown hair is covered with a knit cap.*

We have here the feeling of community that we always wanted. When we lived in Jerusalem, we felt guilty because we weren't doing more. Once we came here we felt fulfilled. And honest.

JLA: Do you ever feel lonely on this hilltop, surrounded by empty hills and Arab villages?

Batya: To tell you the truth, I feel less lonely than I did in the city. The people here, it's the community feeling that we really wanted, and I love it. I couldn't . . . manage without it . . . gets you through rough times. It's instead of family, especially for immigrants. It's what one looks for, both in terms of the need for family and companionship. And also, when you dream about moving to Israel, with all the ideals, the closest thing to that unrealistic dream is life in a place like this.

JLA: Do you think what you're doing is right?

Batya: I . . . don't see anything wrong in it. I don't harm anyone. I don't hurt anyone. I have a perfect right to live here. I wouldn't tell somebody to live in Queens rather than Brooklyn, and I don't think anyone has any right to tell me I shouldn't live here. And the same liberals who make fusses about closed communities—not letting in blacks, Jews, Orientals, or whatever—shouldn't make Judea and Samaria a closed community, Judenrhein.

Okay, Shilloh is a closed community, but so is Ramallah; Ramallah doesn't allow Jews to live there. All of Jordan is Judenrhein, and that's according to Jordanian laws—Jews are not allowed to be there.

JLA: Judenrhein?

Batya: That's German. That's what the Nazis tried to do to clean up Germany, to make it clean of Jews. So, whether it's the left-wingers in Israel or any outside people saying that Jews shouldn't live here, it's a very Nazi-like and Fascist-like thing to do. Because I'm not throwing anyone out of their home. The hills here are empty; there's room here for thousands more, of both Jews and Arabs! And . . . I want to live in peace. I'm a mother of five. I . . . I believe in the future. I wouldn't have children if I didn't want peace!

JLA: What do you think of the Arabs?

Batya: I don't bother them, and I don't expect them to bother me. I don't have any car or any easy way of doing business with them. . . . There's some who've worked here, and there's some people here who shop with them. . . . We have enough trouble socializing with our neighbors who live down the hill a mile away. I don't see why we should be expected to . . . socialize with Arabs.

Once I participated in a dialogue with one, and when he was asked, "Do your children play with Jewish children?" his reaction was, "Why should they?" You know, it's not convenient. I don't need it. There's no reason why we shouldn't each live in our own homes and be with the people we want to be with and keep our identities and . . . as long as nobody hurts anybody else, I don't see what could be wrong with it.

JLA: So the situation is tolerable?

Batya: The longer it goes on, I think the better it is. I mean, as long as people don't try to make trouble. But Judea and Samaria have been under Jewish rule longer than it was ever under Jordanian rule. And the Arabs here are living on a very, very high standard—I'm always amazed as we go by; the houses that are going up are unbelievable!—and life for them is very good. I'm sure that most would really like to keep the status quo. There's certain things they don't have, but the levels of their hospitals have gone up.

We have this land, and we may as well use it! It was a miracle that we won the war, won two wars under unbelievable odds, and you have to see the hand of God in it. You don't have to be someone who speaks in Messianic terms but . . . if God gives us this message, then we should take the hint and do something about it; otherwise, you know, you're sort of insulting God.

*At the end of our conversation, we asked the plump, silver-haired woman her name. She looked thoughtful, then said with a smile, "Call me Jihad [Holy War]; it's a good name."*

*Jihad lives on a hillside in Israeli-annexed East Jerusalem. Her house is homey and filled with pictures of her children. In the windowsill of the dining room is the mark of a stray bullet from one of Jerusalem's battles. In her small patio are two trees laden with lemons; before leaving, she insists we take several of the largest ones with us.*

My father was a very big merchant. We were all educated; all of us know the English, the Arabic, so many languages. We are not as they say; they say we are rough people. And we were friends for the Jews at the time. The Jews used to buy all their equipment from my father, because my father was a landowner and a very big merchant. And that's what happened. We lost everything to the Jews. They stole everything from my father.

I am a refugee. That happened in Mandate. In Mandate, we were living nicely, peacefully with everybody. Then the Jews started. We didn't have weapons; we have nothing, nothing at all. If one had bought a pistol or something like that, he has to hide it, he can't show. The British Mandate gave all the weapons, everything, to the Jew. Everything, even the guns. And we were having nothing.

So they start killing people and shooting in the sky and frightening the people. For instance, we were having a shop, and just beside us was a shop belonging to the Jews. What happened was the English commandants came, break the Jewish shop, took the very expensive things from it, and they said, "The Arabs have broken the shop of the Jews," and so the war broke out in that place. It always started like this; all the events, all of them started this way.

So my mother was very sick. She was having a dead baby boy, you know, and we were very young. We were nine people in the house, but we were living peacefully. So they started killing the people and we were without water. My mother was very sick and we can't take her to hospital.

My father remained in this place, but the family left. We were having no men to fight, not a single Arab. We were closed off. After the Jews had entered our place, my father went to the shop to take the money from the iron place [safe], but they had opened a hole through the wall and come in and stolen everything. Everything, all his goods, his money and passport, were gone.

So after the war we were living in Jordan. It was forbidden to go back. My father wanted to go back to his home and shop, but he couldn't. They said, "No, it's finished. You have to manage. The Israelis have taken all this area, and you can't go back."

And now, if we go back, everything is with the Jews. And if anybody comes and asks for our identity card, they will see we are Arab and they will take us to prison and make us trouble. If any event happens, although it wasn't from the Arabs—sometimes it is between the Jews—so they collect hundred Arabs, two hundred, and they take them. (laughs) And they want to know everything about everybody. So (laughs) that is life. There is no place you can go. You are just in here, stranded. It's terrible. (laughs) We laugh because we have to laugh. When a person is very angry, he has to laugh. This is life. As long as we can stay on our feet, it's good.

We are very good people. We are civilized. We have good heart. We are very good people. You know, in '67, they do statistics. They found out that ninety-nine percent of the Palestinian people are civilized. Ninety-nine percent! They said in the whole world you won't find such a well brought up people. We love everybody. If we see a Jew in the street needs help we help them. Believe me! Here, I don't know who you are. Whoever needs help, we help them. We don't damage. Every day, I do something good. This is life. We must help out each other, look after each other. We help everybody. We help everybody. We don't differentiate between this and that.

JLA: So you don't feel bitter?

Jihad: Of course! In heart, (laughs) but not in words. If I take this briefcase from you, will you be angry or not? They took our souls, our children, our families, our land, our means of living, our places of residence, our everything. What do you think? Would you be angry or not?

It's because we worship God. We believe in all good things; that's why we are continuing our lives. We want to live peacefully, happily. If a person loses one dinar, he keeps thinking all day, "How did I lose it, who took it from me?" What about us? But still we are standing on our legs.

It's not so easy to live. It's not so easy. It's not so easy to live. Tell me, we have to live, what can we do?

We suffered. We suffered much, and still we are suffering.

*Munir Fasheh, the dean of students at Bir Zeit University, is a slender, energetic man of 46 with a ready smile. He lives in Ramallah, an Arab town outside Jerusalem where his family has lived since 1948. He is a graduate of the American University of Beirut, Florida State, and earned a doctorate at Harvard in social policy and planning.*

I was born in 1941 in Jerusalem. We were driven out in '48. Our house is still in West Jerusalem. It's occupied by European Jews who came to civilize us, of course. We still have the papers to it, though, even the keys. They've changed all the locks, of course, but my father never had the heart to throw them away.

When I grew up, when someone asked me, "Who are you?" I would hesitate. I had, and I have, a Jordanian passport, but I knew I was a Palestinian. But I was confused. If you look at our youth now, their sense of belonging is much greater than my generation. They're not confused; they know they are harassed for being Palestinians, that their problems are because they are Palestinians. There is a sense of common cause, common future, common past. These are positive things that the Occupation has brought.

The problems are handed down to the young at a very early age. Last week, a man here was arrested. The next day, his three-year-old son was going around, proudly telling the neighbors, "The Jews took my father."

You see eight- and ten-year-olds rushing towards the Army, the tanks, and you wonder if they have lost the meaning for life. They run, not even to throw rocks, just to shout.

The Army is afraid of them. Why? Because it's taken their land and left them with no future. But this lack of options has brought with it hope for the future. There is no youth in the West Bank who doesn't have hope about the future. They feel that, though they don't know when, there will be a Palestinian state.

When people talk about hostages, basically we here are hostages. What is a hostage? It's always having a gun pointed at you, telling you when to move and when not to move. You get shot if you don't follow the rules. It's hostages at a much larger scale and with a more profound impact on people's lives. The Occupation challenges people to try and make sense out of an absurd situation, that of ruling absolutely over another people. They even rule over what we can or can't plant; at one point, the Israeli traders needed strawberries, so our farmers had to grow them. There are such challenges; constantly you are reminded of the absurdity of the situation.

*Haithan Hanna, 26, a Palestinian Catholic, is an architectural draftsman who wears a traditional red-checked kaffiyeh headdress. After working in Saudi Arabia and Finland for six years, he has returned to his West Bank home village of Taybeh, where he is working for its development council.*

*Hanna married a Finnish woman with whom he had a child in 1986. When the wife and baby came to join Hanna in Taybeh, they were only given temporary visas, and told to apply for residency. The catch is that no decision on their application will be made for two months, thirty days after their visas expire.*

*The Hannas' dilemma highlights the predicament of thousands of Palestinian families scattered across national boundaries who are victims of an international bureaucratic nightmare, resulting in their enforced separation.*

After all these problems that they cause for me, so I must start to cause problems for them! Maybe with our voice and our pressure, they will start to talk about it and Israel will start to take it into consideration, to think about this family union paper, about these people, about—It's not only a file, not just a name and papers, written in black or in red, it's a human. There is a family inside this file!

They say, "After two months you come to know the answer, if it's rejected or not." So . . . you have to hope for these two months, but . . . it is like playing in somebody's feelings and life, like you are not a human, you are a kind of football in the field. They are just kicking you from one place to another. That's what they are trying to do, but I don't like it and I don't ever let anybody to do this with me.

By this, they are trying to make people get fed up and just leave your country; you leave your house, your relatives, your family, your . . . everything you have here. And when you get fed up you just have to go to where your wife is living. Maybe there is a better life and you can stay there, but why I can't have this here? First I must try it in my country; I must have this! So maybe I can't, but I'm not going to give up, either!

I want for my wife, and for my child at least, to stay here sometimes so she can speak Arabic, and know more of our traditions and food and everything. For the child. She's now seven months. If we stay here two or three years, at least she'll catch the language, she can speak Arabic. But if we are just living in Finland, then my daughter is just a European, and just by name she'll have had a father from Arabia or something. Then what for I am Palestine? What I've done? Nothing! Then, as they want us to be . . . just a kind of paper, in a file.

This is the first year I have been working in my country. And I think this work that I'm doing, this planning and developing for my village, I can say that I have done something, that my name is connected with this kind of thing, that Haithan Hanna was part of this group who made this and my name is there. So I can say I have done something for some time to the good of myself, my family, and my people here. At least something.

*Zvi Al-Pelege, 61, has a pronounced military bearing: short-cropped hair, stiff-backed, and with piercing blue eyes set in a weathered face. A wealthy Tel Aviv businessman, Pelege has for decades been chosen by the Israeli government to be its initial military governor in the areas it has occupied in the wake of wars: in Gaza after the 1956 Sinai Campaign, the West Bank after the Six-Day War, the west bank of the Suez Canal after the Yom Kippur War, and in southern Lebanon after the 1982 invasion.*

If you come to ask me whether I am happy about the Occupation, no, I'm not happy. One, because I feel that a very long occupation brings about a de facto annexation, and since there is only one small Jewish state, I would like to keep it as such. Two, because no people in the world in the present era likes to be governed or ruled by another nation.

But no one can call this a brutal occupation. When the United States occupied Japan, did the Americans ever let a single Japanese apply to the Supreme Court in Washington against the deeds of a military governor? Never. But anyone in the areas here can apply every day against the prime minister, against the governor.

You have six universities now in the West Bank and another two in Gaza Strip, more than in Israel, three times as many as in Jordan. You had forty-five percent unemployment in the Gaza Strip before; you have nothing now. You had ten to fifteen percent unemployment in the West Bank. You had about fifty percent illiterate people in the border areas in 1967. Do you know how many new schools we have built?

Now if you come into an area and you just ask a man in the street how is the situation here, he will say, "It's a horrible situation, the Israelis are oppressing us, we have no freedom whatsoever," and so on. Is there anywhere in the Arab world as much freedom as there is in the occupied areas? The PLO has thirty newspapers in the West Bank! Each of them has its own youth organization, its own labor unions.

Now, if you ask me if this makes the lives of people under occupation better, no. They would rather live in total poverty and have Arabs as their governors, not Jews. No doubt about that. But talking about improving the quality of life, never, never will they have the situation they have now.

They say, "Keep your favors to yourself and get off our backs." Okay. I'm with you, but don't tell me there have been no favors. Let's first agree on the favors, and then, okay, we should get off your back.

*Mohamed Khass is a native Gazan in his late sixties. As a young teacher, he joined the National Liberation League, an Arab Communist party. Because of Moscow's support of the partition of Palestine in 1947, his party endorsed the UN plan. When the Egyptians occupied Gaza in 1948, Khass was detained along with other Palestinian communists who had supported the partition and imprisoned in the Sinai Desert. Seven months later, the Israeli army captured the area and took the prisoners to detention camps in Israel, where Khass spent nine more months.*

*Unable to return to Egyptian-occupied Gaza, Khass was eventually released to live in Israel. He spent the next twenty-three years in Haifa, as a journalist for the communist newspaper there. There he met and married Mary Khass, a Palestinian Christian. He broke with the Communist Party and returned to Gaza in 1970 to work for the Palestinian cause. Today he and his wife have a spacious home one block from the sea on a sandy back street of Gaza, and Khass is the editor of Gaza's leading newspaper.*

There is no good occupation and bad occupation; there is only one occupation, which is bad. And not only bad for Palestinians—it is bad for any other nation. When you go through the history, you don't find any people who accepted occupation. Why should the Palestinians accept? There is no logic in it. Any nation under occupation has struggled against the occupation. It is natural.

My family has been here for nearly eight hundred years. Gaza was a small town before 1948; it was inhabited by nearly fifty thousand people, and now there are three hundred thousand. There is no place left here. The only place to breathe is the sea, and you are not allowed to be there after seven o'clock. Even the people who are living along the beach, they are not allowed. To see the sea, to breathe the fresh air, you are not allowed.

I consider myself a Palestinian who looks to be equal with other nations, to have my state. And I want to tell you that we are suffering more from the Arabs more than from the Israelis. Thousands of people from Gaza are working in the [Persian] Gulf area. If I finish my work in the Gulf area, I have no place to go. Israel will not accept me to come back to Gaza, and the Jordanians are not willing to have more Palestinians. Syria the same. If we go to Iraq we have to join the war with Iran. If we go to Libya, they won't let you back in here ever.

We . . . we are not speaking about a state; we are speaking about a home. To have a home! Never mind the state, but to have a ceiling of your own and to sit under it!

*Hamdi Farraj, 31, is a thin, tough-looking Palestinian journalist who lives in the Dehaisha camp on the edge of Bethlehem. He has spent the last three and a half years in either town arrest or prison on state security violations. By his own count, Farraj has been arrested at least fifteen times by Israeli authorities.*

I was born in Dehaisha. Most of the people in the camps today are educated people. Because the fathers lost their lands and they haven't money to do other projects, they depend on another idea, which is to send their sons to the school. An example: in my family we are seven brothers. One of them is a doctor, graduated from Athens. An agricultural engineer graduated from Jordan. A lawyer, he graduated from Lebanon. And me, I graduated from here at Bir Zeit.

We consider ourselves, as refugees, as the soul of the Palestinian problems. I cannot find a separation between the refugee problem and the Palestinian problem. Both are together.

The Israeleans tried to solve some of the refugee problem, and they wanted to start from Dehaisha, to build houses for the refugees to move there from the camp. But the people of the camp—all of them—they refused.

SA: So when you have children, they will also be raised in Dehaisha?

Farraj: Yes. It's not good?

SA: I don't know. Is it good?

Farraj: No, it's not a good life. We are suffering under occupation in general. Every way and every level we are suffering, so don't think living under occupation is a good life.

At the same time, the Israeleans don't feel any happiness, either. They don't feel they can live in calm or quiet. No. Both, I think, we are suffering. Yes, we are suffering more. . . .

JLA: What made you stay in Palestine and risk constant arrest rather than take the option, like others have, to go and fight?

Farraj: I consider myself a good citizen and a supporter also of the PLO, and maybe the circumstances obliged me to stay here. At the same time, I think the Palestinians outside don't need us as fighters. There's a lot of Palestinians to fight. Inside Palestine, the Palestinian risks more. So the problem is not how many fighters the Palestinians have, because I don't believe that the war between us and Israel will solve the problem. It needs time. We know that our problem will take a lot of time.

We are people, my friend. And if we are people, then we have rights. And we will reach our rights. I am sure. Not today, not tomorrow, but one day we will reach.

And we are good people, also. Even we are poor people, even we are not conscious people, even we are from the Third World, but we are good people. Israel today has twenty-five jails. This is for us. The jails are full, all the time. More than two hundred thousand Palestinian people have been to the jails. But we are good people. We love our homeland and we will work all the time, till we die, to reach our rights.

We know the game. We know. We know that Israel is not just our enemy; we know that we are facing a big enemy, *your* country. Three billion dollars to the Israeleans, this from your government.

Without America and without the official policy, it would be very easy to live together. Very, very easy. Do you think I myself hate any Israelean? Or that an Israelean hates me because I am a Palestinian? You are Americans; officially, you are our enemy, but we are sitting together and speaking together. I have Israelean friends, too, among the peace people, and they are very, very nice—they are better than me, believe me. No problem to live together.

Once, when I was in a cell during an investigation, one of the soldiers, he gave me his cigarette, put it in my pocket, and said, "Smoke one cigarette, two cigarettes, however much you want." Even though the Shin Bet [secret service] officer told him not to allow me to smoke. But the soldier brought me bananas, everything, what I want. And I don't know him, he doesn't know me. I'm a human being; he's a human being. Why not?

*Yitzhak Orpaz, 65, is one of Israel's best-known novelists. A small, soft-spoken man with thinning hair, Orpaz is a direct descendant of the founder of the Hassidic sect of Judaism. He lives in a spartan apartment in Tel Aviv where the major ornamentation is laden bookshelves covering virtually all the wall space.*

I was born in a little town of Soviet Russia, and until the age of fifteen I grew up there; first there and later on in a little town in Bessarabia, a conflicted area between Romania and Russia. So all my life I have lived in conflicted areas.

I came in the end of '38. It was really the last ship coming from Europe, with the youth that came out alive. I came here at the age of fifteen, but I saw myself as an Israeli long before that. I mean, since I first became conscious of myself I knew that I belonged in Israel, that it is my country. It was quite natural for me and it took very little time to feel like I was born here. At that time, I also disconnected myself from my original setting—place, ambition, Yiddish, family. I felt I had been something of an exile [in Russia] and everything that was connected with exile was bad.

I have been born anew in my old homeland, which is Eretz Israel. I have been expelled from it two thousand years ago and I have been dead for two thousand years. I've been born again here, you understand?

So I changed my name. My name was Awerbouch, and I changed it into a very new Hebrew name, symbolizing my renaissance—Orpaz, which means light and good and so on—and cut off my old name, the exiled name. But at a much later time, after the Yom Kippur War, when I came to think about everything, mostly about my origins and my roots, I came to line myself up again with my ancestors, their traditions. So at that time, I also took my old name back, so today I have two names.

I should say there were two reasons for this return. One was a domestic factor. The son of my brother was killed in the Yom Kippur War, on the [Suez]

Canal. . . . It was very unfortunate, because he wasn't just killed; first he was missing, then he was . . . it's a very long story.

He was also a writer, beginning, a storyteller, very talented . . . so he was rather . . . responsive to me more than my brother, although he was his son—my brother is a good kibbutznik, but he is not really an intellectual, not a writer—so I was just . . . we . . . we were very close.

The other thing was the traumatic effect this war had on us. Not only were we surprised, but we were on the point of losing the war, which meant for us extermination. And it was, of course, automatically reminding us of everything we thought we had finished with—the Holocaust, the constant persecution of Jews through history. All these things came alive at once. It was a very deep shock.

For half a year, I couldn't write a word. When I did come back to it, it had a very great effect on my writing. I began to write much more realistically, with a kind of fantastic dimension. I was telling our story. I was connecting our story here with the story of our ancestors, our parents. The main theme of the trilogy I wrote, starting right after the Yom Kippur War and ending just two years ago, was precisely this theme, of being Israeli and being Jewish.

My Jewishness means an extra sensitiveness to suffering of others, and, with it, extra suspiciousness. Especially for Christians—when Christians start talking too much about love, I never know, but somehow I know it must end on my grave. My Jewishness means being restless, soul-restlessness. Being a nonconformist. To be awaiting, expecting some new revelation, looking upon ourselves in kind of intermediate terms, not life for life's sake, but life as leading toward something. That means not letting things freeze as they are, to strive for change, constant change.

It is my fate to be in a disputed area with so many enemies around and, in an existentialist way, in danger of perhaps being exterminated—you must not forget that almost every other Jewish person, perhaps two out of three, have some family connection with the Holocaust. If it is not their mother and father and sister—like myself—it's an uncle, an aunt, a grandfather, a grandmother. It's a thing that happened yesterday. So it's like a fish; without knowing it, a fish feels all the sea. A fish must certainly feel the difference between being in the big seas and being in the shallow waters. I myself feel that difference.

SA: Does the memory of the Holocaust make it more difficult for you to consider compromising today with the Palestinians?

Orpaz: It goes back to my second point: extra suspiciousness. We are entitled to have it; with such a biography, individually and as a people, we are justified to be suspicious. That explains much of the hard-liners. They may be very good people in themselves, and liberals in their general stand, but when it comes to existential fears and anguishes you can just feel this sort of transfiguration. The same with me; I'm aware of it.

But, you know, the Palestinians, they double-talk. I just don't understand their ways, what they mean, what they say. Sometimes, we have been sitting and drinking together and after they had a couple of glasses, they were saying things that were different, entirely different, opposing to things they had said before.

One day a Palestinian writer friend called me and asked me to give my name to a petition against some administrative detention of a Palestinian intellectual. I said, "All right, but let's sign together a petition which will include also our opposition to the atrocious terrorist act that has been done yesterday in Cinema Chen in Tel Aviv in which civilians were killed by a grenade by a Palestinian terrorist." She said—she was a very fine poet, by the way—she said, "How can you mix these two things; this is a liberation movement." (laughs) So I said, "Well, it's the liberation movement on the lives of civilians who have nothing to do with it." She didn't want this. So then my suspiciousness began to work, and I thought, "Is that the kind of peace you mean to introduce here? A peace on my grave! Is that the peace you are striving at?"

So that's why I say we have to be suspicious. You have to be liberal, you have to be humane, but you don't have to be a fool. You don't want, just out of liberalism, to make your partner your grave-maker.

But I believe that things must always change and always change for the better. Which is something that gives so much force to the Jewish existence; otherwise, how would you explain that so many strong countries have vanished and the Jews are going on all this time being chased away and persecuted? It must be some inner optimistic force, an optimistic . . . talent for surviving. It's a kind of talent.

*Jamal Saleh is a handsome 22-year-old Palestinian from Nablus. He is studying business administration at Bir Zeit University. His friend, Quais Hodali, is a student of engineering from Tulkarm who speaks in a low monotone.*

*The radicalized, pro-PLO Bir Zeit campus is frequently shut down by the Israeli authorities. In the student council office, there is a large photo of Yassir Arafat, an illegal symbol of the students' defiance.*

Saleh: Sometimes I think that the best way is to leave this land. But the strong belief that this is my land prevents me from going outside. Any American or Englishman, bring him here and let him live these situations; he will curse everything and he will go abroad. But because of the strong belief that this is my land, I will bear everything and I will be patient.

And I will stay until a solution will happen, for me and for others. I think that this is the same for a good percentage of Israelis. They don't want to keep living in Jerusalem or in Tel Aviv and waiting for a bomb or some bullets to be shot.

There is a characteristic of the Palestinians, that if you give him something, he will give you more and more back. So this feeling of destroying Israel is carried now because of what Palestinians see from Israel and its soldiers. Show them that you want peace, that you want a solution to the struggle in the Middle East, and this feeling will dissolve. It will dissolve itself. And I guarantee that if you give the Palestinians only one kilometer square it will be sufficient, because they only want something good. Nowhere, not in Lebanon, in Syria, in Egypt, and Tunis—or here in the West Bank—no one is treating them gently, you know?

JLA: What does being a Palestinian mean for you?

Saleh: If I was not a Palestinian, I would wish to be a Palestinian.

JLA: Why?

Saleh: To see what's the . . . the taste of life. What's the taste of getting something to eat, or getting something happy. If you are living comfortable you will feel nothing that tastes good, but if you live in this struggle and in this very, very bad situation you will know the meaning of life. You will know the meaning of getting a very simple right. I think that Americans don't care for their right to vote, for example, or they see that's it's very simple to say, "I'm not interested to vote." But when you are forbidden to vote, when you are forbidden to walk in the street after six o'clock, when you are then allowed to do so you will see what is the taste of life.

JLA: Do you think you will see an independent Palestine?

Hodali: Yes.

JLA: Why?

Hodali: Why. This is a thing you must not ask about. (laughs) Because our struggle is to get Palestine. Our struggle, in Lebanon, in Syria, in Jordan, is to get our land, our state.

I'll give you an example: the Zionists had a dream. They said, after fifty years or five hundred years there will be an Israeli state. We have the right to dream also! They can't forbid us our dream also, they can't! (laughs)

*Surica Braverman, 68, is a small, sturdy woman with short gray hair and intense, thoughtful eyes; in her blue cardigan, corduroy pants, and leather tennis shoes, she displays a youthful vitality. Braverman lives in Kibbutz Shamir, her home for the past forty years, on a sloping hillside of the verdant Galilee Valley.*

*The parklike grounds of the kibbutz are ringed with concertina wire and dotted throughout its grounds are stone bomb shelters. Until the 1967 Six-Day War, the Syrian border lay but a few hundred yards away; now, that part of the Golan Heights has been annexed by Israel. A few miles across the valley is the embattled Lebanese border.*

*Braverman is one of Israel's true pioneers. As a young Zionist, she emigrated from Romania in 1938. She joined the underground Palmach militia at the age of 23 and in 1944 parachuted into Yugoslavia as part of a plan to rescue Jews; of the three woman involved in the operation, only Braverman survived. After six*

*months, she slipped back into Palestine and took up duties in the Haganah, the
umbrella organization fighting for Jewish statehood. Besides training women
fighters during the 1948 war, she helped establish Kibbutz Shamir.*

What I have learned in my long life is that war didn't solve any problem.

At a very young age, I was in a Zionist movement that educated for "folk
loving," as we called it: that this land will be promised to the Jews and to the
Arabs. We thought about a binational country. The idea was that this country, Eretz
Israel, belongs to two nations, the Jewish nation of those who returned back to the
country and the Arab nation for the people who were living here.

When we came into this desert, the Arabs in this area came to us. They didn't
believe that someone would come into this area; there was a very big swamp here,
with malaria. The relationship was very good. The Arabs, they came here, they
brought bread. Our nurse treated them to save some of them bitten by snakes. They
brought us things for agriculture because we had no farms, no cows.

I can say that during the independence [war], when I was commander of this
place, with a white flag came the Arab village opposite to us and they asked us not
to attack them, and we agreed. We asked them if they will give shelter if forces
attack us, and they agreed. We had nothing against them. In the independence war
I'm speaking, and we didn't attack anyone at that time. After the war, these people
fled away.

JLA: You say that you have seen in your long life that war doesn't solve
anything, and yet war has followed you all your life. Even now in this beautiful
place, you are surrounded by barbed wire and bunkers. What do you feel about
that?

Braverman: It's a terrible feeling. I hope the children will not go to war, but I
believe that my nephew will go to war. I am terribly afraid of the extremism of both
sides, we and also the Arabs. Therefore, for me to see to the future, and I haven't
many years to see before my eyes, I can't see friends on the land.

Until 1967, the tension was a way of life. It meant to raise children in shelters. I
will give you an example:

We built our dining room. It was a glass wall facing the Syrian border, but then
we had to build before this window a wall in order that the Syrians will not shoot us
in the dining room.

To be honest, I have to say that we learned to live with this situation.

I'll tell you a story. There was a very big bombing. Three hundred and fifty tons
of cannons fell on this kibbutz. Fifty days. Most of the people were living in wood
houses at that time, and we didn't have enough shelters. There wasn't one house
that wasn't damaged at that time. We were lucky that no one was wounded. We did
everything to make life for our children possible, because the shelter was like a
home, a second home. In the shelters we played with the children. We took care

about the atmosphere. During the Six-Day War and the Yom Kippur War women cooked all the time. We cooked hot food and we divided the food between the children and the fighters in the bunkers. In the Yom Kippur War the Syrian planes would pass right over us, but the women would continue to cook. During the Six-Day War, the Syrian Army was just there in their positions, six hundred meters away. . . .

And . . . (long pause) something happened here in '74.

There was a pregnant woman from the kibbutz. There was another young member of the kibbutz who didn't feel well in this day, so they decided to stay at their work and not to come to the dining room for breakfast. They stayed in the beekeeping place. Close to the graveyard.

It was eight o'clock. A boy entered the dining room, crying. "Terrorists are near to the children's house!" Accidentally, this day I was working in the children's house. The terrorists came near the children's house and were seen by a child, eight years old, sitting on the steps in front of the house, and the child entered the house and cried, "Terrorists are shooting us." I took the children to the shelter, and from the dining room all the sons of the kibbutz, reserve soldiers, they ran, took their weapons from their homes—everyone has his weapon in his home; I also have a weapon here in my home now—and they begin to search for the terrorists.

So, one of the volunteers—she was from New Zealand—and two boys were walking. They didn't know the terrorists were near to the beehouse, so they were returning normally to their work. One member was wounded and the volunteer they killed on the way as they [the terrorists] ran to the beehouse.

At that time, the children who are fighters, our sons, came. Two of the terrorists were wounded or killed by sons of the kibbutz, close to the swimming pool. The other two ran back to the beehouse. We still didn't know what had happened inside the beehouse.

We took a microphone. We tried to speak Arabic to them, the terrorists inside, to make a dialogue with them. There was one fighter whose wife was inside the beehouse. The answer to our offer to negotiate was an explosion in the beehouse. And we don't know if they explode themselves or there was an accident. In the beehouse was the two women. One of the terrorists had stayed in the beehouse. He killed them from the back. We found them on the worktable with their heads on the table.

It was the most hard time. It's different, a war and . . . sabotage like this. I think the kibbutz passed through one of the hardest periods after this. First of all, to bury three women in one day. That mothers of children were killed in such a way . . . it was stronger than anyone at that time. (tears come to her eyes)

We have done everything to have a safety feeling. We guard twenty-four hours now around the kibbutz. We were helped at that time by people who came, kibbutzim from all over the country. Every week, ten people came to guard here, returned back to Tel Aviv, and then ten new people. They encouraged us in this. We felt that we are not alone . . . it was a hard period.

SA: Did anyone leave the kibbutz because of it?

Braverman: No. People left for other reasons, but not for this. At this moment, people didn't . . . dare to leave for such a reason.

I want to tell you of the Yom Kippur War in 1973. A unit of the army which included our sons, they passed this kibbutz on their way to the Golan Heights. Members of the kibbutz, parents, ran after them with food, milk, cakes. And gave them to drink . . . The children had gotten up as soldiers.

I remember that I was very distressed. We saw the battle on the TV, and I felt in my heart that I was there. . . . All the women in the world live so close to the frontier . . . they know that her husband or her brother, in all these battles, this fighting. . . . They don't expect them to return back home, all the children, the soldiers, at the end of the war, and we don't know where they are.

When I say children, I'm a mother. I remember also that when I was fifty years old I was still a child of my mother. So one of the sons of the kibbutz, I remember I gave him the blessing of a grandmother; he was twelve years old when he came from Europe as one of the children escaped from the war. I called him also my son. He is now fifty-two years old. . . .

I don't want to show ourselves as heroes; we are only blood-and-flesh people. There was one son from the kibbutz. During the Yom Kippur War, he decided to return back to the army to serve. He went to the Golan Heights with the army. His mother is my close friend and his father was one of the founders of the kibbutz who—it was terrible—who fought to his fate, so my friend was a widow.

Every two days the mail came from him. One day a letter came, and the mother said, "It's not right; it's not from him." It was a postcard I had sent to make her feel better; I was sending her the letters. I saw she was so distressed that I decided I had to take her to him, to show her that he is still living. I took one of the members of the kibbutz, and we took the van. We didn't know exactly what unit or where he was. (tears come to her eyes)

There were roadblocks in the Golan. I was astonished that they allowed me to cross. I arrived to the battle itself. I found twenty-five very high commanders sitting in a bunker in a meeting. I went inside, and they were astonished to see a woman in such a place! One colonel came outside with me and I told the story. He took me to the radio tent. All the units began to search their bunkers for our son. In a moment, they told me they know where he is. They promised me that tomorrow morning they will send him home for a half an hour. To see his mother . . . And I think in my heart, "Where in the world can you find such an army that can be so influenced from the stress of a mother, to allow a son to return back for one half an hour." (voice cracks)

And the next morning, a car came, and he arrived and saw his mother and returned back. . . .

(Braverman rises to make coffee; she is fully composed when she returns)

To live on a kibbutz, a person needs a very strong outlook. We came with an idea that was strong in our hearts. Our kibbutz was formed when Russia was in her glory time, our youth. After this, disappointment came with the Russians. They didn't fulfill socialism; they did it by barbarity and we are trying to live in a humanistic socialism. We wanted to build, not by war, but by understanding between people and nations. And now the fate of our children, every Jew, from eight, nine years, they are candidates for death. I'm not believing in Zionism and the existence of this country if the chance of peace will not be chased, for a chance to live. We call it love between nations, war against racism . . . difficult.

I'm not pessimistic. I still think we will find the political powers in Israel and also the Arab nations, and that we will understand once and forever that war does not solve problems. Prisoners, concentration camps, there is no end.

We are closer to Damascus than Tel Aviv. If there would be peace, it's possible to drive, to visit. Why lies this wall between? When I look at Lebanon, this country was called the Switzerland of the Middle East. What has happened? How they kill each other? Why? In Iran and Iraq, how many were killed? They have no answers; their answer is to kill. To kill and destroy, to send seven-year-olds as fighters. . . .

In time of war, it is very hard to keep a nice soul. War is the highest test of our soul. I ask, in how many wars can a man participate and stay being a man?

# Conclusion:
# Jon Lee Anderson

It should be straightforward; you go to a place, ask people about their feelings, listen, and then leave. Their words are supposed to be all you carry away with you. But no, I have carried something more of them with me. Too often, my questions dug up those intimacies locked by the heart in the dark recesses of memory. These people expected far more than questions. They wanted help, answers, and solace of a kind beyond my ability to give them.

At times, I have been troubled by the apparent perversity of our project; to journey through a world exclusively at war, its wounded inhabitants hostage to a separate reality. And this reality has become mine, as well, because in a war zone, you delve into the whole netherworld of emotions that exist there, and in yourself.

I now know that you can't go in and come out unscathed. There is an emotional baggage I have accumulated and brought back. It is still here now; I feel it in me:

I am euphoric with the unrelenting idealism of the young terrorist; I share the horror and shock of the woman about to be executed as a spy; yet, I understand her executioner's practical motives. I reel with the grief of the mother who has lost her son, and my blood stirs in fraternity with the man who has taken a life in vengeance. I am weighed down, wearily ancient, with the cynical burden of those who have seen and felt it all and who know it will never really change.

There is no conclusion to *War Zones*. It is not something that has a beginning and an end. It has always been here; we have just touched it for a brief moment.

# Conclusion:
# Scott Anderson

With the book now over, I'm not sure what to conclude from it all. My thoughts are rather personal, and fragmentary at that. I don't feel I have any unique insight about war. I better understand some of the basic maxims—that war is hell, that man has a tremendous will to survive anything, that it doesn't take very much for a man to pick up a gun—but to furnish something new?

Most of all, I feel exhausted. From the pressured work and the often-depressing subject matter, of course, but also from things I hadn't really thought about before.

Opinions I had, about who was right and wrong in a conflict, blurred, then vanished, when becoming friends with people on both sides of a divide. To spend an afternoon in the genuine warmth of an Israeli kibbutz, and the evening being royally feted by Palestinian hosts, is not the proper breeding ground for a dogmatist.

I had a vague image of the face of evil and a belief in my ability to recognize it, only to have it torn away by the kindness of killers when meeting them. I spoke, drank, and ate with men who had placed bombs in cars, gunned down civilians, orchestrated massacres. Often, they were very good company.

I'm tired of being constantly lied to. That's something new, perhaps: that war makes liars out of everybody. It's wearying to be with people you enjoy, whom you consider to be friends, but always to know that any "fact" they give about their conflict is often so grossly exaggerated that it bears little resemblance to truth. And there are the more subtle lies, the outrage at atrocities committed by the other side, justification of atrocities committed by one's own.

Perhaps most, I feel spent from the role I was placed in for so many months, alternately an accuser, a recorder, psychologist, friend, exorcist. There were times when someone I was interviewing was on the threshold of a terrible pain—the memory of horror, the death of a child—as a result of my questions. Sometimes I spared them crossing that threshold; other times I didn't. There were times when I could have eased someone's grief with a soft assurance, with a touch, with silence. Sometimes I did; sometimes I didn't. I don't think there was any pattern to it.

But along with my general confusion, there is one moment, one quick vision, that will stay with me forever, and forever be my lasting image of war. It was a pair of little green shoes held up by K. Alvis, the lotus blossom seller, in his tiny, dirt-floor home in Anuradhapura. They were the shoes of his five-year-old son, who had been shot by guerrillas two years before. One of their bullets had torn away four inches of the boy's leg bone, and this was now compensated for by a four-inch heel on one of the little green shoes.

In the middle of the interview, Alvis suddenly grabbed the shoes and held them in the beam of sunlight that passed through a crack in the front door. In the light, the father stared at the shoes in disbelief. The mother peered over his shoulder and, as if understanding for the first time, clutched her cheeks and burst into tears.

And I suppose for me that is war: that for a variety of reasons, all of which sound good, men shoot the children of lotus blossom sellers and leave behind them little green shoes.

# Afterword

Since we completed our travels for *War Zones*, there have been noteworthy developments in each of the five conflicts we visited:

In Northern Ireland, where little progress has been made toward political reconciliation, radicals like "Jerry" have seized the initiative. In the spring of 1987, his Irish National Liberation Army (INLA) was fractured as the more doctrinaire Young Turks went on a killing spree against the old leadership. At least thirteen INLA members died in the purge.

In mid-1987, the more mainstream Irish Republican Army (IRA) played and failed at a new political gambit. For the first time, Sinn Fein fielded candidates in the Irish Republic's parliamentary elections, and was trounced. What it wasn't winning at the polls, the IRA didn't gain on the battlefield, either. Its style was further crimped when a huge arms shipment destined for it was intercepted.

An act by its own hand, however, did more to hurt the IRA than any British dragnets: the November 1987 bombing at a veteran's memorial ceremony in Enniskillen killed eleven civilians. The world's outrage had a resounding local echo, as the incident brought closer cooperation between the Irish and British governments to curb the IRA's activities.

Two men we interviewed, Loyalist hardliners John McMichael and George Seawright, were assassinated in separate attacks in December 1987. Both were men who had espoused violence and who, in their interviews, had spoken of their lives as marked men.

El Salvador's conflict seemed to abate, intensify, and take bizarre, new twists by turns, but came no closer to an end. A Central American peace plan, signed by El Salvador's President Duarte and his neighbors in October 1987, seemed at first to herald a possible end to the region's endemic conflicts. In El Salvador, however, neither side seemed willing to make the necessary compromises for a cessation of hostilities.

An ambitious ceasefire agreement failed, but a sweeping amnesty for political crimes set free many of the militants, both of the left and right, who were held in jail. New talks between the FMLN and Duarte's government—the first since 1984—were held, then faltered, in September.

Then, perhaps the most dramatic event occurred, with the temporary return from exile of leftist politicians Guillermo Ungo and Ruben Zamora. Their visit, inconceivable only months earlier, reflected the new dynamics at work in the country.

While the talk of political settlements took center stage, there was a resurgence of the right-wing death squads, a sign of restiveness in the conservative armed forces. A prominent human rights activist was gunned down, and several leftist suspects died of torture while in government custody.

In Uganda, there is every indication that this bedeviled country is sliding into a new cycle of bloodshed. While Museveni's government continues to wage war against the Karamoja tribesmen and their Obote and Okello allies in the northeast, it has also had to combat one of the more bizarre "liberation armies" of this century.

In the fall of 1987, some 6,000 disciples of self-styled Princess Alice Lakwena, an Acholi sorceress, began a march from the north toward Kampala. After rubbing an ointment on their chests which they thought made them impervious to bullets, the rebels launched a series of suicidal frontal attacks on Museveni's soldiers. Their chief weapon was rocks, which they believed would turn into hand grenades when thrown; the rocks didn't and they were slaughtered.

There were ominous signs that the country's early confidence in Museveni was misplaced. In October 1987, Amnesty International issued a report charging the Ugandan government with extra-judicial killings and the torture and murder of prisoners. At year's end, mounting border tensions with neighboring Kenya led to shooting, and the frontier was closed down temporarily.

A more personal illustration of the deteriorating situation is the plight of one Ugandan we interviewed for *War Zones*: human rights activist Sera Mwanga was an early Museveni supporter, but in our meeting with him he warned of the growing danger signs coming from the government. In February 1987, Mwanga was arrested by the Museveni government and is still being held without charge.

Much more quickly than we imagined, Sri Lanka has made vast strides towards "burying its future." Nearly three thousand people have been killed in the year since our visit.

Among the dead are several people we spoke with. The Batticaloa government agent, Marianpillai Anthonimuthu (he was the senior civil servant, "Tony" in our Sri Lanka chapter for safety reasons), died in a land mine explosion set by the Tigers in October 1987. With him, died police Coordinating Officer Sumith de Silva, with whom we had such a confrontational encounter. Tiger leader Kumarappa, of course, died long before both of them, just eleven days after we interviewed him.

Instead of achieving peace, the July 1987 peace deal which Prime Minister Jayewardene signed with Indian Premier Rajiv Gandhi has only widened the island's conflict. In return for Colombo's granting of limited autonomy to Tamil areas and a full amnesty for the Tigers, New Delhi promised to disarm the Tamil militants with a temporary contingent of peacekeeping troops. The Tigers didn't sign the agreement, but promised to go along with it.

Initial sounds of mutual compromise gave way to the usual crackle of gunfire, however, as the Tigers refused to relinquish all their weapons, and attacked rival guerrillas, sparking a massive mobilization of Indian troops—now numbering over 20,000—throughout the Tamil areas. In October 1987, after bloody fighting, the Indians succeeded in trading places with the Tigers as the occupying force in Jaffna.

Now, the Indian troops have become part of the conflict, as they shoulder most of the burden in fighting the Tigers. Already, hundreds of Indian soldiers have been killed, and there is no end in sight to their presence on the island.

And where the government in Colombo only faced the Tamil guerrillas before, it must now contend with the murderous resurgence of the Sinhalese extremist JVP organization, inactive since a 1971 counter-insurgency campaign ended its first bid for power. Resurrected, the Janatha Vinukthi Peramuna has embarked on its own killing campaign in opposition to any concessions for the Tamils. A JVP bomb in the presidential palace nearly killed Jayewardene himself.

The list of outrages is long; every week, it seems, there is a new bus massacre or bomb set off in a public place. Inevitably, most of the dead are civilians, their only crime that they are either Tamil or Sinhalese.

In late 1987 and into 1988, Israel dealt so harshly with an outbreak of Palestinian rioting in Gaza, the West Bank and among its own Israeli Arabs that it earned the condemnation of its closest ally, the U.S. Using live ammunition, Israeli troops shot and killed over thirty Palestinians in the first month of disturbances and conducted mass arrests of over 1,000 suspects. Cruel images of Israeli troops beating suspects and using captured Palestinian men tied to the fronts of trucks as human shields, spawned public disgust at the tactics and lent new international legitimacy to the Palestinian's plight.

In newspapers and on the nightly news, we caught fresh glimpses of people we had interviewed there—Munir Fasheh, former dean of students at Bir Zeit, and Mary Khass of Gaza—condemning the Israeli tactics and commenting on the new generation of pro-PLO Palestinian youths, increasingly radical and organized in gangs called *shabbab*. In Hashem Mahameed's Um-el-Fahem, the rioting was fierce; the militant identification of normally-uninvolved Israeli-Arabs with the Palestinian cause was a new source of worry for the Jewish state.

If anything, the unapologetic attitude of the Israeli government showed its desperation, a retrenchment in the face of its increasing internal problems and international political isolation. The riots were also a watershed, signalling the need for Tel Aviv to actively deal with what has become an untenable situation—its continued occupation of Gaza and the West Bank.

If we have heard about a few of the people we met during our journey for *War Zones*, it is because their nation's conflicts have continued, and they have found a place in them. Most of them we have heard of only because they were officials of some sort, and because they were assassinated, their positions meriting a news item upon their deaths.

The other people we spoke with are still there in their war zones, perhaps alive, perhaps not. As with civilians in conflicts everywhere, they have already sunk back into that space reserved for the vast majority, anonymity.

—New York City
January 1988

# Index